Battle of the Little Big Horn Series
Volume Five

Vanishing Victory
Custer's Final March

by
Bruce R. Liddic

UPTON & SONS, PUBLISHERS
El Segundo, California
2004

For Cherry E. Hoyt

Also by Bruce R. Liddic
I Buried Custer: The Diary of Private Thomas W. Coleman (College Station, TX, 1979)
Camp on Custer: Transcribing the Custer Myth (Spokane, WA, 1995)

Library of Congress Catalog Number
2003117161

ISBN 0-912783-39-7

UPTON & SONS, PUBLISHERS
917 Hillcrest Street
El Segundo, California, 90245

Contents

Maps

Get your facts straight first, and then
you can distort 'em as you please.
—*Mark Twain*

Acknowledgments

In November, 2000, I received a phone call from Richard Upton of Upton & Sons, Publishers inquiring if I would be interested in writing a book to be included in the publisher's "Battle of the Little Big Horn Series." At the time, I was just finishing my graduate studies and replied, at present, I wasn't able to devote the time required to do justice to this impressive series, and besides there are any number of other battle scholars who could do a far better job than I. I suggested he might want to contact one of them. Mr. Upton persisted and stated he wanted me to author the fifth book in this series, concentrating on just the twenty-four hour period of June 25th. He then asked me when I could sign the contract he was putting in the mail. After this conversation, I concluded Richard's sanity had departed and he finally had gone around the bend. But, early the following year, with my Master's degree requirements fulfilled, I returned the signed agreement to Upton & Sons. Thus, I began to write the book you are reading.

For my reconstruction of the Custer battle, there are scores of students who will take exception to my development and explanation of the battle. Nearly every point I made will be counterpointed by the research they have undertaken and the conclusions they have drawn from these inquiries. I'm sure the decades of study done by Bill Boyes, 'Dutch' Hardorff, Bob Doran, Dr. Richard Fox, Greg Michno and many others, will challenge my conjectures. They are probably thinking Richard Upton's sanity has yet to return, as he actually published this book, and furthermore I have sought his companionship around the bend. To their alternative theories, I can only concede, you could be very well right, and I wrong. I look forward to the day when their own further investigations of the Custer Battle are published. Perhaps then we, who study this subject so diligently, will be closer to a more complete understanding of how and why the events unfolded as they did. The late Dr. Edgar I. Stewart, who when questioned about his classic book *Custer's Luck,* appropriately replied to the writer, "No two Custer students ever agree on anything, it is against the rules to agree, also, it isn't any fun to agree, then you can't argue about your disagreements." Part of the attraction this battle has held upon the general public and the battle students, for better than 125 years, has many of its roots in these concise comments by Dr. Stewart.

The expression that "no man is an island" most assuredly applies to everyone who aspires to be an author.

As is customary and usual, the author is listed on the title page as the major domo of the work. However, in most instances, he/she is beholden to many others who materially assisted in transforming a concept into the book the reader has in his hands. This was especially true in my case. I have been extremely fortunate in having a number of recognized experts of the Custer battle freely give of their time and advice to make this book a reality. I would like to express my appreciation to Richard Upton who asked me to contribute to his distinguished publishing company. To Steve Moses whose maps have visually made the printed word understandable and his permission to use his extensive Custeriana collection; to Tom Bookwalter, Bill Boyes, Richard Hardorff, John S. Manion, and Major General Hoyt S. Vandenberg, all master battle scholars in their own right, who spent many hours reading and critiquing the manuscript, my heartfelt thanks. Their suggestions and comments, especially those of Mr. Bookwalter and Mr. Boyes, have vastly improved the book. In particular, I would like to mention Mr. Hardorff, who in spite of his busy schedule took time off to give a final critical read to the manuscript. Without his insightful suggestions and comments this would indeed be a subjacent book. This assistance, freely given, does not imply these distinguished scholars subscribe to the conclusions I have reached or to my reconstruction of the Battle of the Little Big Horn. I am solely responsible for these explanations.

For Roger Darling, who allowed me the use of his Darling Research materials, thank you. To Warren Van Ess, who gave authorization to use a number of his fine line drawings from *Little Big Horn Diary,* along with Peter Leers of Hastings House Publishers for permission to use several of the drawings from their book, *A Picture Report of the Custer Fight,* I am indebted. My appreciation also extends to the Little Big Horn Associates, Inc., who likewise permitted the use of various drawings and maps which appeared in their fine publications. To John D. Mackintosh who kindly permitted the use of his Reno Battlefield map from his book *Custer's Southern Officer.* This thanks is also extended to Ron Nichols, who has authored the best biography of Major Reno to date, Mike Koury, President of Old Army Press, and to Stackpole Books, publisher of *Legend Into History,* and other works, who allowed reproductions of material from their publications.

My thanks to Jim Court and the Custer Battlefield

1

Preservation Committee who had the foresight to buy and hold many acres of historical significant land which surrounds the National Park Service's Little Big Horn Battlefield enclave. Their efforts have allowed researchers to walk and study this land at their leisure without interference. I would also like to extend my appreciation to Robert Doran whose knowledge of the battle is encyclopedic. He presented me with many insights and theories of how the Custer Fight unfolded. I look forward to the day he writes a book on the Little Big Horn. There could be only one person who I would want to inscribe the introduction for my book, and that is the "dean" of western book men and long time lynch pin of the Little Big Horn Associates, Frank Mercatante. I made my request to him as soon as I returned the contract, and he graciously accepted.

I have used different spellings of the various Indian tribes; for example, I used "Uncpapa" instead of the more common "Hunkpapa" and "Ogallala" instead of "Oglala." I believe there is historic, as well as linguistic rationalization for my decisions.

To the Syracuse, NY Public Library, especially Jean Palmer in the local history department and adult services librarian, Mitchell M. Tiegel; the Onondaga County (New York) Historical Society whose collections I have used, thank you. To my sister, Cherry E. Hoyt, for whom this book is dedicated, a long overdue recognition from her admiring younger brother, and finally, to my wife Dianne and sons Matt and Jim, your patience in enduring all my quirks and the attention I have paid to this long dead man and this battle, over better than four decades, is beyond all reasonable understanding.

BRUCE R. LIDDIC
Syracuse, NY
2004

Introduction

Colonel Graham, in introducing his readers to fellow scholar Fred Dustin referred to him as a "master of research." Now let me introduce to you another master of research, Bruce R. Liddic. Here for the first time, in my opinion, is perhaps the most meticulously researched and detailed account of what happened to Custer on June 25, 1876.

Liddic's account is heavily based on notes of the late Walter Camp who, by the way, never majored in penmanship or ever bought a pad of paper. His notes were written on every conceivable type of paper he could get his hands on. How Liddic deciphered these here-to-fore unknown privately owned Camp's notes, (and he did over one thousand pages of them), is a miracle bigger than the loaves and fishes! It is not my intention, in this introduction, to give you the slightest clue of what this fantastic book is about. I want you to enjoy every page as I did.

Much has been written about the Custer Battle. You often wonder if another book is necessary. The answer to that question is, "YES," especially this book, for the depth of research and the startling new facts presented here make it a worthwhile contribution to the Custer story. This book, a labor of love, is designed for the serious Custer student rather than the casual reader. But I am sure both will enjoy it.

I first met the author in 1970 in Monroe, Michigan at the home of the late Dr Lawrence Frost. Looking at Bruce at that time he reminded me of a beanpole. If he turned sideways, you could barely see him. Today, next to me, he is still a beanpole, but with less hair. Bruce is a graduate of the State University of New York (Cortland) and holds a Master's Degree from Salve Regina University in Newport, R.I.

He is the author of nearly two dozen magazine articles and two previous books on Custer and the Battle of the Little Big Horn. He is a well known Custer historian and for many years has served on the Board of Directors for the Little Big Horn Associates, Inc. This group, founded in 1967, is the premier organization devoted to the study of this famous battle.

One of his articles, published in the *Marine Corps League Magazine* entitled, "A Marine Who Died With Custer," comes to mind. On telling this story to a good friend and fellow marine, whom I had served with in the Corps during World War II, he looked at me rather puzzled and said, "Well, I just can't understand how they lost."

Custer's last day with Seventh Cavalry, a unit he molded from 1866 through 1876, was fashioned by his personality and fortitude. This molding formed the reputation of his regiment. Custer, the "Boy General of the Civil War," the hero of many hard fought battles, a young major general at twenty-five, and finally, Custer, the Indian fighter, died on heights above the Little Big Horn river.

Looking deeply into the history of the regiment, we find it was no better than any of the other Indian fighting cavalry regiments of the west. Its greatest popularity was due to its lieutenant colonel and to its last stand. For who has ever heard much of the Fourth, the Fifth or Sixth Cavalry's? There were 209 officers and enlisted men killed under Custer's personal command. Four of them were West Point graduates. They were Lt. Col. Custer, Lt. Harrington, Lt. Porter and Lt. Sturgis. Those who study this battle have heard these names mentioned so often in reading about this engagement that at times we assume they all should have been generals. But in reality, most were just run-of-the-mill officers and a few should have been cashiered!

Finally, I remember the words of my good friend and fellow Custer collector, Steve Moses, who once said, "You know, somewhere up there in Fiddler's Green, all the past historians and participants stand around endlessly arguing about what really happened at the Battle of the Little Big Horn. Then there is a little commotion over there in the middle, and 'ole Gorgeous George himself rises to his feet, holding up his hand for silence. He'll carefully look around at the faces in the crowd before he begins to speak. He'll probably say something like this, "Now listen here people—if you really want to know (and don't we all) what actually happened—just read Bruce's book. He's gone over it all very carefully, and he's got it all figured out!"

FRANK L. MERCATANTE
Grand Rapids, Mich.

1
Overview

Early on this partially sunny Sunday morning the 25th of June 1876, the citizens of a small central New York State city began to arise to begin the day's activities. The people of Syracuse would start their observance of the Sabbath as they had done so many times before. Yesterday, had been a typical Saturday for the 48,000 inhabitants nestled along the banks of the Erie Canal. The temperature was normal for this time of year peaking to 70 degrees in mid afternoon, partly cloudy, with a light breeze out of the northwest. Much the same weather was expected for the next several days. It was a picture perfect day for going to church and praising the Lord for the bounty He had bestowed upon the city, state, and nation. At the end of the services, many of the preachers in the towns and villages surrounding the city reminded their flocks that Syracuse was planning a stupendous celebration for the 4th of July. The newspapers were reporting that a procession of 10,000 citizens were expected downtown that evening for the birthday of the nation to view an "unparalleled magnificent pyrotechnic display costing $3,000."

Yesterday was busier than usual for the merchants in the heart of the city on Salina Street. All week long the newspapers carried advertisements of unheard of bargains and sales that couldn't be missed. Many women had been discussing the public invitation, specifically directed to them, by Hancock's Dry Goods Store. All of their stock of colored dress goods priced at 75 cents a yard would be sold on Saturday for 25 cents a yard. The invitation implied this was a monumental event as great as the upcoming 4th of July celebration. Not to be outdone, D. McCarthy's Men's Store was offering their dress shirts by "Fruit of the Loom," normally selling for a dollar apiece, for only 75 cents. There was little doubt the place to be on June 24th was shopping for "buys" in Syracuse.

The whispered gossip around much of the city was a scandal which had surfaced during the business meeting of the Advent Church on Wednesday. Much to the dismay of the elders, the wife of their Pastor M. R. Petteplace, stunned this august body with a revelation charging her husband "with adultery, abuse, and lying." It was reported when Pastor Petteplace entered the room he "was taken by surprise" at the charges. He then broke down completely and "confessed to the truth of the charges" and revealed he had "committed adultery with the housekeeper in his employ." It was smugly reported by Syracuse's *Morning Standard*, he forthwith "resigned his pastorship and the Christian ministry." In addition, the same newspaper recounted from the police court dockets, the arrest of Lucy Green. It seems Officer Sevencake observed what he thought was suspicious behavior on the part of Mrs. Green. Upon stopping her, it was discovered she had a bottle of whiskey secreted under her bustle. Mrs. Green was unable to provide any explanation as to how the alcohol came to be there or why her speech was "faltering" and her gait unsteady. She was immediately brought before the bar of justice and fined $5.00 for such a public display. In true journalistic fairness, opposite this police court action, the newspaper printed an advertisement by Fanley's Distributors for Greenway Ale, Porter, and Lager, a ½-pint case of 25 bottles, delivered right to your door for the bargain price of 90 cents. Perhaps Mrs. Green should have first read this announcement before venturing outside and saved herself the "sawbuck" by having Fanley make a house call.

Besides the local gossip, religion, and politics, most of this Sabbath's discussion was still centered on the Centennial Exhibition in Philadelphia. It had opened on May 10th to overflow crowds and much speculation and debate. The slogan adopted by the exhibition committee was: "1776 with 3 million people on a strip of seacoast; 1876 with 40 million people from ocean to ocean." It was to be America's coming out party to the world and possibly, her proudest moment.[1] Syracuse, like many other cities, tried to cash in on the excitement being generated by the City of Brotherly Love. *The Morning Standard* announced the ladies at the Church of St. Johns were planning on holding a festival the following Saturday, in honor of this Centennial Exhibition, and admission was just 10 cents. Everyone was invited to stop by the church and "partake of their endeavors."

But the celebration in Philadelphia almost didn't happen. As 1875 came to a close, it was clear the Centennial Committee was frantic. The much expected and ballyhooed exhibition was only half completed, had already overrun its projected costs, and without backing from a higher source the committee made it known they didn't have the resources to finish the job. So like the special interest groups of today, the committee made an appeal to the Grant Administration. The President wasn't sure about backing their request, but he believed in light of the recent Panic of 1873, the celebration of the one hundredth birthday of the country was just too important an

---

[1] Suzanne Hilton, *The Way It Was—1876* (Philadelphia, PA: Westminister Press, 1975), 184.

event not to support. The exhibition just might be the thing to help lift the nation out of its doldrums. The opposition argued it wasn't a project that tax dollars should be supporting. It was a close vote in Congress, but the extraordinary backing, in the amount of $1,500,000, was approved. It marked one of the first times when Congress had directly approved public funds for a strictly private enterprise. The debate over this extension of the government's role in the Centennial Exhibition's business was still a source of discussion among both Democrats and Republicans six months later.

Politics always seemed to take center stage, and among the men there was much talk on the upcoming presidential election. The newspapers were full of accounts concerning the upcoming Democratic and just concluded Republican Conventions. This discussion was even more prevalent than usual, for in New York, the leading candidates for both parties were from the Empire State. The Democrats were pinning their hopes on their Governor, Samuel Tilden. The Republican front runner was Senator Roscoe Conkling of Tammany Hall fame. Although others would argue the odds on favorite was Senator James Blaine of Maine. The truth was, after a decade and a half in power, the Republicans were beset with scandal and riddled with fractions who were more interested in keeping power than doing the country's business. It was just nine days ago the Grand Old Party had met apprehensively in Cincinnati, at the time the country's eighth largest city, for their once every four year celebration party. On the first roll call, Blaine, showing early strength, led the balloting with Conkling coming in fourth place, and a number of lesser candidates finishing far down the list, including Rutherford Hayes, the Governor of Ohio. But in later balloting there appeared to be a subtle shift in sentiment away from the front runners. It began with Michigan as their delegates moved to support Hayes. By June 23rd, the shift was complete, and Hayes edged Blaine by 30 votes to gain the nomination. Hayes was pushed over the top by the New York delegation, led by Conkling, who by custom was given the honor of picking the Vice Presidential nominee. Therefore, it was no surprise that a fellow New Yorker, Congressman William Wheeler was selected. No less controversial or colorless public figures could be found in the entire country.[2] However, after the trouble-plagued Grant Administration, this was probably the attraction the ticket of Hayes and Wheeler held for the Republicans.

The Democrats were scheduled to begin their convention on the 27th in St. Louis. The citizens of Syracuse and New York had reason to be proud in this presidential election year as their state was the power in the land. The Democrats were now resurgent, and in the election of 1874, had captured both houses of Congress for the first time since the Civil War. Tilden was expected by everyone to be the nominee and probably the next President of the United States. True to the predictions, the following day, on the second ballot, Tilden was chosen, and his running mate was Governor Thomas Hendricks of Indiana. The canvas for votes, heated discussions, and the partisan debates were already beginning.

Some of the more erudite and informed citizens of the "Salt City" were aware that there was a military operation underway out in the western territories, nearly 1,800 miles away. This undertaking was begun in March 1876 to enforce President Grant's policy for removal of the hostile Indians from these uncharted lands and force them back to their assigned reservations. If they had given any second thoughts to this seemingly minor Presidential executive decision, it probably involved the perceived leader of the expedition Lieutenant Colonel, Brevet Major General, George Armstrong Custer. These folks would have recalled how, over a decade earlier, the famous Civil War commander and his wife Elizabeth Bacon Custer had played, enjoyed the pleasures of life, and even honeymooned in the Syracuse area among his new bride's family and friends. In fact, Custer's father in law, Daniel Bacon, had been born in a nearby township and had resided there for twenty-four years before moving to Michigan in 1822.

Thus the citizens of Syracuse spent this last Sunday in June going about their lives unaware that ten days, hence, they would not be reading or discussing the local news, the Centennial Exhibition, or the upcoming presidential election. Over the next several weeks, their attention would be focused on of all things, as *The Morning Standard* reported "an Indian War now fully inaugurated." The Syracusans and their fellow countrymen would be dumfounded to read in their newspapers the reprinted telegraphic dispatches from the far distant Montana Territory, that in this 100th year of American independence, their Army had battled the Red Man and had been defeated. It was said the public shock at the news of the "Custer Massacre" was only matched by the news of President Lincoln's assassination eleven years earlier.[3] How could this

[2]John D. Bergamini, *The Hundredth Year* (NY, NY: G.P.Putman Sons, 1976), 160–161.

[3]Edgar I. Stewart, *Custer's Luck* (Norman, OK: University of OK Press, 1955), 5.

have happened? Wasn't the much hyped and expensive Centennial Exhibition supposed to demonstrate to the world the United States' time had come? The country appeared to be on the brink of international greatness, and now a few tribes of "uncivilized savages" had defeated one of the army's elite regiments led by, supposedly, the country's premier Indian fighter. Suddenly, not only Americans but people from London to Paris to Berlin were reading about this abrupt reversal of fortunes in the young republic. Someone had to be at fault, and blame needed to be assessed. The newspapers had a new catch phrase to explain what happened: "John Bull 1776—Sitting Bull 1876;" a simplistic answer at best.[4]

During the nearly three hundred years from the founding of Jamestown to the dawn of the Twentieth Century, first the colonies, then later the United States, fought many battles with various Indian tribes. The citizens of New York State could recall their full share of bloody engagements from the pillage of Schenectady, to the battles at Fort William Henry and Fort Ticonderoga, to the deadly ambush at Oriskany. In these memorial battles many outstanding leaders were involved, but by 1876 few Syracusans (or Americans) could name even one leader or his battle. These New Yorkers were, for the most part, aware of Custer's name from his Civil War leadership, past Indian fighting exploits, and his local connection. Better than a century later little has changed. For the general public, then or now, one leader and his battle have come to symbolize all the conflict between the Red Man and White. George A. Custer is that leader and his Last Stand on the banks of the Little Big Horn River are both so deeply rooted in the American conscience as to become the archetypal Indian fight of all time. From generation to generation, this interest has little abated and still today "his name alone will start an argument. More significant men of his time can be discussed without passion, they are inextricably woven into the tapestry of the past, but this hotspur refuses to die. He stands forever on that dusty Montana slope."[5]

The story of the Battle of the Little Big Horn is much more than just Custer standing on that "dusty Montana slope," even though most Americans and many history buffs think this is the case. The Little Big Horn Battle was only one part of the Campaign of 1876, albeit, the campaign's most famous event. It is on this event where all the attention is fixed, due in no small part to the confluence of the event's personalities and the circumstances

which led to what was to be a sure victory, which disappeared once the gunsmoke had cleared. The Campaign of 1876 was only a natural extension of the westward expansion, the Manifest Destiny, of the United States. This expansion, always to the west, began almost as soon as the pilgrims landed at Plymouth Rock. From the start the "new" Americans kept up a constant and unrelenting pressure upon the native Americans. Those tribes who wouldn't acquiesce to the white man's insatiable hunger for land were pushed aside, killed, or were driven further to the west. A world wide historical pattern repeated many times over, since the dawn of time, when a more technologically advanced and stronger civilization covets something in the possession of one who is less advanced and weaker.

Long before the Centennial Campaign began, it had been the policy of the government through the Interior Department's Bureau of Indian Affairs to have all the Indians live on the reservations assigned to them. When various Sioux bands who were residing off their reservations refused a government summons to return by January 31, 1876, they were declared hostile and the Interior Department shifted the responsibility for these Indians to the War Department for appropriate action. It was evident from this stance taken by the Grant Administration, it had already decided that it was past time for these Indians to join their fellow tribesmen and "walk the white's man road."[6] Lieutenant General Philip H. Sheridan, one of the three great captains who had saved the union was in command of the Military Division in which these now declared hostiles were residing, immediately began preparations to implement his government's orders. The general's strategy was to converge upon the area with three columns and strike the Sioux and their Cheyenne allies wherever they could be found and force them to comply with the President's decision. On February 7, 1876 Sheridan ordered Brigadier General George Crook, commanding the Department of the Platte, and Brigadier General Alfred Terry, commanding the Department of Dakota, to organize their forces and begin the government's response.

General Crook, employing Fort Fetterman in the present day Wyoming as his base, was the first to take to the field and approached the hostile Indians' camping grounds from the south. On March 17th, 1876, sixteen days after leaving their base, a column of Crook's troops under the command of Colonel John J. Reynolds discovered and surprised a winter camp of Northern Cheyennes near the

[4]Hilton, *The Way It Was—1876*, 199.
[5]Evan S. Connell, *Son of the Morning Star* (San Francisco, CA: North Point Press, 1984), 106.
[6]Stewart, *Custer's Luck*, 76.

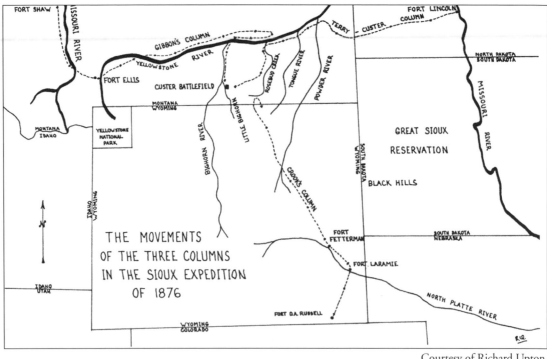

THE MOVEMENTS
OF THE THREE COLUMNS
IN THE SIOUX EXPEDITION
OF 1876

Courtesy of Richard Upton

present day town of Broadus, Montana. But through ineptitude and bitterly cold weather, Reynolds abandoned his wounded, the village he had so recently occupied, later the pony herd and allowed victory to slip through his hands. By this winter action, the tribes were put on notice, this time the white man would stop at nothing to bend them to their will. In view of this unforeseen reversal, Crook could do little but return to his base, resupply the troops, and begin again at the first signs of Spring. General Terry, due to the harsh winter conditions in his department, was unable to duplicate Crook's early start, and it wasn't until April that Colonel John Gibbon was able to lead the Montana Column of troops to the east from Fort Shaw, near Great Falls, Montana. His command consisted of five companies of the 7th Infantry and four companies of the 2nd Cavalry under Major James Brisbin. The strongest unit of the converging columns was to be the 7th Regiment of United States Cavalry based at Fort Abraham Lincoln, across the Missouri River from Bismarck, Dakota Territory. This regiment and its supporting infantry companies were to march to the west and link up with Gibbon somewhere along the Yellowstone River deep within the Indians' favorite haunts.

This force from Fort Lincoln was further delayed due to the absence of its field commander, who was supposed to lead the Dakota Column. Lieutenant Colonel Custer was in Washington, DC, embroiled in a controversy involving his appearance before a congressional investigating committee. By testifying before a Democratic House committee, he had publicly criticized the Republican president and his administration. Grant retaliated by removing him from the campaign. It was only through the intercession of several generals that the President relented and permitted the humbled Custer to take the field. But instead of being in command of the eastern strike force, he was relegated to command only the 7th Cavalry as Grant had directed Terry to assume overall command of this column as well as the campaign.

On May 17th, the Dakota column finally got underway, more than a month behind schedule. The column marched across North Dakota and reached the Montana border. No one had seen a single Indian. Even though on May 30th, Custer was ordered to lead a scouting party down the Little Missouri River on a rumor there were Indians in that direction. On June 7th they reached the mouth of the Powder River where troops met the supply steamer "Far West." This riverboat had been contracted by the government to supply both the Montana and Dakota columns. Terry boarded the boat and went up the river to meet Gibbon. Gibbon's column, after leaving Fort

Shaw, had earlier marched to Fort Ellis and was joined by Brisbin and the 2nd Cavalry. The combined units proceeded along the north bank of the Yellowstone River, and on April 20th arrived at the mouth of the Big Horn River. Terry's objective was to block any attempted escape of the Indians to the north and link up with him upon his arrival in the area.

Terry arrived at Gibbon's camp on June 9th, and the General and his ranking officer discussed the tactical plans for the summer campaign. Terry took the steamboat back to Custer's camp and before he departed, ordered Gibbon to move his column and join the 7th Cavalry near the mouth of the Rosebud where it emptied into the Yellowstone. Terry had established a supply base near the mouth of the Powder River, and he directed a battalion from the 6th Infantry, stationed at Fort Buford, to guard it. At the same time upon arrival back at the 7th's camp, Terry, still without any concrete information as to the Indians' location, decided to send out a major reconnaissance detail. This was in spite of the many indications of the Indians whereabouts which had been reported to Gibbon by this excellent chief of scouts. Lieutenant James Bradley and his Crow scouts had been keeping track of the Indians ever since the Montana Column arrived on the Yellowstone. But little had been done to confront them. Terry's plan was to split up his major strike force for this reconnaissance. Custer was to take the left wing of the 7th Cavalry and march up the south bank of the Yellowstone and join Gibbon at the mouth of the Tongue River. On June 10th, Major Reno was ordered to take the right wing (Companies B, C, E, F, I, and L) and scout up the Powder River as far south as the Little Powder River, then turn west to Mizpah Creek and move down that creek to the Tongue River, following its course until it joined the Yellowstone. However, in an effort to capture a degree of glory, Reno exceeded his orders and bolted clear over into the valley of the Rosebud where a very fresh hostile trail was discovered that appeared to lead across the Wolf Mountains and into the valley of the Little Big Horn. On June 18th, upon his return, Reno reported he thought there were no more than one thousand Indians camped somewhere in the area of the Big Horn and Little Big Horn watersheds. Reno, in this case, whatever his ulterior motive was in disregarding Terry's orders, did provide valuable intelligence which was previously unknown as to where the Indians were not. In the absence of any other reliable information, Terry acted on Reno's presumptions that this was the extent of the Indian force he faced, their presupposed location and altered his plans accordingly.

Reno had discovered this trail on the very same day (June 17th) where forty miles to the south and west, General Crook learned first hand of the fighting prowess and numbers of the Sioux and Cheyenne. The Battle of the Rosebud was a day long fight, and the Indians had forced Crook to retire and establish a base camp near the present day town of Sheridan, WY. Thus, unknown to Terry, $\frac{1}{3}$ of the army's columns were neutralized at the very beginning of the summer's campaign. Custer, leaving his new recruits and sick at the Powder River supply depot, marched to join Reno and link up with him on the 21st where together they marched to the mouth of the Rosebud. Custer was called to an officer's conference on board the "Far West" and that afternoon met with Terry, Gibbon, and Brisbin to learn the final details of Terry's tactical plan. Terry explained to these officers that he hoped to place the Montana and Dakota columns in co-operating distance to each other. If the Indians were in fact to be found on the Big Horn River, the columns would be in a position to launch a co-ordinated attack. Terry instructed Custer to follow the Indians' trail Reno had discovered, march up the Rosebud, then cross over the Wolf Mountains and approach the Little Big Horn valley from the south. Later it was supposed, Custer was to have timed his march so as to arrive in this valley on Monday, June 26th. Terry, himself, would march with Gibbon traveling up the Big Horn River and enter the Little Big Horn valley from the north. Terry told his senior officers that hopefully the Indians would be caught between the two columns, and the Army would be victorious. Perhaps this was only wishful thinking on Terry's part that both columns would be able to reach a specified area about the same time. Custer had been rationed for fifteen days, and it's possible he could be on the Indians' trail until July 6th. No one ever claimed, except after the battle had been lost, that Custer was on any kind of time table. More likely, Terry's intent about this specific date was to let Custer know about where he (Terry) might be found.[7]

It is apparent from Terry's plan, that he expected the Indians to try and flee from the troops rather than engage in a stand up fight. It is also apparent Terry expected Custer to engage the Indians, and he didn't expect Custer to wait until the infantry could get into position. The general did expect "that Custer should attack the savages wherever found and as to the manner of the attack, of course, was left to the discretion and judgment of Custer."[8] That the columns were to converge from different directions,

[7] Stewart, *Custer's Luck,* 250.

[8] Col. William A. Graham, *The Custer Myth* (Harrisburg, PA: The Stackpole Company, 1953), 225.

each one supposedly strong enough to overcome any resistance they would meet, indicated a belief that a beating of the bushes and a final round up of sorts would be all that would be required. If any fighting would be undertaken, it would be more in the manner of a Civil War after battle mop up operation.[9] The column would no doubt have to contend themselves with corralling the prisoners and shepherding them back to the reservations, it was all fairly simple. There seemed to be no way the army could fail.

Also evident in Terry's latest tactics, this plan was a modified version of his earlier thinking, in that the best chance he had of bringing the Indians to bay could be accomplished by turning Custer, his only Indian experienced field commander, loose with a strong highly mobile strike force. Custer could then pick up the trail and follow it back to the Indians' camps wherever they might be found. Only by a stroke of luck could Gibbon's infantry block the Indians . . . if such a thing was possible against the highly versatile Red Man. One column would have to make the first contact. Lieutenant Bradley wrote in his diary the true intent of Terry's plan, and it was "understood that if Custer arrives first he is at liberty to attack at once if he deems prudent."

Terry had given Custer his written instructions outlining what he wanted his strike force to accomplish, and at noon on the 22nd, the 7th Cavalry broke camp. On a small knoll overlooking the camp site, Terry, Gibbon, and Brisbin gathered to review the troopers as they departed. Custer soon joined them for a final "pass in review." Major Reno rode at the head of the column, accompanied by the massed trumpeters, followed by twelve companies of what was universally perceived as the flower of the American cavalry service. Terry could sense Custer's pride in the regiment and his pleasure at "having the post of honor."[10] But it was Gibbon who put into words the private thoughts of the senior officers and admonished: "Now Custer, don't be greedy. Wait for us." Custer, as he put the spurs to his mount, turned his head and quickly answered, "No, I won't."[11] One of the 7th's junior officers later wrote there never was a more eager command who had been ordered off after Indians. There was nothing that could save the Red Man except by "rapid flight" and "the general belief was that when the Indians found that the whole 7th Cavalry was coming, they would run, and then the hard stern chase would begin."[12] After Terry returned to the now reduced camp, he was heard to remark, "Custer is happy now, off with a roving command of fifteen days. I told him if he found the Indians not to do as Reno did, but if he thought he could whip them to do so."[13]

The regiment marched only twelve miles before going into camp around 4 o'clock at the base of a steep bluff on the Rosebud River. There was good grazing for the horses and adequate wood and water. It was here Custer held an officer's conference and told them that they would be directly responsible for their own companies. Headquarters would only direct the regiment as to when to begin the march and when to stop. Custer told the assembled officers they could expect to meet about one thousand warriors but no more than fifteen hundred at the most.[14] The officers checked their watches to insure they were all set alike. Easy marches would be made and would only average twenty-five to thirty miles a day. He instructed the officers not to get too far ahead or lag behind the rear guard but to keep well closed up and in supporting distance at all times. The next day at 5 AM, the cavalry continued further south along the Rosebud valley. Several deserted Indian campsites were passed by, and after marching about 33 miles, camp was made by 5 PM. About six miles into the day's march the regiment started seeing the first signs of the Indians' previous campsites. It was remarked that "Every bend of the stream bore traces of some old camp." By mid afternoon Custer had reached the point in the Rosebud valley where Reno, six days prior, had ended his scout and turned back to the north. At this time, one of his officers overheard Custer saying, "Here's where Reno made the mistake of his life. He had six troops of cavalry and rations enough for a number of days. He'd have made a name for himself if he had pushed on after them."[15] About 4:30 PM on this rather warm afternoon the regiment halted. They had covered about thirty miles in the past twelve hours. It was nearly sunset before the slow moving packtrain arrived at the camp. Today, a stone marker twelve miles north of Lame Deer, Montana marks this supposed site.

[9]Roger Darling, *General Custer's Final Hours* (Vienna, VA: Potomac-Western Press, 1992), x.

[10]Wayne Michael Sarf, *The Little Bighorn Campaign* (Conshohocken, PA:Combined Books, 1993), 157; Frazier and Robert Hunt, *I Fought With Custer* (NY,NY: Charles Scribner's Sons, 1954), 71. Hereinafter cited: *I Fought . . .*

[11]Frederic Van de Water, *Glory Hunter* (Indianapolis, IN: The Bobbs-Merrill Co:1934), 324.

[12]John M. Carroll, ed., *The Gibson and Edgerly Narratives* (Bryan, TX:NP, ND), 6.

[13]Frances Chamberlain Holley, *Once Their Home* (Chicago, IL: Donohue & Henneberry, 1892), 262.

[14]Graham, *Custer Myth*, 134.

[15]Van de Water, *Glory Hunter*, 328.

Courtesy of MacMillan (The Bobbs-Merrill Company)

On June 24th, probably in response to the number of Indian camp sites observed the day before, Custer had the scouts up and about early to explore the narrowing valley ahead. The regiment followed at 5 AM. Undoubtedly, Custer thought he was in hot pursuit as the trail was fresh. The Lieutenant Colonel intended to follow up every trail, and the troopers remembered "We rode hard, too. There was no foolishness."[16] Custer, two companies, and the scouts now took over as the advanced guard, about a half a mile ahead of the rest of the regiment, but close enough for support by the rest of the companies should

any trouble develop. Obviously, for Custer and many men in the 7th Cavalry, the edge of darkness had been reached. After this Saturday, one out of every two American soldiers who rode behind Custer would not live to see another sunset. In their death, they created an unsolved mystery of "how" and "why" did the anticipated victory suddenly vanish. Since then, literally thousands of people and hundreds of history students have searched long and hard for the key that would unlock the secret of this "how" and "why." Perhaps this is a major part of the reason for the world wide attention paid to what would be an otherwise minor event in American history.

---

[16]Hunt, *I Fought . . . ,* 73.

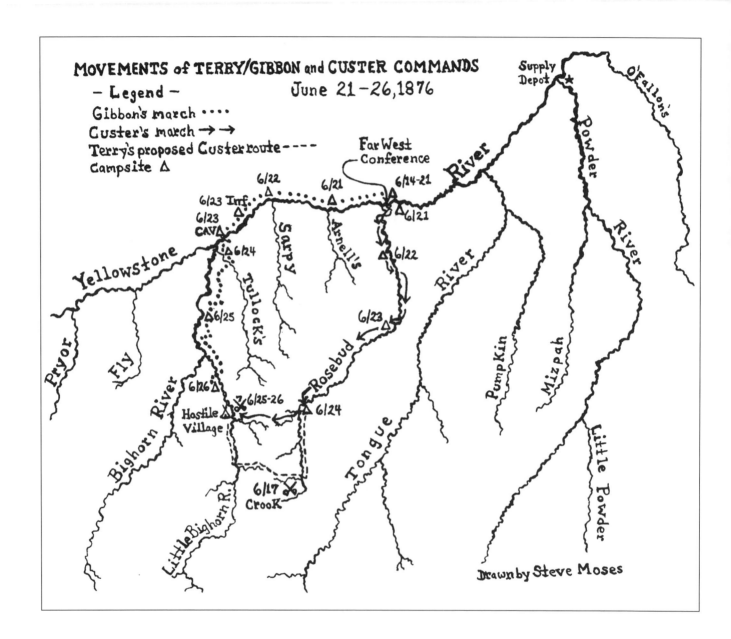

2
Crow's Nest

Dawn was just beginning to break over a rocky promontory in southeastern Montana Territory called the Crows Nest. Red Star, an Arikara, poked Second Lieutenant Charles Varnum awake and when the groggy lieutenant struck a sulphur match, opened his watch, its hands showed 4:00.[1] He had been asleep for only two hours. It had felt like two minutes.

Yesterday, June 24, 1876 had been a particularly trying time for the 7th Cavalry's Chief of Scouts. Varnum had been up again before dawn and had ridden 70 miles that day supervising the Crows and Arikara scouts in checking out every Indian trail no matter how insignificant, and he had been looking forward to the afternoon's halt for a much needed rest. The day proved to be both long and irksome. The weather had turned uncomfortably warm, and the dust kicked up by the horses covered everyone in a chalky, choking blanket of beige. All day long the twelve companies of cavalry moved slowly along the trail in jumps and starts due to the vigilance of Lieutenant Colonel George A. Custer, commanding. This day he was especially guarding against any of the Indians moving around his column's left flank thereby making good their escape from him into the vast unchartered regions of the Tongue and Power Rivers. This resulted in Varnum being ordered to follow up every trail no matter how small.

By doing so, Custer insured he was following Brigadier General Alfred Terry's written instructions he was given two days prior. Terry, the expedition's commander, had directed Custer to feel "constantly however to your left so as preclude the possibility of escape of the Indians to the south or southeast by passing around your left flank."[2]

On this Saturday, Varnum, who was to enjoy a long and distinguished military career, had probably wished Custer would have assigned another officer when they left Fort Lincoln to manage the scouts. These scouts assigned to Varnum were a very important element in the campaign. Among their responsibilities were to scour the front and flanks during the day's march to detect any unusual activity and during the night to guard against any surprise incursions by the enemy. In addition, they were expected to search for enemy trails, conduct reconnaissance missions, act as messengers, engage in fast skirmishing, and when the villages were encountered to raid and capture the pony herds.[3] Make no mistake, these 37 Arikaras who enlisted for the campaign were veteran fighters. Their average age was twenty-nine, and they had previously served no less than nineteen months and averaged at least three separate army enlistments before taking the field with Custer.[4]

During this brief afternoon halt, Varnum learned to his chagrin the importance Custer had placed on all trails leading from the left flank. Varnum in his autobiographical reminiscences remembered that First Lieutenant Edward Godfrey, Company K's commanding officer, had reported to the Lieutenant Colonel that he had seen a small trail leading off east (left) several miles back. Custer inquired if his scouts had made a report of it. Varnum told his commander they hadn't, and he didn't believe this report.[5] Although Godfrey probably spoke to Custer about the small trail, George Herendeen told a reporter from the *N.Y. Herald* on January 22, 1878, it was he who informed the commander about the divergent lodge trail.

No matter who acquainted Custer with the information, he became angry with his lieutenant's neglect, and ordered him to retrace his route and thoroughly conduct an investigation and then inform him of the results.

[1] Throughout this book I will be referring to various clock times. There were no time zones or standard times back in the 1870s. Each locality pretty much kept their own time or relied on railroad time. The army watches were originally set to the Department of Dakota time to which the personnel at Fort Lincoln reported. To find out how this would correspond with the current Mountain Standard Time at the Little Big Horn you would need to deduct 1 hour and 13 minutes; for sun time deduct 1 hour and 10 minutes. As a person travels east or west by more than 15 degrees one's watch is off by one hour from "sun time." Thus, when Colonel John Gibbon's Montana column joined the Dakota column no ones' watch agreed. So what time was the campaign following? It was probably sun time. A clue is found by the times in the official itinerary kept by Lieutenant George Wallace; on the night of the 24th he wrote camp was made at 7:45, others recorded it was nearly sunset. On June 24th at the Custer Battlefield (local sun time) sunset was at 7:53. It would appear the watches of the command were adjusted to sun time before Custer departed Terry's and Gibbon's combined camp on June 22nd. Other incidents during the camapign will confirm the difference between the sun time and the men's watches varied by only a few minutes. Local sun time for sunrise on June 25, 1876 was 4:13 AM. Therefore, I have Red Star poking his "Chief" awake at 4:00, so he could be in position as the sun rose. For a more detailed description of these time frames refer to John S. Gray, *Custer's Last Campaign* (Lincoln, NE: University of Nebraska Press, 1991), 221–25.

[2] Stewart, *Custer's Luck*, 249.

[3] John Gray, "Arikara Scouts With Custer," *North Dakota History*, Vol.35, #2, Spring 1968, 457.

[4] Ibid, 474–475.

[5] John M. Carroll, *I, Varnum* (Glendale, CA: Arthur H. Clark Co., 1982), 60–61.

Instead of a rest, this back tracking added additional miles to an already long weary day. Even more frustrating for the saddle sore Chief of Scouts was the fact that in retracing this small trail, it led up a ravine for a ways, then over the prairie, down in the valley and returned back upon the trail the command had been following.[6] The back tracking had been for nothing, causing Varnum to sharply comment on this aggravating wild goose chase even forty years later.

However, this concern about the column's left flank didn't extend to Varnum's scouts. Besides his Dakota column's Arikaras on June 21st, Terry assigned six of the Montana column's Crow scouts along with Mitch Bouyer, their half breed interpreter who also possessed intimate knowledge of the country, to Custer while in camp on the Yellowstone. This was because the Arikaras did not know the country west of the Tongue River where Custer was expected to operate.[7] The soldiers as well as the Arikaras knew they were outsiders and unacquainted with the country, and the Crows knew every nook and corner of it.[8] These Crows were to provide valuable service throughout the rest of the campaign. The scouts knew there were more than enough Indians ahead, their camps were cohesive and only increasing in size. During the past two days, ever since the command left Terry's camp on the Rosebud River, they had uncovered signs which showed there were already more Indians ahead than "the soldiers had bullets in their belts." The Crows didn't understand why the soldiers wanted to find more. Although the white men didn't know where the Indians were, the scouts were aware the Sioux and Cheyenne had been watching the soldiers and knew where they were.[9]

In fact, years later White-Man-Runs-Him, a young Crow scout who did most of the advance scout work to prove his worth, claimed many times he was close enough to speak with the Sioux by means of sign language. He further related "From the time Custer's command left the military camp at the mouth of the Rosebud Creek, it was under the surveillance of Sioux scouting parties."[10]

This one o'clock afternoon halt lasted for three hours while Varnum checked out the divergent trail. The 7th Cavalry's resting place was about four miles north of the present day town of Lame Deer. Varnum, in an effort to make up for his perceived morning negligence had the scouts range further ahead even after it was discovered the side trail doubled back on itself. This extra effort yielded results. Lt. George D. Wallace, a West Point classmate of Varnum and the regiment's official itinerarist, explained in his report what information Varnum had unearthed.

> The scouts got back about 4, and reported a fresh camp at the forks of the Rosebud. Everything indicated that the Indians were not more than thirty miles away. At 5 PM the command moved out; . . . The trail was now fresh, and the whole valley was scratched up by trailing lodge-poles.[11]

First Lieutenant Godfrey would later recall Custer ordered the command to move even more cautiously, and many halts were made so as to not impede the scouts in their work. Custer had ordered Varnum to pay particular attention west toward Tullock's Creek whose valley was in view from the divide.[12] However, Varnum reportedly told Colonel Robert Hughes twenty years later

> in all his instructions from Custer in regard to scouting he never heard of Tullock's Creek . . . and any examination whatever was made of the Tullock Valley, it was made without his knowledge and by someone not under his control.[13]

Fred Dustin, an early Custer student who saw no good in anything the Lieutenant Colonel did, used this later recollection by Varnum to bolster his case for Custer's disregard of Terry's orders.[14] However, as we will read later Custer didn't disregard this area; Hughes simply failed to inquire if any one else had gone there, as Varnum indicated could have happened, and Dustin didn't follow his sources closely enough.

After following this trail up the valley of the Rosebud for the next two hours they had only moved about 6 miles and had arrived at a point not far below the present town of Busby. Custer knew the trail leading to the location of the hostile Indians continued on ahead, but in which direction did it eventually go? Was it west to the Little Big Horn? Or did it keep on a southward course up the Rosebud, and if so would it be discovered to turn southeast or in an easterly direction? Did it divide itself and branch out in many different directions as these trails did

[6]Charles Townsend Brady, *Indian Fights and Fighters* (NY, NY: Doubleday, 1904), 357.

[7]James Willert, *To the Edge of Darkness* (El Segundo, CA: Upton & Sons, 1998), 147.

[8]Charles Robinson III, *General George Crook* (Norman, OK: University of OK Press, 2001), 167.

[9]Stewart, *Custer's Luck*, 261. [10]Ibid.

[11]John M. Carroll, *General Custer and the Battle of the Little Big Horn: The Federal View* (New Brunswick, NJ: The Garry Owen Press, 1976), 65. Hereinafter cited: *The Federal View*.

[12]Graham, *The Custer Myth*, 136.

[13]Col. William A. Graham, *The Story of the Little Big Horn* (Harrisburg, PA: The Stackpole Company, 1959), 31.

[14]Fred Dustin, *The Custer Tragedy* (NP: NP, 1965), 97.

so often? After two days on the march, the commander still had no precise knowledge, and it was now about 7:45 PM. Custer ordered Varnum to dispatch three of his Crow scouts to ride ahead and try to read which direction the trail led, and was it still conjointly before darkness enveloped the command?[15] If as close to the Indian camps as the signs attested, perhaps the information the Crows could expose would allow the command to draw even closer with a tricky night march, gathering further intelligence.

It is interesting to speculate if Custer had not been so diligent in uncovering the direction of the hostile Indian trail and had indeed chosen to follow the Rosebud away from them, he probably would have come upon some interesting discoveries. Without a doubt Varnum's scouts would have found the site of General George Crook's Rosebud fight seven days earlier. If the scouts would have pursued Crook's after battle trail, the two commands would have joined forces on Goose Creek near the present day Sheridan, WY. If Custer would have turned to the right, he would have moved towards the headwaters of the Tongue River. The country was very rough and broken in this area with water non-existent, and he would not have been able to extract his command in time to be in any position to coordinate with Terry. This was the same general area in which Terry, himself, had become engulfed during his march to the Big Horn River to meet the 7th Cavalry and was barely able to escape.[16]

There have been many students of the Custer battle who have argued long and passionately about the "orders" given the Lieutenant Colonel by Terry at the mouth of the Rosebud. There have been extensive monographs and numerous articles written about this question with as many different opinions as there were authors. However, one constant theme runs through the pro and con argument of whether Custer ignored his written instructions and these are their personal opinions of the Lieutenant Colonel. These authors' individual biases, from the very beginnings of the Little Big Horn battle controversy, have colored their accounts regardless of what the record shows. Those who judge Custer as a glory hunting, self promoting, reckless commander who would do anything will hold he willfully disobeyed his "orders." Those who judge Custer's character as bold and daring but willing to take a calculated risk and act as the situation unfolded will hold he only interpreted the instructions in a manner consistent with what was expected of him. Most Americans now pride themselves in being "non judgmental," except apparently where personas such as Custer's are concerned. As noted, Evan Connell took a fair measure of this polemical man and stated the passions his name invokes. It was so with Custer during his lifetime, as it is contemporarily decades after his death. Custer's character is as much today as yesterday the hotspur, the lightning rod, to which all that was and is wrong with our government's Indian policy is assigned for blame.

There are some students of this battle, who subscribe to a conspiracy theory, who believe that Custer was the victim of some deep and dark Grant Administration plot to remove him from the army. To help accomplish this, Custer was given a set of "orders" which damned him if he complied with them or damned him if he didn't.[17] I am not in agreement with such theorists. I don't believe history can be explained through a conspiracy framework. But what of Terry who gave the Lieutenant Colonel these orders; did he consider Custer acted within his instructions? If in Terry's (or his superior's) view Custer hadn't and he preferred charges (or was so directed) against him, it would have been up to Custer to defend himself on the disobedience charge. It is impossible to know what Terry really thought before the battle and he might have been deceiving himself in giving these "orders" to Custer. Subsequently his views on Custer's compliance or lack thereof were given heavy consideration, but if the Little Big Horn had been a victory, would Terry's views even been solicited? It should be noted, Terry was an attorney by profession, and the words of the order were written to favor Terry should there be any disagreements.

The Montana column's senior officer, Colonel John Gibbon of Civil War "Iron Brigade" fame, Terry's second in command, and privy to all the of internal workings of the campaign, stated the only thing Custer was ordered to do was pursue Indians. Everything else was left to Custer's discretion. In addition, Gibbon said it would have to be kept in mind, by those who study the question, that the letter of instructions declared it was impossible to bind him (Custer) down by any "definite instructions." Furthermore the Colonel declared, "A military commander in the field is supreme over everything within his reach. . . . he may act upon his own responsibility if he so chooses."[18] No matter what today's battle students believe, all the parties then knew and understood the campaign could not be based on written instructions by themselves

---

[15]Carroll, *The Federal View . . .* , 65.

[16]Roger Darling, *Sad and Terrible Blunder* (Vienna, VA: The Potomac Western Press, 1990), see chapters 4 & 5.

[17]W. Kent King, *Massacre: The Custer Cover-Up* (El Segundo, CA: Upton & Sons, 1989), 25–32.

[18]Col. John Gibbon, "Comments on Custer's Orders," *Little Big Horn Associates Newsletter*, May 1998, Vol 23, #4, 5.

but augmented by the commander's judgment relative to what he encountered in the field. Dr. Edgar I. Stewart, as fair and knowledgeable of a chronicler who ever studied the campaign, concluded there was no plot and Custer acted within Terry's instructions. The only exception was his failure to scout and report on the upper reaches of Tullock's Creek.[19] However, if one studies the whole record they will find even this "failure" bears closer scrutiny.

It has been recorded that Terry had assigned the white scout George Herendeen, who was familiar with the area, to Custer exclusively for this purpose. Herendeen, however, stated the way he came to be assigned to Custer was the Lieutenant Colonel inquired of Terry at the Yellowstone Camp, where he could get a good man to guide him. Major Brisbin told Custer he knew of just such a man. "So they sent for me and when I appeared, Custer placed his finger on the map and asked me if I could lead them to that place, Tullocks Forks. I said yes. He said: 'You are just the man I want.'"[20] In compensation for scouting the Tullock's for signs of the enemy and delivering the information to Terry, Herendeen claimed he was promised a bonus of $200. Despite the maps provided to them, neither Terry nor Custer had a very good idea of the topography the command would encounter after leaving the camp on the Yellowstone. According to some sources Custer was vague as to exactly where Herendeen was to take his departure from the cavalry. Custer was to depend on Mitch Bouyer for guidance regarding the point of Herendeen's exit. The commander intended to go beyond just sending Terry's scout north, he also planned on forwarding Charlie Reynolds, then the best white guide on the Northern Plains, with Herendeen so a two way communication could be probably undertaken between the columns with any further directions Terry might impose. Thus Custer did have every intention of complying with Terry's instructions in this regard as evident from the story Herendeen related to the Bozeman (MT) *Herald* on January 4, 1878:

> On the morning of 24th, we broke camp at five o'clock and continued following the trail up the stream. Soon after starting Custer, who was in the advance with Bouyer, called me to him and told me to get ready, saying he thought he would send me and Charlie Reynolds to the head of Tullock's fork to take a look. I told the General it was not time yet, as we were then traveling in the direction of the head of the Tullock, and I could only follow his trail. I called Bouyer, who was a little ahead

and asked him if I was not correct in my statement to the General, and he said, "Yes; further up on the Rosebud we would come opposite a gap, and then we could cut across and strike the Tullock in about 15 mile ride." Custer said, "All right; I could wait."

By the time the column reached the point where it was practical to dispatch Herendeen to Terry, the situation had changed in ways which precluded Custer from doing so. First are the geographic features of the region. Many things have changed in southeastern Montana since the 1876 campaign but one thing hasn't, the foothills of the Chetish Mountains are the same today as they were then. With this range blocking Herendeen's quick egress the only logical place for Custer to dispatch the scout was from a point near the Crows Nest about where the Camp Marker today marks the divide between the Rosebud and Little Big Horn watersheds. In addition, from the nearby hills the area around the forks of the Tullock's are plainly visible for miles. Mitch Bouyer knew this, and as Herendeen remembered, he concurred with his reasoning.

Secondly, Custer had been following this warm cohesive trail for two days but he still was not sure where it led or if it was breaking up. He would have no concrete information to report. He could only relate as Major Marcus Reno, the regiment's second in command, had at the termination of his scout on June 19th when he said to Terry, "I can tell you where the Indians are not."[21] What good would it do to send anyone with this type of message? Custer's best course of action at this point was to attempt to fix the Indians' exact location, insure the trail didn't split apart, then dispatch Herendeen to advise Terry. Herendeen fully concurred with this thinking as he told Walter Camp, an oral historian par excellence and the greatest Indian War information collector, that Custer didn't know until the early hours of the 25th that the trail had left the Rosebud.[22]

Some students of the battle who believe Custer didn't follow Terry's instructions regarding the Tullock's will point to the fact Varnum was ordered to keep his scouts employed mostly to the east and very little attention was paid to the west where the forks of the Tullock's lay. Godfrey would later write Custer did pay attention to both directions. He recorded:

> During the second or third day (23rd or 24th) up the Rosebud, several times we thought we saw smoke in the direction of the Tullock, and finally we spoke to the Gen-

[19]Stewart, *Custer's Luck*, 264.

[20]Lee Noyes, "Sketches of the Frontier . . . ," *The Battlefield Dispatch*, Vol. 21, #1, Winter 2002, 13.

[21]Willert, *The Edge of Darkness*, 173.

[22]*Walter M. Camp Papers* (Bloomington, IN: Indiana University), box 2, 63. Hereinafter cited as: *Camp, IU.*

eral at one of the haults. He said it could not be, that he had scouts over on that side and they most certainly would have seen any such "signs" and report to him, and he reiterated that there were scouts out looking toward Tullock's valley.[23]

Godfrey then dismissed this smoke as clouds as well he should. Custer had told Godfrey correctly; the Crows had already been to the forks of the Tullock's. The scout Curley informed Dr. Joseph Dixon in a 1909 interview, "We followed the trail and we waited at the head of Tallec [sic] Creek for the command to come up."[24] But the command stopped at Busby and the Crows rejoined the regiment there.

Fred Girard, a frontier scout on the campaign with many years of experience, also weighed in on the Tullock's question. He related:

I have heard Gen. Custer criticized for not sending Herendeen to scout Tullock's fork. Gen. Custer did not overlook this and the subject came up for discussion while we were on the divide. From the Crow's Nest we had a good view of the valley of Tullock's creek, which takes its rise not far from where we were. We could see all over that part of the country, and as no trail led that way we concluded there were no Indians in that part of the country.[25]

About 9 o'clock Custer received word from these returning scouts the trail had crossed over the divide to the Little Big Horn River. White-Man-Runs-Him explained, "We knew the trail and the way the Sioux were moving but not sure which way they went."[26] Custer had no choice now but to again send his scouts forth, Red Star recalled Custer told them:

tonight you shall go without sleep. You are to go ahead. You are to try to locate the Sioux camp. You are to do your best to find this camp. Travel all night. When day comes, if you have not found the Sioux camp, keep on going until noon. If your search is useless by this time, you are to come back to our camp.[27]

Custer was trying to comply with Terry's wishes, since he couldn't be sure of the Indians' position he would keep the command in camp, even until noon on the 25th. This is not the action of a man many times portrayed as headstrong and impetuous in leading men into battle. It was

the action of a man who was displaying the required caution and military professionalism the situation demanded. It was analytic to camp near Busby and be astride the Indians' trail and not lose sight of a known issue. Terry had said to proceed southward if the trail turned towards the west and the Little Big Horn. When the scouts reported what he needed to know, the commander could determine the best course to employ.

Custer was now on the horns of a dilemma. On one hand, should he break off contact with the trail he had been following to comply with Terry's wishes to go further south along the Rosebud then swing back north to the Little Big Horn valley? If he did so, would he be able to find the trail again and would it still be as fresh? What would happen if he was unable to pick up this thread and had to spend several days in re-scouting the country? If so, any general perceived cooperation, two days hence with Terry, would surely be lost. What would happen if all this marching would alert the Indians and the trail would break up and the camps scatter? How would contact be reestablished?

On the other hand, if Custer continued to follow the trail he could do so at his convenience, not the Indians', giving the regiment plenty of time to rest while the scouts fixed the exact location and size of the Indian camps. This option also permitted Custer to keep an ever watchful eye to the east to prevent any movement around his flank. Custer probably dismissed any escape southward by the Indians as he and Terry were both aware General George Crook's much larger force was in that area to intercept any movement down in that direction.

Custer chose the second option, and decided to follow the trail. No doubt Custer rationalized his decision not to go southward as in effect complying with Terry's strategic instructions, while adding his own tactics to the evolving and fluid situation. After all didn't Terry verbally inform him, "Use your own judgment and do what you think best if you strike the trail"?[28] To Custer's mind this gave him a wide latitude in executing Terry's wishes. Given what Godfrey and Varnum would later write, Custer was not being abrupt in making this decision to deviate from what he had been directed to do 72 hours earlier. The presence of an intact hot trail, the distances between the commands, the geography, and the consequences for his not acting, showed Custer was doing exactly what was expected of him. As noted previously, Lieutenant James Bradley, Terry's Chief of Scouts, recorded in his journal

---

[23]Graham, *The Custer Myth*, 136; Brady, *Indian Fights and Fighters*, 379.

[24]Joseph K. Dixon, *The Vanishing Race* (Glorieta, NM: Rio Grande Press, 1973), 162.

[25]*Walter M. Camp Papers* (Provo, UT: Brigham Young University), roll 5, box 6, folder 19. Hereinafter cited as: *Camp, BYU*.

[26]Graham, *The Custer Myth*, 21.   [27]Ibid, 32.

[28]John S. Manion, *General Terry's Last Statement to Custer* (El Segundo, CA: Upton & Sons, 2000), 26.

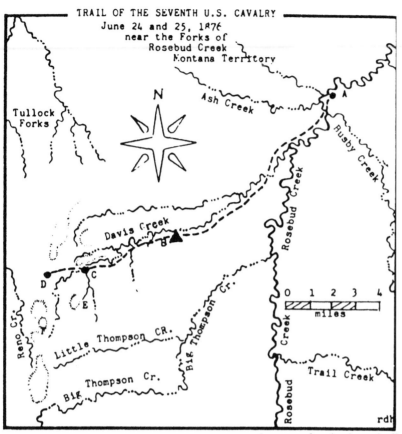

TRAIL OF THE SEVENTH U.S. CAVALRY
June 24 and 25, 1876
near the Forks of
Rosebud Creek
Montana Territory

A. Regiment halted near Busby at 7:45 P.M.; Varnum detached to Crow's Nest at 9:30 P.M.; regiment advanced at 11:00 P.M.; marched about eight miles.

B. Regiment halted at 2:00 A.M., June 25; Custer to Crow's Nest at 8:30 A.M.; march of regiment resumed at 8:45 A.M.; advance about five miles.

C. Regiment halted at 10:07 A.M.; march resumed at 11:45 A.M.; advance about one mile.

D. Regiment halted at 12:05 P.M..

E. Crow's Nest

F. Rocky promontory, identified faultily sometimes as the Crow's Nest.

Courtesy of Richard Hardorff

on the 21st "it is understood that if Custer arrives first he is at liberty to attack at once if he deems prudent."

Walter Camp wrote he had long studied whether Custer had disobeyed Terry's instructions and he had discussed this very point with many men of long military experience. Camp concluded it was left to Custer's judgment and he used his judgment. The only thing he could be charged with was nothing more than bad judgment but not disobedience.[29] I believe it is difficult to find fault with Custer's decision to continue in "hot pursuit." One must also take into account the military never formulated any campaign plans into "a systematic, coherent policy towards the Plains Indians."[30] It was left up to the individual field commander to reinvent the wheel with each campaign. How much this lack of any methodical planning affected the Little Big Horn is still being debated. In spite of this military void, what both Terry and Custer didn't figure in the 1876 campaign's equation was the Indians' might and their belief their 'medicine' was strong

combined with their determination to stay together and resist the white man. Not only did Terry misinterpret the intentions of the Indians in drawing up his plans but they were also seconded by John Gibbon, Terry's ranking subordinate. Gibbon was one of the Civil War's premier combat commanders and he, too, never expected the Indians to fight. The Colonel remarked the object of the campaign was "to prevent the escape of the Indians." Along with this flawed perception regarding the enemy's temperament, one could also add the ethnocentrism of the army, itself, whose leaders believed they were invincible against the hostile Indians. The General, his Colonel, and his Lieutenant Colonel all concluded whatever force they fielded would be victorious no matter what the Indians' reaction. Vanity and prejudice can transform into deadly combinations. Replace Indians with Viet Cong, add ninety years and the carry over of this culturally superior mindset is complete.

It was Custer's Crows scouts, who knew the country much better than the Arikaras, who told him of a quicker way to uncover the enemies' location. Varnum later recorded:

[29]*Camp, BYU*, roll 5, box 6, folder 16.

[30]Lee Noyes, "The Guns Custer Left Behind," *The English Westerners Society*, Summer 1999.

the General (Custer) sent for me. He said that the Crows believed we would find the Indians in the Little Big Horn Valley. That in the divide between the Rosebud and that stream was a "Crow Nest," a big hollow, where the Crows used to go and hide . . . that from there they could see in the early morning when the camp fires started and tell whether they were there or not and estimate their strength.[31]

What the Crows had told Custer was from this point they could tell by the smoke if there were or were not any Indians in the Little Big Horn Valley. The trail itself had so far shown the column this much, but it didn't reveal if there was a village ahead or its exact location. The Crows knew, as we do today, standing on the Crow's Nest one can't see a great deal of the Little Big Horn valley, but the benchlands beyond are visible and the scouts knew if a village was along the river, the horse herds would be seen grazing out there.

Custer took their suggestion and decided to further augment this important scouting detail and directed Mitch Bouyer and six Arikaras to report to the Chief of Scouts. According to Varnum, he wanted an "intelligent white man to go with them & get what information he could from them & send him a message with that information."[32] Varnum who knew this trip would add more hours of hard riding to an already impossible day now made a request of his own. He wanted Charlie Reynolds to accompany him. Varnum told his commander he needed "one white man to talk to." Besides Varnum recalled he didn't feel he was in the safest kind of an expedition with all these Indian scouts and at the first sign of trouble they might just scatter leaving just Charlie Reynolds to depend on. Custer told Varnum he would move the command about 11 PM to be close to the divide by sunrise and he expected to receive information there "as early as possible."

White-Man-Runs-Him recalled he acted as the guide for Varnum's expanded detachment; he probably did so but it was only under the watchful eye of the older more experienced scouts. He said they "followed down Lodgepole trail which was the regular trail from the Rosebud across the Little Big Horn."[33] Red Star remembered the horses trotted most of the way and the party tried to get as close as possible to the Crow's Nest while there was still a faint glimmer of daylight on the horizon. However, as the inky darkness surrounded the party, its pace slowed and White-Man-Runs-Him and the scouts had to stop

several times to regain their bearings.[34] The Arikara further said:

they rode on and on and reached a small grove of trees where they smoked and a Crow scout told them they were near. They came on to the foot of the mountain and the same Crow scout, the leader (White-Man-Runs-Him), told them they had come to the mountain and they were to climb up.[35]

The Crow's Nest and the divide between the Rosebud and Little Big Horn valleys are not in the strictest sense mountains. As anybody who has been in that country can attest, it's a rough and broken land of elevations with sharp sides and deep narrow ravines. A geologist would probably say the "mountain" referred to by the scouts was not formed by the volcanic activity which created the Rockies but rather by water and wind erosion. There is still some dispute from exactly which elevation the scouts made their discovery. Today the students of the campaign know about the conventional peak called the Crow's Nest and the marker upon it. But in fact, this viewpoint's exact location is a source of puzzlement and debate among historians almost since the beginning.

It would appear its location had been forgotten over the years as Walter Camp was not sure of the spot where the scouts discovered the Indian camps on the Little Big Horn. In 1909, he wrote to Varnum trying to get clarification and was told it was located "near the summit of a high ridge in the divide between the Rosebud and the Little Big Horn." Captain Myles Moylan, 'A's Company commander who would fight in the valley as part of Major Marcus Reno's battalion, stated the village and pony herd were seen from "a point on the divide."[36] Camp concluded after studying all the evidence, interviewing the participants, and personally traveling over the back country, the point the scouts climbed in the early hours of the 25th was close to the divide and is what we know today as the Crow's Nest. He stated the: "Crow's Nest is about a mile east of the divide at the lowest point of the divide. Crow's Nest is a spur running 10 degrees west of N. The base of it is about ½ mile south of Custer's trail over the divide."[37]

Although this lookout is east of the geographic divide and is part of the Rosebud drainage area, nevertheless

[31]Carroll, *I, Varnum*, 61.

[32]Ibid.
[33]Graham, *The Custer Myth*, 21.

[34]Ibid, 32.
[35]Ibid.

[36]Col. William A. Graham, *The Official Record of a Court of Inquiry convened at Chicago, Illinois, January 13, 1879, by The President of the United States upon the request of Major Marcus A. Reno, 7th U.S. Cavalry to investigate his conduct at the Battle of the Little Big Horn, June 25–26, 1876* (Pacific Palisades, CA: NP, 1951), 184. Hereinafter cited as: *Reno Court*.

[37]*Camp, IU*, box 3, 188.

Camp and other campaign students believed Varnum and Moylan had remarkable memories to describe the terrain precisely as they did years after the event. In 1919 General Hugh Scott, a former officer in the 7th Cavalry, was taken by White-Man-Runs-Him to this same hill as Camp recorded.[38] The late Henry Weibert, a local rancher who devoted a lifetime to the study of the Little Big Horn battle, used this picture General Scott had taken on the Crows Nest to "rediscover" this site in 1966. His extensive field research has also helped many other students in their understanding of the events on June 25th.[39] Since then, it has been the generally accepted location for their viewpoint that Sunday morning and although it isn't the highest peak on the divide, but by its position it's the most advantageous relative to the surrounding topography.

Despite Camp's and then Scott's inquires ten years earlier, campaign student Albert Johnson still wasn't sure the right peak had been discovered. In 1929 he explored the country around the divide in an effort to verify, for his own satisfaction, this lookout. He told a reporter for the Billings *Gazette* after crossing over Little Thompson Creek, his party came almost directly upon a pass which is recognized as where Custer's command reached the top of the divide. About 1800 yards south of this pass, he reported, is the Crow's Nest.[40] In addition Fred Dustin, an early expert on the Custer Battle, during his only trip to the area in 1938 had questioned if Johnson had found not necessarily *the* Crow's Nest but the right viewpoint. Dustin confirmed Johnson's conclusions with Russell White Bear who was later a friend and interpreter for White-Man-Runs-Him. White Bear said his friend told him during the night march they passed up the left branch of Davis Creek around a high hill to the Crow's Nest. The reason why they traveled by this route was "to avoid any hostiles that might be coming up Reno Creek." Dustin inquired about the higher point south of the Crow's Nest, sometimes identified as such, but White Bear said it is too far out of the way and even if you were there you could not see any more.[41]

There has been additional research done by Vern Smalley which places into question, not that peak we have known as the Crow's Nest isn't the Crow's Nest, but rather is it really the peak from which Varnum, then Custer, looked into the valley of the Little Big Horn? He determined Varnum was led to a peak on the divide, just as

the Chief of Scouts recalled to Camp, (Smalley refers to it as "Varnum's lookout") and wasn't near the conventionally accepted place known as the Crow's Nest. This "lookout" is nearly a mile away to the west.[42] Notwithstanding Smalley's interesting deductions, most campaign experts believe Camp pin pointed the elevation and it is the same hill we call the Crow's Nest that Varnum ascended early on the 25th. All this is interesting for debate among historians but what effect did it have on the coming battle? What difference did it make if the scouts ascended this hill or "Varnum's Lookout' or another unknown hill? The view reported would be the same and the actions of the regiment was based upon the scene described from whatever the viewpoint. Its location would not have changed anything on this Sunday.

Varnum's party arrived at the Crow's Nest about 2 AM. The Lieutenant was worn-out. He had spent almost 20 hours in the saddle and had ridden nearly seventy miles in the past 24 hours; he recalled, "I was so completely exhausted that I could hardly sit in the saddle."[43] While his scouts kept watch for the beginning of sunrise, he laid down to sleep and with the first sign of dawn breaking he was awakened. Varnum climbed up the steep crest of the hill to join the Crow scouts while leaving the horses with the rest of the Arikaras in the "Nest."[44] With dawn becoming more pronounced with each passing minute, the scouts were astonished with what they could see.

The terrain precluded a full view of the Indian camp but it didn't prevent their sharp eyes from detecting the flats of the Little Big Horn valley being covered with lodges. They also noted to the north and west there was a distinct haze from many campfires which hung over the valley. In addition, to their complete wonderment, the bench land on the west side of the river was "black with Sioux and Cheyenne horses, as far as they could see."[45] Unfortunately for Varnum, physically fatigued, his eyes red and tired from the previous day's exertions, he could not confirm what the Crows told him. He later said his eyes were never very good for long range viewing.[46] The Crows implored him to look again, the horses were "like

---

[38]A photograph of this site can be found in *The Custer Myth*, 112.

[39]Henry Weibert, *Sixty-six Years in Custer's Shadow* (Billings, MT: Bannack Publishing Co.,1985), xii–xvii.

[40]Billings *Gazette* (Billings, MT), July 23, 1929.

[41]Dustin, *The Custer Tragedy*, vii–viii.

[42]Vern Smalley, "Where was the Crows Nest?," *13th Annual Symposium Custer Battlefield Historical & Museum Assn.*, June 25, 1999, 77–90.

[43]E. A. Brininstool, "I Was There—Varnum's Experience," *Winners of the West*, Vol. 13, # 4, March 30, 1936.

[44]Carroll, *I, Varnum*, 62.

[45]Frank B. Linderman, *Pretty-Shield* (NY, NY: The John Day Co, 1972), 234.

[46]Robert P. Hughes, "The Campaign Against the Sioux in 1876," *Journal of the Military Service Institution*, Vol.43, #79, January 1896, 29.

worms crawling in the grass." But the Lieutenant could distinguish nothing except some smoke and "on a branch between me and the river one teepee standing and one partly wrecked."[47] Varnum then turned to Red Star and asked him to tell him what he had observed. Red Star told the officer he saw:

> a dark object and above it light smoke rising up from Dakota tepees.It was the upper end of the village, the tepees hidden by the high ridge but the smoke was drawing out and up. Beyond the smoke he saw black specks he thought were horses.[48]

Varnum knowing his limited distance vision asked Charlie Reynolds for confirmation. The frontiersman possessed a good pair of binoculars and after looking through them for what seemed a long time returned them to their case and nodded his head in the affirmative.[49] The Chief of Scouts was now convinced. He took out his note pad. It was almost 5 o'clock and Varnum decided to send two of his scouts, Red Star and Bull, with a message to Custer. His note contained only the information he could personally verify that of smoke, probably from the Indian village, and a lone standing teepee about twenty miles away in the valley of the Reno Creek.[50]

---

[47]Carroll, *I, Varnum*, 62.
[48]Graham, *The Custer Myth*, 32.

[49]Ibid.   [50]Carroll, *The Federal View*, 65.

Courtesy of Warren Van Ess

3
Advance to Battle

It was about 10 PM when Varnum's scouting detail left the camp near Busby. Custer called his officers together for new orders. In the flickering candlelight of their commander's tent, the officers were informed of the situation as reported by the scouts and of the Lieutenant Colonel's decision to cross the divide before daylight. From here the regiment would be concealed on the 25th while the scouts would gather intelligence in preparation for a surprise attack Monday at dawn.[1] Reno wrote in his July 5th report, Custer notified the assembly it was necessary to cross the divide at night as "it would be impossible to do so in the daytime without discovering our march to the Indians." Reno also stated Custer said, "beyond a doubt the village was in the valley of the Little Big Horn."[2] Lt. Winfield Edgerly, "D" Company's junior officer, confirmed Custer told the assembly that "the Indian's village had been located in the valley of the Little Big Horn and the object (of the night march) being to cross the divide between the Rosebud and the Little Big Horn before daylight."[3] In addition, Custer was aware of the possibility of a great many Indians ahead and he told the officers they would have the fight of their lives.[4] Custer probably obtained this information from Frederick Girard who said he could expect to find the fighting strength of the enemy between 2500 to 3000 warriors.

If Custer told his officers about a village it was not any information he had from personal knowledge. He had been just following the trails made by a large number of Indians. True they had become more pronounced, were getting larger, and in all probability the trails at some point must come together. But no one on this Saturday evening was sure there was a village or of its location. If Reno and Edgerly were correct, Custer could only be inferring there was a village ahead from the assumptions reported by the scouts. As the conference was breaking up, Custer informed Godfrey he was detaching his junior officer, 2nd Lieutenant Luther Hare, for temporary duty with the scouts. Custer told 'K's commander he knew this left only him to manage the company, but with Varnum away there was no officer in charge of the remaining scouts.[5]

The captains were directed to make their companies ready for a night march to begin about 11 o'clock. How-

ever, ordering a night march and actually starting one are two different events. By the time the troopers were turned out, the horses and mules made ready, it was as Wallace said, closer to 1 AM when the last company left the camp site.[6] This hour and a half delay was mostly due to the problems encountered in getting the pack train across Mud Creek. As with most events associated with this campaign there is a disagreement over which route the command took in its march to the divide. Some have stated they followed Thompson Creek, while others have held it was Davis Creek. Most historians believe it was Davis Creek, as this was the route, according to Wooden Leg, a Cheyenne who later took part in the battle, that was taken by the Indians. In addition, White-Man-Runs-Him told General Hugh Scott in an interview, Custer came through a pass to the head of the north fork of Upper Reno Creek. This pass followed up Davis Creek from the Rosebud.

Godfrey would later recall that this march was particularly trying. It was impossible to see the trail in the dark, and combined with the dust, the only way he could keep in formation was by listening to the sounds of those in advance "sometimes whistling or hallooing" before proceeding.[7] The column moved in fits and starts as the officers and men groped their way forward. Unbelievably, one trooper claimed the night march was made at a trot or gallop most of the way.[8] 'B' Company private Thomas Coleman recorded in his diary, "the night being so dark we could scarcely see the horses ahead of us."[9]

The moon was a crescent (about 12%), and it had set at 11:48 PM. Thus the march was made, as Coleman wrote, in near total darkness. Private John Burkman, Custer's personal orderly, added his confirmation regarding problems the men encountered on this march:

> we were moving quiet through the dark, not in formation, but helter skelter, scattered out, and we advanced the best way we could, every man for himself. It was pitch dark. We couldn't see one another . . . some of us got lost. Some fell, horse and all, into ravines and had to get out alone the best way they could. The moon had gone under a cloud.

Needless to say, very little progress was made toward

---

[1] Carroll, *The Federal View*, 65.

[2] Ibid, 102.

[3] Carroll, *The Gibson and Edgerly Narratives*, 7.

[4] Charles F. Roe, *Custer's Last Battle* (Old Slip, NY: National Highway Assoc, 1927), 8.

[5] Graham, *The Custer Myth*, 136.

[6] Carroll, *The Federal View*, 65.

[7] Graham, *The Custer Myth*, 136.

[8] Daniel A. Knipe, "A New Story of Custer's Last Battle," *Contributions to the Historical Society of Montana*, Vol. 4, 1903, 279.

[9] Bruce R. Liddic, *I Buried Custer* (College Station TX: Young West, 1979), 15.

the divide, and about 2 o'clock the scouts told Custer they could not possibly cross the divide before daylight. If they attempted it after sunrise they would be discovered by the Sioux. Wallace said not more than eight miles were marched, and as dawn was breaking Custer directed the command to conceal itself in a wooded ravine between two high ridges to await Varnum's report.[10] Most of the tired troopers simply slid off their mounts, laid down next to them, and slept.

Some of Custer's detractors point out one of the reasons for his defeat was the tired condition of his command. They claim he had pushed the command with long marches, which exhausted the troops, in an effort to be the first to bring the Indians to battle. However, a check of the official itinerary reveals, for example, the regiment didn't march until five o'clock the morning of the 24th, an hour later than usual. A leisurely and deliberate march was made with frequent brief halts while the scouts ranged out from the regiment. At one o'clock an extended halt of 4 hours was made, and just two hours and forty-five minutes later another halt was made. The total distance covered that day was 28 miles; hardly taxing for troopers who had already spent a month and a half in the field.[11] The scouts however covered many more miles than this in their assignments and were no doubt tired. As related above, the command moved out near midnight and traveled for about two and a half hours. On the morning of the 25th, the regiment was still resting at eight o'clock. Thus Custer's men were in the saddle for about eleven hours out of the day, and there were frequent halts besides the two camps. The average speed was only 2.5 miles per hour, barely walking speed, and it was hardly the exhausting pace as these critics have charged.

Besides exhausted troopers, another criticism directed at Custer has been the tired condition of the command's horses. In April, 1941, Colonel Elwood Nye wrote an article for the Army's *Veterinary Bulletin* in which he noted, "The whole story of his (Custer's) military life shows a brutal disregard of the well being of his men and animals. There can be no doubt that this contributed, in part, to his tragic end beside the 'Greasy Grass.'"[12] As noted, the command and these horses only averaged 26 miles per day since leaving Terry's camp, with frequent stops. Hardly a "disregard of their well being." The point that Colonel Nye neglects is the horses accomplished what they were supposed to do, and that was to deliver a combat force to the

location of an Indian village. But whether or not the horses were worn out is really not an arguable point, as Custer neither chased the Indians nor did he try to run from them. Private Edward Davern probably gave as fair assessment as we are likely to obtain when he stated at the Reno Court, "The horses of the command were in tolerable condition." While the condition of some individuals' horses might have impeded their performance, (however, one set of 'fours' from Company C did drop out), overall it had no effect on the outcome of the battle.

Almost as soon as Red Star and Bull departed the Crow's Nest, Varnum received a disturbing report from his scouts. He was told there were two Indians about a mile in front riding parallel to the ridge but moving in the direction of where the trail crossed the divide. Varnum quickly ordered Charlie Reynolds, Mitch Bouyer and two Crows to join him to intercept and kill the Indians to prevent them from exposing the command.[13] No sooner did the party start than it was called back by the remaining scouts who informed Vanum the pair had changed course. When the party arrived back on the hill, much to their chagrin, the two Indians again changed direction and crossed the trail. Varnum felt sure they had discovered their presence. This feeling was reinforced a little later when Varnum saw seven Indians riding on a hill parallel to the stream (Davis Creek) up which the main command had moved. He said the Indians disappeared and "They had evidently seen Custer's column."[14] Varnum then needed to inform his commander the Indians knew there were soldiers on their back trail, and if there was a village ahead it would surely be warned. The chance of any surprise attack was now remote.

What Varnum and Custer didn't know was before the regiment broke camp for their night march they had been observed by two Indians from Little Wolf's Cheyenne band. In 1927, the two, Big Crow and Blackwhiteman, told Willis Rowland, an interpreter at the Cheyenne Reservation in Lame Deer, on June 24th they were camped on the Rosebud near Busby. The pair were out to hunt in the evening and saw Custer's camp, but they didn't know who the soldiers were. Both were quick to point out Little Wolf's band didn't join the warriors until after the battle.[15] Even if these Cheyennes didn't warn the village, the soldiers did a good job of advertising themselves without Little Wolf's help. Red Star and Bull, upon saddling their horses to carry Varnum's message, saw the smoke from the command's campfires as it rose up in the morning's light. Crooked Horn, an Arikara leader, told them, "Look

[10]Carroll, *The Federal View*, 65.

[11]Carroll, *The Federal View*, 65.

[12]Lt. Col. Elwood Nye, *Marching With Custer* (Glendale, CA: Arthur H. Clark Co, 1964), 13.

[13]Carroll, *I, Varnum*, 63.   [14]Ibid.

[15]Billings *Gazette* (Billings, Montana), May 26, 1927.

you can see the smoke from our camp, just follow it to them."[16] It is little wonder these Indians shook their heads in disbelief; did the white soldiers think the Sioux and Cheyenne had no eyes? These Indians now surely knew the army was hunting them.

Red Bear remembered when he passed through the soldier's camp to get some water for an early breakfast, he saw "the soldiers lying in groups on the ground snoring, for they were very tired and lay down where they had unsaddled."[17] But not all the troopers were sleeping. Company officers had permitted small fires to be started to heat water for coffee, and it was the smoke from these cooking fires Crooked Horn saw from the Crow's Nest. Burkman said small cooking fires were authorized because the troops were in a deep ravine well hidden from the enemy. The morning's light revealed this was not the case. Godfrey said the fires should have never been started as after the coffee was made it was impossible to drink it as the water was so alkaline.[18] However, Captain Frederick W. Benteen, the regiment's ranking captain, recalled he had coffee and all the trimmings for breakfast, and it was "first class."[19] If so, the officers must have had their own private potable water with the pack train.

It was well before eight o'clock and the sun had cleared the horizon when the two Arikara messengers met the sentries from their camp. Ignoring the white man's timetable, and instead of reporting directly to Custer's camp, Red Star remembered they got off their horses and asked for breakfast.[20] Isaiah Dorman, an interpreter and the only black man on the campaign, saw the scouts arrive and went to Burkman and asked the whereabouts of Custer. Burkman told Dorman he was sleeping and wasn't to be disturbed. But the interpreter wasn't to be put off and said, "This is important, Boss. I got a message from Varnum for the General."[21] After listening to Dorman, Custer called for his horse to be saddled and rode over to where Girard was sleeping, woke him up and said he was to accompany him to the scout's camp. Upon their arrival at the scouts' camp, Red Star handed him Varnum's message.

Custer, after reading its contents, decided he needed to go to the divide and see for himself. He couldn't commit his command one way or the other based on the unsure intelligence Varnum reported. So far he had conducted his operations in a careful and business-like manner, and he wasn't about to deviate from this format now.

Custer had Girard tell the scouts to guide them back to the Crow's Nest. Girard also recalled Custer ordered his Adjutant, 1st Lieutenant William Cooke, to keep the command in camp until he returned.[22] Other sources indicate Custer gave instructions to move the regiment closer to the divide, which was still about five miles away. Godfrey remembered the Lieutenant Colonel gave orders to be ready to march at 8 o'clock. Private John Martin, Custer's trumpeter orderly for the day, confirmed this and stated, "the General . . . rode around the camp, talking to the officers in low tones and telling them what he wanted them to do." But it wasn't until 8:30 the command was ready to march."[23] Even if Custer didn't order the regiment to follow him, he could have hardly missed the preparations being made to march and could have stopped it.

It is interesting to speculate why Custer who had been so careful about keeping their presence from being discovered by the Indians would now expose his command to the Sioux or Cheyenne scouts. Especially since he had no knowledge direct or otherwise which indicated the troops had not yet been seen by the Indians. The dust from the moving column would surely be spotted now if the smoke from the cooking fires hadn't already been seen. One of the Lieutenant Colonel's critics expressed his opinion that Custer permitted the fires that morning to "deliberately betray the presence of the regiment, hoping to draw the Indians into combat, or to attempt to cause them to flee towards the Terry—Gibbon command advancing up the Big Horn River."[24] Everyone is entitled to his belief.

A more plausible explanation could be, Custer had given the order exactly as Girard remembered but had changed his mind about moving closer to the divide when he decided to go to the Crow's Nest himself. He simply forgot to countermand the order. This explanation is made more believable as Girard testified at the Reno Court upon Custer's return from the Crow's Nest, he asked Captain Thomas Custer, 'C' company commander, a double Medal of Honor recipient and his brother, "Who moved the Command?" To which Tom Custer replied, "I don't know; the orders were to march and we marched."[25] It is easy to make judgments after the fact, and we now know

---

[16]Graham, *The Custer Myth*, 32. [17]Ibid, 31.
[18]Graham, *The Custer Myth*, 136. [19]Ibid, 179.
[20]Ibid, 32.
[21]Glendolin D. Wagner, *Old Neutriment* (NY, NY: Sol Lewis, 1973), 149.

[22]Graham, *Reno Court*, 43.
[23]Col. William A. Graham, "Come On! Be Quick! Bring Packs!," *The Cavalry Journal*, Vol. 32, #132, July 1932, 303–317.
[24]Daniel O. Magnussen, *Peter Thompson's Narrative of the Little Bighorn Campaign 1876* (Glendale, CA; Arthur H. Clark Co, 1974), 99.
[25]Graham, *Reno Court*, 45.

there was nothing Custer could have done this Sunday to prevent his discovery by the Indians. However, at the time he didn't know this, and some students of the campaign have taken him to task for putting the success of the campaign in peril with the daylight move to the divide.

It was after eight o'clock when Custer left the camp to ride out to the Crow's Nest. In the party who accompanied him were Red Star, Bull, Bloody Knife, Bobtailed Bull, Little Brave, Fred Girard, and John Martin. There is evidence that Tom Custer as well as 1st Lieutenants William Cooke and James Calhoun joined the detail.[26] In about five miles, they arrived at the base of the Crow's Nest; it was after nine o'clock. Varnum saw Custer approaching the hill, and years later he wrote, "I rode down to meet them. When partly down I met General Custer and Tom and Jim Calhoun. He sent Tom and Calhoun back and went with me to the crest of the divide."[27] He immediately told his commander about the Indians they had seen, and that they had spotted the regiment, and they were seen going in the direction of their camps, no doubt to give the alarm.[28] Custer could have hardly been pleased with this information.

Red Star said they climbed the hill and came upon the rest of the advance detail. Charlie Reynolds came up to Custer and they both went off a little ways further and left the others behind. Reynolds was seen pointing out to Custer areas in the Little Big Horn valley. Custer just shook his head and continued to look for a long time. Reynolds was not to be dissuaded, and he continued to point and speak to the commander. At long last, Custer nodded his head indicating he had seen signs of a camp. Just to be sure Custer understood the whole situation, Reynolds took out his field glasses and handed them to him. Custer studied the area once more and told Reynolds he was right, the signs were visible.[29] Girard told Camp he independently looked out over the valley as well through his glasses. He said, "I made out a pony herd on the hills or table land beyond that stream. I could distinctly see a large dark spot or mass, and could even see dust rising, from which I concluded that I was looking at a herd of ponies that were being driven."[30] After watching Custer and Reynolds for awhile, Girard joined the pair and called back to the scouts, "Custer thinks there

is no Sioux camp." What the reactions of the scouts were to this statement wasn't recorded.

Varnum recalled a different story and said Custer told him he had as good of eyesight as anyone but he could see nothing. Mitch Bouyer then entered into the discussion and told Custer to his face, "If you don't find more Indians in that valley than you ever saw together before you can hang me."[31] We will never know if Custer saw for himself and believed the signs of a village in the valley. Godfrey understood Custer thought there was a village ahead. He said Custer expected to find Indians strung out along the river but was unsure whether they would be found upstream or downstream from where he might strike the river.[32] This was in keeping with Custer's past experience in fighting Indians, as in 1868 the villages along the Washita were strung along for some distance along the river's banks. Another possibility was he may not have wanted to publicly contradict Reynolds for whom he had great respect, but Custer could not afford to disregard what his scouts were telling him. Custer was also aware like any human the scouts were not clairvoyant in their observations and assumptions. Even if he didn't see the signs, all the circumstantial evidence pointed to this fact. The scouts said there were indications of a village along the Little Big Horn, the trail they had been following went in that direction, and according to the Crows, it was a favorite camping place for the Sioux.

It can be assumed during the roughly hour and a quarter Custer spent at the Crow's Nest that he also studied the land toward the Little Big Horn valley, as far as he was able. Godfrey wrote, "It was a rare occurrence in Indian warfare that gives a commander the opportunity to reconnoiter the enemy's position in daylight." It would have been an opportune time because he could also ask Bouyer and the Crow scouts to clear up any questions about the topography he might have formed from his observations.

Whether or not Custer was convinced about a village along the Little Big Horn, he was sure the command hadn't been seen by the Sioux and Cheyenne despite what Varnum had told him. A Crow, Half Yellow Face, asked Custer, through an interpreter, if he thought this was true? Custer is reported to have said, " This camp has not seen our army, none of their scouts have seen us. . . . I want to wait until it is dark and then we will march, we will place our army around the Sioux camp."[33] The scout told Custer he was wrong. The smoke from the command had

[26]Graham, *The Custer Myth*, 33.

[27]Letter, Charles Varnum to Albert Johnson, November 13, 1929, Dustin Collection, Custer National Battlefield.

[28]Carroll, *The Federal View*, 66.

[29]Graham, *The Custer Myth*, 32–33.

[30]Kenneth Hammer, *Custer in '76 : Walter Camp's Notes on the Custer Fight* (Provo, UT: Brigham Young University, 1976), 231.

[31]Carroll, *I, Varnum*, 63–64.

[32]Hammer, *Custer in '76*, 75.

been seen, and the camp would be alerted. Red Star agreed with the Crow. They told Custer if he waited the warriors would come out to fight him to give the women and children time to escape, then all would scatter. Godfrey recalled the officers were of the same opinion, and the object would be to intercept and drive the "families, ponies and other impedimenta" back into the village.[34] If they couldn't prevent their escape it would be the campaign's worse case scenario, chasing small groups of Indians all over southeastern Montana with little hope of catching any of them. White Swan said he advised Custer to send two scouts to Terry and tell him what they discovered. Then the cavalrymen should wait for the Indians to attack Terry and Gibbon. Once they did, Custer could hit them in the flank. White Swan conceded, Custer "did not approve of his plan."[35] The other scouts said he should attack the Sioux camp right away before they could react to their presence; capture their horses so they couldn't move; they would not expect a mid-day battle. It was reported Custer listened to this advice and finally said through the interpreter they were right and he would march on the village.[36] Wallace recorded, Custer's order to move the column was complied with and at 8:45 the regiment marched to get as close to the divide as possible without crossing it. It was about 10:15 when the command arrived about one mile from the divide and halted in a timber lined ravine. Godfrey recalled the troopers were "ordered to be quiet, keep concealed, and not do anything to reveal our presence to the enemy." The officers "had generally collected in groups and discussed the situation." There was nothing to do but await Custer's return.

Before the command moved toward the divide that morning, one of Captain George Yates' non-commissioned officers, Sergeant William Curtis, requested permission to take a detail and go back along the trail to look for some lost personal items. Captain Myles Moylan related:

> While at the second halt at the foot of the divide . . . a Sergeant returned on the trail some miles for the purpose of recovering if possible some clothing of his that had been lost from a pack mule the night before.[37]

Permission was granted, and the Sergeant after riding several backtracking miles found more than he expected. In topping a small knoll, the five troopers saw several Indi-

Courtesy of The Little Bighorn Associates, Inc.

ans about four hundred yards in front, sitting on a box of hardtack and examining the contents of the Sergeant's lost bag. The Indians upon seeing the soldiers rode quickly out of range, and the detail didn't try to pursue them but rejoined the regiment immediately, arriving shortly after it stopped for the second time. Curtis reported to his company commander the information of being seen by the Indians, and Yates told Captain Myles Keogh, the rider of Comanche and 'I' Company's commander, who in turn reported to Captain Tom Custer who said he would inform his brother.[38]

The Sioux Black Bear explained the Indian side of this incident:

> While crossing the divide early on the morning of June 25, 1876 we discovered soldiers marching toward the village. We ran into the high hills and watched them, holding bunches of grass in front of our heads as a disguise. While here three Cheyennes came up to us and said they had been following the soldiers all the way from the Pow-

---

[33]Graham, *The Custer Myth*, 33.

[34]Ibid, 138.   [35]*Camp, IU*, box 2 folder 10.

[36]Graham, *The Custer Myth*, 33.

[37]Robert Utley, *The Reno Court of Inquiry : The Chicago Times Account* (Fort Collins, CO: Old Army Press, 1972), 207. Hereinafter cited: *Reno Court—Chicago Times*.

[38]Graham, *The Custer Myth*, 137–138.

der River. That morning they had come upon a box of bread lost by the soldiers and were in the act of opening it when soldiers appeared and they ran off. After the soldiers marched the Cheyennes left us and followed the soldiers towards the L.B.H.[39]

It was about quarter after ten when Custer rode down from the observation point and rejoined his command. He traveled less than a mile before he arrived at the regiment's second halt of the day about 10:30. As noted above, Custer was angry the regiment had moved thereby increasing the chances of discovery by the Sioux and Cheyenne. The news his brother related about the run-in Curtis had with Indians on the backtrail probably did little to improve the commander's disposition. Custer was now certain the Indians were aware of his presence, and it ratified his earlier decision to attack. If he waited, the alarm would surely be raised in the village, and by Monday at dawn there would be no village to attack. Godfey later would inform Camp, Custer was "possessed" with the idea the Indians would not stand and give battle but would run at the first sight of the cavalry.[40]

Custer was fully aware he could not make the proper reconnaissance, and he was taking a chance in marching towards an indefinite location in broad daylight. The alternative was less appealing, a scattered village and a hard chase after the Indians that would punish the chasers more than the chasees. The campaign could end in a failure. It would appear Custer's major concern was to keep the Indians where they were until he could launch his attack, and judging from his past performance, attack and victory were inseparable.[41] Years later, Godfrey agreed Indian fighting was an inexact science:

> At all events his attack must be made with celerity, and generally without other knowledge of the numbers of the opposing forces. . . . The dispositions for the attack may be said to be "made in the dark" and a successful surprise to depend upon luck. . . . In Indian warfare the rule is "touch and go."[42]

Custer had officer's call sounded by his trumpeter and told them about what the scouts had reported during his visit to the Crow's Nest. The Indian camps were about fifteen miles away in the valley of the Little Big Horn. His previous plan of concealing the regiment until Monday was no longer feasible as he had a number of reports which indicated the Indians had seen the command and were no

doubt at this very moment riding to warn the village. Custer told the officers he had no choice but to strike at once. Today, there are some students who believe there has been little attention paid to the assumptions that the discovery of the troops necessitated and justified an immediate attack.[43] Even given the campaign's mind set was on "fleeing" Indians, the command was at best hours and miles away from any possible interdiction. What could an immediate attack accomplish? Custer no doubt assumed by making forthwith to the suspected village location, a few Indians might escape but the majority would be stopped or driven north into Terry's command. Custer probably would have preferred to attack at dawn but he was also well aware of Colonel Ranald Mackenzie's late afternoon attack on a Comanche village in the Red River Campaign in 1872. Likewise, Lt. Colonel Eugene Carr's successful daylight action against a Cheyenne village at Summit Springs in 1869 was conducted against a numerically superior Indian force. Custer probably wasn't happy he had to modify his plan but a broad daylight attack wouldn't have caused him a great deal of concern. It was also evident Custer was ignoring the signs of a very large village ahead, with possibly more Indians than had been contemplated. But by 1876 army officers knew from experience, a small village would scatter the same as a large one. Whatever flawed assumptions we, today, believe Custer was operating under, they weren't apparent to him at the time, or if they were he dismissed these assumptions as part of the risk he was willing to accept. There is another salient point which is often brushed aside by Custer's detractors. He is the only western Indian war commander who was ever able to bring an entire cavalry regiment undetected to within striking distance of an enemy village. Not only did he accomplish this remarkable feat in broad daylight, but Custer did it during the Indians' greatest period of mobility . . . the summer. One must remember the commander's contemporary critics took him to task for many of his actions on this day but one decision they have not disputed, then or later, is not one regimental officer questioned Custer's determination to attack when he did.

The campaign's planners all feared even if they were able to find the Indians, they would scatter before they could be engaged, and the prospects of trying to track down, then capture the dispersed inhabitants was historically impossible. As noted, this thought was foremost in Custer's mind. It was the justification for his ordering the regiment into immediate action. He believed the troops had been discovered, the village would be warned,

[39]*Camp, BYU*, roll 5, box 6, #634.
[40]Hammer, *Custer in '76*, 75.
[41]*Army and Navy Journal* (Washington, DC), July 22, 1876.
[42]Graham, *The Custer Myth*, 136–137.
[43]Darling, *Sad and Terrible Blunder*, 192.

and the Indians would decamp. Some sources claim a second report by Varnum caused Custer to act even quicker than he had originally planned while at the Crow's Nest. After Custer had left to return to the command, the scouts had seen a dark mass which they took to be a band of Indians moving downstream. From this they inferred the village had been warned and was in the first stages of breaking up. We now know this was only a small camp near the Lone Teepee site moving towards the larger village, but the scouts didn't know this. Second Lieutenant Charles Woodruff, 7th Infantry, later wrote:

> it was thought that about sixty lodges were a few miles up the Little Big Horn above the main village, and in the early morning, when Custer's proximity was discovered, that this small village, knowing that they were but a mouthful for Custer's command, hurriedly packed up and dashed down the valley. It can readily be understood that sixty lodges with the horses and paraphernalia, moving rapidly down the valley, might well create the impression that a very large force was in retreat.[44]

Varnum made sure this latest intelligence was relayed to Custer.

If Custer was going to follow Terry's instructions to send Herendeen through with updated intelligence, now was the time to dispatch the scout. The pass where Herendeen could move through was near, and Custer had definite information about the Indians. Interestingly, Reno and Benteen testified at the Reno Court of Inquiry, Custer said he had not seen the village himself and although the scouts said there was a village he didn't believe it. However, their suspicious self-serving testimony is offset by the recollections of Lieutenants Gibson, DeRudio, Godfrey, and Edgerly who clearly remembered Custer said the scouts reported a village and pony herds in the valley. In addition, the Arikara and Crow scouts positively declared Custer saw the signs of a village from the Crow's Nest.[45] If Custer didn't believe there was a village along the banks of the Little Big Horn why would he commit 600 men to attack an illusion?

Why didn't Custer send George Herendeen to General Terry? Girard told Walter Camp after Custer found out the Indian scouts had discovered the command, he decided to attack the camp that day, and Girard believed Custer saw the futility of sending a scout through a valley where there were no Indians, to inform Terry of this

fact after Custer had made his attack.[46] Herendeen himself addressed this question and answered:

> Early on the 25th we lay in camp in the hollow east of the divide, I said to Custer: "General the head of Tullock's Creek lies just over those hills yonder." He replied rather impatiently: "Yes, but there are no Indians in that direction—they are all in our front, and besides they have discovered us. It will be of no use to send you down Tullock's Creek. The only thing to do is to push ahead and attack the camp as soon as possible."[47]

Thus we have two people who were present when Custer made his decision not to send Herendeen and his reasons for the decision. They remembered he didn't forget or ignore Terry's instructions as has been claimed; the situation had changed from when they were written, and Custer used his judgment. We can debate forever if it was sound or not. Custer didn't dispatch Herendeen because: (1) he wouldn't reach Terry in time before the regiment attacked, (2) there were no Indians on the upper reaches of the Tullocks, and (3) with Indians on the backtrail it is doubtful a lone rider could escape from them. Could Custer have reasoned that with the rapid advance on the village, Herendeen might have been dispatched later from a more advantageous, safer, and closer point? For instance, after the attack he could have been sent, not down the Tullocks but north down the Little Big Horn Valley with the intelligence Terry requested. Custer employed a similar messenger service when he forwarded California Joe with the information to Major General Philip Sheridan after the Washita Battle. George Herendeen was without question a brave and competent man. But it is interesting to note Herendeen never verbally complained then or in his later writings regarding not being given the opportunity to earn his $200 bonus. I suspect he placed more value on his scalp than earning this reward.

There are some students of the campaign who believe Custer made two trips to the Crow's Nest. These students base their belief on the statements by Hare and DeRudio in their interviews with Camp. Hare told Camp, "Before this Custer had been out ahead with scouts viewing valley of Little Big Horn. . . . Lay concealed less than ½ mile from divide for more than an hour. During this halt Custer again went to Crow's Nest to look at Indians."[48] DeRudio explained why Custer returned to the Crow's Nest:

> In the morning of June 25 Custer came back and said he had been up ahead with the scouts but his glasses were

---

[44]Brady, *Indian Fights and Fighters*, 383.

[45]Orin Libby, Ed., *The Arikara Narrative of the Campaign Against the Hostile Dakotas, 1876* (Bismarck, ND: North Dakota Historical Collections, Vol 6, 1920), 91. Hereinafter cited: *The Arikara Narrative*.

[46]*Camp, BYU*, roll 5, box 6, #511.

[47]Ibid, #562.   [48]Hammer, *Custer in '76*, 64.

not strong enough to discover anything. DeRudio had the strongest glasses in the regiment . . . and Cooke came to DeRudio and asked if he would lend them to Custer. . . . Custer took them and went ahead again.[49]

From this one could agree Custer made two trips. However, Hare wasn't in a position, personally, to know what Custer did when he returned from the Crow's Nest. His statements to Camp were hearsay. Hare was assigned to be with the remaining scouts, and he was with them on picket duty in front of the regiment. Without a doubt, Custer borrowed DeRudio's glasses, as the Lieutenant recalled with some bitterness thirty-four years later; his glasses were given to him by an Austrian optician, and he really didn't want to lend them but he finally consented. DeRudio made sure Camp recorded Custer took these glasses with him to his death, and he never saw them again.

DeRudio was never known for his veracity; why would Custer want to borrow his glasses for a second look at the Crow's Nest? Charlie Reynolds had as good a pair of glasses, and we know from Varnum and Red Star, Custer borrowed these and looked through them. A more likely occurrence was when Custer came back from the Crow's Nest he knew about DeRudio's pair and sent his Adjutant to borrow them as he saw what good binoculars would reveal. In addition, was it possible based on time and distance factors for Custer to make a second trip to the Crow's Nest? Custer returned to the command about 10:30; he called the officers together and spoke to them. This meeting would have consumed another 20–25 minutes. Custer would have then had to ride back about a mile to the Crow's Nest over rough terrain, make his observations, and ride back to the regiment all before 11:45, the time Wallace recorded Custer led the troops forward. Furthermore would Custer have ridden back to the Crow's Nest alone? There is no record of anyone, trooper, officer, or scout accompanying him on this second alleged trip.

Walter Camp was puzzled by Hare's and DeRudio's statements regarding the Crow's Nest and wrote a letter to then Lt. Colonel Varnum. In Camp's opinion the Chief of Scouts was in the best position to know the facts and pointedly asked him if Custer had made two trips to the Crow's Nest? In reply to Camp's question, Varnum wrote:

Hare & DeRudio are probably right in their statements of the length of time & places of Custer's halt. I don't think Custer went a second time to the hill. I am in fact quite if not absolutely sure of it. . . . Something was said by either Custer or myself about DeRudio's having a fine pair of field glasses. & Custer probably borrowed them from DeRudio as he says but I am certain he did not go back to the hill again.[50]

Camp considered this to be an authoritarian answer to his inquiry if Custer returned to "the hill again." All of this makes for an interesting debate and argument among battle students who question almost every detail of the campaign, but that's all it is. What effect did it have on the future outcome if Custer went to "the hill" once, twice or ten times? He based his decision to engage in battle upon the reported intelligence and what he personally gleaned while on "the hill," no matter how many trips. The number of times had no effect upon Custer ordering the regiment into immediate action.

The officers listened intently to Custer's decision to attack. He ordered each company commander to assign a non-commissioned officer and six privates from their ranks to guard the pack train. One can be certain the 1st Sergeants, with a battle looming, detailed the company's privates who could be best spared; the young, the inexperienced, and the slackers. In addition, Custer directed the officers to make sure their troops were well supplied with ammunition and it be carried on their person. As an incentive, he said the order in which they reported their company ready would be the order they would be assigned on the march. Benteen at once informed Custer that 'H' Company was ready as his company had strictly adhered to all the requirements since the campaign started. Benteen recalled, "I feel quite sure it wasn't expected of me; but he (Custer) stammered out, 'Well, Colonel Benteen, your troop has the advance.'" According to Private John Bailey, 'B' Company was the last to report because his commander, Captain Thomas McDougall the son of a former Army doctor, who was supposed to have the advance, was asleep when Custer gave the instructions and thus was assigned to guard the pack train.[51]

[49]Ibid, 84.

[50]*Camp, BYU*, roll 2, box 2, folder 16.

[51]Bruce R. Liddic, *Camp on Custer* (Spokane, WA: Arthur H. Clark, Co: 1995), 81.

4
Separation of Forces

Custer had made and executed the first of four critical decisions that would significantly affect the outcome of events that afternoon. He had reached a conclusion that he must immediately attack the village and had advanced the 7th Cavalry, in their usual column of fours with intervals of about 60 feet between companies, towards the divide. In spite of what some studies have suggested, Custer wasn't particularly hampered by untrained and inexperienced troopers. This was indeed a veteran regiment being led into battle. The recent recruits made up only about 10% of the regiment, and many of these were dismounted and left behind at Terry's Camp. Nearly 75% of the command could claim one or more years of service; 27% had served a minimum of one prior five year enlistment, and seventeen men had been in the army for fifteen or more years. The troopers average age was 27, and the vast majority were German and Irish immigrants.[1]

All the intelligence Custer had received, combined with his experience, led him to believe the regiment had been discovered, and upon receipt of this news the village would break up and scatter in all directions. He must have known he was throwing the dice in attacking a village of unknown size without fixing its precise location.

Whatever plans he had formulated while at the Crow's Nest would now have to be modified or totally discarded. Custer would have to improvise on the march, and his tactics would be formed as the situation unfolded. He no longer had the luxury of resting the command for a day while his scouting parties provided him with the intelligence to craft and communicate his tactics. At the Reno Court of Inquiry, Custer's officers criticized him for not telling them his battle plan; some in fact stated he had none. But without knowing the exact location of the village, the surrounding terrain, or its size, no workable plan could be drawn up; thus Custer as he crossed the divide had no tactical plan to communicate. Once he made his decision to commit his force, Custer had no other choice, as Dr. Charles Kuhlman so aptly observed, but to advance the entire regiment on a "reconnaissance in force."

The sun was at the meridian as the regiment and the trailing pack train crossed the divide. From the top of the divide the troopers could only see a small part of the Little Big Horn Valley. About eighteen miles away in a northwest direction there were opaque clouds which the scouts said marked the location of the Indian village. For western history students, it is one of those defining exciting moments in the time line of history . . . the 7th Cavalry was marching towards immortality that would turn its commander into a folk hero of world wide proportions. However, the soldiers were under no illusion about any "glory" which might await. Charles Windolph, a private in 'H' Company who would win the Medal of Honor the next day, recalled:

> We were tired and dirty and hungry. . . . Our horses hadn't had a good drink of water since the day before. It would be easy to say we were thinking of only glory on this hot June Sunday afternoon, but I reckon what most of the plain troopers were thinking about was how good a nice cold bottle of beer would taste.[2]

Windolph also recalled the men knew they were going into battle. This was *the* day they would "see the elephant." His company commander, Captain Frederick Benteen, used to tell his men, "the government pays you to get shot at." Windolph believed even "the dumbest, greenest trooper in that regiment figured that this day he'd get shot at plenty."[3] Private Coleman agreed with Windolph and wrote in his diary entry for June 24th "every Man feeling that the next twenty four hours would decide the fate of a good many men."[4]

The command crossed over to the western slopes of the divide and halted fifteen minutes later. Custer and Adjutant Cook rode off by themselves for a short distance, dismounted and the two officers were seen with pencil and paper, making notes.[5] Custer was dividing the regiment to begin his reconnaissance. It could not have taken more than a few minutes to draw up the battalion assignments as they hadn't changed much since the campaign began. Although Custer has been charged with favoritism with the assignments, the battalion configurations were based mainly on the seniority system so sacred to the old Army. Cooke then announced the assignments to the regimental officers.[6] Reno would later write in his official report that very little attention was given to him, and he merely "assumed command of the companies assigned to me and without any definite

[1]Robert M. Utley, *Cavalier in Buckskin* (Norman, OK: University of OK Press, 1976), 113.

[2]Hunt, *I Fought . . .* , 77.

[3]Ibid.

[4]Liddic, *I Buried Custer*, 16.

[5]Graham, *Reno Court*, 388. For a very good overview of this division, refer to Larry Sklenar, *To Hell With Honor* (Norman, OK: University of OK Press, 2000), 114–119.

[6]Ibid.

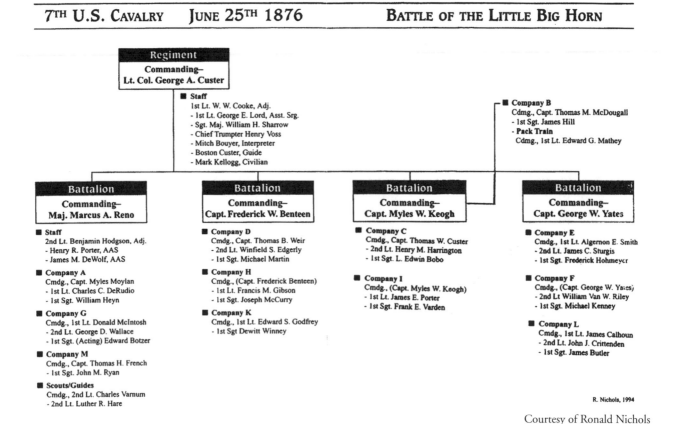

Regiment
Commanding–
Lt. Col. George A. Custer

■ Staff
1st Lt. W. W. Cooke, Adj.
- 1st Lt. George E. Lord, Asst. Srg.
- Sgt. Maj. William H. Sharrow
- Chief Trumpter Henry Voss
- Mitch Bouyer, Interpreter
- Boston Custer, Guide
- Mark Kellogg, Civilian

■ Company B
Cdmg., Capt. Thomas M. McDougall
- 1st Sgt. James Hill
- **Pack Train**
Cdmg., 1st Lt. Edward G. Mathey

Battalion
Commanding–
Maj. Marcus A. Reno

■ Staff
2nd Lt. Benjamin Hodgson, Adj.
- Henry R. Porter, AAS
- James M. DeWolf, AAS

■ Company A
Cmdg., Capt. Myles Moylan
- 1st Lt. Charles C. DeRudio
- 1st Sgt. William Heyn

■ Company G
Cmdg., 1st Lt. Donald McIntosh
- 2nd Lt. George D. Wallace
- 1st Sgt. (Acting) Edward Botzer

■ Company M
Cmdg., Capt. Thomas H. French
- 1st Sgt. John M. Ryan

■ Scouts/Guides
Cmdg., 2nd Lt. Charles Varnum
- 2nd Lt. Luther R. Hare

Battalion
Commanding–
Capt. Frederick W. Benteen

■ Company D
Cmdg., Capt. Thomas B. Weir
- 2nd Lt. Winfield S. Edgerly
- 1st Sgt. Michael Martin

■ Company H
Cmdg., (Capt. Frederick Benteen)
- 1st Lt. Francis M. Gibson
- 1st Sgt. Joseph McCurry

■ Company K
Cmdg., 1st Lt. Edward S. Godfrey
- 1st Sgt Dewitt Winney

Battalion
Commanding–
Capt. Myles W. Keogh

■ Company C
Cmdg., Capt. Thomas W. Custer
- 2nd Lt. Henry M. Harrington
- 1st Sgt. L. Edwin Bobo

■ Company I
Cmdg., (Capt. Myles W. Keogh)
- 1st Lt. James E. Porter
- 1st Sgt. Frank E. Varden

Battalion
Commanding–
Capt. George W. Yates

■ Company E
Cmdg., 1st Lt. Algernon E. Smith
- 2nd Lt. James C. Sturgis
- 1st Sgt. Frederick Hohmeyer

■ Company F
Cmdg., (Capt. George W. Yates)
- 2nd Lt William Van W. Riley
- 1st Sgt. Michael Kenney

■ Company L
Cmdg., 1st Lt. James Calhoun
- 2nd Lt. John J. Crittenden
- 1st Sgt. James Butler

R. Nichols, 1994

Courtesy of Ronald Nichols

orders moved forward with the rest of the column and well to its left."[7]

Custer basically re established the two wing formation constituted at Fort Lincoln, but discontinued upon leaving Terry's Rosebud Camp when Custer ordered all the company commanders to report individually to him. In May, when the 7th Cavalry left their fort, the right wing of the regiment consisted of "B, C, E, F, I, and L." It had been under the command of Major Reno where the battalion commanders were Captains Keogh for "B, C, & I" and Yates with "E, F, and L." The left wing was under the command of Captain Benteen, third ranking officer present, with battalion commanders Captains Weir with companies "D, H, & K" and French with "A, G, and M." Custer would personally assume command of the right wing. The first battalion would consist of 'B,' 'C,' and 'I' Companies with Captain Myles Keogh in charge ('B' was detached to guard the pack train). The second battalion was comprised of E, F, and L Companies with Captain George Yates in command. Custer has been taken to task

for tying himself down with only part of his regiment when he should have been overseeing the entire unit to coordinate one part with another.[8] However, other military leaders have defended his actions stating that Custer was doing what he had always done, being on the front line. In this way "he could see with his own eyes the rapid changes of cavalry situations and instantly form and execute his plans."[9]

Major Reno was assigned the left wing, but he was only in nominal command, as in reality this wing was employed as two separate and distinct components. Reno was ordered to take charge of the first battalion comprised of Companies A, G, and M. The second battalion was formed by Companies D, H and K under Captain Benteen's leadership.[10] It was recounted when Custer and Cooke were figuring out the assignments, Custer originally had D Company as one of his five companies. Benteen, however, wanted 'D' with his battalion as it was among

[7]Loyd J. Overfield, II, *The Little Big Horn 1876, The Official Communications, Documents and Reports* (Glendale, CA: Arthur H. Clark Co, 1971), 43.

[8]Col. T. M. Coughlan, "The Battle of the Little Big Horn," *Cavalry Journal*, Vol. 43, #181, Jan.–Feb. 1934, 17.

[9]Maj. Joseph M. Hanson, "The Civil War Custer," *Cavalry Journal*, Vol. 43, #183, May–June 1934, 30.

[10]Graham, *Reno Court*, 388.

the strongest in the regiment. Benteen protested to Custer, and he "rather impatiently" told his senior captain to "take D Company."[11] Some battle students have questioned why Custer would create such a distribution given the animosity displayed by both Benteen and Reno towards him. However, in establishing these assignments Custer, for better or worse, was appropriately following Army procedures and regulations regardless of any personal reservations the Lieutenant Colonel might have felt about their loyalty or competence.[12] It's within the realm of possibility that his adherence to these customs contributed to the afternoon's disaster. Custer, ever the optimist, expected his orders to be carried out faithfully by his primary subordinates. Full obedience to orders requires confidence and respect for the authority issuing them. Neither Reno nor Benteen had confidence in or respect for the commanding officer, and they reacted about as one might expect in this situation. We know Custer was aware of their feelings and should have taken into account his orders would be executed grudgingly and made allowances for it.[13]

It was shortly after the command had been divided that Custer sent Benteen's battalion off to the left. Benteen directly questioned the wisdom of further command division when he said to Custer, "Hadn't we better keep the regiment together, General? If this is as big a camp as they say, we'll need every man we have." Custer was said to have replied, "You have your orders."[14] Benteen's orders, according to his testimony at the Reno Court of Inquiry, were to proceed to a line of bluffs four or five miles distance. Benteen claimed it was ten minutes after noon by Wallace's watch when he left the main trail. Reno remembered as Benteen rode past him, the senior Captain related he was "to sweep everything before him." Custer subsequently dispatched two additional orders to Benteen. The first told him to go on to the second line of bluffs if he found nothing from the first line, and a second set told him to go into the valley if he still found no Indians after the second line of bluffs. Benteen wrote in his official report, Custer also said to send a well mounted officer with six men who should ride rapidly to the line of bluffs with instructions to report at once if any Indians could be seen from that point.[15] This would indi-

cate Custer wanted the intelligence about any Indians on his left flank as soon as possible.

When Custer sent Benteen off on his mission, he still possessed no definite knowledge of what lay ahead of the regiment. He could have reasoned the next couple of hours might result in a running fight. Dispatching Benteen's force on a left oblique movement would provide him with three benefits: 1) it would confirm where the Indians were or were not; 2) if they were to the left, the battalion would be in position to block any escape to the south and hopefully drive them towards the main command; and finally 3) Custer would be following Terry's instructions to feel constantly to his left. However, Custer could have reaped all the above benefits with none of the risks by delaying Benteen's departure until he had better intelligence of what lay ahead. In other words, Custer could have accomplished the same desired results if he had dispatched his senior captain from a closer point to the Little Big Horn River.[16] This would have given Custer the advantage of keeping his command together for a longer period should the situation suddenly change. In addition, he would maintain direct control over the four battalions and shorten the supporting distances should he be forced to commit one part or the other.

Another scenario as to why Benteen at this point was dispatched to the left was given to Dr. Thomas Marquis by some of his Cheyenne informants. They said this was the route the Indians took in going to and returning from their fight with General George Crook on June 17th. The Cheyennes thought perhaps Custer or his scouts saw the trail and not knowing there had been a battle on the Rosebud Creek, reasonably concluded this trail on Reno Creek had been made by Indians encamped in that direction and this needed to be explored.[17]

To accomplish this undertaking, I believe Custer felt he was assigning some of his best companies to the mission, and he gave Benteen a great deal of discretion in carrying out his charge. Custer did not, as some of his critics claim, send Benteen out on a useless endeavor to keep him out of any meaningful action.[18] Although there is evidence to suggest Benteen might have felt this way, and Lieutenant Roe told Walter Camp that he, as well as Benteen's friends, thought "Custer's object in sending Benteen to the left from the divide was to keep Benteen out of the fight, as Benteen had the advance and should reg-

[11]*Walter M. Camp Papers* (Denver, CO: Denver Public Library, Robert S. Ellison Collection), item 108. Hereinafter cited: *Camp, DPL.*

[12]Brady, *Indian Fights and Fighters*, 232.

[13]Tal Luther, "Benteen, Reno, and Custer," *The Trail Guide*, Vol. 5, #1, March 1960, 9.

[14]Charles K. Mills, *Harvest of Barren Regrets* (Glendale, CA: Arthur H. Clark Co, 1985, 52–53.

[15]Carroll, *The Federal View*, 105.

[16]Custer was always impatient for results and probably couldn't have waited this long before dispatching a battalion to his left.

[17]Thomas B. Marquis, *Keep the Last Bullet for Yourself*, (NY, NY: The Two Continents Publishing Group, 1976), 95–96.

[18]Hammer, *Custer in '76*, 249.

ularly have been with headquarters." Camp noted succinctly, "I think their view will bear criticism."[19]

At the time, Benteen undertook the mission in the spirit that Custer intended as evidenced by his remarks as he passed Reno. Furthermore, on July 2, 1876, long before any controversy arose, he wrote his wife: "Custer divided the 7th Cavalry into 3 Battn's.— about 15 miles from an Indian village, the whereabouts of which he did not know exactly. I was ordered . . . to the left for the purpose of hunting for the valley of the river—Indian camp— or anything I could find."[20] This private statement to his wife probably aligns with what Custer intended for Benteen's mission. Thus it would appear, regardless of his later denouncements of Custer's "senseless" orders, at the time they were given, Benteen understood them completely. Lieutenant Edgerly, D Company's junior officer, also believed this was the mission assigned to them: "The idea I had was if they ran out of the village we would strike them on the left; and if to the right, then some other part of the command."[21]

Again this aligned with the campaign strategy of preventing the village from scattering. Since a ridge line blocked the view to the south, I believe Custer's primary reason for sending a force out in that direction was to insure no Indians were there or were making their way to the upper Little Big Horn. Once this needed intelligence was revealed and communicated, this battalion was to rejoin the rest of the regiment farther down Reno Creek.

It was only afterwards and at the Reno Court of Inquiry that Benteen changed his mind and testified: "When I received my orders from Custer to separate myself from the command, I had no instructions to unite at any time with Reno or anyone else. There was no plan at all. My orders were valley hunting ad infinitum."[22] Benteen was right about one thing in this testimony . . . Custer didn't have a complete plan. The strategic part of the plan was complete. His strategy was to surprise the village, capture it, and prevent as many Indians as possible from fleeing. In their traditional response, when confronted with soldiers, the Indians made a lot of noise, raised a lot of dust, but in the end fled or fired a few annoying but generally harmless, long range shots.[23] This escape would need

to be intercepted. The tactical part to accomplish this strategy was still not distinct in Custer's mind. What Benteen overlooked was his responsibility to provide Custer with intelligence that would permit his commander to complete his plan. In addition, if one can believe Benteen's testimony in 1879, it reflects how he really felt at the time about his orders, and tends to confirm that Custer was still framing a plan as he rode along.

There were some participants and a few writers who claim Custer had early on formulated a plan to have Reno charge the village at the upper end, while he himself would go down and attack at the lower end, with Benteen clearing away any Indians who tried to escape to the south.[24] One of those who so advocated this theory was Private John Donoughue who went into considerable detail in a letter to the *Bismark Daily Tribune*. He said Custer ordered:

> "Major Reno you will charge down the valley and sweep everything that will come before you; Captain Benteen will take the extreme left. I will take the extreme right myself with five companies." General Custer here described the point that Major Reno should strike the camp supported by Captain Benteen and his three companies. "I will strike them on the opposite point and we will crush them between us."[25]

A very neat and tidy plan; Custer should have won!

Despite what some heard or thought they heard, Custer as yet had no tactical plan, and their reasoning is deeply flawed. Benteen, one of Custer's harshest critics, admitted Custer was correct in not having a plan at this point. He said, "Not knowing where they were, I do not know whether there was a need of a battle plan."[26] As Benteen stated, Custer had no clear knowledge of exactly where the village was located, nor its size, so he was moving on as wide a front as possible. If he kept the command together he might lead them to the wrong place, and since the battle would probably be over very quickly, speed was of the essence to strike the village before it had a chance to flee. It was possible, however, that Benteen could encounter the extreme southern edge of the village; if so, the division of his force would pay big dividends. Custer and his officers knew from experience, Indian villages most often camped in groups for sanitation purposes and better pony grazing, separated from each other by some distance, all along the river's banks.

What of the Indians for whom the soldiers were

---

[19]Ibid.   [20]Graham, *The Custer Myth*, 187.

[21]Graham, *Reno Court*, 404.

[22]Col. William A. Graham, *The Reno Court of Inquiry, Abstract of the Official Record of Proceedings* (Harrisburg, PA: The Stackpole Company, 1954) 147. Hereinafter cited: *Reno Court—Abstract*.

[23]Maj. Robert E. Morris, "Custer Made a Good Decision: A Leavenworth Appreciation," *Journal of the West*, Vol. 16, #4, October 1977, 97.

[24]Liddic, *I Buried Custer*, 17.

[25]Bismarck *Daily Tribune* (Bismarck, ND), January 1, 1888.

[26]Graham, *Reno Court—Abstract*, 149.

searching? Did they know the whereabouts of the white men? There is evidence to suggest the Indians were cognizant of the Dakota column since it marched from Ft. Lincoln. As we have read, White-Man-Runs-Him stated the Indians kept close track of the troops, checking on them almost daily. Sitting Bull later told James McLaughlin, noted Indian Agent, he knew where Custer was the morning of the 25th.[27] Gall, a leading Uncpapa warrior, related further details on what the Indians knew of the soldiers' presence:

> We knew where the soldiers camped on the night of June 24th. Buffalo scouts brought this word to us late at night on the 24th. We were surprised at this information because we did not expect any soldiers unless they came from the South where we knew General Crook was. The Buffalo scouts reported these soldiers northeast of us.[28]

Was an ambush prepared in advance for Custer? Several battle students believe this was the case and have based their battle reconstructions upon it. Several interviews with Sitting Bull tend to support this sentiment. The Uncpapa, less than a year after the battle when he was in Canada, related to Lieutenant Colonel Acheson Irvine of the Northwest Mounted Police how for twelve days his scouts had shadowed Custer. On June 25th they all rode unwittingly into a trap prepared for their destruction.[29] He further elaborated on this story in an 1878 interview. In it, the Uncpapa medicine man related how he assembled the village's young men and had them put up the oldest teepees and place dummies around lighted fires to fool Custer, then he sent all the women and children to a place of safety. Custer would think the village was caught off guard and would fire into empty teepees. "When he did, I fell upon him from the rear and in less than two hours destroyed him."[30] It's strange that Sitting Bull didn't keep his family informed of this plan, because as the attack began, Four Robes, one of his wives, was so surprised and scared she fled the leader's teepee with only one of his two infant sons. Four Robes, after reaching safety, realized her mistake and rushed back to the village to retrieve the other baby.[31]

Everett McVey in his story of Mitch Bouyer claimed Custer's Crow scouts as well as the Sioux and Cheyenne conspired to trap Custer. These scouts fulfilled their role and led the command into a well prepared ambush. Rain-In-The-Face likewise told David Barry, the noted frontier photographer, how "they all got together on the Little Big Horn ready and waiting to fight. . . . They were wild for battle."[32] P. E. Byrne stated he learned from the Indians the details of Crazy Horse's plan to insure there would be no escape for Custer. He had Gall "completely screened and had massed his warriors within easy striking distance" to await Custer "in a circle of death."[33]

The Indians were no doubt aware there were soldiers looking for them. But even when the above recollections are added to the knowledge of the white man movements, the overwhelming body of attestations demonstrates the Indians didn't expected any early attack from the east. Knowing where the soldiers were is one thing, but it doesn't necessarily follow that it was transformed by the Indians into knowledge of an impending attack with a detailed ambush planned as a countermove. For example, Beautiful White Buffalo Woman (Mrs. Spotted Horn Bull) related: "I have seen my people prepare for battle many times, and this I know: that the Sioux that morning had no thought of fighting. We expected no attack, and our young men did not watch for the coming of Long Hair and his soldiers."[34]

Wooden Leg, a young Cheyenne warrior, confirmed Beautiful White Buffalo Woman's recollections, and further related their camps were not arranged for defense, and that there were many women and children present, and the night before (the 24th) there were numerous parties and dances in all the camp circles. Many of the inhabitants were still feeling the effects of the late night activities even as Reno was charging upon the village.[35] A number of women and children were bathing and swimming in the river when the dust clouds from Reno's battalion were seen. This was not the disposition of a village expecting an attack.

In addition, White Bull, Sitting Bull's nephew and one of the Minniconjou band's greatest warriors, must have missed his famous uncle's pre-battle meeting. He told his

[27] James McLaughlin, *My Friend The Indian* (Boston, MA: Houghton Mifflin Company, 1920), 137.

[28] Usher L. Burdick, ed., *David F. Barry's Indian Notes on 'Custer's Last Battle'* (Baltimore, MD: Wirth Brothers, 1949), 23. Hereinafter cited: *Indian Notes*.

[29] Paul F. Sharp, *Whoop-Up Country* (Helena, MT: Historical Society of Montana, 1960), 254.

[30] Ft. Benton *Weekly Record* (Ft. Benton, MT), July 12, 1878.

[31] Albert Marrin, *Sitting Bull and His World* (NY, NY: Dutton Books, 2000), 144.

[32] Burdick, *Indian Notes*, 24.

[33] Patrick E. Byrne, *Soldiers of the Plains* (NY, NY: Minton, Balch and Co, 1926), 102–103.

[34] McLaughlin, *My Friend The Indian*, 44.

[35] Stanley Vestal, *Sitting Bull : Champion of the Sioux* (Norman, OK: Univ. of OK Press, 1957), 158.

[36] Stanley Vestal, *Warpath: The True Story of the Fighting Sioux* (Boston, MA: Houghton Mifflin Co, 1934), 193.

biographer, Stanley Vestal, when the soldiers attacked "All through that great camp was confusion of complete surprise."[36] This sentiment was echoed by the Ogallala chief Low Dog who said, "I was asleep in my lodge at the time. The sun was about noon. I heard the alarm, but I did not believe it. I thought it was a false alarm. I did not think it possible that any white man would attack us." Uncpapa Chief Crow King related much the same thing, "We were in camp and not thinking there was any danger of a battle, although we had heard that the long-haired chief had been sent after us."[37] Kate Bighead, a Northern Cheyenne, recalled that on June 25th she joined other women bathing in the river. "All of us were having a good time. . . . Nobody was thinking of any battle coming."[38] Finally, the Indians didn't want the soldiers coming anywhere near their "homes." If they had kept as close of tabs on the white man as some have claimed, they surely would have challenged Custer miles away from their village just as they did with Crook on the Rosebud eight days earlier. This precaution was necessary to provide a margin of safety for the women and children should they suffer a reversal.[39]

With representative samples of both the pro and con argument of either side a ready and waiting village, or one that was shocked and surprised, the pronouncement of one General should be taken with a great deal more than the proverbial grain of salt: "the narratives of the Indians should be read with a considerable degree of allowance and some doubt, as Indians generally make their descriptions to conform to what they think are the wishes of those who interview them."[40]

The remaining eight companies of the 7th proceeded down the middle fork of Reno Creek. Reno took his three companies and turned slightly to the left and moved down the south bank. The five companies with Custer followed the Indian trail along the north bank. Custer moved the command out at a walk.[41] He was taking a slow, deliberate pace so as not to out distance Benteen, and to give him the time needed to complete his assignment and report. Custer's and Reno's companies traveled along side each other as they rode along each side of the creek. This was the same small creek which flowed from the divide,

and it appeared to be moving in the approximate direction towards where the scouts had observed the village. The country was somewhat broken, but White-Man-Runs-Him remembered the command "going at a fast trot down" the creek.[42]

Reno's companies began to fall back due to the terrain on his side of the creek until he was now across from Custer's rear most soldiers. With the horses showing signs of becoming tired and no village yet visible, Curley remembered that Custer ordered a halt. Curley said, "We stopped by some pines for a little while, about 4 miles from the mouth of the creek."[43]

Varnum gave perhaps another reason for the halt besides giving the horses "a blow" and the others time to catch up. He and 2nd Lieutenant Hare had been scouting ahead of the command. Hare and his group of scouts took the right front of the advance, while Varnum took the left. "From every hill where I could see the valley I saw Indians mounted."[44] Varnum stated he reported this information to Custer several times.[45] In addition, Varnum saw the main Indian village and more Indains than he had ever seen before from the high bluffs while the command had been moving down the creek. But it was impossible to get a good view of it unless one got out on the valley floor because of the bends in the river and the timber around on the left bank.[46] He told the Reno Court that the village was seen about an hour or more before Reno was ordered forward. Thus the information was relayed to Custer about the time the halt was made.[47] It is interesting to note that Varnum made it very clear that what he saw was the main village not the smaller camp where the Lone Teepee stood. He said he "had passed these some distance over to the left and had gone southwest to a point on the high ground where he could overlook the valley."[48]

Some battle students concluded that Varnum couldn't have seen the main village due to his line of sight limitations from his known observation points. They claim the most he could have observed was "A few isolated teepees . . . at the far western edge of the valley indicating some minor evidence of . . . Indian habitation."[49] Yet, as noted above, this is not what Varnum said he saw and then told his commander. He said it was the "main village" and so reported.[50] In addition, Custer received a similar report collaborating Varnum's from one of Hare's scouts. Hare

[37]Leavenworth *Times* (Leavenworth, KS), August 18, 1881.

[38]Thomas B. Marquis, *Custer On The Little Bighorn* (Algonac, MI: Reference Publications, 1933), 84.

[39]Jay D. Smith, "What Did Not Happen At The Battle of the Little Big Horn," *Research Review: Journal of the Little Big Horn Associates*, Vol 6, # 2, June 1992, 12.

[40]Graham, *The Custer Myth*, 116.

[41]Graham, *Reno Court*, 122.

[42]Graham, *The Custer Myth*, 23.

[43]Ibid, 13.   [44]Carroll, *I, Varnum*, 64.

[45]Ibid.   [46]Graham, *Reno Court*, 121–122.

[47]Ibid, 121.   [48]Hammer, *Custer in '76*, 61.

[49]Darling, *Custer's Final Hours*, 11.

[50]Carroll, *I, Varnum*, 64.

had been given the Crows to supervise while Varnum took the others. Harry Moccasin, one of the Crows, said he went to "a butte on the head [sic] of Reno Creek" and he saw the village. That he was in this area was only natural as he was with Boyer and the other Crows, observing the area around the Lone Teepee. He immediately reported this information to the commander. Custer asked Harry Moccasin if the camp was breaking up and he was told no. This intelligence was delivered about the time the halt was ending because this scout remembered that the soldiers "then came on down to the forks of Reno Creek."[51] If correct, there can be little doubt that an hour before Custer ordered any action, he knew that an intact village was ahead on the left bank of the Little Big Horn and it, according to his chief of scouts' information, contained an "immense number of Indians." Custer must have been pleased with the scout's report, the village had yet to be warned and was still intact. He had advanced the regiment to about six miles from the river, and its presence still hadn't been made known. His objective was the main village, not the small camp which was ahead. This camp

Courtesy of The Little Bighorn Associates, Inc.

would hardly be a bump on the trail for eight companies of cavalry. All he needed to do was prevent these Indians from further spreading the alarm. Custer couldn't have planned it any better. His decision to attack at once was bearing fruit. "Custer's Luck," indeed; but how long could he count on his good fortune?

The Lieutenant Colonel now changed the pace of the march and the scouts were seen riding in and out reporting to him. Sometimes he would ride out with them a short distance and look around.[52] The scouts could have been giving Custer information of their observations from the location where Varnum had seen a small camp from the Crow's Nest. It was located near the forks of the creek they had been following. Bouyer and the four Crow scouts had been perched on a high rocky bluff overlooking this small camp site since the early afternoon, watching the

Sioux and the lone teepee which remained standing just opposite the bluffs.[53]

This intelligence was confirmed personally by Custer when he sighted the Lone Teepee about a half mile away and decided to make the site of the small camp and its Lone Teepee his focal point.[54] With the camp now bolted, Custer assumed it had had broken up in response to the warnings just as he had feared as it was the closest to the advancing troops. Now he would have to overtake these fleeing Indians before they had time to panic the village, or the worse case scenario would happen. In response to this visual sighting, Custer, shortly after 2:00, motioned for Reno to cross over to the north side of the creek and fall in behind him.[55] The lone teepee was less than a mile ahead and beyond that, the Little Big Horn River was four

[51]Coughlin, "Battle of the Little Big Horn," 48.

[52]Hunt, I Fought . . . , 85.

[53]Hammer, Custer in '76, 156, 161.

[54]Roger Darling, Benteen's Scout (El Segundo, CA: Upton & Sons, 1987), 37.

[55]Carroll, The Federal View, 66; Charles Kuhlman, Legend into History (Harrisburg, PA: The Stackpole Company, 1952), 51.

and a half miles away. The Lieutenant Colonel picked up the pace with his five companies. Hare remembered the column almost overtook his scouts, and Custer seemed very impatient.[56] Reno's Battalion had again fallen behind Custer's command due to the rougher terrain he traversed, and after crossing the creek the major found it difficult to keep up with his commander's increased gait. He could only follow in Custer's wake.

As Benteen's battalion rode out of sight from the main column, the senior captain, in accordance with Custer's orders, dispatched his second in command of H Company, First Lieutenant Francis Gibson, and six troopers to ride point about 300 yards in front of the unit to scout for Indians. The lieutenant was directed to continue until he could see the valley of the Little Big Horn.[57] There was no reason for the whole battalion to ride up and down the hills when a small detail could accomplish the same results. This would conserve the energy of both man and beast of the rest of the battalion. The dedicated Gibson went to the top of the bluffs four seperate times; in doing so he discovered the information the battalion was sent to find.[58] From the top of the last bluff, marking his farthest advance, the lieutenant had clearly seen a long distance up the valley with his field glasses, and no Indians were visible. Private Windolph remembered it was rough and hilly country and very hard on the horses. He saw the Lieutenant signal after reaching each hilltop that there were no Indians. Even the troopers now thought the mission was "a wild goose chase."[59]

Benteen had received the reports and had seen the same signals as Windolph, and after winding through two separate valleys and ridges with their associated bluffs, Benteen turned to the right. In a candid moment he wrote, "as I was anxious to rejoin the command, as there was no sign of Indians, I decided to rejoin the main trail."[60] Contrast this to his testimony at the Reno Court three years later when he stated he scarcely knew himself "what I had to do." In addition, Benteen swore he had no orders to unite with anyone; the reason he returned was because he thought he might be needed, and he was separated from the command by possibly fifteen miles or more.[61] This statement was only self serving and an attempt to deceive the Court. The Court of Inquiry was made aware of it when the Recorder asked Benteen if there was anything in Custer's orders to him that would lead the captain to

believe he wasn't to rejoin or come up with the column if he found no Indians? In an introspective moment, Benteen let his guard down and revealed the lieutenant colonel's tacit trust in him and replied: "I don't think General Custer would have told me that. He would have known that I would come up"[62]

In reality, Benteen's scout covered, in total, about seven and a half miles and occupied a little over two hours in time. This was probably within the range of what Custer expected, and Benteen did accomplish what Custer had ordered. He discovered the upper valley of the Little Big Horn was empty and had been empty. There were no villages strung out as it had been at the Washita. The problem was Custer probably wasn't aware of this intelligence nor would he be. According to Benteen's testimony at the Reno Court, Custer's orders were to only let him know if he (Benteen) had found any Indians and "to pitch into" them.[63] Later, Benteen shifted his story and told the court, Custer would have known if he hadn't found any Indians he would have rejoined the trail and "come up."[64]

But is it reasonable to assume, when Custer heard nothing from Benteen, that Custer would have known he was on his way to "come up" and there were no Indians to the left? I believe a more logical response, on the part of this senior officer, would have been to send a messenger to his commander with this information. For whatever reason, this thought never seemed to cross Benteen's mind. If, in fact, Custer did expect Benteen to rejoin the trail if no Indians were seen, then what Custer didn't expect was the pace Benteen undertook to catch up with the main column.

That one of Custer's most experienced officers would fail to keep his commander informed or, at least, "come up" in an expeditious manner, when he knew what was expected, borders on irresponsibility.[65] We have no idea if Custer was able to infer the village wasn't strung out upsteam. But is it possible if he had definite knowledge of this fact he might have deduced they were in a more compact area downstream and would not have divided his forces again?[66] As noted before, it is little wonder Benteen's testimony shifted about constantly with half truths, evasions, and falsehoods; by the time the Inquiry ended he had spread enough whitewash to cover Chicago. There can be little doubt Custer's senior captain dramatically changed his story three years later when called to the witness stand at the Reno Court.

[56]Hammer, *Custer in '76*, 65. [57]Ibid, 80.
[58]Graham, *Reno Court—Abstract*, 157.
[59]Hunt, *I Fought . . .* , 80.
[60]New York *Herald* (NY, NY), August 8, 1876.
[61]Graham, *Reno Court—Abstract*, 147–149.

[62]Graham, *Reno Court*, 380. [63]Ibid, 356.
[64]Ibid, 380. [65]Darling, *Benteen's Scout*, 32.
[66]Luther, "Benteen, Reno, and Custer," 6.

Lt. Edgerly remembered the battalion kept going from the time Gibson made his last observation, and no further effort was expended to go to the left as there were no Indians in that direction. The unit rode around the hills and finally came into the valley and the main trail. The pack train was just descending into the valley about a mile away.[67] There is a question as to where Benteen rejoined the main trail. In the best study of this scout to date, Roger Darling's *Benteen's Scout to the Left*, the author reasoned Benteen crossed Custer's trail less than a mile east of the morass. It was a little after two o'clock.[68] At this point Custer was near the Lone Teepee area, two miles ahead.[69] According to Benteen, his route back to the trail was the same as going from it, that is, bearing to the right and at the same angle. He said, "I struck the trail about a mile ahead of the pack train. I followed the trail to a kind of morass. My horses had not been watered since six or eight o'clock of the evening before and I formed them around this morass and watered them."[70] Darling concluded the morass was just a little to the east from where the south fork of Reno Creek joins the creek itself.

While Benteen's Battalion was at the morass, Custer's youngest brother, who had been hired as a guide and had been on duty with the pack train, galloped past to catch up with his brother. McDougall told Walter Camp he saw and talked to Boston when he came back to the packtrain.[71] McDougall and 'B' Company were at the rear of the pack train, along with the few extra horses, trying to keep it closed up. It appears that Boston didn't want to miss any of the action that George was sure to start, and besides it wasn't much fun trying to keep mules in line while eating their dust. Edgerly recalled that "He (Boston) had stayed back with the pack train and was now hurrying up to join the general's immediate command. He gave me a cheery salutation as he passed, and with a smile on his face, rode to his death."[72] The youngest Custer must have gone back to select a fresher horse before he started after the commander. However, Fremont Kipp, a private in D Company, explained that Boston had been detached by his brother to act as a messenger between the other battalions and was with the main column from the start. This is the reason McDougall had seen him in the rear and Boston had been riding to catch up.[73] Nevertheless, there is no concrete evidence which supports one way or the other where Boston Custer was supposed to be or what

he was supposed to be doing. In all probability, it wasn't with the main column, despite Kipp's recollections.

It was nearly twenty minutes after the main column began its movement to the Little Big Horn Valley that the pack train started downhill from the divide. The hundred twenty men who would guide and guard the mules would have their hands full this afternoon. The pack train from the very beginning of the march had been an embarrassment to the regiment. Godfrey recalled the mules assigned were badly used up and compounding the problem was novice packers with inadequate equipment. The whole enterprise was questionable at best.[74]

Private Peter Thompson of C Company, whose later actions in the battle would win him the Medal of Honor, said, "I don't think there were a half dozen men . . . who know how to pack a mule without having the pack work loose."[75] The men and the mules got a little more proficient over the next several days, but it was only from experience. Nevertheless, the 7th Cavalry's pack train was always an amateur affair. But what effect did this "circus in the rear" have on the battle's outcome? It's true the pack train drained off about 20% of the regiment's fighting strength on the 25th, and it contributed to the scattering of the battalions, but no matter how inefficient it was, the pack train itself was not a determining factor in Custer's Last Stand.[76]

According to McDougall, he was unaware that three separate trails were being made, and he endeavored to keep the train in the middle set of tracks. The train had been under way a little over a mile when Lieutenant Cooke rode back with an order to Mathey from Custer to keep the mules off from the trail as "they made so much dust." Mathey implemented the order, and when Cooke returned to check on the order, Mathey asked him how was the dust now, and Cooke said "much better—they were not kicking up so much dust."[77] Many battle students have remarked that in spite of the congenital problems with the packs, both Captain McDougall with the escort and 1st Lieutenant Mathey as the officer in charge were saddled with a difficult and tedious assignment on this Sunday. They completed their responsibilities as well as any of the other officers, and better than most, in keeping the pack train together, accounted for, and within reasonable supporting distance if needed.

[67]Graham, *Reno Court—Abstract*, 158.
[68]Stewart, *Custer's Luck*, 382.   [69]Darling, *Benteen's Scout*, 35.
[70]Graham, *Reno Court*, 356.   [71]Hammer, *Custer in '76*, 69.
[72]Carroll, *The Gibson and Edgerly Narratives*, 5.
[73]*Camp , DPL*, #108.

[74]Graham, *The Custer Myth*, 130.
[75]Jesse Brown and A. M. Willard, *The Black Hills Trails* (NY, NY: Arno Press, 1975), 139.
[76]John S. Gray, "The Pack Train on George A. Custer's Last Campaign," *Nebraska History*, Vol. 57,# 1,Spring 1976, 67.
[77]Graham, *Reno Court*, 456–457.

Just as Custer had sent additional instructions to Benteen's battalion after they departed, he likewise was keeping track of the pack train as evident by his Adjutant's visits. Custer knew the slower moving pack train couldn't keep up with the main column's pace, and it would make an inviting target if any Indians were on his back trail. Therefore, Custer was trying to minimize the tell tale dust from the 175 mules. After moving the mules to the side of the trail, the column continued to follow the main trail. McDougall, seeing they were falling further and further behind Custer, began urging Mathey to increase the pace. Mathey reluctantly did so. But he knew by moving faster, it would only loosen and shift the inexperienced packing to which the mules had been subjected since they had left Terry's Camp.[78] Mathey was correct, and they had to repack "a great deal." He stated, "When a mule became unpacked, I would leave two men to pack him, and go ahead with the train and leave them to bring up that mule. We pushed along with a good deal of trouble."[79] Private Coleman confirmed this fact and wrote in his diary "we were moving so fast the packs would slip off and the packers had to put them on again."[80] The pack train was very much scattered when they observed the tail end of Benteen's column leaving the morass. At the time, Mathey judged the train was spread out over two to three miles from front to rear.

It was towards 2:45 PM when some of the mules, mad with thirst, made a break for the morass. Some of these mules evaded their handlers and rushed head long into the spring and became mired in the sticky mud. McDougall ordered his company to dismount to help the packers extract the animals. Mathey continued on with the rest of the train.[81] This task took 'B' Company nearly thirty minutes to pull the mules out, straighten the loads, and follow the rest of the packs.

The Lone Teepee, which Custer approached, stood on the north bank of the middle fork of Reno Creek, about three and one-half miles in a straight line from an excellent crossing of the Little Big Horn River. Most accounts speak of a single teepee; however even these details are in dispute among battle students. This is because it's one of the major landmarks that was constantly referred to by the participants making it an excellent reference point. Many authors' battle scenarios are based on the location, time, and distance factors from this geographic place. In addition, Lt. Wallace recorded the last official time near this site; thus we know for certain where Custer was at

2:00 in relation to this landmark. This has important implications for the testimony of Reno and Benteen who believed the Custer fight was over by the time they were able to reach Weir Point. Nevertheless one can't escape the relationship between time and distance no matter how much distortion is attempted.

In their excellent study of this controversy, Ray Meketa's and Tom Bookwalter's research pointed to the fact the Lone Teepee was an elaborately decorated burial lodge which contained the body of a warrior killed at the Battle of the Rosebud. The dead warrior was a Sans Arc, Old She Bear, wounded in the belly and carried back to the village where he died several days later.[82] This teepee stood near the lower end of the general encampment on Reno Creek when the Indians went to fight Crook (June 17th). The mid point of this village was at the present day bridge crossing of the creek, and it extended about two miles in length.[83] It was also the camp site on the night of the 24th for a small group of Indians who were traveling to the main village. It was these teepees which were spotted by Varnum and others from the Crow's Nest. This small camp had started to break up upon hearing reports of soldiers on their back trail. They broke camp in such a hurry they left cooking pots on still smoldering breakfast fires. It was this activity which the scouts had witnessed while on the peak.

The argument regarding the location stems from the fact that many students believe the Lone Teepee was at the North Fork of Reno Creek, about a mile from the Little Big Horn. They base their site on the testimony of Fred Girard at the Reno Court. He stated it was about a mile from the River. In addition, his description of the land around the teepee appears to match the North Fork area. Lately some interesting theories have been advanced which builds upon the field research of Keith McDougal and Bill Boyes who believe there were two different sets of teepees, and that this accounted for the confusion. One stood at the south fork and another single one at the north fork area. McDougal recorded the "burning (our Lone Teepee) teepee was located farther east where the Indian camp was located on the day of the Rosebud Battle." He believed it was one of several lodges containing dead Indians. McDougal's years of research led him to believe the Lone Teepee meant what it says . . . single. It was off by itself about two miles from the other teepees and only about a mile from the river; again he used Girard's statements in his proof. This line of reasoning was recently

---

[78]Ibid, 457.　　　　[79]Ibid.
[80]Liddic, *I Buried Custer*, 17.　　[81]Graham, *Reno Court*, 471.

[82]Graham, *The Custer Myth*, 98; Hammer, *Custer in '76*, 205.
[83]Ray Meketa and Thomas E. Bookwalter, *The Search For The Lone Tepee* (NP: Little Horn Press, 1983), 47.

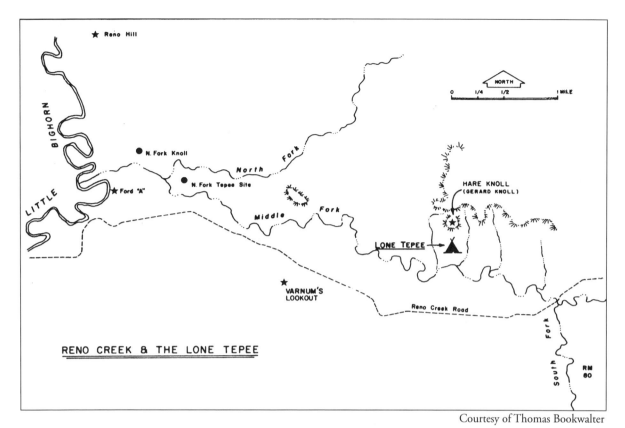

RENO CREEK & THE LONE TEPEE

Courtesy of Thomas Bookwalter

expanded upon by another student. By analyzing the various accounts of events happening around a "lone teepee," Vern Smalley concluded all these references couldn't possibly be associated with the Lone Teepee. He reasoned there were two distinct groups of teepees. He labeled them "Eastern Lone Teepee Cluster" and "Western Lone Teepee Cluster." The traditional Lone Teepee stood about four miles from the River and contained the body of Old She Bear. The other "Lone Teepee" actually consisted of three teepees; it was near here that Reno was given the order to attack, and Girard spotted the Indians. Mr. Smalley believes the focus on a single Lone Teepee has resulted in a confused sequence of events and hinders any ability to fully understand the occurrences on this part of the battlefield.[84]

His deductions are different.

There was one individual whose statements about the Lone Teepee should be given considerable weight when determining the number and location(s) of the Lone Teepee. It is Sergeant Daniel Knipe (Kanipe) of 'C' Company. This native of North Carolina was twenty-three years

old at the time of the battle. Knipe was to play an important roll in the early stages of the engagement as one of Custer's messengers. He later married the widow of his company's First Sergeant Edwin Bobo. According to Walter Camp, Knipe was one of his most valuable informants. He told his story straight and the same way each time when questioned. Knipe was also intelligent and accurate in his descriptions. Knipe, as will be explained, was the only individual in the regiment who passed the Lone Teepee three times that day. Thus he would be in a better position to remember what he saw: "About halfway down this Creek (Reno) we came to a vacated Indian Camp at which one teepee remained, containing a dead Indian."[85] He made no mention of any other "clusters of teepees," other than the one which was about half way down the creek. I believe that what Knipe recalled was about as close to the truth as we'll ever come regarding the location and number of lodges at the Lone Teepee site.

As noted, Custer had seen only one standing teepee at the abandoned camp site. He had hoped to prevent these Indians from alerting the main camp which Varnum had reported. As the troopers approached the camp it had become apparent from the amount of debris on the

[84]Vern Smalley, "The Lone Tepees Along Reno Creek," *12th Annual Symposium Custer Battlefield Historical & Museum Assn.*, 1998, 1–11.

[85]Knipe, "New Story of Custer's Last Battle," 279.

Courtesy of Hastings House Publishers

ground that the inhabitants had recently fled. This was confirmed by Hare, who was with the scouts on the right front of the column, when these fleeing Indians were seen on a rise between him and the Little Big Horn River. It was apparent that these Indians had seen the troopers as well.[86] Lt. DeRudio, riding in the center of Reno's Battalion, also saw these same Indians from the abandoned camp.[87] As these Indians moved towards the main village and spread the alarm, the pony herders began to round up the horses and move them north to the safety of the village. This movement raised a large amount of dust and this was seen by a number of soldiers including Hare, Girard, and Herendeen who reported the motion to Custer.

Some of the scouts had stopped at the Lone Teepee to examine its contents. They were expected to be ahead of the troops looking for Sioux and Cheyenne, but a few of the Arikaras, including Young Hawk and Two Strikes, had

ridden down from the ridge where they had been when they saw the soldiers advancing. Young Hawk dismounted and drew his knife and slit the teepee open while Two Strikes struck the lodge with his whip. Red Bear said One Feather went into the teepee and drank the soup left for Old She Bear and also ate some of the meat as well. One Feather recalled they stayed around the lodge about a half hour.[88] It's little wonder Custer caught up with the supposedly advance scouts. Daniel Knipe said that as Custer reached the burial lodge, he ordered his soldiers to set it on fire. This action was confirmed by White-Man-Runs-Him.[89] But with nearly every detail of this day in contention, some accounts claim that the scouts set the lodge on fire. This recollection might have merit as Knipe stated the command never halted at the lone teepee, although Custer could have ordered the scouts to set it on fire. Whoever ordered the Teepee burnt, it wasn't very successful because when Benteen came along later it was relatively unscorched. However, the fire and smoke from this burning lodge was seen by the Uncpapas in the village.

Custer was not pleased the scouts had stopped to investigate the teepee. In 1912 Strikes Two told Camp, "At lone teepee Custer became impatient and said that we were slow and if he had to urge us again to go forward he would take our guns and horses and put us afoot."[90] Herendeen, who was with Hare on the top of a hill overlooking the Lone Teepee, told Hare he could see the Indians "riding very fast and seemingly running away." He told the Lieutenant "we would have to hurry up, or we would not catch them." The scout remembered Hare wrote a note to Custer and "presumed he thought, as the rest of us did, that the Indians were getting away."[91] Hare confirmed at the Reno Court that he told Custer about the Indians they saw: "I spoke to Custer about it. He told me to take the Indian scouts and he would follow."[92] But the scouts would not go. Many authors have questioned the bravery of the scouts in refusing to take the lead. It was not an issue of bravery but a lack of understanding that caused them to hold back. One Feather, an Arikara, told Camp the scouts would have charged ahead after the Indians if they had only known what Custer wanted. Their interpreter, Girard, was off on a rise above the teepee. When he returned, One Feather said, "I scolded Girard for not staying with us so as to give us orders. Girard . . . left us without an interpreter."[93] When asked to describe the

[86]Graham, *Reno Court*, 236.   [87]Ibid, 267.

[88]Libby, *Arikara Narrative*, 121.
[89]Hammer, *Custer in '76*, 92; Graham, *The Custer Myth*, 23.
[90]Hammer, *Custer in '76*, 183.   [91]Graham, *The Custer Myth*, 263.
[92]Graham, *Reno Court*, 248–249.
[93]Liddic, *Camp on Custer*, 128.

duties of an Indian interpreter, Girard replied "to communicate between the scouts, and whoever was in command of them, and with the commanding officer; and with any Indians that might come in. Any news I received through the scouts I reported."[94] He would have better served the campaign if he had adhered to these duties instead of acting as a scout. As soon as it was made known what the lieutenant colonel expected, the scouts rode off in pursuit following Reno's battalion.

It serves no purpose, except the author's own bias, to claim these Arikaras were cowards because they "refused" to ride after the fleeing Indians.[95]

Cowardice was not a trait of the Indian warrior whether, Eastern or Western. They had a different concept of how and when to wage battle, and many times this was in conflict with the white man's tactical battle plans. Being unable to understand and then relate to this "foreign" mindset caused many in the army to assert these "friendly" Indians were "good for nothing" and poltroonism. It simply wasn't the truth and their devotion was amply demonstrated in the valley when ten of the scouts went beyond their call of duty and fought bravely beside the troopers and suffered heavy casualties. Moreover army records charge none of these scouts with desertion,

and in the aftermath of the Custer fight, they continued to serve a badly dispirited army faithfully and well for the remainder of their terms of enlistment.[96]

After crossing the creek, Reno's companies were behind Custer's troops, and when they reached the Lone Teepee Custer, through Cooke, directed Reno to take the lead. Reno's battalion never slowed down and passed the nearly halted right wing, becoming the head of the column. Fred Girard had ridden to a small elevation northwest of the teepee and saw a large dust cloud rising from the river valley. Custer must also have seen the dust about the same time as he asked the leader of the Crow scouts, Half Yellow Face, what caused the dust. Half Yellow Face replied, "The Sioux must be running away."[97] Girard probably saw the same Indians Hare had seen, and he then took off his hat, waived it, and yelled to Custer: "Here are your Indians, running like devils."[98]

---

[94]Graham, *Reno Court*, 110.

[95]James Willert, *Little Big Horn Diary* (El Segundo, CA: Upton & Sons, 1975), 217–272.

[96]Gray, "Arikara Scouts With Custer," 473.

[97]Graham, *The Custer Myth*, 23.

[98]Graham, *The Custer Myth*, 258; Graham, *Reno Court*, 112. It should be noted Girard made it very clear to the Reno Court of Inquiry that he told Custer about the Indians 'running' from a knoll near the Lone Teepee. There are others who claim this incident occurred from another knoll much closer to the Little Big Horn River. See Graham, *The Reno Court*, 96 Vs. John S. Gray, *Custer's Last Campaign* (Lincoln, NE: University of Nebraska Press, 1991), 275.

5
Turn to the Right

Girard's words struck Custer as would a fire bell in the night. Custer at this point became a victim of reacting only to what his senses told him and what his eyes saw; not the information he had been presented. He believed the Indians were running because his scout(s) said they were, he saw for himself the dust moving away from the troops up the valley, and all the campaign planning was based on this premise. It is analogous to among the first things taught a pilot in training, for an instrument rating, is to ignore what you see or think you see from the cockpit's window. But always trust what your instruments tell you. This is one of the hardest things for a pilot to practice. You want to believe what your senses tell you is happening, not what the outside imput reveals is happening. Like the pilot at dusk who thinks he is flying level when his artificial horizon instrument tells him he is really dangerously descending, so Custer began his descent into tragedy. Custer had information the trail was growing larger and larger the further they followed it. Mitch Bouyer told him there were more Indians ahead than he had ever seen before, and by the signs the scouts read the Indians were ready to fight, not run. But Custer's mind-set couldn't assimilate this imput as it conflicted with what he was experiencing and conceptualizing a short distance below the Lone Teepee. The Crows described their leader as "going to his death, and he did not know it." They said he was "like a feather blown by the wind, and had to go."[1]

Custer now made his second critical decision and ordered a battalion of his command forward to arrest this Indian flight.

What had been so promising an advance just thirty minutes ago, was now turning upon itself. The Indians were running, as the village had no doubt been alerted, and soon they would disappear like a ghost at cock-crow. An attack on the families and the capture of the pony herds were counted upon to strike consternation into the hearts of the warriors and were the key elements for success.[2] But, with a scattered village, the victory General Terry and he expected would vanish. The scouts couldn't understand what Custer wanted them to do, so in frustration, no doubt, he ordered Reno's Battalion in pursuit. This is another indication Custer didn't believe there was an intact village ahead. If he had, Custer would have never sent the scouts ahead to "attack a village." The Indians to their front were thought to be only a rear guard. (Speculation abounds in the study of the Little Big Horn, and here it's fascinating to suppose what might have happened if the scouts would have ridden off in pursuit of the Indians. This would have enabled Custer to arrive at the river with both battalions in check, and Benteen's within an hours' ride away. But it's difficult enough to discover what really happened, let alone create "what ifs" scenarios.) Cooke rode some distance ahead to the Major and delivered the order. Custer's commander, Terry, wrote in his report after the battle, "He (Custer) thought, I am confident that the Indians were running. For fear they might get away, he attacked without getting all his men up and divided his command."[3]

There is nothing clean or clear cut with any event associated with this battle, and exactly who told Reno what, is also a subject of controversy. Reno himself wrote: "Lieutenant Cooke, adjutant, came to me and said the village was only two miles above, and running away; to move forward at as rapid a gait as prudent, and to charge afterward, and that the whole outfit would support me. I think these were his exact words."[4] Major Reno told the Court of Inquiry he made no comment when Cooke delivered Custer's orders, he just moved off as directed.[5] This was contradicted by Dr. Harry R. Porter, a civilian under contract to the army, a graduate of Georgetown University Medical School, and the only surviving surgeon from the battle, who said the orders were, they (Indians) were just ahead, and he was to charge them. Reno then asked Cooke if Custer was going to support him. The adjutant said "yes." Reno, still not satisfied with the reply, asked if the General was coming along; again he was told "yes."[6]

Reno's two questions to Cooke regarding any assistance would tend to indicate Reno had no question about what he was ordered to do, but he had difficulty in understanding what role Custer was to play, whether it was to be in a supporting or reinforcing position.

In light of what was later to happen in the valley, Reno's vacillation may have been the result of a misunderstanding between was what said and what was meant. Reno appears to have wanted Custer as "reinforcement," but Cooke told him he would be "supported." Both Custer and his vice commander understood that there is a difference between the words. One battalion can "support" another without actually being "reinforced" by attacking

---

[1]Linderman, *Pretty Shield*, 235.
[2]Peter Panzeri, *The Little Big Horn, 1876, Custer's Last Stand* (NY, NY: Reed International Books, 1995) 71.

[3]Graham, *The Story of the Little Big Horn*, 113.
[4]Carroll, *The Federal View*, 103.
[5]Graham, *Reno Court*, 500.   [6]Ibid, 159.

the enemy from another direction.[7] At the Court of Inquiry in 1879, Reno stated he believed there was no other way that Custer could have supported (reinforced?) his battalion *except* from the rear.[8] However, it is strange that just ten days after the battle, Reno was able to clearly make this distinction—support Vs reinforce—in his after-action report: "it was evident to me that Custer intended to support me by moving farther down the stream and attacking the village in the flank;"[9] What exact words Custer gave to the Adjutant, and the meaning he wanted attached to them, are lost to history.

Reno's orderly, Private Edward Davern 'F' Company, agreed with the Major's story and related how Cooke gave the order. Cooke said: "Girard comes back and reports the Indian village three miles ahead and moving. The General directs you to take your three companies and drive everything before you." Davern also added Cooke further stated that "Colonel Benteen will be on your left and will have the same instructions."[10] But Reno, in a letter published in the New York *Herald* less than six weeks after the battle, contradicted his orderly's testimony given later, and said there was "No mention of any plan, no thought of junction, only the usual orders to the advance guard to attack at a charge." The Major further wrote that the Adjutant's exact words were: "Custer says to move at a rapid gait as you think prudent, and to charge afterward, and you will be supported by the whole outfit."[11] Custer's orderly trumpeter John Martin remembered that Custer told Cooke to direct Reno to go down and cross the river and attack the Indian village. Martin further said Custer would support him with the whole regiment. According to Martin, the plan was for Custer to go down to the other end and drive them, and he would have Benteen hurry up and attack in the center.[12]

Martin, as an orderly, would have been in an excellent position to be privy to any conversation between the lieutenant colonel and his adjutant.

Interestingly, both Girard and Herendeen claimed Custer gave the order in person. Girard stated that he personally heard Custer give Reno the order to advance. He recalled he (Custer) "beckoned to him with his finger and the Major rode over, and he told the Major Reno: 'You will take your battalion and try and overtake and bring them to battle, and I will support you.'" He further said that as Reno was going off, Custer told the Major to take the scouts along with him.[13] Herendeen told the Court of Inquiry he also heard Custer personally give the order to advance to Reno; he was to lead out, and Custer would be "with him." Herendeen also heard Custer tell Reno to "take the scouts with you, too," and he said, "Custer talked to him direct."[14] Lt. George Wallace supported part of these scouts' recollections regarding the Indians in front, but said Cooke transmitted the order. Wallace related that soon after they passed the Lone Teepee, the Adjutant came to Reno and said, (the) "Indians were about two miles and a half (miles) ahead, and Major Reno was ordered forward as fast as he could go and to charge them and others would support him."[15] Captain Myles Moylan also said Custer sent for the Major and received the order to move forward with his battalion, as the Indians were supposed to be a few miles ahead and retreating.[16]

For the number of people who claim they heard the orders, congestion was a very mild term for the immediate area around the Major, and it's a wonder Cooke or Custer was able to get through the crowd to speak with Reno.[17] At the Court of Inquiry, the possibility was raised that the confusion as to whether Custer or Cooke gave the order directly might have resulted from the similar dress worn by both men, which caused Girard and Herendeen to mistake the identity of the person.[18] One might say this just emphasizes the point that intelligent and honest individuals can see the same event entirely different; each attaching his own perspective. They can hear the same words spoken at the same time, yet manage to relate a different understanding to what was spoken and then swear to its truthfulness. Or is there another exegesis for the confusion, as Reno should have known who delivered his order?

There is an alternate explanation to this confused sequence of events as to what whom did or said, and it doesn't reflect well on Major Marcus Reno. At the Court of Inquiry, Reno swore under oath he had never received any direct orders from Custer, and the only order he received was to 'advance' from the Adjutant beyond the Lone Teepee.[19] However, we know Cooke assigned Reno his battalion at the divide, his battalion was brought to the head of the column by Custer as they approached the Lone Teepee, and, of course, the order to advance. It would seem Benteen was not the only one at the Court of Inquiry who dipped into the whitewash bucket. Daniel Knipe remembered that Custer called Reno over to his side, and

---

[7]Edward J. McClernand, *With Indian and the Buffalo in Montana, 1870–1878* (Glendale, CA: Arthur H. Clark Co, 1969), 70.

[8]Graham, *Reno Court*, 520.   [9]Carroll, *The Federal View*, 105.

[10]Graham, *Reno Court*, 286.   [11]Graham, *The Custer Myth*, 226.

[12]Graham, "Come On! Be Quick!" 306.

[13]Graham, *Reno Court*, 76.

[14]Ibid, 212; *Camp, IU*, box 2, folder 8.

[15]Graham, *Reno Court*, 19.   [16]Ibid, 185.

[17]Stewart, *Custer's Luck*, 327.   [18]Graham, *Reno Court*, 545.

[19]Ibid, 499.

Reno and Custer rode together for some distance.[20] In addition, Hare said he thought Custer personally repeated the directions given by Cooke.[21] Thus it would appear, at the Court of Inquiry, Reno conveniently forgot the two other orders he received from Custer. Moreover, his concern over what Custer's role would be caused him to seek out the commander in person. Reno, himself, confirmed speaking with Custer and wrote in his account of the Little Big Horn "as I rode back to my command, the last remark I ever made to him (Custer) was— 'Let us keep together.' In his jaunty way he lifted his broad brimmed hat as much as to say, 'I hear you.'"[22]

In light of the above information, everyone was correct as Cooke first gave the order, and Custer then repeated it to Reno who had ridden back for clarification.

Reno's action of seeking out Custer for further discussion and telling him they should keep together, speaks volumes about the Major's view of the developing situation and his expected role. What Reno and Custer spoke about is unrecorded, but it is possible Custer believed Reno's battalion was strong enough to stand on its own. Reno, from his actions, might not have concurred and might have protested, much like Benteen had, and wanted to keep the two units together or at least within close "support" of each other. Reno had a very exaggerated opinion of his own importance and thought of himself as an executive type.[23]

Unfortunately, this day he was neither. Under the direction of a superior, Reno probably would have acquitted himself in an acceptable manner, but in the forthcoming battle, he lacked the "aggressive and controlling leadership" required for an independent command.[24] It has been written that the courage to follow is one thing, while the courage to lead is something different.[25] Custer couldn't have had a very good feeling about his second in command as Reno rode after his advancing battalion, now a few hundred yards ahead.[26]

I believe Girard, Herendeen, and Porter were correct in what Reno was directed to accomplish. Custer's orders to Reno were to bring the fleeing Indians to battle, and he didn't imagine he was sending him to attack a village. The reports Custer heard indicated the presence of a village, but there was still no specific knowledge of its size or exact location, except it was about three miles ahead, with plenty of inhabitants, and they were probably dis-

mantling the village. The immediate circumstances confronting Custer would indicate he never expected his Major to do any serious fighting. It would appear the commander intended Reno's mission would be to harass, delay, and stop these Indians who didn't possess the will to confront the soldiers in a standing battle.[27] Thus Custer's orders to "attack the village" was an afterthought by those who so heard, and consequentially, in a very human trait, they telescoped the village they were soon to confront with what they had been ordered to achieve a half hour earlier.

Whether Custer or Cooke, or both, directly gave the orders is of little importance. What was conveyed in these directions is of importance. To reiterate, if Reno was correct and was ordered to attack a village, it must have been based on inference by Custer or Cooke, as neither had seen a village. What the two did have personal knowledge of was that a group of Indians had been observed moving in the direction of the reported village, and the scouts didn't react quickly enough to the order to chase them. As noted above, the civilians said the orders were to "pursue the Indians," while most of the soldiers said the "village was to be charged." However, all were in agreement about the three parts of the order, namely: 1) Reno was to follow the Indians; 2) he was to stop them through military action; and 3) he was to expect 'support.' The only thing left to Reno's discretion was the speed of his advance. There was no provision in the orders for any other deviation on the part of the Major; Custer's order was "positive and peremptory."[28]

About the time Custer ordered Reno to advance, he told Mitch Bouyer to take two Crow scouts and ascend the hill to the ridge and report as to what they saw. However, by the time the scouts had nearly reached the ridge line, Reno's battalion moved out, and the scouts turned to join this advance. It was at this point, Custer told Reno to take the scouts with him as they were not following his orders.[29] Besides, with the pony herds across the river and the importance of their capture, they would be more useful to Reno than himself. However, Hairy Moccasin said Custer deliberately took four Crows with him and gave Reno two. He said Custer did this because the Crows were better informed about the country.[30] Thus with the scouts all going with the advance by direction or otherwise, Custer retained just Mitch Bouyer and four of the Crows . . . Goes Ahead, Curley, White-Man-Runs-Him and Hairy Moccasin. Young Hawk, and the Arikaras who were still at the Lone Teepee and who now understood

---

[20]Hammer, *Custer in '76*, 92.　　　[21]Ibid, 65.

[22]Hunt, *I Fought . . .*, 165.

[23]John M. Carroll, *The Custer Autograph Album* (College Station, TX: The Early West, 1994), 147.

[24]McClernand, *With the Indian and the Buffalo in Montana*, 72.

[25]Stewart, *Custer's Luck*, 351.　　　[26]Ibid, 236.

[27]Charles Kuhlman, *Custer and the Gall Saga* (Billings, MT: Privately Printed, 1940), 9.　　　[28]Graham, *Reno Court*, 546.

[29]Graham, *The Custer Myth*, 13.

[30]Hammer, *Custer in '76*, 176–177.

they were to pursue the Indians, rode around to the north side of the teepee at full speed and turned into the dry coulee just beyond. A little further down the trail they overtook Reno's Battalion.[31] That is, all except the Arikara scout, Soldier, who because of his tired horse (he claimed his horse was "lazy") was left behind. He saw that a messenger had met Custer who rode up and down the column talking to the men. Soldier's friend Stabbed, another Arikara, "Came up behind me and explained that he had been out with a message to the soldiers to (the) east."[32]

The only soldiers over to the east were those of Benteen's Battalion.

It wouldn't have been unusual for Custer to wonder about Benteen's whereabouts. Why hadn't he rejoined the main trail, or why hadn't he reported what he discovered? If Stabbed's account is accurate, he must have been dispatched as a messenger to find out the answers. If Custer dispatched this messenger, his request would have had to have been in writing as Stabbed spoke no English, and no interpreter accompanied him. One battle student suggested that the messenger was the Sergeant Major, and that Stabbed escorted him.[33] What would have the message contained? Probably, as noted, Custer would have asked why he had not heard from the senior captain? What were the conditions on the back trail? Were there any camps in the lower valley? In addition, could Custer have given Benteen further orders, such as, he was to join in the attack or to come in on the left of the eight advancing companies? The possibilities of Stabbed going to Benteen and returning would create enough interesting scenarios to keep battle historians busy for the next hundred years.

It was about 2:15 in the afternoon when Reno's battalion moved forward; one trooper remembered Company I was abreast of Company M when Reno started off.[34] The major was about three and half miles from the Little Big Horn River. Varnum had rejoined Custer and saw Reno's Battalion moving off at trot. He asked his commander where they were going, and Custer replied, "To begin the attack."[35] He asked Custer for further orders and was told that he could go with the advance if he wished. As he rode past his lieutenant colonel for what would be the last time, Hare and the scouts around him joined Varnum. While the small party passed the main column, Varnum noticed his friend and roommate George Wallace riding at the head of the troops and called out,

"Come on Nick, with the fighting men. I don't stay back with the coffee coolers."[36]

Custer just smiled and waived his hat, and Wallace also joined the advance. The invitation by Wallace's friend saved his life. In addition, Varnum's recollections strongly imply that Wallace perjured himself at the Reno Court of Inquiry when he stated he always rode "near Major Reno" and gave testimony as if he had.[37]

After catching up with his battalion, Reno rode at a steady pace toward the Little Big Horn River, following the Indian trail. The route to the river was fairly open and treeless. As shown on the map in Chapter 4, the north fork of Reno Creek, where some claim the Lone Teepee was located, enters the creek on its right, less than a mile from the Little Big Horn River and a little over three miles south of the Lone Teepee. On the left bank at the mouth of Reno Creek is a natural ford used by the Indians for years. This ford was one of the best ones on the river, for if one goes north, the river moves through some very steep and formidable bluffs, which can reach 150 feet above the water. These bluffs extend northeast for a couple of miles and are interspersed by several other fords. At the Court of Inquiry, the Reno Creek crossing was designated Ford 'A;' I will use that terminology here. Reno kept his command in a column of fours, with each company following the other, and tried to conserve the horses' energy as much as possible until he established visual contact with the Indians. Herendeen, who assumed Custer's order regarding the scouts also applied to him, rode next to Reno and heard him instruct the troopers to keep their horses "well in hand." The battalion settled into a slow lope.

It took less than a half an hour for the troopers to reach the mouth of the North Fork, cross over to the left bank of Reno Creek, and reach Ford 'A'. Girard and most of the Indian scouts were about a half a mile in front of the advance, and the scouts crossed the river before Reno had arrived. They quickly galloped up the valley. Reno now changed his front from column of fours to column of twos in order to cross the Little Big Horn. At this time in June, the river was about twenty-five to thirty feet wide and "belly deep to the horses;" Company 'M' was first across, then 'A' with 'G' last.[38] Along the river's western bank, groves of thick trees obscured the view of the valley both to the north and west, so the men could see little of what lay ahead. Although the battalion was supposed to cross and form up on the other side as rapidly as possible, the horses had not been watered since the night before. Many of them could-

---

[31]Graham, *The Custer Myth*, 34.

[32]Hammer, *Custer in '76*, 188.

[33]Pennington, *The Battle of the Little Bighorn*, 203, 279.

[34]Neil C. Mangum, "Reno's Battalion in the Battle of the Little Big Horn," *Greasy Grass*, Vol. 2, May 1986, 4.

[35]Carroll, *I, Varnum*, 64.

[36]Carroll, *I, Varnum*, 65.   [37]Graham, *Reno Court*, 19.

[38]Graham, *Reno Court*, 21; E. A. Brininstool, *Troopers With Custer* (Harrisburg, PA: The Stackpole Company, 1952), 48.

n't be held back in spite of the tight reins and thrust their heads forward into the water.[39] The troopers also took advantage to fill their empty canteens, and the crossing took all of ten minutes before the troops were closed up on the western side of the Little Big Horn; it was nearly 3 o'clock.

While Reno was moving to the advance, Custer followed at a much slower pace. He was still giving Benteen time to catch up with the rest of the regiment while Reno carried out his assignment. Varnum remembered that when he left the main column, "Custer was moving at a walk," and he followed behind Reno, using the same route.[40] Custer, after his brief interview with Reno, might have hoped Reno would now display the same confidence, imagination, and aggressive personality as he did when he first wrote to Terry, asking him to be given command of the 7th Cavalry when he (Custer) was delayed in Washington two months before. To insure his orders to Reno were being carried out, Custer asked Cooke to follow after Reno. The regimental adjutant is an extension of the commanding officer; he is in effect a second set of eyes and ears. In addition, battalion commander Myles Keogh also joined the Adjutant. These two key figures from the right wing weren't just "pirating on their own hook." They were sent by Custer with a specific mission to accomplish. It is conceivable, at this point, Custer intended to follow Reno, probably in a reinforcing position. It's doubtful the Lieutenant Colonel would have ever sent these two important officers to follow up on the advance if he expected to change his plans to a supporting position and move in a different direction. This is another indication that Custer closely followed Reno almost to the ford itself and did not turn to the right several miles or more from the Ford 'A,' as some battle students claim.

The reasons for dispatching his Adjutant were twofold: 1) it would goad a reluctant and possibly confused Reno to stop the flight of the Indians expeditiously, and 2) since he hadn't heard from Benteen, Custer was making allowances for Reno's temperament and took a proactive approach to insure this wouldn't happen twice, and he would have quick feedback on the situation ahead. Some battle students have asserted Keogh, who was the regimental's senior captain after Benteen, was sent to provide Reno with some moral support, in effect saying, "Custer is not going to forget about you." I believe a more likely reason for Keogh going forward was to conduct a personal reconnaissance of the area. Keogh would be able to see first hand the terrain and what was happening with the idea of his battalion being committed if the Major

didn't execute his orders in a prompt and military manner. If so directed, this would leave Custer with only three companies. However, with Benteen expected momentarily, the "right wing" would return to its original six company strength. Reno confirmed that both Cooke and Keogh rode with him for "some time," but he had lost track of them in getting his command across the ford and didn't see either of them afterwards.[41]

It would be very surprising indeed if Reno and Cooke and or Keogh didn't converse about the situation. Reno would have us believe he was acting as a spectator and not as commander of an independent action. Reno never revealed what was discussed. Keogh turned back to the main column right before he reached the Little Big Horn. He observed and noted all that was required and was ready to remain with the right wing or proceed to Ford 'A'. Godfrey, however, insisted that Keogh rode with Cooke all the way to the ford, and both of them observed the crossing of Reno's troops.[42]

Cooke was right at the river's crossing; in fact some troopers remember he even crossed to the western side of the river.[43] Ferdinand Culbertson, a Sergeant in Company 'A', said Cooke was at the river trying to keep the men closed up, telling them there was "hot work ahead of them."[44] Thus Cooke was at the crossing long enough for at least two of the three companies to reach the western side and was able to know first hand the conditions encountered so far. As Reno's Command was forming on the river's western side for the advance down the valley, Cooke turned away from the Little Big Horn and moved towards a small knoll about 75 yards away on the eastern bank to observe the situation and wait for the main column which was about ten minutes away on the back trail.[45]

Most of the scouts had ridden out onto the valley floor, and the Arikaras, who were riding to his left with a clearer view down the valley, saw a large numbers of warriors coming out to meet them from around a bend of trees (near the present day Garryowen). They also saw the village was intact and wasn't being dismantled.[46] At the same time, several scouts rode upstream along the river's high bank and looked to the north over the tree tops. They quickly informed Girard, who was just east of the ford, that a number of Indians were coming up the valley to meet the soldiers.[47] Herendeen recalled that one of the Crows called

[39]Graham, *Reno Court*, 237.
[40]Ibid, 122; Knipe, "A New Story of Custer's Last Battle," 280.

[41]New York *Herald* (NY, NY), August 8, 1876; Graham, *The Custer Myth*, 228. [42]Graham, *The Custer Myth*, 139.
[43]*Camp, IU*, box 2, folder 10.
[44]Hammer, *Custer in '76*, 148; Graham, *Reno Court*, 333.
[45]Graham, *Reno Court*, 77. From the river, Custer's companies were blocked from the view because of a knoll.
[46]Ibid, 77. [47]Kuhlman, *Legend into History*, 53–54.

out the Sioux were coming out to meet us. Reno was in the river at the time, and the interpreter called out, "hold on the Sioux were coming."[48]

Girard sought out Reno and informed him of what they had seen. However, Reno said he received no such information, and even if Girard had told him he wouldn't have believed him because of their past problems.[49] He further postulated the scout "had no right to speak to me officially."[50]

Girard knew Custer was under the assumption the Indians were fleeing as he had told him so less than an hour before, and this new information, he thought, might change his plans.[51] He felt it was his duty to inform Custer since Reno was impervious to any intelligence he might impart. Girard started back to Custer's command, which was less than three quarters of a mile away. He had just recrossed the river and had ridden towards the small knoll when he saw Cooke coming around the same knoll, about 80 yards from the ford.[52] Girard didn't see Custer's column; he was of the opinion Custer was right behind the knoll which blocked his immediate view, because if Custer had been further out on the trail the scout could have seen him.[53] Cooke asked him where he was going. Girard told the adjutant that the Indians were showing fight and were coming out to meet Reno, and he thought it was of sufficient importance that Custer be informed. Cooke said, "All right, I'll go back and report."[54] Girard turned his horse back toward the ford and rode off at a gallop. Just before Girard reached he river, which was about three minutes after his meeting with Cooke, he met Reno's striker, Private Archibald McIlhargy of 'I' Company, "hurrying east," whom the Major had dispatched to Custer "with my compliments, and to say that the Indians were in front of me and in strong force."[55] By the time Girard crossed the river, he saw Reno's battalion moving down the valley several hundred yards ahead.[56]

After hearing Keogh's assessment of the situation that Reno was carrying out his orders and was by now across the Little Big Horn, Custer, who was still following behind Reno, halted for about ten minutes to water his horses in Reno Creek.[57] That Custer thought they would be chasing, not fighting, Indians is evident when he told his officers not to permit the horses to drink too deeply,

as he expected a hard afternoon's ride ahead to bring the Indians to bay.[58]

While there, Custer saw two riders approaching the command. McIlhargy found Custer before Cooke. Private Edward Davern also saw McIlhargy cross back to the eastern side of the river and spoke to him. McIlhargy told Davern he "was going to General Custer."[59] Cooke was within eighty yards of the Ford when Girard turned back and met McIlhargy who, as Davern said, had already recrossed the Little Big Horn. Based on Girard's and Davern's statements, Reno's striker was less than five minutes behind Cooke, and it would have been only natural for the messenger to holler, "hello," then speed up to overtake the adjutant while Cooke slowed down to receive the message, and together they rode to the main column. It has been suggested that McIlhargy didn't meet up with Cooke as soon as has been portrayed; that he must have ridden a longer distance to deliver his message, thus precluding any safe return to Reno. I believe an equally valid explanation is he returned and stayed with his own company ('I'); also that there was a greater chance of action and "glory" riding with Custer, rather than Reno, shouldn't be discounted.

Custer listened to both reports and believed them to be entirely plausible as to the reaction of the Indians, because they had enough warning to mount a delaying action so the village could escape. The village ahead was probably in a state of confusion, with panicked inhabitants, undefended in their flight. The Indians would have no reason to expect another column of soldiers to be near, and if the reports were correct, by concentrating their warriors against Reno, the village would be left wide open for a flank attack, or even better, a strike at the end of the encampment to put a stop to any further flight. Custer knew from combat experience how quickly the confidence of any fighting force becomes subverted when the enemy appears in a place unexpected and attacks. Their spirit would crumble, and Custer would capture many noncombatants and ponies within reach, kill any warriors still showing fight, and destroy the village. It would be the Washita on a grander scale.

At about 3 o'clock, as all this was happening near the Little Big Horn River, Benteen's Battalion was just pulling out from their watering stop at the morass. These animals also hadn't had a good drink of water since the previous afternoon. The lengthy halt had lasted long enough for one of the officers to remark, "I wonder what the old man is keeping us here for so long."[60] Some suggested it

[48]Graham, *Reno Court*, 213.

[49]Ibid, 524.

[50]Graham, *Reno Court—Abstract*, 223.

[51]Graham, *Reno Court*, 100.

[52]Ibid, 80.

[53]Ibid, 77.

[54]Ibid.

[55]Ibid, 80; Hammer, *Custer in '76*, 232. At the the Reno Court of Inquiry, Girard said he did not see McIlhargy. Ibid, 92; 500.

[56]Ibid, 101.

[57]Ibid, 340.

[58]Ibid.

[59]Ibid.

[60]Hammer, *Custer in '76*, 75.

was to allow the men to fill their canteens. Captain Thomas Weir, commanding officer of 'D' Company and destined to play a major role in the battle, became more and more uneasy over this half hour stop. Weir rode over to 'K' and spoke to Godfrey about the delay. He said they ought to go to Benteen and tell him to move out. Godfrey said he agreed, but it wouldn't do any good as Benteen would tell both of them to mind their own business.[61]

Company D's captain said he didn't care and was going to advance anyhow and proceeded to mount his company.[62] This uneasiness could have been made acute, supposedly by hearing gunfire ahead.[63] Charles Windolph remembered they began to hear firing right before they left the morass. Likewise, Private William Morris, 'M' Company, reported Jan Muller (Moller), Private 'H' Company, told him they heard "heavy firing" as they were watering the horses.[64] To complicate the situation, Fremont Kipp said they heard no firing, and the first gunshots the battalion heard was when they got closer to the river. Camp noted he thought Kipp was right and the others wrong on this point.[65] Camp came to this conclusion because the origin of any gunfire heard by Benteen's troops is problematic. At this time, no one from Custer's wing nor from Reno's was yet engaged. We know that some of the scouts who crossed the river ahead of Reno had exchanged a few shots with the Indian pony herders, but that would hardly qualify as heavy gunfire. In addition, this action would be almost seven miles from the morass; a near impossible distance to hear this sporadic gunfire.

I believe Camp's conclusions are accurate, as will be established later. For if gunfire was heard at this point, Benteen is shown as being even more neglectful of his duty for not riding at once and quickly "to the sound of the guns." Whether Captain Weir just became impatient to take some sort of action, or the improbable gunfire was heard, he, nevertheless, led his company forward. In spite of the fact, D Company had been second in the marching order.[66] In an effort to make up for his extended dithering and resume control, Benteen galloped past 'D,' with 'H' now in the center and 'K' in the rear, and rode about a hundred yards in front of the advance.[67]

According to Private Morris, Benteen then moved at a pace "as slow as though he was going to a funeral." Godfrey agreed with Morris and recorded in his diary: "After

we watered we continued our march very leisurely."[68] Within two miles, Benteen arrived at the Lone Teepee, which was still smoldering; it was about 3:30. Custer was less than six miles away in the vicinity of Sharpshooter's Ridge, and Reno was down in the valley about five miles ahead, heavily engaged.

It was a little after three o'clock as Mathey drove the mules past their half dozen others mired in the morass. It was all he could do to keep the entire train from making a break to the waterhole. He knew it would take the rear guard some time to put things back in order. The forty-five men in Company 'B' pulled, cursed, and prodded the mules out of the mire. The troopers then had to repack or adjust the loads, line them up, and start them after the rest of the train, which was about a mile ahead.[69] McDougall did very well in getting these wayward animals back on the trail in less than a half hour. He kept the mules at the front in a "sort of a jog trot." The reluctant mules had one trooper assigned to pull them along with a lariat and another to ride behind them with a whip "to get them along."[70] The Captain lost track of time, and sometimes he would pick up one stray animal, sometimes five, but McDougall was determined not to lose a single mule. At the same time, he was concerned about Indians on his back trail and thought about methods to resist an attack.

When Lt. Mathey, with most of the mules, arrived at the Lone Teepee he saw a great deal of smoke ahead. He assumed the regiment was engaged from the report of a half breed scout who passed the train and said there were "too many (Indians) for him (Custer)" to whip.[71] The lieutenant halted the train and sent word back to McDougall that there was probably fighting ahead, and he would wait for him. That potential action was ahead, although Mathey wouldn't admit it, was confirmed by Daniel Knipe as he rode past the head of the train on his way to deliver Custer's order to McDougall, whom he met a short distance east of the lone teepee. McDougall had done well in pushing the stragglers forward. He was only 15 minutes behind the Lieutenant and closed as rapidly as possible with the rest of the unit.[72] This was only a natural reaction by Mathey to halt the train and concentrate the command if action was expected. It would also give him the opportunity to water the mules who had been denied as they had been driven past the morass. However, the

[61]Ibid.

[62]John M. Carroll, *The Benteen-Goldin Letters On Custer And His Last Battle* (NY, NY: Liveright, 1974), 16–17.

[63]Hammer, *Custer in '76*, 75.

[64]Brady, *Indian Fights and Fighters*, 404.   [65]*Camp, DPL*, #108.

[66]Hunt, *I Fought . . .* , 81.   [67]Ibid.

[68]Edgar I. Stewart and Jane R. Stewart (Eds), *The Field Diary of Lt. Edward Settle Godfrey* (Portland, OR: Champoeg Press, 1957), 11. Hereinafter cited: *The Field Diary . . .*

[69]Graham, *Reno Court*, 471.   [70]Ibid, 472.

[71]Ibid, 458; *Camp, IU*, box 2 folder12.

[72]Graham, *Reno Court*, 459.

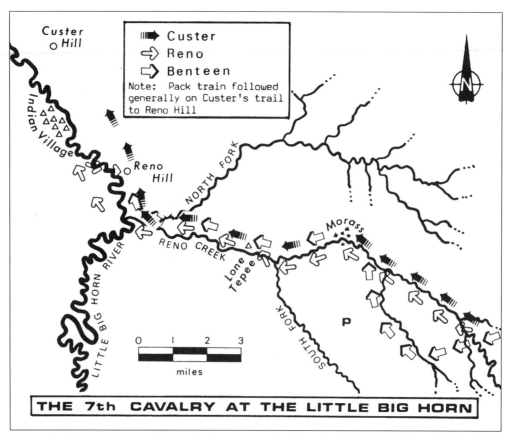

Courtesy of The Little Bighorn Associates, Inc.

quarter of an hour halt belies the fact Custer wanted the pack train brought forward as rapidly as possible. Perhaps, in Mathey's opinion, he could do no less as the mules would start to break down unless soon watered.

Upon McDougall's arrival, with Knipe in tow, the entire command was together for the first time since crossing the divide. The Captain dismounted and examined the smoking teepee, while Mathey, whose attention was taken up by the pack train, didn't notice much about this landmark. The command now being a cohesive unit, it proceeded down the trail towards the river. McDougall said they traveled about two miles when he saw some dark objects on a hill at a right angle from the trail and thought they were Indians. He imagined the train would have to cut their way through. McDougall gave orders to further close up the mules and placed "one of 'B's platoons in front and in the rear."[73]

He then gathered all the ammunition mules together and told the front platoon, if attacked they were to stand them off, and if they couldn't, the men with these mules were to lead them into a circle and shoot them down. They could hold off any number of Indians as they had plenty of ammunition and mule meat for rations.[74] McDougall then ordered 'B' Company to draw pistols and moved towards the objects on the hill. Custer should have had McDougall take the advance and Reno the pack train.

After receiving the Adjutant's and McIlhary's report, Custer continued on for another three hundred yards until he was about a quarter mile from Ford 'A.'[75] It was before three o'clock when Custer made his third critical decision. At this point he abruptly turned 90 degrees to the right; he was no longer following in Reno's rear. However, the Crow scout, Curley, claimed Custer turned north about one and a quarter miles east of Ford 'A.'[76] He further explained that they went to the north fork of Reno Creek, and crossed it, going to the hill, and turned westward along the ridge.[77] Hank Weibert who lived in the area for years also claimed Custer turned several miles from the ford after watering his horses in the North Fork, as it offered an ideal place to water the animals.[78] Varnum and Girard believed Custer separated from Reno a mile or less

[73]Graham, *Reno Court*, 471.

[74]Hammer, *Custer in '76*, 70.   [75]Graham,, *Reno Court*, 341.

[76]Hammer, *Custer in '76*, 156.   [77]Graham, *The Custer Myth*, 19.

[78]Weibert, *Sixty-Six Years in Custer's Shadow*, 1–19, 42.

from the Little Big Horn.[79] Varnum further elaborated that Reno's companies were crossing the ford when he reached the river, and this was at the most fifteen minutes after he had left Custer.[80]

What caused Custer to change from what had seemed to be a reinforcing role to one of supporting? There are no clear cut answers, and it probably was a combination of factors. Knipe always claimed he was the cause of this change in his commander's plans. Camp recorded:

> Knipe says as soon as he saw 60 to 75 Indians on hill north of where Reno was corraled, he reported it to 1st Sergeant Edwin Bobo who in turn reported it to (Second Lieutenant) Harrington and he to Tom Custer then to his brother. General Custer immediately turning to the right in the direction of Indians.[81]

Knipe further said Custer would not have wanted to follow after Reno and attack the village without first disposing of these Indians. Knipe recalled his exact words to 1st Sergeant Bobo were "There are the Indians."[82] Knipe elaborated on the information he told Camp in the account he gave to the Montana Historical Society. In this earlier account, he said Custer "turned squarely to the right charging up the bluffs on the banks of the Little Big Horn, when he saw a number of Indians." Knipe made no mention of first spotting the Indians, then giving the alarm.[83]

Girard gave two reasons why Custer might have turned to the right. First, because of his report about the Indians coming up to meet Reno, he thought it might change Custer's plans. When questioned at the Court of Inquiry as to why he so thought, the scout replied, "by pressing forward; and if there were any parties out, he might call them in; or he might have recalled Major Reno for all I knew." When asked because of his report if he thought Custer would cross the river to support Reno, Girard said he didn't think he would.[84] The second reason was Custer no doubt saw the same large trail he had noticed on the eastern side of the small knoll during his ride with Reno's Battalion to the Ford 'A.' Girard said there were two trails behind the knoll, one going left towards the ford and another "going to the right—quite a large one."[85] He further stated it was a lodge trail, and it was larger than the trail Reno was following.[86] Trumpeter Martin, who was riding near Custer, also saw this same trail; he said, "It looked like teepee poles had been dragged along there."[87]

A lodge trail would indicate the presence of women and children. These Indians could very well have been the inhabitants of the camp site at the Lone Teepee.

In addition, we need to take into account Custer's aggressive nature; to him, attack and victory were the same. If the warriors were moving against Reno, then he, Custer, could move against an undefended part and hit them before they had realized it. It would be the old Indian ambush trick in reverse: force the Indians to confront a small force as a feint, then unexpectedly hit them with a larger force on their flank. He would attempt to hit them from this direction by the shortest route possible. Custer knew that a lodge trail would eventually lead to a good river crossing, and these trails always took the path of least resistance and would be the fastest route for a body of horsemen to move quickly across unknown terrain.[88] Of course, we might be overlooking the simplest reason that Custer just might have wanted to see for himself what was happening in the valley and rode to the high ground for a better look. Any of these reasons, a combination of them, or others unrecorded, could have caused Custer to turn to the right, with major consequences resulting from the turn.

By going to the right, Custer has been roundly criticized for not informing Reno of his change in plans. Custer knew Reno wanted to be reinforced; he had sent Reno to stop the flight of a body of Indians, and now he received two reports they were coming out to meet Reno in "strong force." If Custer's intent was to reinforce rather than support (and we have no way of knowing what additional instructions were given to Major Reno), then his failure to apprise Reno of "this sudden and variant" change at best "constitutes a lack of good faith."[89] However, Custer might have thought he could execute his attack well before any messenger would get though to his vice commander. Also, without a doubt, Custer still believed the village was breaking up and the "strong force" Reno reported was only the rear guard.[90] There is one soldier and a scout who claimed to have been a messenger from Custer to Reno. This soldier was Private Theodore Goldin of Company 'G,' and the scout was Curley. In addition to these better known claimants, Sergeant Thomas Harrison of Company D wrote that Private Henry Jones, Company I, was sent back by Custer with dispatches to Reno. Jones, however, denied he was a messenger, and Harrison was mistaken, as he

[79]Graham, *Reno Court*, 77, 122, 125.   [80]Ibid, 125.
[81]*Camp, IU*, box2, folder 7.   [82]Graham, *The Custer Myth*, 249.
[83]Knipe, "A New Story of Custer's Last Battle," 280.
[84]Graham, *Reno Court*, 100.   [85]Ibid, 79.
[86]Ibid, 80.   [87]Ibid, 350.

[88]Letter, Robert Doran to Bruce R. Liddic, December 6, 2001, author's collection.
[89]Coughlan, "Battle of the Little Big Horn," 17.
[90]Kuhlman, *Custer and the Gall Saga*, 12.

was one of the men detailed from his company to the pack train.[91]

Curley said, as Custer crossed the creek to commence his right turn, he gave him a message to take to Reno. The Crow said he didn't know what the message said, and he delivered it to Reno when he was on the skirmish line. He then brought back Reno's reply to Custer.[92] To many battle scholars, this seems incredible, but it was corroborated by the scout Goes Ahead. This Crow said, "Curley I did not see because he carried the last dispatch to Reno."[93]

Curley told so many different stories to so many different people that many historians have discounted large parts of his reminiscences. Regarding his carrying a message to Reno, I believe their skepticism is merited. Of the enlisted men in the five companies who were riding to their death with Custer, none, with the possible exception of Peter Thompson, is more a conundrum than Theodore Goldin. Goldin, if one believes all the tales subscribed to him, did, saw, and heard everything possible at the Little Big Horn with the lone exception of actually dying with Custer.

Goldin stated he was assigned on the morning of June 25 as an orderly to the Adjutant. Never mind the fact he was at the time just 18 years old, an illegal, underaged recruit, with two and a half months of service. In 1886, he wrote the following to The Janesville *Daily Gazette* as Custer:

> dashed along, spoke a few words to Capt. Cook, his adjutant. Cook checked his horse, dashed off a few words on a piece of paper and turning in his saddle called for an orderly; being nearest to him, . . . with the hurried instructions "Deliver this to Maj. Reno, remain with him until we effect a junction and report at once to General Custer."[94]

Goldin also wrote that as he turned his horse, he heard Custer say to Keogh, "Keogh, those Indians are running. If we can keep at it we can afford to lose every horse in the 7th Cavalry." Goldin stated that after a ride of five or six miles, he delivered the message to Reno who looked it over and put it into his pocket.[95]

There has been and still is a great deal of controversy about this messenger. Compiler Fred Dustin first accepted the story, then wrote later, "I began to feel some doubts," and even later in a letter to Albert Johnson, an early Custer student, "instead of becoming more skeptical as to his carrying that note to Reno, I have become satisfied that he did carry it."[96] Larry Sklenar, author of *To Hell With Honor*, wrote a very interesting article in which he believed Goldin did carry a message, but never delivered it, due to a number of circumstances, not the least of which that he was scared stiff.[97]

The problem with accepting anything Goldin claimed he did at the Little Big Horn is that he had a definite and lifelong predisposition for lying. For example, in July 1878, while Goldin asserted he was with 'G' Company in the Black Hills to intercept Indians near Bear Butte (South Dakota), his hometown newspaper in Janesville, Wisconsin recorded Goldin, along with a number of the town's young ladies, celebrated his 21st birthday with an ice cream party at his residence.[98] Others have maintained Goldin was with the pack train, a not unusual assignment given his youth and inexperience, but they have never been able to prove this theory. However, it's not an impossibility that Custer would have tried to communicate with Reno. Godfrey was doubtful any message was sent, but he did declare if it was, "who knows but this message contained important instructions, hastily glanced at, that were pocketed, ignored, destroyed and never revealed?"[99] And what of Major Reno; did he expect Custer to reply to his messengers? Judging from his post battle report, he attached no blame for this lack of communication from his commander: "But he (Custer) was fully confident they were running away, or he would have not turned from me."[100]

As Custer rode away from Reno Creek, his command was in a squadron formation (company front) of column of twos, moving at a trot and gallop all the way up the bluff.[101] As he did so, Custer's column was seen by Standing Bear and several other Minneconjou as they began this maneuver. The Indians were on Weir Point with some women who had been digging wild turnips.[102] The dust

[91]*Camp, BYU*, roll 1, box 1, folder 20.

[92]Dr. Joseph K. Dixon, *The Vanishing Race* (Glorieta, NM: The Rio Grande Press, 1973), 163.   [93]Ibid, 167.

[94]Janesville *Gazette* (Janesville, WI), July 8, 1886.

[95]Brady, *Indian Fights and Fighters*, 271.

[96]Dustin, *The Custer Tragedy*, 149–150; Letter Fred Dustin to Albert Johnson, January 9, 1941, copy in Moses Collection, Otsego, MI.

[97]Larry Skenlar, "Private Theodore W. Goldin : Too Soon Discredited," *Research Review : Journal of the Little Big Horn Associates*, Vol. 9, #1, January 1995, 9–17.

[98]Lt. Col. Melbourne C. Chandler, *Of Garryowen In Glory* (Annandale, VA: The Turnpike Press, 1960), 76; The *Janesville* Gazette (Janesville, WI) , August 2, 1878.

[99]Graham, *The Custer Myth*, 295.

[100]Carroll, *The Federal View*, 105.

[101]*Camp, IU*, box 2, folder 8.

[102]Richard Hardorff, *Lakota Recollections of the Custer Fight* (Spokane, WA: Arthur H. Clark, 1991), 143–145; Raymond J. DeMallie, *The Sixth Grandfather* (Lincoln, NE: University of Nebraska Press, 1984), 185.

from this compact formation, which had attracted the attention of the Minneconjou, would be natural if Custer was chasing the Indians on the bluffs. Heading to the north, the company front from left to right was "E, F, L, C, I." This arrangement would tend to confirm the assignment of the right wing, with Keogh as battalion commander of 'C' and 'I,' while Yates continued as battalion commander of "E, F, and L." This compact body of horsemen was 10 horses, about 50 feet across and 20 horses, about 200 feet deep.[103] The disturbed ground and dust left by this five-company squadron formation could have been followed by a blind man. Custer was in the center at the head of the companies, not over fifteen yards from 'C.'[104] Peter Thompson, of this Company, had a good view of his commander and said he was dressed in buckskin pants shoved into long legged-boots, and his buckskin jacket fastened to the rear of his saddle. He wore a blue flannel shirt decorated with a white narrow braid, with a broad-brimmed white hat with the brim turned up on the right side.[105]

Despite riding hard, by the time the troops "reached the top the Indians were gone."[106]

When Custer reached the top of the bluffs, a large part of the Indian village was in plain view. He also saw Reno and his battalion to the left, moving very quickly down the valley and heading towards the village.[107] Custer was also observed by Reno's men in the valley, and they provide us with the strongest evidence of Custer's route along the bluffs. Any attempt to understand and reconstruct this battle would have to take into account the route taken by the soldiers. Whatever faults Varnum exhibited in his testimony at the Court of Inquiry, his estimates of distances are very close to the actual distances. He stated when riding with Reno on the valley floor, he first " saw "E" Company about a quarter of a mile, some little distance like that, from the point where Major Reno was when we struck the hill."[108]

Varnum further explained that where he saw Custer, the bluffs are not as high as they are further to the north. Anyone who has been on this part of the battlefield will note that about a quarter mile north of the National Park Service's (NPS) boundary line on Reno Hill, the land begins to rise until it reaches the summit of the divide. There are two additional high peaks still further north,

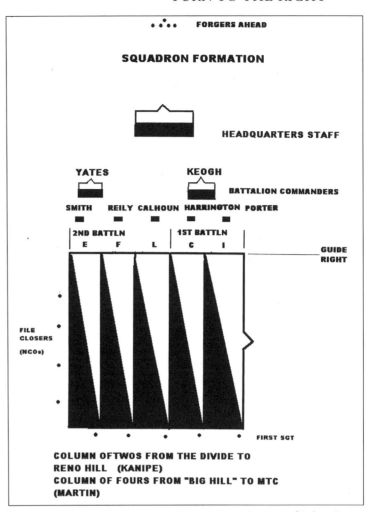

Courtesy of Robert Doran

the farthest one being Weir Point. Therefore, as one travels from the high point on Reno's Hill towards Weir Point, where the land slopes down, the terrain is higher. On the current topography map of the area where the "3500" elevation is marked above Reno's retreat ford is the summit of Reno's Ridge. From Varnum's description, he saw E Company just to the south of this landmark.

Girard also saw Custer's battalion about a half a mile below what would later be Reno's entrenchments. He said he noticed the troops on the bluffs at about the time Reno halted his command to form a skirmish line because of "the cloud of dust" being raised by their fast trot. He estimated it would have taken Custer about 15 or 20 minutes to reach that point from where he last saw Cooke.[109] Custer's survey of the valley would have been well after 3:00. In addition, DeRudio's testimony serves as a further check as to Custer's route along the bluffs. He said he saw Custer while standing at the edge of the timber near the

[103]*Camp, IU*, box 2, folder 2, #32; Also see the map by Lt. Edward Maguire, "Plan of the Battlefield of the 7th Regt. Cav.," *Report of Chief of Engineers*, Appendix, Washington, 1877.

[104]*Camp, BYU*, box 1, folder 2.   [105]Ibid, box 1, folder 5.

[106]Graham, *The Custer Myth*, 249.

[107]Knipe, " A New Story of Custer's Last Battle," 280.

[108]Graham, *Reno Court*, 147.

[109]Ibid, 108.

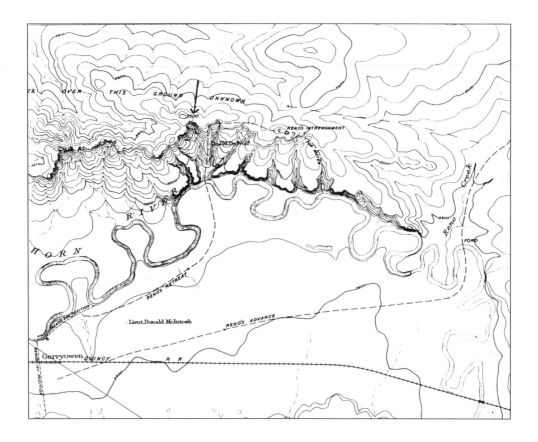

river. "It was on the highest point on the right bank, just below where Dr. DeWolf was killed . . . he was about a 1000 yards from where I was."[110] DeRudio further said he could see only Custer, Cooke, and another man whom he couldn't identify. At no time did he see "any part of the column of General Custer."[111] A number of battle students have debated if DeRudio could have identified anybody at such a distance. The distance aside, with all the dust and blackpowder smoke around during the timber fight, it's questionable if anyone in Reno's command could have identified individuals on the bluffs. Be that as it may, DeRudio repeated to the Court that even though Custer borrowed his field glasses, he was able to recognize Cooke and Custer by their dress . . . they were the only ones who wore buckskin pants and blue shirts.[112] The reason why the Lieutenant didn't see any other part of the command was because his view from the valley floor was limited to the edge of the bluffs, which blocked the view of the area around the summit of the ridge, which is about a quarter of a mile in the rear. Consequently, DeRudio's testimony places Custer on the edge of the bluffs about 1200 feet west of the summit. The Crow Scouts also tend to confirm this as Custer's lookout point.[113]

This observation point is important as it provides us with a point of reference from where Custer's first messenger was dispatched and his subsequent actions and route to the battlefield. After Custer returned to his command, they rode a short distance north, to about where the NPS's entrance fence to Reno Hill is located, and Knipe's captain, Tom Custer, turned, motioned him along side in response to the Adjutant's request for a messenger. As noted above, most of the teepees were visible all along the river, and when the troopers saw them, Knipe remembered they began to shout and became excited. Some of the horses became unmanageable and took their riders past Custer. The last words Knipe heard Custer speak were "Boys, hold your horses, there are plenty of them down there for us all."[114]

Prior to this, Sergeant August Finkle had been riding near the company commander. But Finkle's horse was giving out, and he fell back, putting Knipe in a more prominate position. His Captain verbally told him: "Go back to McDougall and bring him and the pack train straight across the country. Tell McDougall to hurry the pack train to Custer and if any of the packs get loose cut them and let them go; do not stop to tighten them."[115] Knipe also told Camp about an afterthought Captain Custer had and called out to him, "And if you see Benteen tell him to

---

[110]Ibid, 291. [111]Ibid. [112]Ibid, 296. [114]Ibid, 249. [115]Hammer, *Custer in '76*, 93–94.
[113]Graham, *The Custer Myth*, 13, 17, 24.

come on quick—a big Indian camp."[116] Knipe saluted, checked his horse, and started on the back trail. It was after 3:15. The young sergeant thought it was tough luck, as he would miss all the action, but he later admitted, "it proved to be my salvation."[117] Knipe started back on the trail, but cut across the back country when he saw the dust "rolling up like a little cloud," raised by both Benteen's column and the pack train. Using the dust as his compass, he rode rapidly towards it.

Private Peter Thompson, riding near Knipe, confirmed his sergeant's story in his 1914 account of the battle. He said the troops were in columns of twos, and Custer had learned there were Indians down the river, and it was his intention to keep out of sight when he left Reno, so he turned and followed, "in parallel lines," with the Little Big Horn. When the command reached the top of the bluffs, they had a good view of the surrounding country, and "we were ordered to form into a set of fours." A half a mile further they finally saw the Indian village and a black mass of ponies grazing beyond the valley.[118] Custer kept the command moving north, but at a steady pace. It was about at this point, Custer directed that a five man detail be sent ahead to the eastern divide to form a reconnoitering flank guard in front of the battalion. These men came from Captain George Yates' 'F' Company.[119] These soldiers from 'F' were dispatched because Custer now had only the services of Mitch Bouyer and four Crow scouts, he had ordered all the other scouts to go with Reno. Custer had directed Reno to take the scouts with him below the Lone Teepee; he then sent the Crow Scouts Half Yellow Face and White Swan to go over to a ridge and report if any Indians could be seen. However, these Crows went in with Reno on the advance and fought bravely with the soldiers for the next two days. It's possible Varnum or Hare could have gathered these two up with the rest of the Arikaras by mistake, as they were unaware of Custer's instructions.[120] Curley didn't think this was the case, as he saw the two scouts go almost to the foot of the ridge when the "trumpeter sounded a call and the left wing started moving. The scouts then turned to the left and joined Reno."[121] Bouyer saw what had happened to Half Yellow Face and White Swan and called out to the remaining four Crows, saying, "Let us go over to the ridge and look at the lodges." They rode over to the ridge and saw the lodges were in the river's valley, extending quite a ways down the Little Big Horn. They then rode ahead of Custer to the bluffs. After they reached the bluffs, Custer ordered the scouts to stop and directed them to the high hill just north of where Reno was later entrenched.[122]

There are some battle students who believe Custer took an alternate route to reach the bluffs, and it wasn't near their edge.[123] As mentioned before, Curley stated that Custer turned to the right much sooner, about one and a quarter miles from the river before Cooke and McIlhargy had a chance to report. Knipe's report was the cause of this turn. After watering their horses and crossing the North Fork, the command rode up a ridge running northwestwardly in the direction where the Indians had been reported. The ridge line provided a good view all the way around. The Crow Scout further said Custer's trail went "directly across the country, on the crest of a long ridge, running to the bluffs and coming out to a point about 500 feet north of the Reno corral."[124] According to these students, Curley conveyed that Custer rode directly to Sharpshooters' Ridge and did not pass over Reno Hill, but was about 500 yards northeast of this landmark. Hare seems to reinforce this position by saying he didn't see any evidence of Custer's trail coming anywhere near Major Reno's position on the hill.[125] This was contradicted by Reno who, soon after arrival on his hill, said he saw Custer's trail of shod horses.[126] It is little wonder that Hare, with all the commotion on Reno Hill, along with the hundreds of animals arriving with Benteen's battalion, followed by the pack train, added to the Weir Point attempt, would have seen any evidence of Custer's earlier trail. General Terry wrote in his offical report that Custer's trail was on the back side of the bluffs, and probably a short distance east of where Reno later established his hospital site. But, if in fact they had ridden east of the future hospital site, they would not have been visible from the valley. Nevertheless, I believe the weight of the testimony of the individuals in the valley along with Reno's recollections, confirms the route along the bluffs near Reno Hill despite the lack of any observable tracks left by the column.

Goes Ahead remembered that during this time Custer stopped "dismounted and said prayers to the Heavenly Father."[127] While it's dubious this incident occurred, if Custer didn't halt to say his prayers, he most surely should have.

[116]*Camp, IU*, box 2, folder 8.

[117]Graham, *The Custer Myth*, 249.

[118]Brown and Willard, *Black Hills Trails*, 153–154.

[119]Ibid, 154.   [120]Graham, *The Custer Myth*, 13.

[121]Ibid.

[122]Ibid, 25.

[123]Doug McChristian, "Hurrah, Boys! We've Got Them!": An Analysis of Custer's Observation Point," *3rd Annual Symposium Custer Battlefield Historical & Museum Assn.*, 1989, 69–77.

[124]Hammer, *Custer in '76*, 156.   [125]Graham, *Reno Court*, 264.

[126]Ibid, 517.   [127]Dixon, *The Vanishing Race*, 167.

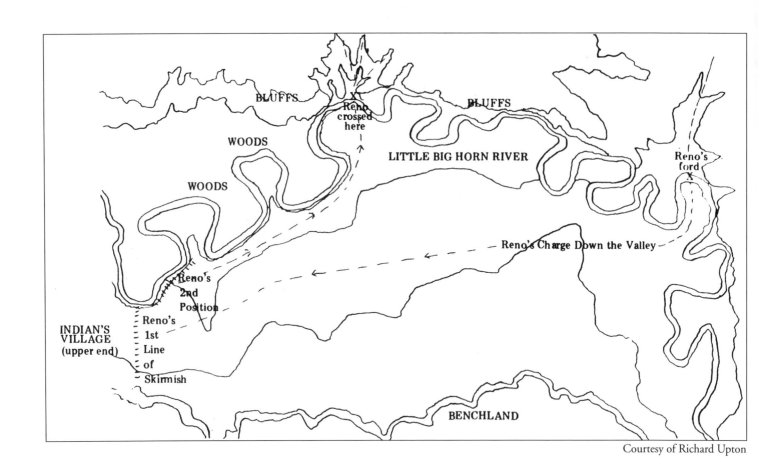

BLUFFS

BLUFFS

X
Reno
crossed
here

WOODS

LITTLE BIG HORN RIVER

Reno's
ford
X

WOODS

Reno's Charge Down the Valley

X Reno's
2nd
Position

Reno's
1st
Line
of
Skirmish

INDIAN'S
VILLAGE
(upper end)

BENCHLAND

Courtesy of Richard Upton

6

Into the Valley

As Lieutenant Carlos DeRudio approached the Little Big Horn, he noticed the command was mushrooming along the river's eastern bank, on both sides of the ford. In spite of the efforts of the officers and the company sergeants to keep the ranks closed up, it was difficult for many of the soldiers to keep their horses from slowing down to drink, thus creating this spreading effect. In addition, Lieutenant Hare recalled that Reno didn't push the crossing and gave the men plenty of time to water.[1] Some of the men simply lowered their canteens by the straps so as to fill them as they rode across. One of these men must have been Private William Morris, Company M who later was wounded and became a future New York City judge, Morris stated emphatically that neither the troops nor the horses were allowed even a mouth full of water.[2]

Trumpeter William Hardy, Company A, remembered that it was about this time he saw Adjutant Cooke on the eastern bank at the ford intently watching their progress.[3] Major Reno had taken a position in the middle of the river supposedly to keep the column of twos closed up, but by the time 'A' Company was entering the ford, DeRudio saw that Reno's attention was diverted in another direction. De Rudio observed Major Reno drinking heavily from a whiskey flask.[4] It wasn't the first time on the campaign that Reno had been drinking. In fact, Reno was "intoxicated on June 22 the day the command left the mouth of the Rosebud."[5] In addition, Private William Taylor, Company A, also saw Reno drinking but said it was right before Reno ordered the advance. He remembered that Reno was in the rear of his company "perhaps 30 or 40 feet away, possibly more but certainly a very short distance, as I looked back Major Reno was just taking a bottle from his lips . . . in appearance it was a quart flask, about half full or two thirds full of an amber colored liquid."[6]

Private William Slaper, Company A, defended the Major and stated positively that at no time did he note any evidence of drunkenness "nor did I see him use any liquor."[7] Reno, under questioning at the Court of Inquiry, admitted he had about a quart of liquor on his person but he quickly added he didn't "drink a drop of whiskey until after the firing had ceased—about 12 o'clock at night (the 25th)."[8]

The Arikara scouts had preceded Reno to the ford, and a number of them were now angling off in search of the Indians' pony herds. While Reno was watering, Hare went down the valley with the scouts. They had advanced about a mile when they saw a herd of ponies.[9]

These scouts had crossed the river at a point where there was no regular ford and attempted to fulfill their mission to capture the horses.[10] The young Sioux horse herders found themselves between the charging scouts behind them and the soldiers by the river. They raced ahead of the herd to the safety of the village. By doing so, they left a number of horses to run free. The Arikaras immediately circled the unguarded animals and broke them down into small herds. Among these scouts were Boy Chief, Red Star, Strikes Two, and Little Sioux. They succeeded in rounding up a number of these horses and drove them back towards the Little Big Horn. But the Sioux were quick to react and chased the Arikaras, forcing them to relinquish some of their captured prizes. More scouts joined them, and together they shepherded the ponies across the river just ahead of the Sioux and into a ravine "east of the ridge."[11] However, the majority of the scouts chose to remain with the battalion as it crossed the ford, and eschewing the potential horse plunder, decided to give battle to their traditional enemies, the Sioux; age or sex wasn't a factor to be considered. One of Custer's favorite scouts, Bloody Knife, did both. First, he rode ahead and captured three ponies, then drove them back to his nephew Little Sioux and told him to watch the prizes for him and then turned back to catch up with the advancing battalion.

Gall, an Uncpapa, claimed the scouts were also looking for easy and cheap kills, as his two wives and three children were their victims. Although Little Sioux spoke about the horses they had captured, he also related how the four Arikaras saw three women and two children "running and hurrying along as best they could." Then they "rode through the timber to kill them."[12] After dispatching the women and children, Little Sioux and the three other scouts saw, as related above, a number of Sioux ponies; they went after these prizes. Horses were worth more than the prospect of additional scalps. Besides, the Indian scouts had learned that the white soldiers didn't like to hear about this type of killing, "a guilt complex absent from the Indian's frame of mind."[13]

[1]Hammer, *Custer in '76*, 65.
[2]Mangum, "Reno's Battalion in the Battle of the Little Big Horn," 5.
[3]*Camp, IU*, box 2, folder 10.   [4]Ibid, box 8, folder 4.
[5]Ibid, box 2, folder 11.   [6]*Camp, BYU*, roll 1, box 1, folder 1.
[7]Brininstool, *Troopers With Custer*, 53.
[8]Graham, *Reno Court*, 511.

[9]Hammer, *Custer in '76*, 65.   [10]Graham, *The Custer Myth*, 39.
[11]Ibid.   [12]Libby, *The Arikara Narrative*, 151.
[13]Richard G. Hardorff, *Hokahey! A Good Day to Die* (Spokane, WA: Arthur H. Clark Co, 1993), 34.

Herendeen confirmed this tragedy, as the bodies of six non combatants were found in a little ravine. He further said, "Our men didn't kill any squaws, but the Ree (Arikara) Indian scouts did."[14]

Interestingly, the Cheyennes didn't blame the Arikaras for the deaths of these women and children, but said they resulted from the gunfire of Reno's skirmish line.[15]

Reno declared to the Court of Inquiry that he sent a messenger to Custer before all the companies had crossed the river "as I had been a good deal in Indian country and was convinced they were in overwhelming numbers I sent word back."[16]

In actuality, Reno had spent little time in Indian country, so one must question this self serving statement in light of what he heard from both Girard and Herendeen at the start of the crossing. Private Tom O'Neil, Company G, remembered a little rise of ground near the ford as a few of the Arikaras were there discussing the situation. One of the scouts picked up "handfuls of grass and dropping it and pointing to the Sioux, who could be seen down and across the river , indication that the Sioux were as thick as grass."[17] Probably Reno considered what both these civilians and scouts had attested and decided he had better inform Custer to speed up his "reinforcement." His striker, McIlhargy, was ordered to do so at once.

Reno's battalion was still in the act of crossing the Little Big Horn when McIlhargy was dispatched. This was confirmed by both Sergeants Ferdinand Culbertson and Davern as they remembered seeing the striker as he emerged from recrossing the river and rode past them with Reno's message to Custer. Aside from Reno's own self admitted Indian country experience, another catalyst for Reno sending a messenger to Custer was the possible report from his forward vedettes or outriders. It was a standard tactical procedure to send a non-commissioned officer and five privates (more if the situation demanded) ahead of an advancing column to gather intelligence on what lay in front of the troopers and to guard against any ambushes. Private Daniel Newell, Company M, who was later wounded leaving the timber, said there were ten men dispatched with 'M's Sergeant Charles White in charge.[18] This vedette would have been 500 to 600 yards in advance of the battalion. Without a doubt, these outriders saw the dust ahead, ponies being round up on the flats above the valley, and possibly some teepees. A private could have easily ridden back to the Major with this report, arriving about the same time as Girard's warning.

When the three companies had finished crossing the river, they were reformed into columns of fours along a narrow stand of trees, a short distance from the river's bank. Reno wrote that after the last of the companies had crossed to the western side of the river, he "halted about ten minutes to gather the battalion."[19] That Reno was aware that Custer was close behind is evident from Reno's statement that he received no response from his first messerger. McIlhargy had been gone less than fifteen minutes, but it was more than enough time to reach Custer, whom Reno believed was less than two-thirds of a mile away, deliver the report and return. So Reno said, "Receiving no instructions in response to that, I sent a second time—a man named Mitchell (John Mitchell, a private assigned to I Company), who was about me in the capacity of a cook."[20] We know both that McIlhargy and Mitchell delivered their message, as the bodies of both were later found along Custer's battle ridge.[21]

Reno delayed his advance on purpose to receive an answer. Several more minutes passed, and while tarrying, Hare recalled he had enough time to dismount and fix his saddle blanket.[22] First Sergeant John Ryan, Company M, confirmed Hare's statement and recorded when "we got on the other side, made a slight halt, dismounted, tightened our saddle girths and swung into the saddles."[23] About ten minutes had passed since the last company had crossed the river, Reno was convinced his opinions were correct about the Indians, and since "I heard nothing to guide my movement, and I went on down the valley to carry out my orders."[24]

If one can believe Reno's testimony about "nothing to guide my movement," there is little doubt there was a complete misunderstanding between Custer and Reno regarding his mission. It would appear they attended different meetings together. Clearly, Custer was operating under one set of perceptions and had directed his subordinates according to his intended tactical plan(s). The fear the village was escaping, I believe, drove these perceptions and deployments. Did this correspond to Reno's percep-

[14]Bismarck *Tribune* (Bismarck, ND), July 7, 1876.

[15]Peter J. Powell, *People of the Sacred Mountain*, Vol. II (San Francisco, CA: Harper & Row, 1981), 1011.

[16]Graham, *Reno Court*, 500.

[17]Hammer, *Custer in '76*, 106.

[18]John M. Carroll, *The Sunshine Magazine Articles* (Bryan, TX: NP, 1979), 9.

[19]Carroll, *The Federal View*, 103.

[20]Graham, *The Reno Court*, 500.

[21]Coughlan, "The Battle of the Little Big Horn," 18.

[22]Graham, *Reno Court—Abstract*, 89.

[23]Sandy Barnard, *Ten Years With Custer* (Terre Haute, IN: AST Press, 2001), 291.   [24]Graham, *Reno Court*, 500.

tions, and what in reality awaited ahead of him? Allowing that Reno was correct in his recollections and the rest wrong, Reno was ordered to advance at a pace he was to select, look for and to charge the village/Indians. The major hadn't any personal knowledge and had only been given reports of Indians ahead, one of which he dismissed. Before asking for "support," a more prudent course would have been to carry out the orders given until the true situation in the valley was disclosed. When asked if he had obeyed Custer's orders to "overtake and bring these Indians to battle," Reno said yes. He then clarified this affirmation by explaining, "I don't consider that I charged the enemy, but I went near enough to discover it was impossible to do so."[25] Custer's tactical perceptions tragically clashed with the reality of what transpired before Reno's eyes. But weren't these very Indians his objective, as well as the campaign's? Custer dispatched his second in command to look for a village of recalcitrant Indians, and since the Major hadn't lost any of these Indians, he didn't feel he needed to find any . . . unless his commanding officer was with him.

As the battalion emerged from the timber onto the valley floor, Reno gave the order "Left into line, gallop—forward, guide center." This had the effect of bringing the companies from their column of fours into a line with 'M' and 'A' on a left to right formation and 'G' was placed in line as reinforcement at the rear. Accompanying Reno, as per Custer's orders, were Billy Jackson, Isaiah Dorman, Fred Girard, George Herendeen, and Charlie Reynolds.[26] There has been a continuing controversy over the number of men that Reno had in his battalion as he started down the valley. Reno stated he had 112 officers and men, not counting the Indians scouts, and he declared that as soon as the fighting started "they (Indian scouts) cleared out, and I didn't see them any more." Reno remembered this was an actual count as he requested the company commanders to report the number of men they had in the saddle.[27] Reno's count was confirmed by Wallace who said the number of men who advanced down the valley was between 112 and 115, including the scouts.[28] Wallace also said the scouts numbered twenty-two.[29] Thus by the Lieutenant's count, Reno had only 90 to 93 officers and men in his battalion. Wallace then contradicted himself and said when the three companies were "marching in column of twos: probably in each company there were twenty files" or about forty men each."[30] For an engi-

neering officer, his calculations on this day were sadly inadequate. However, Reno's actual count is contradicted by his later testimony at the Court of Inquiry, stating he "supposed" Company G had about 40 men. Captain Myles Moylan supported Reno's supposition and stated his Company A rode into battle with thirty-eight men.[31] If these figures are accurate, then French's, M Company strength would be an unlikely thirty-four men.

A number of battle students have made detailed studies and from these sources, including the regimental muster rolls, a different count of the actual strength of Reno's battalion emerges. Their findings show that Company A had 3 officers and 47 enlisted men; Company G had 2 officers and 38 enlisted men; Company M had 2 officers and 47 enlisted men. To this total would be added 21 scouts and 7 civilians, for a total of 174 men.[32] In retrospect, it would appear that the officers had understated the number of men Reno took into battle, so as to give the impression the force allotted by Custer was insufficient for the assigned task. Therefore no blame could be attached to their subsequent actions in not being able to carry out Custer's orders.

Even as Reno crossed the ford and formed his companies, a number of men were having problems with their horses. The training of the men in horsemanship was left to the company officers and the senior non-commissioned. Some commanders were more diligent than others in cavalry drills. In addition, the men exhibited all different levels of riding expertise and when matched with horses of every temperament it made for some very interesting actions. It would seem 'M' Company had the least skilled horsemen and the most unruly horses because this company suffered disproportionally from this problem. In fact, DeRudio was of the opinion that the men weren't the problem but the horses of this company "were rather unruly and the men couldn't check their horses."[33] For example, Roman Rutten remembered he couldn't control his horse, and after he crossed the ford he had even more trouble. No matter what he tried, the horse just kept going around the three companies in a big circle. His mount continued this behavior all the way down the valley, much to the amusement of Rutten's fellow troopers.[34] Private John Wilber (a/k/a, James Darcy), later wounded in

---

[25]Ibid, 590.   [26]Ibid, 74.   [27]Ibid, 527.
[28]Graham, *Reno Court—Abstract*, 14.   [29]Ibid, 15.
[30]Graham, *Reno Court*, 71.

[31]Graham, *Reno Court—Abstract*, 74.
[32]Dale T. Schoenberger, *End of Custer* (Blaine, WA: Hancock House, 1995) 64; David C. Evans, *Custer's Last Fight : The Story of the Battle of the Little Big Horn* (El Segundo, CA: Upton & Sons, 1999), 425–446, 210–211; Gray, *Centennial Campaign*, 289, 296.
[33]Graham, *Reno Court*, 268.
[34]Hammer, *Custer in '76*, 118.

action, also had issues with his mount as the horse just wanted to run and wouldn't be restrained.[35] In addition, M Company Privates John Meier, George Smith, and James Turley also experienced problems with their fractious horses.[36] This level of horsemanship, combined with the animal's character, would produce tragic consequences for two of these M troopers this Sunday afternoon.

The three companies started off down the valley at a trot, then changed over to a slow gallop.[37]

It was before 3:15 PM. As a precaution against any Indians lurking along the river's bank, M Company's Captain Thomas French ordered First Sergeant Ryan to take ten men from the right of the company and form a skirmish line "so as to cover the brush from our right to the river bank."[38] With the vedettes out in front, the scouts on the left flank and with Ryan on the right flank, the advance was conducted in textbook fashion. In leading off, Reno was guided by an old, unused Indian trail. However, he failed to note that this trail near Ford A was not the main entry into the Little Big Horn Valley from the Sundance Creek trail.[39] When Reno began his advance from the west side of the ford, he missed the main trail which went further to the west, before turning downstream. This main trail to the village followed the current Interstate highway. Reno struck an older trail that paralleled the river to the east. In a few minutes, this overlooked trail would have major consequences in the valley fight.

Varnum, who was riding with Reno about 75 yards in front of the battalion, recalled the bottom opened wider as they moved downstream. The officer noticed a large body of Indians quite a distance ahead, moving back and forth, sometimes advancing, sometimes retreating, all the while raising as much dust as they could so that no one could tell exactly how many were in their front.[40] That the Indians were able to raise this dust was due to the fact that the vegetation had been eaten off by the pony herds, and the ground was cut up by their hooves to the extent the prairie resembled an ash bed that was a "mile or two wide."[41] Hare remembered there were probably fifty Indians riding in front of them who were firing. They would ride towards the troops and stir up more dust, fire, and then move back.[42] After moving downstream about a mile, according to Captain Moylan, Companies A and M increased their gait to a very fast trot, causing G Com-

pany to break into a gallop to keep pace. Private Morris wrote afterwards that they moved down the valley faster than he had ever ridden before.

Even the soldiers noticed the increasing numbers of Indians circling about, and the force had become "thicker in the front" before moving off towards the bluffs on the left.[43] It didn't appear to Major Reno these Indians were retreating, and because of their aggressive tendencies, Reno felt he needed to strengthen his two company line and brought up 'G' on the right flank of 'A.' The pace remained unchanged. It had been about 10 minutes since the advance began; the command was less than a mile from the Uncpapa teepees. Varnum remembered he could see a number of teepees but "the Indians didn't uncover the village much."[44] Reno claimed he detected a disposition on the part of the Indians to lead his battalion on. He saw Indians were coming out of a ravine where they had evidently hidden themselves in ambush. He remarked, "The ravine as I saw it was 8 or 900 hundred yards in front of me . . . I said to myself I could not successfully make an offensive charge. Their numbers had thrown me on the defensive."[45] Reno ordered the battalion to halt. Hare contradicted the Major as Reno couldn't have seen the Indians in the ravine before he halted and deployed. This was because Hare was in a better position to see the ground in front of the command than Reno. Hare was positive the command had halted before any of them came out.[46] It should be noted that nowhere in the Indian sources is there an account of a large body of warriors laying in ambush for Reno in a ravine or otherwise. There are also no accounts by any of the participants who said they were in this "ravine." To further complicate the issue, Varnum didn't even see any "ravine" ahead of the troops. He recalled it was all open prairie, but afterward he was told there were ravines beyond, but as far down the valley as he was able to see, there were none. He added that the terrain of the valley floor ahead of them was the same as the battalion had just passed over.[47]

With all the dust being stirred up, Reno couldn't have seen anywhere near a half mile down the valley to recognize a "ravine" or any other terrain features. He later corrected his earlier testimony under cross examination and said: "It was afterward developed that if I had gone two or three hundred yards further, I should have thrown my command into a ditch."[48]

Reno further acknowledged to the Recorder that he

[35]Ibid, 148.

[36]Brady, *Indian Fights and Fighters*, 402.

[37]Barnard, *Ten Years With Custer*, 291.

[38]Ibid.

[39]Letter, Robert Doran to Bruce R. Liddic, August 28, 2001, author's collection.

[40]Graham, *Reno Court—Abstract*, 46.

[41]Graham, *Reno Court*, 22.

[42]Ibid, 237.

[43]Graham, *Reno Court—Abstract*, 113.

[44]Ibid, 47.

[45]Graham, *Reno Court*, 501.

[46]Graham, *Reno Court—Abstract*, 104.

[47]Graham, *Reno Court*, 127.

[48]Graham, *Reno Court*, 526.

"knew nothing about the topography of the country," and that he didn't make an examination of the "ravine" until after the battle when he "crossed it in two or three places . . . I think."[49] Reno's sudden halt, as he admitted, wasn't due to his eyesight or his knowledge of the country but because of the vedettes riding ahead of his battalion. These outriders had suddenly stopped, because if they had continued they and the command would have stumbled into this "ravine." Should the companies blunder into this depression at the speed they were traveling, it would be cataclysmic. They signaled to Reno that there was an obstacle directly to their front. The ravine was actually a small unnamed tributary which emptied into the Little Big Horn from the west. Today, this small tributary is the present irrigation canal located east of the defunct Reno Battlefield Museum. This tributary has since been reconstructed, narrowed, and straightened, but in 1876 it had the characteristics of a small running stream. If Reno had swung more to the west before starting down the valley, he would have followed the main trail, but by staying close to the river, he encountered this obstacle, and to his misfortune, he was about to strike it near its mouth. Here it was about five feet deep and about ten feet wide; it was indeed a "ravine" as described by the Major.[50]

The stocky Reno had been sweating prodigally on this 90 degree afternoon, and the whiskey he consumed was of little assistance. It was reported that he had lost his hat and had tied a red handkerchief around his head at the river's crossing to keep the sweat out of his eyes. When the men sighted the Indians, during the charge, they had begun to cheer, but the unimaginative Major quickly shouted at them to "stop that noise."[51]

With the order to halt, he turned over the initiative to the Sioux by placing his command on the defensive. The Indians knew why the soldiers had stopped, and their actions were no doubt the reason. Their belief in their medicine grew stronger. It would be another Rosebud Fight. The soldiers were scared of them. This decision to halt has been severely questioned by Reno's detractors and just as severely defended by his supporters. Almost before the gunfire had died away, Reno's critics couldn't understand why he halted the command.

Lieutenant Edgerly told a fellow officer that if Reno had charged through the village, Custer and Benteen would have been with him shortly with an expensive vic-

tory as a result.[52] Mrs. Spotted Horn Bull, who was in the village that afternoon, agreed with Edgerly. She in effect informed Indian Agent McLaughlin that the soldiers had the camp at their mercy, and if Reno had charged, he would have been victorious.[53] Captain Charles King, 5th Cavalry, wrote that a bold and dashing charge was required, but that "Reno had no dash to speak of, and the sight that burst upon his eyes eliminated any that might have been latent. He attacked but the attack was spiritless and abortive."[54] Lieutenant Edward McClernand, 7th Infantry, which was part of Terry's column, heard from the 7th Cavalry officers that it was Reno's lack of aggressive and controlling leadership that had allowed the troops to slip from the offensive to the defensive.[55] Captain Thomas French, Company M, had no idea why Reno halted as it wasn't the kind of fighting he was used to; "When you saw your enemy you went right at them." He thought the only chance Reno had was to "charge headlong through them all."[56]

One must bear in mind the fact that only one of the above critics was in the valley fight. However, the battalion hadn't made any real contact with the Indians at the time of the halt. Varnum told the Court of Inquiry, prior to the halt: "There was no absolute contact between the command and the Indians." Only a few scattered shots had been fired by either side, and the nearest Indians were at least 500 yards away. The numbers of Indians seen through the dust was estimated from as few as 50 to as many as 500. No one was sure. Most of the battalion officers defended the Major's decision to abandon the charge. Lieutenant Hare was of the belief Reno couldn't have lasted another five minutes if he had not halted, and not a man would have gotten through the village. Hare thought Reno's order to halt was "the only thing that saved us."[57]

DeRudio was in complete agreement with Hare, for when Reno gave the order to halt, he exclaimed to no one in particular, "Good for you as I saw if we had advanced another 500 yards we all would have been killed."[58] DeRudio was also quick to add that he thought the position the troops took after the halt threatened the village, and the Indians would not have left a command the size of

[49]Ibid.

[50]Letter, Robert Doran to Bruce R. Liddic, August 28, 2001, author's collection; Sandy Barnard, *Custer's First Sergeant* (Terre Haute, IN: AST Press, 1996), 258–259.   [51]*Camp, BYU*, box 6, folder 2.

[52]Lt. Col. O. L. Hein, *Memories of Long Ago by An Old Army Officer* (NY, NY: G. P. Putman's Sons, 1925), 145.

[53]James McLaughlin, *My Friend The Indian* (Boston, MA; Houghton Mifflin Co, 1926), 170.

[54]Charles King, "Custer's Last Battle," *Harper's*, #81, August 1890, 383.

[55]McClernand, *With the Indians and the Buffalo in Montana*, 72.

[56]Graham, *The Custer Myth*, 341.   [57]Graham, *Reno Court*, 259.

[58]Ibid, 282.

Reno's in this position so near their village.[59] Private Morris was of the opinion that Reno "very properly, gave the command 'Battalion halt—prepare to fight on foot—dismount' . . . to continue to charge down the valley meant the immediate destruction of the battalion."[60]

Just as Reno couldn't have known about the "ravine," he also could not have known how many Indians were to his front at the time he halted. He stated he saw between 500 to 600 Indians to his front. Wallace estimated the total was over 200, and they were all in or near the ravine which was about five hundred yards from where they halted. He added later that their numbers increased only after the command to dismount was given. [61] Varnum didn't venture a guess as to the number, but he said the valley was "full of Indians" and they were riding in every direction. However, as the troops advanced towards them, they "retired before us."[62] Sergeant Ryan wrote there were few Indians until they reached the area of heavy timber and dismounted.[63] Sergeant Culbertson also said there were few Indians near the troops. He estimated there were no more than 250 altogether to their front.[64] Girard recalled there were really no Indians to speak of until Reno dismounted, and even after the line was formed the Indians remained about 1,000 yards from the troops. Girard, who had experience in judging Indian numbers, said there were less then 100 warriors in front of the skirmish line.[65] Hare agreed with Girard and testified that up to the time the command halted there were probably only fifty or more Indians riding up and down to their front. But he added as soon as the command had stopped, hundreds of Indians "moved down to the left and rear."[66]

Herendeen, who was in position on the extreme left and about 100 yards in front of Reno's line, was in an excellent place to observe the whole panorama down the valley, but he didn't see any Indians in the immediate front of the command. In fact, Herendeen remembered even after Reno established his line, "There were no Indians near enough to shoot at" and they were few in number. The Indians were all further downstream and they didn't move toward the battalion until the troops halted.[67] Herendeen said the entire number of Indians that Reno fought in the valley "could not have exceeded 200 warriors."[68] Hare concurred with Herendeen's numbers and

estimated there were 200 Indians, maybe more, constantly in Reno's front.[69] Dr. Henry Porter supported the scouts, and said that the nearest Indians, only 75 or 100 of them, were fully 800 or 900 yards away and "there might have been 50" who confronted the troops. He added there were a good many more down river, but he could not see how many.[70]

Just as the question over who gave Reno his orders to advance after the Lone Teepee, the numbers of Indians confronting Reno broke down between the company commanders and the civilians and junior officers. The captains agreed with the Major and saw many Indians. While the civilians and junior officers saw very few. Who was right? I believe a close examination of the record will show that Reno encountered very little opposition as he advanced down the valley. What Indians were ahead of the troops stayed out of effective carbine range. When the battalion dismounted and a line was formed, there still was no serious opposition until the Indians realized that the troops had stopped their attack, and they were no longer a threat to their women and children. Even then, the number of warriors accosting the command numbered no more than 300. Probably Lieutenant Hare said it best when he attempted to answer the question as to how many Indians they saw in the valley. He responded it was impossible to know for certain as they were always moving and never stayed in one place long enough for someone to count.[71]

But what reason(s) did Reno, himself, give for halting his advance? It was his opinion that the troops couldn't have advanced any further against the Indians than they did. If the troops had tried, most of the saddles would have been emptied and the horses killed by the Indian gunfire.[72] He further elaborated in his official report:

> I, however, soon saw that I was being drawn into some trap, as they would certainly fight harder and especially as we were nearing their village which was still standing; besides I could not see Custer or any other support, and at the same time the very earth seemed to grow Indians. They were running towards me in swarms and from all directions. I saw I must defend myself and give up the attack mounted. This I did.[73]

In this statement, Reno confirmed that the soldiers thought the Indians were running, but instead the village was "still standing." Based on the campaign's planning, Reno expected to see a dismantled village. Reno also agreed

[59]Ibid, 278.

[60]Brady, *Indians Fights and Fighters*, 402.

[61]Graham, *Reno Court*, 41–42.   [62]Carroll, *I, Varnum*, 85.

[63]Barnard, *Ten Years With Custer*, 291.

[64]Graham, *Reno Court*, 321.   [65]Ibid, 81–82.

[66]Ibid, 237.   [67]Ibid, 213–214; Graham, *Reno Court—Abstract*, 81.

[68]Graham, *The Custer Myth*, 264.

[69]Graham, *Reno Court*, 238.   [70]Ibid, 164–165.

[71]Ibid, 238.   [72]Ibid, 526.

[73]Graham, *The Custer Myth*, 139.

with those who saw hundreds of Indians to the front. However, according to his officers, these Indians didn't materialize until the command had halted and a skirmish line had been formed. Crow King said that they weren't ready to fight but only wanted to delay the soldiers. The Indians retreated slowly to give the women and children time to get away. Low Dog agreed that the Indians only held their ground to give the noncombatants time to reach a safe place. Once they were safe, they were also to fall back.[74] White Bull said that all through their "great camp was the confusion of complete surprise." The Indians dashed back and forth, and "everything was smothered in a great cloud of dust" while the women and children ran to get away.[75] We know from hindsight that there were too many Indians in the combined village for Reno's 174 men to defeat. We also know there were not enough Indians in his front to seriously hinder a battalion of determined cavalry properly led. However, neither Reno nor his officers knew this at the time. Reno was also to write in his official report that he thought "we were fighting all the Sioux nation, and also all the depreadoes, renegades, half breeds, and squaw-men between the Missouri and the Arkansas and east of the Rocky Mountains."[76] In the fog of war, it was this uncertainty of what lay ahead, combined with the perception the very ground was growing Indians, along with other possible perceptions that led to Reno's fateful decision. In turn, this decision transformed the Indians' posture from passive acceptance to one of active engagement. It was only after the troops stopped that the Indians acted on Reno's irresolution, they ceased their retreat and began their own charge.[77]

How much did the lack of Custer's support influence Reno's decisions in the valley fight? Reno recorded his thoughts on this matter when he first penned his official report ten days after the battle: "it was evident to me that Custer intended to support me by moving farther down the stream and attacking the village in flank."[78] Hare understood what was "evident" to Reno when the Major wrote his report. Hare said that Reno knew Custer had not followed him up and everybody "supposed that he would attack the villages somewhere. If he did not follow up, he would attack it somewhere else and that was the only other way he had of going to the village.[79] Pri-

vate Newell remembered that he saw Custer's battalion on the bluffs as they charged down the valley.[80] In addition, Varnum said he saw Custer's troops "going on the bluffs" about the time the skirmish line was formed. He knew they were giving support by "going to attack the lower end of the village, either from the bluffs or into the village."[81] DeRudio agreed with Hare and Varnum and said when he saw Custer on the bluffs about five minutes before the battalion retreated, he thought Custer was looking for a place to ford the river "down those bluffs." In DeRudio's opinion this would probably be "an effective assistance" to Reno.[82]

Not withstanding what he officially submitted to his superiors, Reno testified three years later at his Court of Inquiry that he had "official information" that he would be supported by the "whole outfit." When asked if he believed Custer would have supported him in some "other way except by following in your rear," Reno replied, "There was no other way to support me." Making sure that the Court understood what Reno meant, the Recorder asked if a flank attack could be considered as support? The reply was "Not under the circumstances." With Reno's battle report in hand, the Recorder asked if Reno did not state that very thing in his report? Without changing his expression, Reno answered, "I may have said that."[83] Recorder Lee was not to be put off by this answer by the Major. Lee was searching for the reason behind the decisions Reno made and his apparent failure to understand what were Custer's objectives, laid before the Court. The Recorder then asked if Reno went into the fight with any confidence in his commanding officer. Ordered to answer after trying to evade the question, Reno replied, "I had no confidence in his ability as a soldier."[84] A Chicago *Times* editorial summed up what, in their opinion, the Court was thinking about this declaration. The editor said Reno's dislike of Custer was not founded on "Custer's record, but on his own feelings toward that officer. Reno did not like Custer; . . . this dislike sways his judgement . . . and influenced by this feeling only half carried out Custer's orders in attacking the Indians."[85]

In view of what these officers thought about the "support" Reno could expect, Custer was providing it for him but from a different direction. Numerous officers and men had seen Custer on the bluffs and with very little mental

[74]Ibid, 75, 77.

[75]Vestal, *Warpath*, 193.

[76]Caroll, *The Federal View*, 103–104.

[77]For a defense of Reno actions refer to Dennis Clark, " Reno's Charge Out of the Timber," *8th Annual Symposium, Custer Historical & Museum Assn*, 1994, 1–11.

[78]Caroll, *The Federal View*, 105.

[79]Graham, *Reno Court*, 248.

[80]Carroll, *The Sunshine Magazine Articles*, 10.

[81]Graham, *Reno Court*, 137.

[82]Ibid, 292.

[83]Ibid, 520.

[84]Graham, *Reno Court—Abstract*, 225.

[85]Utley, *Reno Court—Chicago Times*, 466. Others have said it wasn't this "dislike" of Custer which influenced Reno, as his actions were based more on fear and self preservation.

agility understood what he was trying to accomplish. Reno's sudden blindness on the valley floor is as inexplainable, as would be his later deafness on the bluffs. Probably the Major and certainly many of his soldiers were aware of the direction this "support" had taken, and ten days later Reno so admitted in his report. I doubt if Custer's failure to follow behind Reno had much to do with the latter's decision to halt at the point he gave the order; shortly, however, this perceived lack of "support" would loom large in Reno's decisions. I submit it was only afterwards, with the need to provide a cover story for his failure to press the attack, Reno began his construction of excuses: he was not given the manpower to accomplish his mission; Custer failed to answer his messengers; he had nothing by which to "guide my movement;" there was an insurmountable obstacle in front of his troops; there were too many Indians ahead of his troops; hundreds and hundreds were lurking in the ravine, and they were waiting for him to come closer before springing their ambush.

But what should Reno have done? Should he have halted when confronted by the "ravine" ahead when the nearest Indians were a third of a mile to his front, facing no serious opposition, and with Custer being spotted on the bluffs across the river? Godfrey was to comment later, "I doubt if Reno had ever before seen a hostile Indian, he certainly had not in any campaign with the Seventh Cavalry." There is no question Custer had expected his orders to be executed. However, if the situation which presented itself is very different from the assumed situation, when the orders were given, the field commander has the ability to change the execution while trying to carry out the orders' intent. I believe this inexperience in confronting a "savage" enemy was only part of the defect in Reno's decision process. He was excited, confused, and uncertain, and these emotions overrode any leadership abilities he had. In my opinion a prudent course for Reno, in keeping with Custer's expectations, would have been upon learning of the "ravine" ahead, he should have demonstrated good horsemanship. This, along with sound tactics to slow the command down and a signal for an oblique to the left around the obstacle. Then once cleared of the "ravine," he should have straightened out his line and proceeded with his orders until he had reliable information of what really lay to his front. Once this information was revealed, Reno then could use his discretion, if warranted, to change the orders' execution. After a half an hour had passed and with no main column in his rear, Reno should have known his "support" was to come from another direction. But in fairness to all parties, after more than a cen-

tury of analyzing the participants' every word and action in this battle, an equitable conclusion regarding Reno's order to halt is, it was done in the battalion commander's best judgment. We will argue forever if it was good or bad, but a commander should be given the benefit of the doubt when in combat. Even though some Indian accounts claim that the soldiers let victory slip through their hands, and that they then took advantage. Reno very well might have done the only rational thing in light of his mental state, his lack of confidence in Custer, and his perception of the unfolding situation presented to him.[86]

Reno's adjutant Lieutenant Benjamin Hodgson, who was detailed from Company B and who would be killed in less than an hour, gave the order to halt first to Company G, while Reno personally gave the order to 'A' and 'M.'[87] As Private Morris recalled, the order was "Battalion halt—prepare to fight on foot—dismount." It was before 3:30. DeRudio was very much surprised when he saw the command promptly halt, the troopers dismounted quickly and then deployed in the standard five-yard intervals as if on a parade ground.[88]

He thought the battalion had done well in light of little experience in a combat situation and considering the speed they had been traveling. Sergeant White recalled that despite their horse issues, 'M' under Captain French was the only company properly deployed when the skirmish line was formed. The other two companies were all bunched up, and they never were completely straightened out.[89] It was about this time, as noted when the skirmish line was forming, Custer was seen on the bluffs by several officers, troopers, and civilians. In addition, a little later Varnum saw a good part of the Gray Horse Troop, Company E, along the edge of the bluffs across the river.

A number of men in 'M' Company did not do as well. John Meier's horse would not be stopped and carried him down the valley through the Indians to their front, who in turn gave chase. The private was able to turn his horse, draw his Colt .45 and shoot his way past the Indians and made a circle back, escaping with only a wound in the neck.[90] Private Rutten's horse continued with his familiar circle patterns, but before the horse could make this design through the Indians, Rutten got his head turned, but in doing so received a gunshot to the shoulder.[91] How-

[86]Stewart, *Custer's Luck*, 352.   [87]Graham, *Reno Court*, 501.
[88]Ibid, 268.
[89]Barry C. Johnson, "A Captain of Chivalric Courage," *English Westerners*, Vol. 25, #1&2, 1987/1988, 13.
[90]Brady, *Indian Fights and Fighters*, 402; Richard Hardorff, *The Custer Battle Casualties, II* (El Segundo, CA: Upton & Sons, 1999), 117.
[91]Ibid, 402.

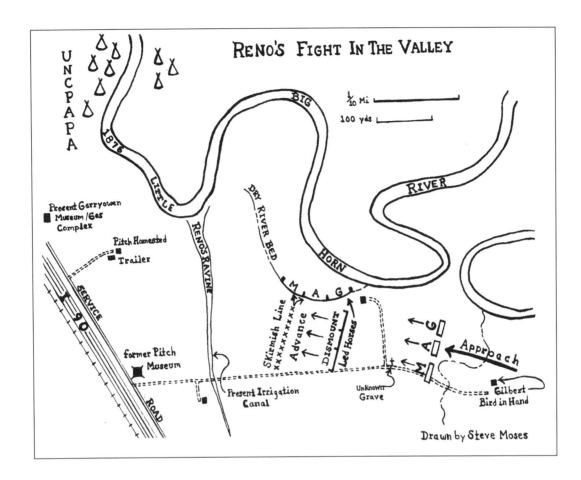

RENO'S FIGHT IN THE VALLEY

Drawn by Steve Moses

ever, Rutten said he wasn't wounded until the next day on Reno Hill.[92] Private Turley wasn't as lucky with his horse. With the order to halt, this horse kept on going straight into the Indians; it was the last anyone ever saw of the trooper until two days later when his body was found in the timber area downstream with a hunting knife driven to the hilt in his right eye.[93]

The same was true for Private Smith; his horse also became unmanageable and sprang right for an opening among the Indians. But unlike Turley, Smith was never seen again alive or dead. After the battle, when the troops inspected the village, the head of a white man was found that had been separated from the torso as a result of the body being dragged around by a rope until it was pulled off. It could have been this United States soldier.[94]

Morris recalled that he was one of the men selected by 1st Sergeant Ryan, as directed by Captain French, to check out the timber to insure it was free of Indians and safe for the mounts. Ryan found they had to ride down an

embankment to get into the timber. This was where the channel of the river had changed, and it was in Ryan's estimation that it was twenty feet lower than the level of the prairie.[95] After going to the banks of the river and finding the area was safe, Ryan signaled to Reno, "All clear in the woods." In a set of fours, after the two right most troopers snapped their link straps to the horse's bit ring on their left, then the number three man gave his reins to the fourth man, usually a veteran. This soldier then moved the horses into the timber, along the river, to protect the animals. Morris stated they then rejoined their company on the line.[96] First Sergeant Ryan remembered one of the men of his squad, Private Wilber (a/k/a Darcy), after checking out the timber, went ahead of the skirmish line, and he actually advanced into the Uncpapa Teepees.[97] Private Peter Thompson said he observed some of the troops as they "dashed into the village" and planted a company guidon alongside the first teepees.[98] But Ryan's rec-

[92]Hammer, *Custer in '76*, 118.

[93]Kenneth Hammer, *Men With Custer* (NP: Custer Battlefield Historical & Museum Assn, 1995), 352.

[94]Ibid, 325; Hardin *Tribune* (Hardin, MT), June 22, 1923.

[95]Barnard, *Ten Years With Custer*, 291.

[96]Mangum, "Reno's Battalion in the Battle of the Little Big Horn," 5.   [97]Hammer, *Custer in '76*, 148.

[98]Mangnussen, *Peter Thompson's Narrative of the Little Bighorn Campaign 1876*, 130.

ollections agreed with Morris, and he stated that "Reno's skirmish line did not get anywhere near the Indian tepees, although we could see them as we fired from the skirmish line."[99] Wallace said they came to within 100 yards of the closest teepee.[100]

Reno had about 100 soldiers on the line, and ideally the line would have extended about 450 yards, but almost as soon as the troops were deployed, the line began to constrict as the soldiers instinctively started to bunch up. About half way on the advance, the line had contracted to about two hundred yards across the valley. 'G' was on the right flank, away from the serpentine-flowing Little Big Horn River. 'A' was in the center, and 'M' held the left flank. The skirmish line advanced on foot in the general direction of the teepees to the right of their line, the tops of which could clearly be seen on the lower benchland behind the river's next loop (today called the Garryowen Loop). The line advanced about 100 yards while the troopers fired their carbines at long range at uncertain targets. Little fire control was being exercised by either the officers or non-commissioned staff. Five minutes had lapsed since the order to halt. Some of the men laid down, while others knelt. Some ducked behind mounds of a prairie dog village, using them as temporary breastworks.[101] As soon as the skirmish line began its advance, a number of Indians were seen coming towards the troops in an effort to ride through them. The command fired a volley and strung out the attack, forcing the Indians to swerve around the western end of the formation. Reno's volley firing was heard by Moving Robe Woman who was in the Uncpapa camp. Most of these bullets tore through the tops of the camp's lodges, causing little damage.[102] Red Feather said that this charge against the soldier's line was foolish. It was led by young men who "didn't have enough experience and were reckless. The older ones held off for safety."[103]

As with other aspects of the battle, the positions of the skirmish mline, how far the troops advanced, and where the timber was located, are still being argued. Each of the experts, Dustin, Kuhlman, Stewart, and Vaughn had their own ideas of these sites.[104]

But after a careful study of their theories, large variations between them are evident. Based on the best available evidence, I believe the skirmish line was formed about 500 yards to the east behind the former Reno Battlefield Museum, on a slightly diagonal axis. This fort-like building stands to the west, 1/10 of a mile, from the current irrigation ditch or what was then Reno's Ravine. The right flank was about 100 yards from the river and extended out almost to the present gravel road, which enters from the service road paralleling the interstate highway, to the south of the museum building. The line advanced on a west by slightly north basis, about three hundred feet, until the right flank was about five hundred feet east of the present irrigation ditch, and then stopped. There are no accounts which claim the battalion crossed this obstacle to their front. Jason Pitsch, whose family had owned this land, told me that in regards to this skirmish line, Dr. Kuhlman's deductions on this point most closely match the physical evidence he uncovered.[105] Based on an overwhelming number of artifacts uncovered by Pitsch, it would be difficult indeed to dispute his fieldwork and research on the re-discovery of the 1876 timber site and the military positions.

The majority of the Indian scouts were on the western end of the skirmish line and as such had to cope with the Indians forced in that direction by the soldiers' fire. The Indian scouts understood their mission better than did Reno. They were to cripple the Sioux Indians' mobility by capturing their horses. Reno would have us believe the Indian scouts had "cleared out" and weren't seen again until the command reached the Power River, which was ninety miles from the battlefield. By implication, their desertion also contributed to his problems in the valley.[106] This was not true. The scouts knew the purpose of their mission. Custer used his scouts not for a stand up fight but for their ability to find the enemy, lead the troops to them, and then, if practical, capture or stampede their horses. This the scouts did. They made skillful and gallant attempts to drive off the pony herd. However, they only captured about two dozen animals. That they weren't able to completely accomplish their mission wasn't because they ran away to the Power River, but rather it was because Reno failed to hold his skirmish line. When Reno pulled back, the Indians were able to sweep down upon them. The handful of scouts who had some success at driving off the ponies, now were sent scurrying for their own safety. They drove the animals up Reno Creek.[107] The evidence clearly demonstrates the Arikara scouts on the left were overwhelmed by the Sioux moving around the left

[99]*Camp, BYU*, roll 1, box 1, folder 6.   [100]Graham, *Reno Court*, 23.

[101]Sandy Barnard, *Custer's First Sergeant, John Ryan* (Terre Haute, ID: AST Press, 1996) 179.

[102]Hardorff, *Hokahey!*, 34–35.   [103]Ibid, 40.

[104]See J. W. Vaughn, *Indian Fights* (Norman, OK: Univ. of OK Press, 1966), 145–166; Compare this to Kuhlman, *Legend into History*, 48–73 and Dustin *The Custer Tragedy*, 110–114.

[105]Conversation, Jason Pitsch to Bruce R. Liddic, June 18, 1997.

[106]Graham, *Reno Court*, 501.

[107]Libby, *Arikara Narrative*, 12.

of Reno's line. And remember this as well: both the Crow and Arikara said Custer dismissed them as the command was moving to the attack. This left them to go or to stay as each one saw fit, but instead they remained to help their white friends in their battle with the Indians.[108]

The ponies rounded up by the scouts were escorted to the east by their captors. Although they had captured a number of horses in the valley, most of these were lost, by the time they had reached the bluffs because of the Indians' pursuit. From the scout's description, they reached the top of the bluffs about a half mile below Reno Hill. Custer had just passed this point about five minutes previously. This would have been before 3:30 PM. Strike Two recalled that some of Custer's stragglers had fired upon them thinking they were the enemy.[109] Soldier also confirmed there were stragglers from Custer's command, but the soldiers didn't shoot at them. These troopers were too busy attending to their faltering mounts. One soldier was kicking his downed horse and calling him a "son of a bitch."[110] It is believed among this set of fours, whose horses were exhausted and had dropped out of Company C's formation, was Peter Thompson and John Watson. The adventures of these two privates after their comrades disappeared over Sharpshooters' Ridge would rival those recorded by the Brothers Grimm. There are those who subscribe to Thompson's wanderings on foot along the banks of the Little Big Horn. Thompson claimed he traveled nearly as far as last stand knoll before making his way back to Reno Hill. Others dismiss his story as preposterous and wildly imaginative. But as with anything associated with this battle, nothing is all black or all white. Fred Dustin's conclusions about Thompson's account merit much consideration. Dustin wrote, his "story as a whole may be unreliable, but it may furnish a few corroborative facts that might not otherwise be obtained."[111]

The scouts were soon joined by Strike the Lodge and Assiniboine, and they continued to drive their prizes back "and got them in good position."[112]

Strike Two further said they saw a soldier with stripes on his arm on the back trail, and he asked them, "How goes it"? While moving the horses along they saw the pack train come along. "Bull and Share were each leading a pack mule."[113] It would seem McDougall was using all his personnel to keep the mules together and moving forward. The scouts then divided up these horses amongst their tribesmen. A number of them exchanged their tired worn

out horses for the fresh Sioux ponies and rode to the edge of the bluffs to see what was happening. The scouts could hear the firing from the valley floor. What they observed wasn't reassuring. The soldiers were falling back, their line was broken, and the Indians were coming right after them.[114] At this point some of the Arikaras set out for the Powder River Camp. In doing so they were merely following the instructions Custer had given them, that, in case they became separated from the command, they should return to the supply camp and await further orders.[115]

A small number of scouts who had ridden down the valley with the troops now took up a position on the extreme western end of Reno's line out on the bluffs near the present day Denny property; among the small party were the Arikaras Red Bear, Little Brave, Forked Horn, Young Hawk, Red Foolish Bear, Goose, Bob-Tail Bull, and the two Crow scouts, Half Yellow Face and White Swan. As the Indians spilled around the skirmish line this detachment moved quickly to avoid being cut off. As they retreated towards the ford, Bob-Tail Bull, who was the last man on the right, was killed in spite of the efforts of his friends to make a stand to assist him.[116] Little Brave retreated back to the river but was killed before he was able to rejoin the scouts. Goose received a wound in the arm. The scouts gave as good as they received with a resulting number of Indian casualties.

Knipe didn't recall exchanging any greetings with the Arikara scouts; in fact he saw about a half a dozen Indians off to his right and not knowing if they were friend or foe, quickly loaded his carbine. One might question Knipe's sanity with being alone in Indian country, carrying an unloaded gun. However, Army regulations prohibited men from riding with a loaded weapon. The 1873 Springfield single-shot carbines carried by the troops had only two hammer positions—full cock and half cock. When on half cock, the breechblock could be jolted open allowing dirt to enter the breech. If on full cock, with a round in the chamber, it became deadly and a dangerous accidental discharge could result. This was corrected in later models with a three-position hammer that allowed a cartridge to be safely chambered. But in 1876, troopers loaded their carbines only under orders from an officer. Knipe didn't need to worry as these Indians were allies and they drove their captured ponies about 200 yards ahead and across the sergeant's front, raising a tremendous cloud of dust.[117] After the dust had dissipated, Knipe saw Benteen's detachment ahead, watering their horses.

[108]Ibid, 12. [109]Hammer, *Custer in '76*, 184.
[110]Ibid, 188.
[111]Carroll, *The Benteen—Goldin Letters*, 116.
[112]Hammer, *Custer in '76*, 188. [113]Ibid.

[114]Graham, *The Custer Myth*, 39.
[115]Byrne, *Soldiers of the Plains*, 99.
[116]Libby, *Arikara Narrative*, 92–103. [117]*Camp, IU*, box 2, folder 8.

Knipe was riding along the North Fork of Reno Creek when he first noticed the battalion which was over on Reno Creek.[118] He turned his mount over to the right and began to wave his hat to attract attention.[119]

With his battalion trailing behind, Benteen slowed down as he approached the Lone Teepee. The senior captain rode around the lodge, dismounted and looked inside where he saw the body of an Indian on a scaffold.[120] As his command was approaching, Benteen was unable "to investigate as to the causes of his having been made a 'good Indian', I remounted" and continued in the advance.[121] Godfrey recalled that it was shortly after they passed the old camp (Lone Teepee site) that they again stopped to water their horses.[122] This second watering of the horses was confirmed by John Frett, a civilian packer, who stated that "We were at the watering place near the teepee . . . the one with the dead Indian in it when a Sergeant came . . . and said we should hurry up; that General Custer was attacking the Indians."[123] Patrick Corcoran, a 'K' company private, saw Knipe rapidly ride up, halt, and speak to Benteen just as they had finished watering the horses.[124] Dennis Lynch, a private in 'F' company, agreed with Corcoran but added that the command was still watering the animals when Knipe arrived.[125] It is important to note that Knipe was identified with this watering stop and it occurred around the Lone Teepee area. Indians seldom made a dry camp, so it would be only natural for there to be a supply of good water near the former village site. There are some students who question the location where Knipe met Benteen near the Lone Teepee as they doubt there would have been another watering of the horses so soon after they had been watered at the morass. These students believe only a few took advantage of the opportunity to water their animals "or, Knipe may have simply assumed they were watering after seeing them come up and reform on the bank."[126] They hold the premise the three companies had crossed to the south side of Reno Creek, and as they were moving to the west, met Knipe about one and a half miles from the Lone Teepee. Factors weighing against this belief are the statements by a number of witnesses who place the meeting point around the Lone Teepee area when they were watering the horses, or just finishing. In addition, the command had marched two hot, dusty miles since the morass, and they surely would have welcomed a second break, as water had been scarce and of poor quality over the last twenty-four hours. Knipe said he met Benteen soon after he had left the place where he (Benteen) was watering his horses, but that was what the Captain was doing when "I first saw him."[127]

It was from this point that firing was heard from the direction of the Little Big Horn River.[128]

Gunfire was heard while Benteen's command was watering their horses; however, it wasn't at the morass, as traditionally remembered, but at this second watering stop. In retrospect, it is easy to understand how these two separate occurrences became entangled. Memories fade over time, and the halt was insignificant compared to what followed. The water stop was probably overshadowed by their remembrances of the Lone Teepee landmark.[129] Lastly, it would seem that no one but Camp thought to inquire if the gunfire that was reported happened to be in the correct sequence relative to other known events. Camp was right, as was Kipp, in his challenging the early reports of hearing gunfire at the morass. This event occurred much later, and because of this confusion about the second water stop, some of the time and motion reconstructions of the battle's events are not in their proper context.

After speaking to Benteen for a few moments, Knipe was directed along the back trail to the pack train. The Sergeant remembered he was not in sight of McDougall or the pack train when he met Benteen. This could be one reason why he stopped to check with the senior captain regarding their location. Later he was to learn that Benteen "was closer to the pack train when he was at the watering hole than he was when he met me & I would say a ½ mile further from him."[130] Exactly what Knipe and Benteen spoke about wasn't recorded. However, Benteen wrote in his report that Knipe had an "order from the lieutenant colonel to the officer in charge of the rear guard to bring it to the front with as great rapidity as was possible."[131] Without a doubt Benteen told Knipe, he made a mistake in delivering Custer's orders to him and pointed out where he would find McDougall.[132] Since the order applied to the pack train command, the senior captain believed that McDougall "would attend to the order" and

[118]Hammer, *Custer in '76*, 93.

[119]Ibid.   [120]Graham, *The Custer Myth*, 180.

[121]Brininstoll, *Troopers With Custer*, 77.

[122]Stewart, *The Field Diary* . . . , 11.

[123]Graham, *Reno Court*, 448. Frett was assigned to the pack train.

[124]Hammer, *Custer in '76*, 150.

[125]Ibid, 139. Lynch, however, wasn't in the battle and what he reported over the years was all hearsay. On June 22, he was detailed to the 'Far West' on special duty. Ibid, 221.

[126]Wayne Wells, "Knipe, Martin & Benteen," *Research Review—Journal of the Little Big Horn Associates*, Vol 2, #1, June 1988, 10–15.

[127]*Camp, BYU*, roll 1, box 1, folder 14.

[128]Stewart, *The Field Diary* . . . , 11.

[129]Gregory J. W. Urwin, Ed., *Custer And His Times—Book Three* (NP: NP, 1987), 222.   [130]*Camp, BYU*, roll 1, box 1, folder 14.

[131]Carroll, *The Federal View*, 106.   [132]*Camp, IU*, box 2, folder 8.

"did not consider it was an order to me."[133] Knipe knew very well the sarcastic Benteen wasn't in charge of the rear guard and claimed he told Benteen to get up there as quickly as you can as we have struck a big camp.[134] What other details Knipe might have communicated to Benteen is possibly reflected in his comment made to his fellow troopers as he rode down the length of their column: "We've got 'em, boys." Windolph didn't recall these were Knipe's exact words as he passed him, but he did shout something about having "the Indians on the run."[135] From this and other remarks the command justly "inferred Custer had attacked and captured the village."[136] Knipe no doubt thought so himself. How much this affected the troops in believing the fight was over, that they wouldn't get to share in the glory and that they would have to be content with a mopping up operation, is open to debate. It is known only that Benteen kept the command at the same pace as he had since leaving the morass . . . at a stiff walk.[137] Nothing was going to move this officer faster.

Knipe estimated that from the top of the bluff where he received the order, it took him about 25 minutes to reach Benteen's command. After he left Benteen, it took him another 20 minutes to reach the packtrain.[138]

If Knipe's times are accurate he would have met Benteen about a little before 4 PM, about five cross-country miles from his departure on Reno Hill. If so, the sergeant wasn't wasting any time and was probably moving at a faster gait than a trot, which was about seven miles an hour. Knipe said he saw the head of the pack train about two miles from where he had met Benteen just as the latter's battalion approached the Lone Teepee area.[139] According to his time estimates, it would have been shortly before 4:15 PM and with his horse tiring, the next two miles would have naturally been traveled more slowly. Knipe's meeting with McDougall, by his estimate, had taken place just to the east of the Lone Teepee as the captain was closing the distance to the rest of the pack train. Knipe declared that he gave Custer's orders personally to Thomas McDougall, and he then remained with the pack train.[140] But McDougall stated that no one gave him any orders. He did say that he thought Mathey received the order to hurry up the pack train, because "he told me about it."[141] However, Mathey was positive he did not receive orders from anybody. When asked, at the Reno Court of Inquiry, "if a sergeant reported to you with orders?", the Lieutenant quickly responded, "No, Sir."[142]

Nobody has been able to satisfactorily explain why these two officers so testified when, as we shall read, they knew their sworn testimony was false.

Private Augustus DeVoto, of McDougall's Company, did see Knipe. He recalled, "We next met a soldier from Custer's command," but at the time, he couldn't recall his name. DeVoto mistakenly thought "Custer had sent him with a message to Major Reno."[143] As DeVoto was assigned to 'B,' it would tend to confirm Knipe did indeed give the message to McDougall rather than to Mathey. One author agrees with both McDougall and Mathey and based on their testimony, claimed that Knipe didn't ride back to the pack train because he was afraid of encountering Indians in the open country between the two commands. Consequentially, Knipe just rode a respectful distance in the rear of Benteen's battalion, which is an interesting reading of the Reno Court of Inquiry's transcripts.[144] If no order was delivered, it seems more than coincidental that the pack train ceased to follow the main trail about this time and moved to the right across country towards the bluffs where Knipe had last seen Custer.[145]

Another author of the Custer Battle believed that both McDougall and Mathey dipped into the same whitewash bucket, as did Reno and Benteen, at the Reno Court by denying that either one received a message. Because if they had admitted they received a message from Custer, they would have to explain why they didn't respond faster. Mathey said they rested for about fifteen minutes near the Lone Teepee. For, as John Frett claimed, the mules were only walked during the whole time; "We did not trot them any."[146] This author suggests they were part of a cover-up to deflect the blame from themselves, which is another intriguing possibility for the two officers not to have heard of Sergeant Knipe.[147] This writer's hypothesis might be more accurate than many of the other conspiracy theorists.

In late 1896, Daniel Knipe asked the now retired Thomas McDougall to provide him with a certificate as to his character. Knipe was seeking a position with the United States Revenue Service, which he subsequently

---

[133]Graham, *Reno Court*, 357; 410.

[134]*Camp, IU*, box 2, folder 8.　　[135]Hunt, *I Fought . . .* , 81.

[136]Graham, *The Custer Myth*, 140.

[137]Brininstool, *Troopers With Custer*, 77.

[138]*Camp, BYU*, roll 1, box 1, folder 3.

[139]*Camp, IU*, box 2, folder 8.　　[140]Ibid, box 2, folder 3.

[141]Graham, *Reno Court*, 472.

[142]Ibid, 458.

[143]*Walter M. Camp Papers* (Crow Agency, MT: Custer Battlefield National Monument), catalog #11338c. Hereinafter cited: *Camp, CBNM*.　　[144]Willert, *Little Big Horn Diary*, 335.

[145]*Camp, BYU*, roll 1, box 1, folder 12.

[146]Graham, *Reno Court*, 448.

[147]Pennington, *Battle of the Little Bighorn*, 63.

obtained and from which he would retire twenty years later.[148] McDougall at the time was living in Wellsville, NY and on January 9, 1897 he responded with a glowing recommendation about Knipe's reliability, efficiency, and his being an honorable soldier whom he had known since 1873. He closed his testimonial with the following:

> On the afternoon of June 25th, 1876 when the entire country was full of Indians, Sergeant Knipe brought to me an order from General Custer 'to bring the pack train across the way' where I found Major Reno . . . I take great pleasure in giving him this small certificate of merit.[149]

I believe we can safely say Knipe did exactly as he, and others, said—he delivered Custer's message to McDougall, and the Captain probably informed Mathey as well. These officers prior negative attestations of this incident reflect little credit upon themselves and overshadows their conduct at the Little Big Horn.

After advancing about a hundred yards from where Reno's charge had halted, the men were shooting at no particular targets. Even if there had been defined targets, the Springfield carbines "did not carry that far; the bullets were striking short of the Indians."[150] Regarding the lack of fire control by either the officers or non-commissioned, Moylan claimed it was impossible to regulate their fire. One reason may have been that the officers were more interested in shooting at the Indians than maintaining fire control.[151] Because of this lack of oversight, many of the more inexperienced men were firing very fast and some of the excited ones were seen "shooting right up in the air."[152] Hare estimated that the troopers expended about forty rounds per man.[153] Sergeant Davern was, by his own admission, a reasonably good shot, and he claimed to have expended about twenty rounds on the skirmish line.[154] As the troopers began to run out of ammunition, alternate men were sent back to retrieve the paste board boxes containing twenty rounds each from their horses' saddlebags in the timber. This had the effect of further constricting the line until it was only about 150 yards in length. The troopers were starting to feel unsure of the situation, and "The intervals were not kept up well."[155]

Private Slaper recalled he became very frightened "when he got his first glimpse of the Indians, riding about

in all direction . . . yelling and whooping like incarnate fiends, all seemingly naked as the day they were born, and painted head to foot in the most hideous manner imaginable."[156] Slaper might have been a little melodramatic in his description, but it conveys lucidly what was going through the minds of the men on the line. Even with some frightened soldiers, poor marksmanship and the reduced volume of gunfire, the Indians found they were unable to ride over this skirmish line. As John Ryan recalled, "So the Indians began to string out in single file, lying on one side of their ponies from us, and commenced to circle. They overlapped our skirmish line on the left and were closing in on our rear to complete the circle."[157]

Major Reno received a report from Moylan that Indians were seen along the river's bank, heading for the timber area where the horse holders were stationed. Reno placed Hodgson in charge of the line and directed Company G into the timber to counter this new threat.[158] The civilian scouts who rode with the battalion also led their horses into the timber, and Girard and Reynolds had taken position "just in the rear of the skirmish line where it rested on the timber, to watch the firing."[159] There were no Indians close enough to shoot at, so the scouts just watched the soldiers' rapid firing.[160] Girard observed Reno as he left the line and, just before he passed into the timber, "saw him put a bottle of whiskey to his mouth and drink."[161] The skirmish line, which was struggling before to maintain its intervals, was now ordered to increase its spacing from left to right to cover the ground vacated by 'G.' As a result, the line was too thin and consequently the left flank was now seriously exposed and the Indian surround tactics were close to completion. Varnum thought Reno had taken 'G' into the woods to attack the village, as he heard some of the men calling out they were going to charge the village down through the woods. Expecting some kind of movement, he rode into the timber to render assistance.[162] It would appear some of the men and the junior officers were thinking of offensive action even if the senior officers were not.

When Reno arrived in the timber, he could see many scattered teepees to the north. It was also plain to the Major that the Indians were using the timber as cover to creep up on the horse holders. Directing 'G' to spread out to protect the animals, he rode back to the skirmish line only

---

[148]Hammer, *Men with Custer*, 180.
[149]Bill Boyes, "Tarheel Survivor of Custer's Last Stand," *Research Review—The Journal of the Little Big Horn Associates*, Vol. 7, #2, June 1993, 30.   [150]Graham, *Reno Court*, 269.
[151]Brady, *Indian Fights and Fighters*, 402.
[152]Graham, *Reno Court—Abstract*, 122; Brininstool, *Troopers With Custer*, 101.   [153]Graham, *Reno Court—Abstract*, 99.
[154]Graham, *Reno Court*, 311.   [155]Ibid, 321.

[156]Brininstool, *Troopers With Custer*, 48.
[157]Barnard, *Ten Years With Custer*, 293.
[158]Graham, *Reno Court*, 501.   [159]Hammer, *Custer in '76*, 232.
[160]Graham, *Reno Court—Abstract*, 81.
[161]Hammer, *Custer in '76*, 232.
[162]Graham, *Reno Court—Abstract*, 47; Carroll, *I, Varnum*, 66.

to be greeted by his adjutant with the news the Indians had passed around their left flank and were now in their rear. Reno believed his command would be safer in a new position along the dry river bank and gave the order to "bring the skirmishers in round the horses" in the timber.[163] Private Morris said Reno was excited and ordered, "Retreat to your horses, men." Sergeant Culbertson said he never did hear who gave the order, but the "line moved by the right flank, every man moving off towards the timber."[164] Captain French modified Reno's order and directed his Company 'M' to execute a flank movement to the right, fall back slowly, with their faces to the Indians, and continue to fire.[165] However, Private Newell recalled, "We went like a bunch of sheep."[166] As the line retreated towards the timber, the Indians didn't come close but remained hundreds of yards away and did not increase their fire. The troopers, however, did continue their rate of firing. The battalion had been skirmishing with the Indians for about fifteen minutes. It was about 3:45 in the afternoon.[167]

Up to this point, the only casualties were the two missing men whose horses had run away with them. However, in the withdrawal, Sergeant Miles O'Hara, Company 'M,' was shot in the chest about fifty yards from the timber. In addition, 'A's First Sergeant, William Heyn, was struck in the left knee, and Sergeant Charles White, Company 'M,' took a bullet in the right arm. Both Heyn and White survived the battle. In O'Hara's case, he pleaded with Private Edward Pigford, whose later accounts of the fight border on the incredible, not to be left behind. Nevertheless, he was, and it has been commonly thought his body was never recovered. Pigford told Camp he could not (did not?) help his sergeant. Another trooper stated the sergeant "was dead or supposed to be when we left."[168] Years later, Pigford told a hometown newspaper reporter that "he (O'Hara) turned to Pigford with the plea, 'Pigford, don't leave me,' and our trooper helped him to a place of safety."[169] With this dramatic change of stories, many battle students thought the former 'M' trooper was just weaving another of his tall tales to enhance his reputation. However, it is possible that Private Pigford's second telling of his assisting O'Hara is accurate.

In 1958, The Custer National Battlefield conducted archaeological excavations at the Reno-Benteen battlefield,

and the remains of three soldiers were uncovered. It was nearly twenty years later before these remains were fully studied.[170] The skull of one of these soldiers was sent for facial reconstruction. The clay model which was returned bored a distinct resemblance to Miles O'Hara. Next, a cast of this skull was made and photographically superimposed over a number of troopers' pictures. No fit was found until the photograph of the sergeant was retrieved; it matched exactly. There are several explanations which could account for O'Hara being buried on Reno Hill. One possibility is his body was recovered from the valley, along with others, then buried on the hill. Another that O'Hara was aided, as Pigford later claimed, and he was one of the wounded retreated to the hill and later died in the swale which served as Dr. Porter's hospital during the battle.[171] Against the former possibility, Varnum said O'Hara died near the timber, and when they went to look for his body, it couldn't be found. Morris stated positively O'Hara was killed, not wounded, as he was "the next man on my right."[172]

First Sergeant Ryan, who would be particularly interested in one of his own men, thought the head of one soldier found in the village belonged to the unfortunate trooper, but they never found the body.[173] Camp, in fact, questioned Ryan on this very point that perhaps the body was buried, and Ryan didn't see it. Ryan reluctantly admitted it was possible.[174] Of one thing we can be certain, in this confusing chain of events . . . if Myles O'Hara was alive when he reached Reno Hill, at battle's end, he remained there.

The troops now were in a new line along an old dry cut bank of the Little Big Horn facing to the west and southwest about 300 yards from their former skirmish line. In a rough alignment, 'G' occupied the right flank near a dry bend of the river, 'A' was in the center, and 'M' held the left flank. The new line extended for about 150 yards. The area in front and around the battalion contained some very heavy timber and dense underbrush, and behind the troops was a "rather open glade or grassy place," a park like setting where the horses were being held.[175]

The protection afforded by the cut bank was much better than the exposed line on the valley floor. With a little work, it could have been made into a defensive position which could have been held indefinitely. Reno, as a pro-

---

[163]Graham, *Reno Court,* 502.   [164]Ibid, 321.

[165]Brady, *Indian Fights and Fighters,* 403.

[166]Carroll, "The Sunshine Magazine Articles," 10.

[167]The length of time remembered by those who were on the skirmish line varies from fifteen to thirty-five minutes.

[168]Liddic, *Camp on Custer,* 86.

[169]Earle R. Forrest, *Witnesses at the Battle of the Little Big Horn* (Monroe, MI : Monroe County Library System, 1986), 18.

[170]For a different interperation of the finding and examination of this skull see Hardorff, *Custer Battle Casualties, II,* 115–116.

[171]Douglas Scott, " Nameless Faces of Custer Battlefield," *Greasy Grass,* Vol 4, May 1988, 3–4.

[172]Brady, *Indian Fights and Fighters,* 402.

[173]Hardorff, *Custer Battle Casualties, II,* 115.

[174]*Camp, IU,* box 7, folder 3.

[175]Brininstool, *Troopers With Custer,* 99.

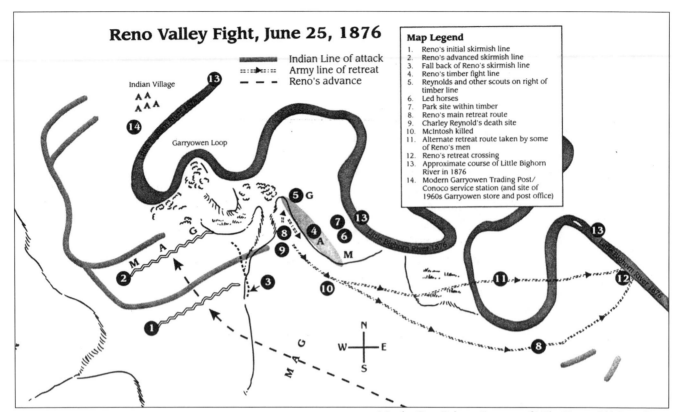

Reno Valley Fight, June 25, 1876

━━━━ Indian Line of attack
┅┅►┅ Army line of retreat
━ ━ ━ Reno's advance

Map Legend
1. Reno's initial skirmish line
2. Reno's advanced skirmish line
3. Fall back of Reno's skirmish line
4. Reno's timber fight line
5. Reynolds and other scouts on right of timber line
6. Led horses
7. Park site within timber
8. Reno's main retreat route
9. Charley Reynold's death site
10. McIntosh killed
11. Alternate retreat route taken by some of Reno's men
12. Reno's retreat crossing
13. Approximate course of Little Bighorn River in 1876
14. Modern Garryowen Trading Post/ Conoco service station (and site of 1960s Garryowen store and post office)

Map by Gary Raham. Courtesy of Mike Koury, Old Army Press.

fessional military man, should have known there was no precedent for organized troops numbering more than a hundred and armed with breach loading weapons, being overwhelmed by any combination of Indians. Thompson recalled that with the troops in the timber, Reno undoubtedly held a great many Indians in check, and although his numbers were less than the Indians, "his advantages were greater."[176] Likewise, Captain Benteen thought the position that Reno assumed in the timber was a "No. 1 defensible position," and it could have been held with 120 men for 5 or 6 hours.[177] DeRudio was more emphatic and said that the timber was "impregnable and nothing but fear could have prompted his (Reno's) retreat."[178]

But Custer had sent Reno forward for an offensive engagement and not for a defensive standoff. With the troops holed up and the river to their backs, they were now less of a threat to the village than they had been out on the prairie where over 300 yards to the north from the right flank was the beginning of the teepees. The warriors quickly moved to surround the soldiers to insure they remained where they were, a safe distance from their fam-

ilies. Varnum said the Indians couldn't afford to permit the troops to remain so close to the village, and they would be forced to keep a number of warriors there just to watch the battalion. Perhaps unknowingly, Reno was creating just the diversion Custer had hoped for to enable him to attack unnoticed the upper end of the village. When Girard was asked at the Court of Inquiry, how many men would it have taken to check the Indians and drive them from the timber? The scout replied that in his judgement, "ten men could have stopped them from coming in at that one point."[179] Later at the Inquiry, Reno was asked if he didn't think with the number of Indians he claimed to have seen "that Custer might not be in the same predicament as he?" Astonishingly, Reno replied it had not, and men "could hold off quite a number of Indians if properly disposed."[180] It is little wonder the Recorder could only stare at the Major after this incredible admission.

As Reno perceived the situation, he was rapidly running out of viable options. His advance upon the village had been stopped. To save the skirmish line from being overwhelmed, he ordered a retreat to the timber, and now the Indians were pushing against his new line from what appeared to be all directions. The Indians seemed to be

[176]Magnussen, *Peter Thompson's Narrative*, 131.
[177]Graham, *Reno Court*, 366.
[178]Utley, *Reno Court—Chicago Times*, 7–8.
[179]Graham, *Reno Court*, 215.   [180]Ibid, 517.

increasing in numbers, and they began to pour "such a hot fire into our small command, that it was getting to be a decidedly unhealthy neighborhood."[181] Was there safety anywhere? Reno had been apprehensive ever since Cooke then Custer had given him the lead, an hour ago, and one thing after another had piled up. The situation had spun out of control; he had only himself to rely upon, and his shortcoming as a follower, not a leader, was clearly exposed. Reno had counted on Custer's "support," which did not come. If Custer had followed him like he suggested, Custer could make the decisions, and the major would execute them. Reno was looking for a place to shelter his command as well as himself; the timber seemed to offer safety, but in ten minutes it was no better than the open skirmish line. Who could Reno find to save him from himself? He quickly needed another place to retreat and for someone to rescue him. The bluffs across the river held promise; Custer had been seen riding along them, and if Custer wasn't coming to "support" him, Reno would go to Custer, and deliverance would be at hand.

There was no sign of Custer, despite his promise of support. Wallace asked Moylan if there was any chance of getting another messenger through to Custer. Billy Jackson, a half breed scout, was standing near the officers, and the captain asked him if he could ride back with a message. Jackson was reported to have looked around, taking the situation in, and replied, "No one man could get through alive."[182] No sooner had the troops been pulled back to the woods, than Reno now believed himself no safer in the timber than he was out on the prairie, and he sought out French for advice. Indecision and self doubt are volatile combinations, especially when they manifest themselves in a commander while in combat. It endangers not only himself, but all the men for whom he is responsible. Reno asked French what he thought of the situation, and French was reported to have replied, "I think we had better get out of here."[183] This answer reinforced Reno's perception of the situation. But in a letter four years later to Lieutenant Cooke's mother, French denied giving Reno this advice. He wrote that he should have shot Reno when he gave the order to retreat, and French believed he would have been justified in doing so.[184]

French also called into question whether Reno ever spoke to him about leaving the timber. The Captain maintained not that they didn't discuss the situation but,

"When he started to that hill he had told me, not one minute before, that he was going to fight."[185] One battle student declared that the evidence was overwhelming that Reno never left the middle of the open glade area in the timber once he arrived after bringing 'G' off the skirmish line. "The rest of Reno's assertions were a series of contradictory inventions conjured by the major to excuse his headlong retreat."[186] Panic was changing Reno's mind with every heart beat. Ryan wrote in 1923 that he had been standing nearby and heard the two officers discussing the situation. Ryan said to no one in particular, "There is nothing to do but mount your men and cut your way out. Another fifteen minutes there won't be a man left."[187] Ryan remembered both officers just looked at him. However, thirteen years earlier Ryan said he spoke these words only to his Captain, and it was in response to his seeing Indians infiltrating the woods.[188] Varnum claimed he never did learn the circumstances for leaving the timber, and regarding that, he didn't know any details.[189]

Reno said he next went to Moylan to inquire about the best place to which the battalion could retreat. Moylan couldn't remember what he said and Reno "designated a point across the river at some high hills where we could go . . . and await further developments."[190]

Reno said he ordered the skirmishers in around the horses in preparation for the movement, and he knew "I could not stay there unless I stayed forever." Reno believed he was outnumbered five to one, and his only course of action was to get to the high ground away from these Indians.[191] He thought the rest of the regiment could make a junction with his companies at a point upon the bluffs, across the river, where they would be seen and he could "dispose the men . . . until someone came to aid us." Reno claimed the losses he suffered up to this point weren't a factor in his decision, but he only had a desire to prevent further casualties.[192] Up to this point, most of the officers and men in Reno's battalion believed he had done a competent job in directing the battle. None of them had much criticism of his troop movements or his disposition of the skirmish lines. They had extended to the commander every benefit of a doubt. But this was soon to change with the implementation of the major's next decision. Unfortunately, as Reno was to learn to his lifetime regret, the man-

[181]Brady, *Indian Fights and Fighters*, 402.

[182]Graham, *Reno Court*, 211.

[183]Brininstool, *Troopers With Custer*, 30.

[184]W. J. Ghent, "Varnum, Reno, and the Little Big Horn," *Winners of the West*, Vol. 13, #5, April 30, 1936.

[185]Graham, *The Custer Myth*, 341.

[186]Sklenar, *To Hell With Honor*, 245.

[187]*Hardin Tribune* (Hardin, MT), June 22, 1923.

[188]Barnard, *Ten Years With Custer*, 293.

[189]Graham, *Reno Court*, 128.   [190]Ibid, 186.

[191]Carroll, *The Federal View*, 103.

[192]Graham, *Reno Court*, 502.

ner in which he executed this "charge to the bluffs" would result in a never ending stream of critique. This charge was a costly and unmilitary sprawl during which no attempt was made to defend the rear or to cover the river crossing, or even to issue coherent orders. Again, this criticism came from those who weren't present, but now it included those who were with him, and it was just as stringent. This movement directly led to Reno losing nearly a third of his command during his self described "charge."

Reno gave the order to Moylan and First Lieutenant Donald McIntosh, normally with Company A, but assigned to 'G' for the campaign. He also directed Hodgson to relay the same order to French, to mount their horses and follow him. The men were ordered off the perimeter to retrieve their horses. They had been at this position less than fifteen minutes. Reno recalled Moylan was near him when they formed for the "charge," and they left together. However, in spite of what Moylan testified to regarding his discussion of the situation with Reno, it wasn't the case. One reason why Moylan couldn't remember what he said is that eleven days after the battle, he wrote to the brother of Lieutenant James Calhoun, commander of 'L' who was also Custer's brother in law. In that letter, Moylan stated he wasn't with Reno when they left the timber because he was then with his company making sure that it was mounted, and he was among the last, not the first, to leave the timber because of his company's wounded.[193] I believe we can add the captain's name to the growing list of those who blanched over their testimony at Reno's inquiry.

Many of the men in Company G didn't hear the order to move out and only ran for their horses when they saw the other companies so doing. Reno never explained why the order was only given orally and not by the bugle so that everyone could be informed. The troopers from 'G' weren't the only ones who were confused by Reno's decision. As the men were running to their horses, Girard exclaimed to Reynolds, "What damn fool move is this?" He didn't understand the call, and he told Reynolds the soldiers would shortly be returning to the timber.[194] Hare never was informed of any order, and the only way he learned of the proposed "charge" was when his orderly brought his horse to him. The lieutenant later admitted he didn't know by what tactical movement it was executed.[195] As strange as it may seem, even Reno's orderly, Sergeant Davern, only saw the men mounting their horses. He said no orders were given about leaving the timber.[196]

Culbertson stated he knew nothing about any orders "more than that someone said they were going to charge."[197] All in all, it was a haphazard way to assemble a battalion for a "charge." The leadership was befitting a junior militia officer rather than a West Point graduate. That panic was probably beginning or had already taken ahold of Major Reno, is revealed in a letter he wrote nine days after the battle: "I have never seen any Indian fight like it, and no one else ever will, . . . I never expected to get out alive."[198] 1st Lieutenant John Bourke, General Crook's Acting Assistance Adjutant General, who later that summer campaigned with Reno, took the measure of the man and wrote, "He (Reno) saw enough at that fight to scare him for the rest of his life. He will never make a bold movement for ten years to come."[199]

It was before 4:00 PM. As usual, the amount of time the troops spent in the timber has been questioned. Exact minutes were hard to keep track of, and one of the early students said it will never be known for certain as "The Indians are not very clear about it at all, and the military is not very much clearer."[200]

With the troops assembling for the movement, the lack of fire control would again plague the command. A group of warriors had assembled just downstream from Reno's position. From the higher banks of the dry river channel, they moved undetected to within ninety feet of Company 'M's line. They saw the troopers had left the area undefended as they pulled back to their horses. The soldiers were easy targets, and the Indians fired a shower of bullets that wounded Privates Daniel Newell and Frank Braun. In addition, Private Henry Klotzbucher, Captain French's striker, was wounded in the stomach. His fellow troopers dragged him into a clump of sagebrush and yelled for Dr. Porter. But they saw that his wound was mortal, and they left him an extra canteen of water before mounting their horses. After the battle, they found his body where they had left him, unmutilated by the Indians.[201] A bullet from the same volley entered the back of Private George Lorentz's neck and came out through his mouth. The private fell from his horse and hit the ground hard.[202] French ordered two privates to take care of Lorentz, and they braced him up against a tree. Someone yelled, "Every man for himself," and the badly wounded private

[193]Tom O'Neil, "Captain Myles Moylan to Fred Calhoun," *Little Big Horn Associates—Newsletter*, Vol. 25, #1, February 1996, 9.
[194]Graham, *Reno Court*, 84.
[195]Ibid, 238.   [196]Ibid, 301.

[197]Ibid, 322.
[198]*Daily Telegraph* (Harrisburgh, PA), August 7, 1876.
[199]Mark Brown, *The Plainsmen of the Yellowstone* (NY, NY: G. P. Putnam's Sons, 1961), 288.
[200]McLaughlin, *My Friend the Indian*,142.
[201]Brininstool, *Troopers With Custer*, 51.
[202]Hardin *Tribune* (Hardin, MT),June 22, 1923.

motioned for the attendants to go as they couldn't help him anymore.[203] Reno had been in the center of the small clearing, and the Arikara scout Bloody Knife was mounted next to him. Reno had been speaking by sign to the scout, inquiring about the Indians, when a bullet from the volley blew apart the Arikara's skull, splattering his brains and blood on the major's coat and face.[204]

Reno immediately gave the order to dismount, and the troopers slid from their mounts. The Indians who had fired melted through the timber, and there was no return fire. The Major now gave the order to remount. Reno's command was confused. Some men were moving to establish a new position, the horses of others became unmanageable, a number of troopers had just hit the ground, and now they were ordered to mount again; they sensed the fear in their commander. Reno dug his spurs into his horse and yelled, "Everybody follow me." Another account said it was the major who cried, "Every man for himself."[205] The men who were able to regain their saddles, followed their commander though the timber.[206] There was dense underbrush that restricted the number of men who could escape. Many had to go single file on a small trail made by buffalo.[207] Dr. Porter, who had been next to the major, said the "bullets were coming thick and fast and he (Reno) did not know whether it was best to stay or leave."[208] As Reno emerged from the timber, the Indians were all about the west and south sides of the men. Reno explained it was "my duty to be at the head of the column to see about the direction of the column and for observing the ford and the hill on the other side." This statement was self serving. Private Taylor saw it very differently: "When an unlisted man sees his commanding officers showing greater regard for their personal safety than anything else, it would apt to demoralize anyone taught to breathe, almost, at the word of command."[209]

How did the warriors regard Reno's decision to "charge the bluffs?" Red Feather, an Ogallala, said the soldiers were far safer in the timber, and they were glad the troopers were leaving as "We couldn't get at them in there. When they came out of the woods they were excited . . . the Indians mixed with them." Soldier Wolf, a Cheyenne, said if the soldiers had stayed where they were the Indians couldn't have killed them; "but all at once—perhaps they got frightened—they rushed out and started to cross the creek." This was echoed by another Cheyenne, Brave Wolf, who could never understand why they left the timber, "for if they stayed there, they would have been all right but they ran out of the timber." Some Indians had told General Nelson Miles, the last commanding general of the Army, that they would have had to divide their forces if Reno stayed in the timber, and they could not have brought all their strength as they did against Custer. The Indians would have had to abandon their village if the troops had not retreated.[210]

Wooden Leg, a young Cheyenne warrior, said he saw the soldiers come "tearing out" of the woods, and he turned his horse along with his fellow warriors to get away from their charge. "But soon we discovered they were not following us. They were running away from us." Wooden Leg and his companions couldn't believe what their eyes were telling them, and for a moment they simply stared at the soldiers "and then we whipped our ponies into swift pursuit."[211] Iron Hawk, an Uncpapa warrior, had a different opinion and believed the soldiers "would have been run over and could not have lasted but a short time if they had stood their ground in the woods."[212] It would appear from the these recollections that when combined with what did actually happen, the Indians were pleased the troopers emerged, running away from the village, and American Horse, a Cheyenne, recalled, "It was like chasing buffalo, a grand chase."

Reno and his defenders believe it took great courage to "charge the bluffs." They claim he made the correct decision to leave the timber and try to save his command. After all, didn't he take the lead in pushing the troops through the surrounding Indians? Reno was basically "in modern military terms, the point man. Certainly not a position of safety." One defender reluctantly admitted he left his dead and wounded to the mercy of the Indians, but it was only to keep the rest from being massacred.[213] Private Slaper implied that Reno acted correctly and admitted the whole movement didn't present a very military appearance, but he personally saw nothing disorderly

[203]Richard Hardorff, *Custer Battle Casualties*, (El Segundo, CA: Upton & Sons, 1989), 139.

[204]Graham, *Reno Court*, 503.   [205]Roe, *Custer's Last Battle*, 9.

[206]Hammer, *Custer in '76*, 118.

[207]Graham, *Reno Court—Abstract*, 83.

[208]Graham, *Reno Court*, 168.   [209]Graham, *The Custer Myth*, 344.

[210]Nelson A. Miles, *Serving The Republic* (NY, NY: Harper & Brothers Publishers, 1911), 191.

[211]Thomas B. Marquis, *A Warrior Who Fought Custer* (Minneapolis, MN: The Midwest Company, 1931), 220–221.

[212]Chris Summitt, "Warriors in the Valley: Indian Perceptions of the Reno Valley Fight," *11th Annual Symposium Custer Battlefield Historical & Museum Association*, 1997, 21.

[213]Ron Nichols, "A Brief Analytical Study of Reno's Fight In The Valley," *3rd Annual Symposium Custer Battlefield Historical & Museum Assn.*, 1989, 42. Reno, however, did in a candid moment admit for the first and only time his movement out of the valley wasn't a charge. He told Lieutenant Frank Bald- (*continued on next page*)

Courtesy of Warren Van Ess

about it.[214] Hare disagreed with one action and confirmed another when he said Reno made his decision to leave the timber precipitously, but to the uninformed there always "is certainly more or less disorder about a cavalry column moving at a fast gait."[215] Hare then clarified this assertion and said as he rode out onto the prairie he could see "the three companies were individual together—well closed up. They formed three angles of a triangle; A company on one side, G company on another, and M company on the other and they were going at a fast gallop."[216] It is a wonder a brass band wasn't playing. Hare didn't just varnish his testimony at Chicago, he whitewashed it; any resemblance between this part of the lieutenant's testimony at the Court of Inquiry and the truth is purely coincidental. Varnum concurred with Slaper, but only to a point, and further related, "I do not consider Major Reno's retreat from the woods a disorganized rout as to the head of the column, but the rear certainly was."[217] In spite of what

Reno and his defenders believe, the words reportedly spoken by Reno's own adjutant convey a sense of reality, when asked if it was going to be a retreat, exclaimed, "It looks most damnably like a rout."[218] Despite claims to the contrary, Lieutenant Hodgson had spoken the truth.

Not only were dead and wounded men left behind, there were also a number of troopers who were late in learning the command was leaving. Girard observed that the men who were able were in a great hurry to get out. "There seemed to be no order at all. Every man was for himself."[219] Dr. Porter thought there were several hundred Indians in the immediate vicinity of the troops, while Reno said there were nearly a thousand. For the lucky ones, who in the beginning made it out of the timber, encountered less resistance from the Indians. This was because the Indians thought Reno was going to attack them, and they scattered, but when they realized the troops were only trying to escape, they quickly closed in on the flanks and rear of the soldiers. There were few Indians in the battalion's front. Even so, they generally stayed about fifty yards from the troopers, unless they saw a wounded man or a horse go down. One reason they didn't close in for the kill was the dust raised by the horses and ponies was so intense that no one could see any more

(*continued*) -win, 5th Infantry, in the summer of 1876, that "he (Reno) gave the order to retire by the right flank which was done with more rapidity than discipline or the good of the service would admit of." Jim Brust, "Baldwin Talks With Reno," *Greasy Grass*, Vol. 9, May 1993, 20–21.

[214]Brininstool, *Troopers With Custer*, 31.

[215]Graham, *Reno Court*, 254; 259.   [216]Ibid, 239.

[217]Graham, *Reno Court*, 156.

[218]Roe, *Custer's Last Battle*, 9.   [219]Graham, *Reno Court*, 83.

Courtesy of Warren Van Ess

than fifty feet in any direction.[220] The warriors were as apt to shoot one of their own as a white man, which resulted in many of the men escaping.

Charlie Reynolds mounted his horse, while Girard led his, and when they arrived at the edge of the timber, they could see the battalion already far ahead. Girard thought the distance was too great to make up, but Reynolds pushed out into the valley. Girard recalled he saw "him whip up and start on the run up the hill." Girard was right, the troops were too far ahead; the Indians were waiting for any stragglers, and the interpreter saw his friend's horse go down, and "several Indians cut him off, and shot him down and he fell." Reynolds appeared to have his leg caught under the horse. Girard saw that he had lost his gun, and the Indians were moving in for the kill.[221] He could no longer watch and reluctantly turned back into the timber. It was a simliar story with Isaiah Dorman. He was not with Reno, but had left a short time before Reynolds. Runs-the-Enemy, a Two Kettle chief, described what happened next:

> We passed a black man in a soldier's uniform and we had him. He turned on his horse and shot an Indian right through the heart. Then the Indians fired at this one man, and riddled his horse with bullets. His horse fell over on his back, and the black man could not get up. I saw him as I rode by. I afterwards saw him lying there dead.[222]

Herendeen rode to the edge of the timber, but the troopers were passing him as fast as their spurs could make a horse move. The dust was so thick the scout couldn't see where he was going and he "got out about 150 yards and my horse went down."[223] As he tried to return to the woods, about twenty Indians almost ran right over him, but he managed to reach the timber with only a few bruises. Herendeen noticed a number of men at the edge, some mounted and some not, and as he collected them he told the soldiers there was no use in running, and that they needed to try to stand them off. Fortunately, most of the eleven troopers he had assembled listened to him.[224]

Herendeen heard volleys coming from down stream about this time (about 4:15); a great many volleys in fact, and it was originating from the direction of what was to be the Custer Battlefield.[225] The little group with the scout as their unofficial leader hid out in the timber until later in the afternoon. They saw two guidons planted on the bluffs across the river, and the men began to move toward the flags; it was about quarter after five. When the group started for the bluffs, two of the troopers, Privates John Armstrong of 'A,' and John McGinnis of 'M,' refused to move . . . either through fear or in the belief they would be safer remaining behind. These two made the wrong choice. After the battle Armstrong's head was found stuck upon a pole. McGinnis's head was found in the village. It was identified by his red hair.[226]

[220]Brininstool, *Troopers With Custer*, 34.
[221]Graham, *Reno Court*, 79.
[222]Dixon, *The Vanishing Race*, 173.

[223]Graham, *Reno Court*, 217.   [224]Ibid; 219.
[225]Ibid, 218.   [226]Hardorff, *The Custer Battle Casualties*, 135; 140.

Most of those deserted by Reno were from 'G,' but the number also included, besides the above scouts, the officers McIntosh, DeRudio, Varnum and Dr. Porter. McIntosh was late in leaving the timber, as he was trying to organize what few members of 'G' he could find, but he could not find his mount "Puff." He saw Private Samuel McCormick, who was leading his mount back into the woods, as the private thought his chances were better undercover than out on the open valley floor.[227] McIntosh took the private's horse, and he rode out to catch up with the column. It was a bad decision, the column was too far ahead, and the Indians were lying in wait for any stragglers. Private McCormick's horse was shot, and McIntosh found himself too far from the timber to retreat; the warriors swarmed about the officer and quickly killed him. Lieutenant DeRudio tried to stop the head long rush of 'A' out of the timber, much as French did when the first skirmish line pulled back, and he yelled: "Company 'A,' halt; let us fight them; for God's sake don't let us run."[228] The troopers were too far gone in their desire to escape to pay any heed, and they rode right past the officer. DeRudio then noticed a company guidon had been discarded behind on the bank, and he went to recover it; he didn't know the battalion's rear had already been cut off by the circling Indians, and it was now impossible to join the retreat.[229] Believing himself to have been abandoned, he quickly discovered he wasn't the only one left in the timber. Private O'Neil, Girard, and Billy Jackson were near by. About this time, around 4:15, heavy firing was heard downstream, but away from where Reno had gone.[230] Girard said he had also heard the firing a little earlier, but it was only a few shots, then for fifteen or twenty minutes it became general. A group of Indians discovered the party, and Girard separated from them and moved off to the left.[231] DeRudio and his small party moved back into the heavier timber. Later Girard rejoined the other three, and in the evening he and Jackson separated from DeRudio and O'Neil. The two scouts reached the troops on Reno Hill late the following evening. DeRudio and O'Neil took a little longer and didn't reached their comrades until early in the morning of the 27th. Dr. Porter heard no orders to leave; he had been treating the wounded when he saw the men begin to leave the timber. He was late in mounting, and the troopers were running, with Indians all around. When he cleared the timber, Porter "expected to see the command charging the Indians but instead the Indians were charging the command. They were all on the run."[232] The doctor took the situation in at once and gave the horse his head to run as fast as he could run, and Porter hung on for his life as horse and rider raced to catch up with the column.[233]

Varnum had been directing the men during the retrieval of ammunition from their saddle bags, and he had dismounted to speak with Girard and Reynolds. The Lieutenant saw quite a confusion behind him as men were mounting and someone was yelling, 'Charge.' He "jumped up and said, 'What's that?' and started down towards the woods and grabbed my horse."[234]

But his horse was in some bushes, and the men and their animals were all around, preventing Varnum from leaving. It wasn't until they had all ridden past him and were leaving that he was able to get "into the path myself" and exit the timber.[235] While the head of the column might have been a cohesive unit, the rest of the battalion was strung out even in this short amount of time. When Varnum reached the edge of the timber and rode onto the prairie, there was a long gap between him and the head of the column. He had to race his horse to catch up. The lieutenant knew of the jumbled situation at the rear of the column and the need to provide covering fire. If not, men were going to die unnecessarily. He tried to check the troopers' escape by telling them you can't run from Indians.[236] "Besides there are a good many officers and men killed and wounded, and we got to go back and get them."[237] The Chief of Scouts failed to notice Major Marcus A. Reno who was leading this disorganized retreat, apparently with the sole thought of gaining the bluffs. Reno quickly informed this second lieutenant "that he was in command," . . . and indeed he was![238]

---

[227] Another account has McCormick not wanting to give up his mount, but McIntosh appropriated it nevertheless. Lieutenant McIntosh's horse, "Puff," was being led around the timber by his orderly, Private John Rapp, who was searching for McIntosh. Rapp was killed while looking for his lieutenant. The horse was caught by Private John Lattman, who later abandoned him in the river, and the Sioux captured "Puff." Richard Hardorff, *On the Little Big Horn With Walter Camp* (El Segundo, CA: Upton & Sons, 2002), 116.

[228] Graham, *Reno Court*, 217; 269.

[229] In reality, Private Henry Fehler had discarded the flag as he could not get the staff into the end of the flag's boot on his unruly horse. DeRudio saw this and dismounted to pick up the flag, but his horse jerked away from him, leaving the lieutenant afoot. *Camp, IU*, box 2, folder 10.

[230] Graham, *Reno Court*, 273.

[231] Ibid, 285.

[232] Ibid, 161.

[233] Ibid.

[234] Ibid, 124.

[235] Ibid.

[236] Carroll, *I, Varnum*, 67.

[237] Graham, *Reno Court*, 161.

[238] Ibid, 145.

7
Medicine Tail

Sergeant Knipe saluted, turned his horse towards the end of the column, and began his ride across country to find the pack train and deliver Custer's orders. Just before dispatching the courier, Custer had ridden to edge of the bluffs, near Reno Hill, close enough to look down at the Little Big Horn River and they "were in plain view of the Indian camps."[1] It is doubtful if Custer could have seen the full extent of the village from this vantage point but it did confirm exactly where the Indians were and Reno, carrying out his orders, was moving full speed to the attack. That Custer observed Reno's charge is confirmed by Knipe, prior to his departure, as well as the four Crow scouts who were near the commander at the time.[2] Only Custer and one or two others went with him to observe the bottom land from the edge of the bluffs. The rest of the command was traveling along the western side of the ridgeline, a little to the east of Reno Hill, approaching what would be later called "Sharpshooters' Hill." If the troopers had been moving on the eastern side of the ridge line near the bluffs, as some have said their route took them, they couldn't have been seen against the skyline by Reno's Battalion in valley as they would have been hidden from their sight. Custer wanted a better viewpoint to evaluate the situation and from the bluffs rode to the summit of the highest elevation closest to him.

This was Sharpshooters' Hill, and it is located about a half mile north of where Reno later retreated; the hill parallels the bluffs overlooking the river, the point of which juts sharply westward about 1000 feet. It was reported that Custer and some officers spent about ten minutes looking at the village through their field glasses.[3] Goes Ahead said that Custer was at "the edge of the high bank and looked over to the place where Reno's men were, as though planning the next move."[4] Without a doubt, Custer, and probably others, also observed the dust being raised on the back trail about five miles away. With DeRudio's field glasses he perhaps saw a large spread out dust cloud. Whether or not Custer was able to break down the cloud into its two separate components, one from 'B' Company and the pack train, the other from Benteen's battalion, would depend on the strength of the field glasses and what Custer was expecting to find. It could be reasonably argued the distance was too far to clearly distinguish the two commands.

However, Joe Blummer, an early pioneer noted for the re-discovery of the Blummer-Nye-Cartwright Ridge and thoroughly familiar with the terrain, thought Custer was able to distinguish Benteen's battalion. He believed this was the only reason why Custer later dispatched Martin, especially to find the senior captain. "For if Custer had not seen the Benteen column coming, he would not have any way of knowing where Benteen might be."[5] Benteen, for one, never suspected Custer might have been able to see his command from Sharpshooters' Ridge. He later wrote, "When that order was sent to me by Custer, he couldn't tell within 10 miles of where I might be found from the nature of the order I had received from him."[6] Despite Benteen's assumptions, it is very probable that Blummer was correct and that Custer from this observation point had the three other elements of his command in visual sight before he proceeded further to the north and into battle. This is an important point, for if Custer knew where all three of his battalions were before 3:30 PM, the charges that he had scattered his command beyond recall is false. He probably had a good idea where they were and that these troops were in supporting distance. Custer could have estimated from Sharpshooters' Ridge that each unit was, at the most, no more than about thirty minutes from being able to reinforce the other. He could now confidently make any additional tactical depositions based on his knowledge of their locations and distance from the main column.

The battalion didn't pass over this second lookout, but kept to the left of the ridge's base as there was no need to have their horses travel along the hill's rough summit. It was probably here, where there is a breach along the ridge's edge, that some members of Reno's Battalion could have spotted a company passing in front of the ridge. It is interesting to note that Hank Wiebert believed that the battalion was traveling on the reverse slope and the troops observed from the valley just happened to be in the lead and were near the top at the time.[7] Unfortunately for Custer, the war chief Gall said he also saw this battalion: "We first noticed several companies of soldiers about two miles west [sic] of our camp (Uncpapa), marching along the bluffs . . . these soldiers kicked up a lot of dust."[8]

---

[1]Hunt, "I Fought . . . ," 82.
[2]Hammer, "Custer in '76," 94; Graham, "The Custer Myth," 17, 19, 20   [3]Hammer, "Custer in '76," 100.
[4]Graham, "The Custer Myth," 20.

[5]J. A. Blummer Manuscript, *Custer Battlefield National Monument*, A-123, 21.
[6] Thomas A. Holmes, "Benteen: An Unpublished Letter," *Research Review—The Journal of the Little Big Horn Associates*, Vol. 7, #1, January 1993, 4.
[7]Weibert, *Sixty-Six Years in Custer's Shadow*, 43.
[8]Barry, *Indian Notes . . . ,* 82–83.

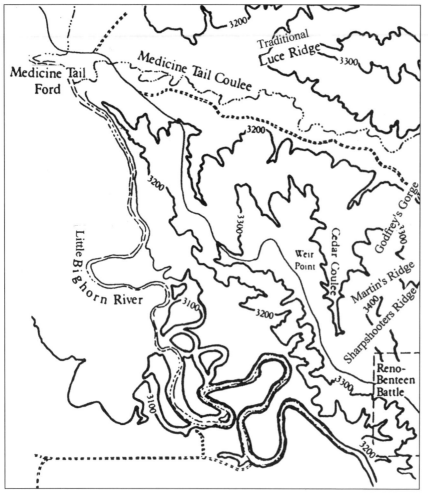

a precise count as to the number of lodges in the various camp circles. He declared that the Uncpapas had 224 lodges, the Sans Arcs—85, Brules—140, Minneconjous—190, Ogallalas—240, and 55 Cheyenne lodges.[10] Each of these different estimates are supported by other remembrances of the participants.

Captain Mills' higher population estimates were seconded by then Lieutenant Hugh Scott, who had attempted to count the sites where the lodges once stood. He stopped at 1500, and from this count he estimated there were at least 7,000 Indians in the camp.[11] Captain Moylan told the Reno Court the number of warriors were about 4,000, and the village must have contained 8 to 9,000 individuals. Lieutenant Wallace agreed with Moylan and believed there were 9,000 warriors.[12] Captain Benteen thought there were at least 8,500 warriors when he testified at the Reno Court, but right after the battle he thought there were no more than 2,500. Lieutenant Edgerly told the Reno Court he believed they fought about 4,000 warriors.[13] However, by 1881 the lieutenant had increased this number by 3,000 and so told the correspondent for the The Leavenworth *Times*.[14] Indian Agent McLaughlin claimed there were between 12 to 15,000 inhabitants with one out of four warriors.[15] In 1877, Captain Philo Clark conducted an examination on the village site with several Indians who took part in the battle, and he wrote to General Sheridan there were 1600 lodges and wickiups which equaled 3,500 fighting men.[16] These higher numbers were confirmed by Flat Iron, the last surviving Cheyenne chief, who in 1915 declared there were 14,000 Indians in the camp, including about 8,000 warriors.[17] Feather Earring, a Minneconjou, said there were 5,000 fighting men arrayed against Custer.[18] Fools Crow, a Blackfoot, remembered there were 5,000 men present

What did Custer observe from this reconnaissance? Today, when one ascends to the area of this ridge, you have a very good and extensive overlook of the valley, and except for anything very close to the river's banks, one can see all the way down to Route 212. The scene which greeted the commander's eyes must have surprised but did not amaze him. Dr. Stewart remarked Custer certainly met more Indians than he had expected to, but he did not meet as many as others thought or would think he had.[9] There has been from the very beginning an ongoing speculation and argument over the population of the Indian village which the 7th Cavalry faced this Sunday afternoon. The number of inhabitants have ranged from Captain Anson Mills' estimate of 20,000 Indians with 5,000 warriors, (Mills was with Crook), to Dr. Charles Eastman, a Carlisle educated full-blood Sioux, who stated there were about a thousand lodges with around 5,000 men, women, and children. There were only 1500 warriors in his total. Dr. Eastman even went so far as to give

[9]Stewart, *Custer's Luck*, 312.

[10]Anson Mills, *My Story* (Washington, DC: Privately Published, 1918), 409; Dr. Charles Eastman, "The Story of the Little Big Horn: Told from the Indian Standpoint by One of Their Race," *Chautauquan*, #31, July 1900, 354.

[11]Hugh Scott, *Some Memories of A Soldier* (NY, NY: The Century Co, 1928), 49.   [12]Graham, *Reno Court*, 72.

[13]Hammer, *Custer in '76*, 58.   [14]Graham, *The Custer Myth*, 221.

[15]Ibid, 130.   [16]Ibid, 116.

[17]Helena *Independent* (Helena, MT), October 15, 1915.

[18]Graham, *The Custer Myth*, 98.

and all of them seasoned warriors.[19] Likewise in 1883, Spotted Horn Bull, when asked about the number of warriors in the village, replied, "after a lengthy and—to a white man—abstruse calculation, said 5,000 would cover the braves and chiefs."[20]

The supporters of the lower population estimates of Dr. Eastman cite Flying Hawk who said there were only about 1200 fighting men in the village, but even with this smaller number only 1,000 took part as the rest were out hunting.[21] White Bull put the number slightly higher and stated there were only about 2,500 warriors who fought in the battle.[22] Lewis Crawford, an old-time pioneer, claimed the number of braves couldn't have been over 2,500, but more probably about 2,000, as the country was not able to support more than this number if they remained cohesive.[23] Chief Red Cloud said there were only 4,000 Indians in the whole camp.[24] To give an example of the difficulty of determining even within a few hundred of an approximation, we will use the size of the Cheyenne camp circle. It is generally conceded by most battle experts that Wooden Leg narrated one of the most accurate Indian accounts of this time period; he was very careful to have everything recorded that he saw or came to his attention. In his book, he told there were 300 Cheyenne lodges on the Little Big Horn.[25] This is agreed to, in the main, by the famous Indian scholar George Bird Grinnell who claimed there were no less than 200 Cheyenne lodges in the village.[26]

However, if one reads Wooden Leg's account closely, a different number of his people's lodges emerge. He said that in March 1876 he was in a Cheyenne camp of forty-two lodges, and that other tribes made up the balance of 105 which were attacked on the 17th by Colonel John Reynolds, 3rd Cavalry, at the Battle of the Powder River. This number of lodges checks out with the Indian Bureau's report of late 1875 in which they stated there were fifty lodges of Cheyennes away from the reservations. Wooden Leg fled with the other Cheyennes, after their village was destroyed, to Crazy Horse's village which had about ten Cheyenne lodges already camped with these Ogallalas. By April 9th, the Ogallalas and the Cheyennes had joined the main camp of Sitting Bull. Wooden Leg recorded the Cheyennes were the smallest of the camp circles—52 lodges. He was careful to make a note when any additional lodges of his people arrived, and there had been no additions since they had joined Crazy Horse a few weeks prior. It wasn't until the end of April when Lame White Man, who would later be killed in the battle, linked up with what was now the main camp with his ten lodges. Two weeks later, about mid May, another Cheyenne chief, Dirty Moccasins, arrived with about ten additional lodges.[27] This tribe's camp circle now contained seventy-two lodges. In early June, while the main camp was on Greenleaf Creek, more Cheyennes came in, but Wooden Leg didn't record the numbers, it was probably Black Elk's band of about ten lodges. According to him, no further additions took place; however John Stands In Timber related that Magpie Eagle's band joined the Cheyenne with about fifteen to twenty lodges, but it wasn't until June 24th. This brought the Cheyenne circle to 102 on the eve of the battle, and no more than 122 on the morning of June 25th. Even this lower figure is disputed. George Hyde, a noted Indian authority, said his informants told him the Cheyenne circle was no more than fifty lodges.[28] This is the same number of lodges John Stands in Timber, the grandson of Wolf Tooth and Lame White Man, said was present on June 25th.[29]

Hyde is backed up in his claim by the fact, that a week before, there were only 87 warriors who rode forth from the Cheyenne camp to attack Crook on the Rosebud. This force would have been too small to have come from the two hundred lodges Grinnell claimed had been assembled a few days later. Using a yardstick of two warriors per lodge, the Cheyenne fighting force arrayed against Custer was about 200 braves. A similar exercise could be undertaken for the Sioux lodges, but remember this, ten days before the battle, Mitch Bouyer estimated that there were about 400 lodges in an abandoned main camp, which was discovered on the Reno Scout.[30] Are we to assume by some sort of magic, the hostile camp in a few weeks, no less than quintupled in size? Particularly, when the Cheyenne camp revealed a pattern of slow growth right

[19] Thomas E. Mails, *Fools Crow* (Garden City, NY: Doubleday & Company, 1979), 20.

[20] Graham, *The Custer Myth*, 84.

[21] M. I. McCreight, *Chief Flying Hawk's Tales* (NY, NY: Alliance Press, 1936), 40. [22] Vestal, *Sitting Bull*, 157.

[23] L. F. Crawford, *Rekindling Camp Fires* (Bismarck, ND: Capital Book Co, 1926), 259. [24] Dixon, *Vanishing Race*, 170.

[25] Marquis, *A Warrior Who Fought Custer*, 210.

[26] Grinnell, *The Fighting Cheyennes*, 356.

[27] Ibid, 383.

[28] George Hyde, *Red Cloud's Folk* (Norman, OK: Univ. of OK Press, 1967), 261.

[29] Father Peter J. Powell, *Sweet Medicine: The Continuous Role of the Sacred Arrows, The Sun Dance, And The Sacred Buffalo Hat in Northern Cheyenne* (Norman, OK: Univ. of OK Press, 1979), 110. Hereinafter cited: *Sweet Medicine*.

[30] Charles DeLand, *The Sioux Wars*, (Pierre, SD: South Dakota Historical Collections, Vol.15, 1930), 345.

up to the Little Big Horn? I believe we will never arrive at a census figure that will prove acceptable to all battle students. But, based on the sources and evidence available, it would appear the estimates of 2,500 to 3,000 warriors confronting Custer are probably high. For those who believe Custer faced thousands and thousands of hostile Indians, it isn't necessary to hold to these inflated numbers as a reason for Custer's defeat. There is no doubt the Indians his regiment did confront were greater than his own. It is not that their numbers were so much greater than the white man's, as it was the white man underestimated the ability, determination, and the "medicine" of the Indian on this Sunday afternoon. But, whatever the size the village, a few or many thousands, it was not large enough to deter Custer. Because, as we know, in spite of what his scouts had told him, Custer decided to move against the camps and strike the Indians who he thought were fleeing, or, in a short time, would be forced to flee.

Some students think Custer made a third observation and obtained his clearest view of the valley from Weir Point. Among the more noted students who thought so were Kuhlman, Dustin, Stewart, and Gray.[31] However, if one places any credence in what Trumpeter Martin recalled and the area's geography, Custer didn't go to Weir Point. Martin described Custer's lookout as "a big hill that overlooked the valley."[32] He further clarified this location as "the highest hill, the very highest point around there."[33] Today, if one is approaching from the south, as Custer did, Weir Point does not appear as the highest hill in the area. The features of Sharpshooters' Ridge are much more pretentious when viewed from this perspective. In addition, Martin was specifically asked at the Reno Court if Weir Point and the lookout were one and the same. He replied they were not.[34] Martin was sure this was the point, not Weir's Peaks, from which they looked over the valley, because on his way to Benteen, he saw Reno's command in action "from the same ridge from which General Custer saw the village."[35] Martin's statements were confirmed by DeRudio, who was also asked about Custer using Weir Point as a lookout: "Was General Custer on that point? He answered 'No' and '. . . I went on the top of it afterwards on the 27th with Captain Benteen.'"[36] Both of these men were familiar with Sharpshooters' Ridge as well as Weir Point, and they knew the difference between the two geographical features. Both declared Custer had not used Weir Point as an observation overlook. But, there is a further check on their veracity, and that is the Little Big Horn River itself. Martin also said they could not see the river from their overlook. This is due to the fact the river flows right at the foot of the bluff, and most of it can't be seen from Sharpshooters' Ridge, as one can attest, today, from its ridge.[37] However, if one is on Weir Point, the river is plainly visible to the north as well as to the south. In addition, as will be noted, the Crows had gone to the edge of the bluffs to view the scene for themselves. As Custer moved along the ridge, the Crows followed the bluff's edge until they reached Weir Point; their accounts do not mention Custer being with them or on Weir Point by himself, or with his staff.[38]

Martin said that after Custer made his observation, he rode back down to where the troops were, and he and the Adjutant discussed the situation. Martin said Custer remarked, "The Indians were asleep in their teepees," and said to no one in particular, "we will get them, and as soon as we get through, we will go back to our station."[39] Many battle experts have taken Martin to task for claiming Custer was under the impression or said that the Indians were "asleep" when a full regiment of cavalry had already begun their attack. They tend to agree with Captain Benteen's assessment of Martin as being "a thick headed, dull witted Italian."[40] Being charitable, Colonel Graham, who later recorded the trumpeter's story, believed Custer probably said, "We've caught them napping," but Martin wasn't used to American idioms.[41] It's possible the village was in the condition Martin so reported and would lead one to assume it was surprised or figuratively "asleep." He told Camp that when Custer was at the observation point, they saw children and dogs playing among the teepees and a few loose ponies. Martin further related the officers discussed where the warriors could be. One of the officers told Custer they might be out hunting buffalo, remembering the skinned buffalo they had seen along the trail.[42] This story of a nearly deserted, unprepared village would appear incredible, based upon the information we have available. But, it was supported by the Crow scout Curley, who said after Custer turned toward the river, the four scouts and Mitch Bouyer looked down upon the village and also noted there were very few Indians around, and Bouyer remarked the Indians were not in the village. He thought they might be out "campaigning somewhere" and the scouts ought to hurry down to fight them.[43]

[31]Dustin, *The Custer Tragedy*, 154; Kuhlman, *Legend into History*, 159; Stewart, *Custer's Luck*, 337; Gray, *Custer's Last Campaign*, 340–344.
[32]Graham, *The Custer Myth*, 289.
[33]Graham, *Reno Court*, 349.　　[34]Ibid.
[35]Ibid, 343.　　[36]Ibid, 291.

[37]Ibid.　　[38]Graham, *The Custer Myth*, 13, 20, 23, 25.
[39]Graham, *Reno Court*, 341–342.
[40]Graham, *The Custer Myth*, 180.　　[41]Ibid, 293.
[42]Ibid, 100.　　[43]Ibid, 13.

This appearance of a deserted village is strikingly similar to Sitting Bull's description of his ambush plan that he prepared for Custer and which he revealed in 1878 to the Fort Benton *Weekly Record*. Mrs Spotted Horn Bull's account tended to agree with the Uncpapa medicine man in that, the Indians had set a trap for Custer, but Reno's attack had caught them by surprise.[44] If these accounts are correct, then Martin, the Crows, and Bouyer did in fact see a village that was 'napping.' The biggest problem with these ambush stories is that there isn't a single Indian who ever claimed to have personally been lying in wait for Custer. For example, Chief Gall, who took a prominent part in the battle and would be expected to be in the forefront of any planned ambush, was with some Cheyennes looking for horses at the time Custer was making his observation on the bluffs. He was nowhere near the rest of the Uncpapa warriors, or even his camp circle.[45] Other hostile Indians told of just being asleep, which is what Martin said they were doing. Wooden Leg said he and his brother were doing just that; also Turtle Rib, a Minniconjou, as well as Chief Low Dog. One Bull and Two Moon, a Cheyenne, said they were at the river watering their horses. Even the renowned Crazy Horse said he was in lodge at the time, but he didn't say he was sleeping.[46] Custer, from Sharpshooters' Ridge, saw a village that was unaware of the approach of his regiment, and comparatively speaking, he had caught them asleep or napping. Martin, by his own observation and by watching his commander's reaction and hearing his comments, concluded this was the village's status as well; so much for being a "dull witted Italian."

Many battle students believe Custer continued along Reno's Ridge until he came to a ravine that led in the direction of the river.[47] This ravine, they claim, was Cedar Coulee; but was it? Cedar Coulee is a tributary of Medicine Tail Coulee. Cedar Coulee goes northward for about a half-mile, then takes a dog leg to the right, away from the Little Big Horn River for another half mile before it joins Medicine Tail. Custer had seen all he needed to from his two lookouts. His state of mind was reflected by what Martin said Custer reportedly told the troopers, "We will go down and make a crossing and capture the village."[48] There was no need to continue on to the north, as it would be out of the way to reach the river, as well as taking up time. Besides, Custer couldn't see what was on the other side of Weir Point. He didn't want to expose his flanks to any possible harassment, and he could see

the area, about what today is identified as Godfrey's Gorge, was clear. That Custer didn't ride on the west side of Sharpshooters' Ridge towards Cedar Coulee, was confirmed by Edgerly, who told Camp that when he advanced to Weir Point, following after Weir, he saw no sign of Custer's trail.[49] Custer was moving five companies abreast, so it's doubtful if Edgerly could have missed the sign. Thus, when Custer returned to his command from the second lookout with his staff, Martin said he gave the order "Attention." "Fours right." "Column right." "March," and the battalion passed down from the hill, and "Column left" was then ordered.[50] We know from cavalry drill manuals that the battalion was at rest when the command "Attention" was given, as it can only be directed to a halted column. In order to prepare for the move into the confines of Godfrey's Gorge, the battalion evolved into a column of fours front with the companies marching behind one another. This was accomplished by the "Fours right," order. If Custer had been headed to Cedar Coulee, he would have ordered, "Fours left." Martin then said, soon afterwards, a "Column left" was ordered. This was no doubt to move around an obstruction, and if one is in this area, you'll see a few small hillocks that lay east of Sharpshooters' Ridge. Even today, one can see the faint traces of a trail that runs over the extreme northern part of this ridge (some people call this Martin Ridge), and it becomes too narrow for anything more than the single set of fours which the battalion had formed. This is why Custer turned more to the east and into the broader Godfrey Gorge. Curley agreed with Martin's description of the route, and said, Custer passed into Medicine Tail Coulee from behind this ridge (Sharpshooters') and went down it, going in a direction directly north, coming out about a mile from Ford B.[51] Russell White Bear told Fred Dustin that the ravine Custer used "comes out two miles up Medicine Tail from the river."[52] This more accurately describes the mouth of Godfrey's Gorge than Cedar Coulee's. It was after 3:30 PM when the movement began.

Hank Wiebert also questioned why Custer would ride over to Cedar Coulee. Wiebert spent a lifetime traveling all over this back country on horseback and was intimate with all the terrain features. He said, "There is nothing but rough going down there."[53] He knew the other ridge running east and close to Cedar Coulee goes "all the way to the bottom, no brush, no sharp ups and downs, and less distance."[54] However, one could reasonably argue the

---

[44]Ibid, 84–88.   [45]Ibid, 92.
[46] Ibid, 57, 75, 102, 104.   [47]Ibid, 290.
[48]Hammer, *Custer in '76*, 56.

[49]Ibid.   [50]Ibid, 100.
[51]Ibid, 156–157.   [52]Dustin, *The Custer Tragedy*, x.
[53]Weibert, *Sixty-six Years in Custer's Shadow*, 46.
[54]Ibid.

battle student, today, knows the terrain much better than did Custer. These students have been all over the battlefield dozens of times, while Custer saw it just once and had to decide then and there which was the best way to proceed. Many have a tendency to know the lay of the land too well and try and use this knowledge for comparison purposes of several different routes. Whereas, Custer could only observe the advantages of one over another from some quick observation point rather than, like us, being able to travel over all the alternatives and then make a judgment. Perhaps the clearest account of Custer's route was related by Curley shortly before he died, in 1923. He said when the soldiers reached the ridge they kept marching on the east side of Reno Hill and went down on the west side of the ridge, down a ravine which runs northward. Custer then went to the ridge and looked into the valley and saw Reno's men riding towards the Indians. He said they could see dust everywhere down the valley. After Custer looked the situation over, he turned and rode back to his command.[55] I conclude, after a careful study of the sources and the area's geography, Custer's route to Medicine Tail Coulee was from Sharpshooters' Ridge, followed to the north by east, down into Godfrey's Gorge. It was here the troops struck Medicine Tail Coulee directly, or possibly crossed over the mouth of Cedar Coulee, into it.

After seeing Knipe riding across the back country and the soldiers with the faltering mounts, Soldier, Stab, Little Sioux, and the other Arikaras intended to continue following Custer's Trail with the stolen Sioux horses. Stab told the others they should join Custer and go where he had gone.[56] Consequently, they traveled along the same bluffs' lines as did the troops. When the Arikaras arrived near Sharpshooters' Ridge, they noticed the "Sioux were coming and getting around us before we got to the end of the Ridge."[57] The Sioux began to press after these horse thieves, and the scouts turned back toward the Lone Teepee area, after exchanging fire with their pursuers. "From this point we started toward the Powder late in the p.m. but before sundown. Struck Rosebud before dark."[58] Meanwhile, Custer, as the battalion was being ordered, "Fours right," told Mitch Bouyer to inform his Crows they had accomplished what he had asked of them. They had escorted the soldiers "to the enemy and need not go into the fight."[59] Bouyer and the Crows rode to a "bluff (Weir Point) beyond the point where Custer had

turned down" where they had an excellent view of the whole valley. Bouyer told the four he was going with the soldiers and would fight with them.[60] Goes Ahead, Hairy Moccasin, White-Man-Runs-Him sat on the top of the high bluff and watched the beginning of Reno's fight, then turned back to the south. Goes Ahead told Camp, "We three Crows did not see Custer after he turned down the coulee" and didn't see any of his battle.[61] For if the scouts had delayed too long at Weir Point watching Custer go into action, they would have met Reno's command as the soldiers made their way to the bluffs.[62] In addition, Herendeen and Girard stated that they didn't hear firing from down river until about fifteen minutes after Reno began his retreat. The three made a circle to the east, met Benteen's battalion, continued on and swam the Big Horn River, and the next day ran across the other Crows scouting with Lieutenant Bradley who was assigned to the Terry-Gibbon Column. Goes Ahead admitted they told their fellow tribesmen about Custer's defeat even though they only believed it to be the case.[63] Goes Ahead justified his telling that Custer was beaten because after they had seen Reno's men being surrounded out in the valley, the scouts concluded all the white men would meet the same fate.[64]

As usual, with anything connected with the Custer fight, there is a dispute as both Hairy Moccasin and White-Man-Runs-Him said they saw the beginnings of Custer's battle before they left. The latter recalled he saw Custer's command turn into Medicine Tail Coulee and go down to the river and out onto the flat. The former said he saw the Sioux working around on all sides of Custer, and "there was much excitement among the soldiers."[65] In 1909, White-Man-Runs-Him told Camp an incredible story about how "Custer sat on bluff and saw all of Reno's valley fight."[66] Two years earlier, this scout gave a more detailed account of Custer's actions to Edward Curtis, a noted Indian photographer who was in the process of compiling his famous twenty volume work *The North American Indian*. He recalled how Custer joined the scouts on Weir Point, and together they watched Reno fight alone in the valley. White-Man-Runs-Him told Curtis how he urged Custer to lead his com-

---

[55]Graham, *The Custer Myth*, 18–19.
[56]Hammer, *Custer in '76*, 189.   [57]Ibid.
[58]Ibid.   [59]Ibid, 175.

[60]Ibid, 179.   [61]Ibid.
[62]These scouts, if they had remained, also would have met some Sioux warriors who were already on top of the bluffs, such as the ones who killed Dr. DeWolf. These warriors then went down towards Custer on the eastside of the Little Big Horn River. The Crows never reported that they met any hostile Indians on the bluffs.
[63]Hammer, *Custer in '76*, 179.
[64]*Camp, BYU*, roll 1, box, 9, folder 11.
[65]Hammer, *Custer in '76*, 179.   [66]Ibid, 178.

mand down from the bluffs direct to Reno's support.[67] Custer reportedly told the Crow, "No, let them fight, there will be plenty of fighting left for us to do."[68] It wasn't until after Reno had fled the field that Custer led his command away from Weir Point and to battle.[69] Curtis claimed he now finally understood the 'why' and 'how' of the Little Big Horn, which had escaped the historians all these years. Curtis believed what he had been told by these scouts and thought Custer had "unnecessarily sacrificed the lives of his soldiers to further his personal ends," and he so wrote in a story to the New York *Herald* on November 10, 1907. Curtis further elaborated in the newspaper:

> When the true story of Custer's fight is told it is probable that the telling will add no luster to the Custer name, unless a willingness to gamble with the lives of others to accomplish a personal end may be considered laudable.[70]

Curtis' version of the Custer fight was immediately set upon by a number of persons including retired Captain Francis Gibson who wrote to the Herald's editor expressing a "solemn protest against such an atrocious charge against an officer who had rendered distinguished service to his country."[71] Another letter to the editor was signed by "Truth." In it, the writer claimed it wasn't Reno who was betrayed, but Custer, by his (Reno's) "bewilderment and incompetency."[72] Walter Camp had heard these stories before and labeled them "preposterous."[73] Camp, the foremost expert on the battle at the time, further explained why he knew this to be the case in reply to a letter he received from then Brig. General Charles Woodruff, who in 1876 was a lieutenant with Gibbon's 7th Infantry. First, Camp wrote that White-Man-Runs-Him told him a different story, and that Goes Ahead disagreed with this scout and stated that Custer had gone out of sight behind the bluffs before all the Reno fight happened. Secondly, Benteen said he met these Crows, all three of them, including White-Man-Runs-Him, "on the first rise of the bluffs north of Sundance Creek," which was over two miles south of Weir Point. This meeting was confirmed by Godfrey and several enlisted men.[74] It would have been impossible to witness the end of the Reno fight and then ride several miles back to Benteen's command and meet these soldiers all before 4:00 PM. Lastly, Camp said that White-Man-Runs-Him specifically told him, "We went back and met Benteen and had some talk

through some soldier who could speak a little Crow."[75] One can not be in two places at the same time, and Camp, through the information he collected, was correct in dismissing this tall tale fostered on Curtis.

And, what about the fourth Crow scout, Curley? Harry Moccasin said this nineteen-year-old youth had left them at Weir Point and "cleared out of the country, and we did not see him again for fourteen sleeps (two weeks)."[76] Curley denied this was true, as it was these three who "shipped out without leave and went south" and they left before the Reno fight, as only he and Mitch Bouyer saw it.[77] It was from Weir Point the three "turned tail and put back up the river following our trail along the bluffs." They left as Custer was going down Medicine Trail Coulee. Curley declared, "Custer did not see Reno fight," therefore, he didn't know what had happened to Reno until Bouyer caught up with the commander in the Coulee and "told Custer Reno had been defeated."[78] Curley stated Bouyer left the three Crows on Weir Point with orders to watch the Indian camp. Bouyer took Curley with him, passed over the peaks, paralleled Custer's course, and together joined him about half a mile from the river.[79] Curley said Bouyer took him when he went to Custer to act as a messenger. He cautioned Curley "to keep out of the skirmish as much as possible, as they might wish to send me with a dispatch to the other troops."[80] Curley said he rode with Bouyer and Custer right up to Calhoun Hill, and it was from here Bouyer told him to leave and save himself "for we will all be cleaned out."[81] The Sioux took exception to Curley's adventures on the battlefield and adamantly and forcefully declared that anyone who crossed the Medicine Tail with Custer is still there.[82] In fact, at the tenth anniversary of the battle, Gall, after hearing Curley's tale, asked the Crow where were his wings? As nothing but a bird could have escaped the Custer field that afternoon.[83]

There are a number of battle students who believe Curley's declarations that he went all the way to Calhoun Hill and saw a good part of the Custer battle. Camp for one thought the Crow was a credible witness: "I have never heard or seen in print the least particle of reliable evidence to prove that he was not in the beginning of the fight . . . his story agrees with other authentic accounts."[84] Camp

[67]James S. Hutchins, *The Papers Of Edward S. Curtis Relating To Custer's Last Battle* (El Segundo, CA: Upton & Sons, 2000), 19.
[68]Ibid, 45.　[69]Ibid, 19.
[70]Ibid, 115.　[71]Ibid, 21.
[72]Ibid.　[73]*Camp, BYU*, roll 1, box 9, folder 11.
[74]Ibid.
[75]Hammer, *Custer in '76*, 179.　[76]Ibid, 177.
[77]Ibid, 162, 166.　[78]Ibid, 166.
[79]Ibid, 157.　[80]Hammer, *Custer in '76*, 162–163.
[81]Ibid, 167.
[82]Thomas B. Marquis, *Memories of a White Crow Indian* (NY, NY: The Century Co, 1928), 251.
[83]Rev. John E. Cox, *Five Years in the United States Army* (NY, NY: Sol Lewis, 1973), 154–155.　[84]Hammer, *Custer in '76*, 164.

continued to believe Curley's stories despite unexplained differences and inconsistencies in both space and time. Curley told Camp that Custer did not stop in Medicine Tail, but went right to the river and then to Calhoun Hill.[85] Camp never learned about the troop positions on Luce and Blummer-Nye-Cartwright Ridges, as he died before these findings were revealed. Camp seems to have accepted at face value what Curley told him in spite of being warned by others not to believe this Crow.[86] It appears he was sort of Camp's protege. In spite of what he related to Camp, Curley told Tom Leforge, a scout with Gibbon's column, "I was not in the fight."[87] Curley also told Leforge when the fight began he was behind with the other Crows. He then left them and hurried away to a distance about a mile away and observed the fighting for a short time. He rode on further and stopped on another hill to take a second look.[88] Curley told Pretty Shield, a Crow medicine woman, that he was sick at the time. She concluded that he probably was, and "Maybe what he knew was ahead of him made him sick," and he left.[89] Just as it was in the past, it continues today; Curley has had his defenders and his detractors. It all depends upon what variation of which story one uses to base his opinion of Curley's veracity. What Russell White Bear told Curley a few days before the scout died, neatly sums up what many students of the battle experience when trying to sort through Curley's statements: "Curley— I have interpreted for you a number of times —I am not clear yet on your stories."[90] Dr. Kuhlman was of a similar opinion, and wrote: "The last word about Curley has not yet been written."[91] There is no doubt Curley could have observed and noted the beginning of 'Custer's Last Stand;' probably with Mitch Bouyer from Weir Point until Bouyer left to join Custer. Then Curly rode away and looked upon the scene again, but this vantage-point, was probably to the south of Medicine Tail Coulee, rather than to the east.

This was because Curley, as he stated, was in a position to note the Arikara scouts had some Sioux horses they were driving and had crossed the river and had brought them up the ridge on the east side.[92] Little Sioux confirmed that he and the Arikaras were pushing a herd of captured ponies up the bluffs about the time of Reno's retreat.[93] This was before four o'clock, and if Curley saw the incident, he couldn't have been with Bouyer riding down the bluffs towards Custer in the opposite direction. In addition, Curley, about the same time, said he saw "some Crow and Arikara scouts were surrounded in some woods on the west side of the river."[94] Young Hawk confirmed that this happened during Reno's retreat as Curley reported. He said the two scouts, Goose and Young Hawk, were in a thick grove of trees and "the Dakotas were riding on all sides of them."[95] Since the other Crows didn't mention these incidents, it would appear Curley had left his brothers and rode to the south as they related. This is despite of Red Bear's recollections who said that when the Arikaras came up to Reno Hill with their captured horses he "saw four riders coming toward them" they were the Crow scouts.[96] In all probability, Curley attached himself to these Arikaras, as White-Man-Runs-Him later said, and this was the only reason Curley survived the fight. He further stated the Arikaras told him Curley was with them.[97]

That Curley was with the Arikaras is further verified by the story that he told to General Scott. He said he left the others to get a drink of water, and they had advised him not to go as it was dangerous, but "I did not listen to them." He rode to the point where Custer watered his horses before he turned to the right and saw the pack train making its way to Reno Hill."[98] It was after four o'clock when the pack train was at this point along the trail, while Custer was in Medicine Tail Coulee. Black Fox, a young Arikara scout, told Red Star it was true that Curley was with him, and they watered their horses.[99] Given the recollections of the other scouts as well as Curley's own admitted observations of the events happening at the time, it is clear he could have seen only the very beginnings of the Custer fight and the final stages of Reno's retreat from the valley. Once he came to the conclusion the soldiers were in big trouble, he began his trek to the south and east toward Reno Creek and safety. He so informed Scott, and, this was verified by the Arikaras. His other statements of riding with Custer down and across Medicine Tail to Calhoun Hill and then almost to the death, are more than doubtful; in my opinion, they were probably a figment of his imagination. But, in defense of this scout, his stories of Custer's Last Stand were no worse than many of the white accounts accorded the public over the years.

As the battalion turned into Godfrey's Gorge, Custer was looking to reach the river and the north end of the village as quickly as possible. He also decided to dispatch

---

[85]*Camp, BYU*, roll 1, box 1, folder 12.
[86]Ibid, roll 1, box 1, folder 2; roll 2, box 2, folder 14.
[87]Marquis, *Memoirs of a White Crow Indian*, 247–248.
[88]Ibid, 250.   [89]Linderman, *Pretty Shield*, 232–233.
[90]Graham, *The Custer Myth*, 18.
[91]Charles Kuhlman, *Massacre Survivor* (Fort Collins, CO: Old Army Press, 1972), 20.   [92]Graham, *The Custer Myth*, 14.
[93]Libby, *The Arikara Narrative*, 152–153.

[94]Graham, *The Custer Myth*, 14.
[95]Libby, *The Arikara Narrative*, 98.   [96]Ibid, 129.
[97]Graham, *The Custer Myth*, 16.   [98]Ibid.
[99]Libby, *The Arikara Narrative*, 119–120.

another messenger. The command moved about a mile since Knipe had been sent with orders to the pack train, and if he saw Benteen, he was to tell him to hurry along. This time the messenger would be sent to Benteen. Martin told the Reno Court that Custer gave instructions to Cooke to send the trumpeter with orders to Benteen. Cooke wrote out a dispatch for him, telling him, "Orderly, I want you to take this dispatch to Capt. Benteen and go as fast as you can." If it was possible, Cooke said, return to the command, but if there was any danger to remain with his company, which was Benteen's.[100] However, in his 1910 interview with Camp, Martin said Custer spoke to him directly and said, "go back on our trail and see if you can discover Benteen and give him this message."[101] Martin further elaborated in 1923 to Graham exactly what Custer's verbal order was: "Orderly, I want you to take a message to Colonel Benteen. Ride as fast as you can and tell him to hurry. Tell him it's a big village and I want him to be quick, and to bring the ammunition packs."[102] In all probability, the correct sequence of events was what he testified to at the Reno Court, as it's unlikely that Custer spoke directly to Martin; Martin no doubt overheard what Custer said to his adjutant. We need to remember all the rest of Custer's orders this day were verbal, and the commander would have no reason now to suddenly put them in writing. But Adjutant Cooke knew Martin better than Custer and was aware of his limited English skills, as Martin had immigrated from Italy just three years earlier. Thus, Cooke stopped Martin as he turned his horse's head for the rear, and said: "Wait, orderly, I'll give you a message." Again, he was told to take the same trail they had used in reaching the bluffs. Martin always maintained he didn't know the content of the message, but he said he just took the paper from Cooke's hand and put it into his pocket. Even if he did open the order, it's doubtful he could read English.

Exactly where Martin received the famous 'last order' has been a subject of speculation among battle authors. Camp said that Martin told him that he left Custer about half way down the coulee. Dr. Stewart, Jim Willert, and Fred Dustin claim Martin left the command at the junction of Cedar Coulee and Medicine Tail. Dr. Gray infers that he was dispatched at the head of the coulee or gorge before the column entered it. Henry Wiebert believed it was at a point just as Custer entered Medicine Tail. Dr. Kuhlman's opinion was that Martin was dispatched after riding 300 yards down the ravine. However, Martin should have known from what point he departed the col-

umn, and while the events were fresh in his mind, he told his story at the Reno Court of Inquiry. Martin testified that about the time the command had executed the "Column Left" a little below the ridge and almost to the head of the ravine, he was ordered to Benteen.[103] Martin admitted he didn't know where "Colonel Benteen was, nor where to look for him."[104] This is why he was directed to follow the command's back trail because both Custer and Cooke knew it would take their messenger to the dust cloud they had observed while at the lookout. At that time, it was less than five miles away to the southeast, and from the movement of this cloud, they estimated it would bisect their trail. Martin recalled that he traveled south about 600 yards and arrived on the same ridge from which he had seen the village with Custer not ten minutes earlier.[105] The trumpeter turned his head to the right and "looked down into the bottom, and saw Major Reno engaged. I paid no further attention to it, but went forward on my business."[106] The reason why Martin suddenly looked to his right was because he heard heavy firing in that direction. He originally thought it was from Custer's command, but the battalion as yet hadn't even reached Medicine Tail.[107] It was before 3:45 PM.

The same Sioux who had exchanged gunfire with the Arikaras with their captured horses must have seen the trumpeter as well. Martin told Graham some Indians had seen him, as they started shooting. "Several shots were fired at me — four or five, I think— but I was lucky."[108] Only Martin's horse was hit, but he didn't know it until later. The back of his blouse was splattered with his mount's blood. As he started along the high ridge, Martin saw a lone rider approaching him and recognized Boston Custer. The commander's younger brother pulled his mount to a halt and asked Martin about his brother's whereabouts. The orderly replied, "Right behind that next ridge you'll find him."[109] Boston then asked if the Indians had attacked yet. Martin said "No," but warned Boston he had better take care "as there were Indians around but the youngest Custer said, 'Well I am going to join the command anyhow.'"[110] Traveling on, the trumpeter met at least one 'C' trooper, possibly two, who also inquired about the command's whereabouts. Martin said he pointed to the north beyond the bluff.[111] The orderly told the soldier(s) the command was heading

[100]Graham, *Reno Court*, 342.   [101]Hammer, *Custer in '76*, 100.
[102]Graham, *The Custer Myth*, 290.

[103]*Reno Court*, 342, 347.   [104]Graham, *The Custer Myth*, 290.
[105]Graham, *Reno Court*, 347.
[106]Ibid, 343.   [107]Hammer, *Custer in '76*, 101.
[108]Graham, *The Custer Myth*, 290.   [109]Ibid.
[110]*Camp, IU*, box 3 folder 3, 130–132.
[111]Hammer, *Custer in '76*, 104.

Courtesy of Old Army Press

saluted and handed Custer's message to Benteen. Martin repeated what Custer had told him about the village and the need to hurry. Benteen took the message, read it, put it in his pocket. Ever the critic of Custer, Benteen noted that it was not dated.[115] He asked the trumpeter, "Where's the General now?" Martin said he was about three miles from them and he supposed the Indians were running and Custer had charged through the village.[116] Martin further related how he was going to tell his captain about Reno's action, but Benteen never gave him the chance. Benteen, lizard cold in his personal relations with his fellow soldiers, believed Martin to be "just as much cut out for a cavalryman as he was for a king." Benteen further recalled that Martin declared the Indians were "skiddaddling." Martin said he told Benteen no such thing.[117]

Benteen ordered the trumpeter to rejoin the company. But as Martin rode past 'D' to fall in with his company, Lieutenant Edgerly heard Martin telling the troopers that Reno had attacked the village and was "killing Indians and squaws right and left."[118] Interestingly, at the Reno Court of Inquiry, Martin said Benteen ordered him to go to the pack train to bring the mules up and keep them together.[119] But later Martin recanted this testimony and told Graham he didn't speak English very well in 1879, and they misunderstood him, and it was a mistake, as he never was ordered to the pack train.[120] He also told Graham another story about his wounded horse. In this account, he didn't know about the wound his horse had suffered. Benteen asked him what was wrong with his horse? Martin said he didn't know but maybe "he's just tired out." Benteen said, "Look at his hip, you're lucky it was the horse and not you."[121] However, in 1910, Martin told Camp it was Boston Custer who called his attention to his wounded horse before galloping north.[122]

Captain Weir was the closest officer to Benteen, his orderly, and Martin and he rode up to them and halted. Benteen took the message from his pocket and handed it to Company 'D's commander.[123] The famous message that Benteen, and now Weir, read, said to come on, there was a big village, and to be quick. Cooke also said to bring packs and then repeated 'bring packs' as a postscript. Ben-

down the coulee to the right but he had better fall back to the pack train as the Indians would cut him off before he could reach the main column.[112]

Martin traveled as fast as his wounded horse permitted, but at pace no less than a trot.[113] After riding on the back trail for a half hour and about two miles west of the Lone Teepee, Martin saw Benteen, with his orderly, riding "two or three hundred yards" in front of his battalion. That Martin was dispatched about ten minutes and a mile after Knipe, is confirmed by the fact that Benteen only advanced about a mile from his meeting with Knipe before meeting the second messenger. Therefore, Martin couldn't have accompanied Custer into Medicine Tail and have enough time to ride back to join Benteen within a mile of the first messenger. Assuming Custer continued on at the same pace, Martin would have had to been dispatched no more than eight minutes or about a mile after Knipe in order for Benteen to meet Martin about ten minutes after he had met Knipe. Martin, much like Knipe earlier, waived his hat to attract the captain's attention and turned his horse in that direction.[114] Martin said he

[112]Ibid.   [113]Graham, *The Custer Myth*, 290.
[114]Ibid.

[115]Graham, *Reno Court*, 357.
[116]Ibid., 343; Hammer, *Custer in '76*, 101.
[117]Ibid.   [118]Ibid., 54.
[119]Graham, *Reno Court*, 343.   [120]Graham, *The Custer Myth*, 291.
[121]Ibid.   [122]*Camp, IU*, box 3, folder, 3, 136.
[123]Graham, *The Custer Myth*, 291.

teen said to no one in particular, "Well, if he wants me to hurry to him, how does he expect that I can bring the packs? If I am going to be of service to him, I think I had better not wait for the packs."[124] Benteen had a good point. Benteen told a similar story at the Court of Inquiry, but looking at the intent of the order, one would reasonably conclude that Custer wanted Benteen's battalion to accompany 'B' and the pack train, and together they would come "quick" to Custer as an integrated unit, not straggling in separately. There are some students who believe Custer only wanted the ammunition packs and not the whole pack train, and Cooke, in his haste to write out the message, left out the word ammunition. Dr. Kuhlman was of the same opinion until he was corrected by General Hawkins, an old time cavalryman, who told him in Army language "'packs' always means the pack train unless otherwise stated."[125] It is clear from Benteen's comments, both private and public, his thinking was not just in the regards to the ammunition mules, but extended to the entire pack train. Edgerly said that he was also shown the message, and he recalled having the same opinion as Benteen, that Custer could not have wanted them "to go for the packs" as they were being brought by McDougall.[126] I do not dispute that Custer wanted the 'packs,' but I believe, along with other battle scholars, that what Benteen and his officers missed was the primary intent of the message. Of course, Custer wanted the 'packs' to be secure and expeditiously brought forward, but what he really wanted more was the nearly two hundred and fifty additional troopers the combined units would represent by 'coming on and being quick.'

The fact was that the Recorder at the Reno Court of Inquiry was thinking upon these same lines. This is evident when he asked just such a question to Benteen: "At the time you received the order in regard to the pack train, did you consider it necessary to take your command and go and bring up the pack train?" The captain answered: "I did not consider it necessary at all, because the Indians could not get to the pack train without coming by me."[127] This was true; but Custer's order said he wanted the 'packs' brought to him, he said nothing about Benteen protecting and defending them. But in fairness to Benteen, Weir, nor any of his other officers questioned Benteen's decision to move forward without the pack train. Incredibly, Lt. Gibson said Benteen thought the pack train had passed them and was now ahead of their companies![128]

The recorder then probed Benteen and inquired if there are two columns searching out an enemy, isn't it the duty of one to inform the other? Benteen replied it certainly was. Once his answer had registered with the Court, the recorder asked him if he didn't receive such a notice from Martin? The senior captain said yes, he had received such order to "Come on, be quick, big village and bring packs. He then had found." Here, Benteen stopped talking, as he was saying more than he wanted to disclose. He quickly changed direction and stated: "I wish to say, before the order reached me, that I believed that General Custer and his whole command were dead." Benteen wasn't a stupid man. If Custer was dead by the time he received the order, by military law he was not obligated to obey it. Therefore, it's not surprising Benteen wanted the Court of Inquiry to be convinced Custer was dead, or at least he thought so, before he received Martin's message. Benteen's verbal "red herring" was an attempt to mask his own disobedience. The Recorder could only stare at the witness in amazement. The Recorder then inquired of Benteen, if after he received the order, did he increase the pace of his battalion? The captain studiously replied, he didn't think the gait was increased at all.[129] It's little wonder the Recorder didn't stare at the judges. Benteen acknowledged the message and its contents to the court and then testified he did little that the order directed him to do. However, the Recorder realized no matter how much he or possibly the court would like to follow up questions of this officer, the Inquiry was impaneled to investigate Reno's conduct at the Little Big Horn, not Benteen's. He could push the captain no further.

However, the Recorder did pursue this line of questioning with Major Reno. He asked the Major if he had read Custer's order to Benteen? Reno replied he had and although he couldn't repeat the exact "phraseology" as he remembered, it said to come on, there was a big village, and to bring the packs. Reno was asked if the message didn't have the words "be quick." Reno casually said, "Yes, I do, now that you called my attention to it."[130] Reno had previously told the Court about the "immense" number of Indians he had faced alone in the valley, and the Recorder asked: "From the number of Indians you saw around you and your estimate of the number that were there, did it occur to you at the time that, with only 225 men, he might need someone to 'be quick?'" The junior major of the 7th Cavalry looked at the Court and then at the Recorder, and answered, "It never occurred to me at all."[131] No further comment is necessary on Benteen's and

[124]Hammer, *Custer in '76*, 54.

[125]Letter, Charles duBois to Charles Kuhlman, May 18, 1954, Moses Collection.   [126]Graham, *Reno Court*, 388.

[127]Ibid, 357.   [128]Carroll, *The Gibson and Edgerly Narratives*, 3.

[129]Graham, *Reno Court*, 382.   [130]Ibid, 517.

[131]Ibid.

Reno's testimony regarding Custer's 'last message;' it defies coherent description.

After Martin rejoined his company, Benteen led his battalion forward at a faster pace than they had been traveling up to this point. It would appear after Benteen received two messages combined with the distinct sound of gunfire ahead, that these events had finally convinced him to join the campaign. The fact that the gunfire was growing in volume and was apparently rolling towards the battalion gave a further sense of urgency. The companies were in the process of being brought into line when the valley of the Little Big Horn opened in front of the troops. Benteen ordered the battalion to draw their revolvers in anticipation of meeting the warriors who Custer was no doubt driving in their direction.[132] When they left Ft. Lincoln, the younger soldiers had thought that this was to be the last major Indian campaign, and after hearing both Knipe's then Martin's optimistic reports of what Custer and Reno were doing to the Indians, the battle appeared to be all over before they could take an active part in it.[133] At the time, they thought they were to be disappointed. Many of the troopers now just expected to help round up the few Indians who had managed to escape.

Benteen's battalion had been following the main trail since Martin had joined them; but now they came to the point where Custer's trail had split off from Reno's, and there was a discussion as to which trail to follow. Weir and 'D' then took the right hand fork and 'H' and 'K' the left. Benteen, who was riding in advance with his orderly, took a position between the two and went almost to the river.[134] What he saw wasn't very reassuring; it appeared it wasn't the Indians who were being driven, but the soldiers. Godfrey said that due to the smoke, dust, and distance it was impossible to tell if the figures they saw in the valley were friend or foe, but that a battle was in progress was unmistakable.[135] However, on the northern bluffs they could distinguish a body of soldiers.[136] At this time, Godfrey said that the Crow scouts had ridden past them with some stolen horses, and they pointed to the bluffs on the east side of the river, motioning for the column to go in that direction. Edgerly told a similar story, and said the Crow scout Half Yellow Face appeared to their right near the ford and motioned for them to turn

to the right.[137] The battalion began its turn to the right and started up the slope that Custer had taken about an hour earlier.

Benteen saw the same Crows (he also said they could have been Arikaras) as did Godfrey, but some of the men wanted to shoot at them, thinking they were the enemy. But Benteen "cautioned them not to shoot, saying they were our own scouts."[138] The scouts told the two officers that there were "heaps of Sioux" below them and Benteen upon having his first clear view of the valley, saw the last of Reno's retreat. The soldiers were recrossing "the river a couple of miles below, and were showing up on the side of the river that my battalion had kept and was then on."[139] In Benteen's report of the fight he wrote that he had seen what appeared to be two separate engagements going on at the same time, one on the bluffs and one in the valley, neither of which appeared to bode well for the troops. Consequently, he directed his battalion to the bluffs; the stories told by Knipe and Martin had not "panned out."[140] Benteen did this because with his estimate of 900 Indians on the valley floor, if he tried to cross at the ford with the number of men in his command, his companies "would stand no earthly chance" against these veteran fighters.[141] Nine days after the battle, the captain had written his wife that he "saw an immense number of Indians on the plain, mounted and charging, some dismounted men of Reno's; the balance of his command was mounted and flying for dear life to the bluffs."[142] It was a little after 4:00 PM. At the Court of Inquiry, three years later, Benteen did not mention the lack of manpower as a reason that prevented him from crossing the Little Big Horn. Benteen answered the question about which trail he had taken by saying he had thought the whole command was defeated, and he didn't think Ford 'A' was a suitable place to cross the river. Instead, he went towards the men he had seen on the bluff.[143] Edgerly agreed the inability to cross the river had nothing to do with the battalion going to the right; the reason was Half Yellow Face not only pointed out where the other troopers were, but also led them north to the soldiers.[144]

Benteen's battalion rode rapidly up the bluffs towards the soldiers. As they neared the crest, Sergeant Windolph remembered that they could see down the valley, about a half-mile away, where there were "figures galloping on

[132]Graham, *The Custer Myth*, 141.
[133]Carroll, *The Gibson and Edgerly Narratives*, 10.
[134]Hammer, *Custer in '76*, 75.
[135]It must be noted, it was difficult for these soldiers to see what was happening in the valley due to the bluffs and the river.
[136]Graham, *The Custer Myth*, 141.

[137]Ibid, 219.
[138]Liddic, *Camp on Custer*, 73.
[139]Graham, *The Custer Myth*, 181.
[140]Ibid.
[141]Carroll, *The Federal View*, 106.
[142]Graham, *The Custer Myth*, 298.
[143]Graham, *Reno Court*, 357.
[144]Carroll, *The Gibson and Edgerly Narratives*, 10.

horseback, and much shooting . . . and there were mounted and dismounted soldiers ahead."[145] They rode swiftly towards them. When Benteen's command advanced to within a couple of hundred yards of these soldiers, Reno came out to meet the senior captain. Some of the men, however, thought it was Custer's battalion coming to their rescue.[146] Reno was excited, breathing heavily, wearing a "red turkey bandanna handkerchief" wrapped about his head, and called out to Benteen loud enough for many of his men to hear: "For God's sake, Benteen, halt your command and help me. I've lost half my men."[147] Benteen thought Reno's battalion had been "badly handled."[148] It was about a quarter after four. Edgerly's attention was drawn to the shaken Major when he turned and fired his revolver at the Indians who were nearly a thousand yards distant in the valley.[149] Reno said he didn't fire his revolver, but he did shoot it during the retreat "across the bottom. I don't think when I got on the hill I had a charge in it."[150] In this, Benteen concurred, as he didn't see Reno fire his gun after they met on the bluffs. Benteen then asked Reno if he knew where Custer was, as he assumed Reno was still part of the main column. Reno quickly informed him: "I don't know. He went off downstream, and I haven't seen or heard anything of him since."[151]

It doesn't take much effort to imagine Reno's mental condition at the time of Benteen's arrival. Dr. Porter caught up with the Major, and they reached the top of the bluff about the same time. The doctor went up to Reno and said, "Major, the men were pretty well demoralized, weren't they?" Reno, who must have been in denial, replied testily, "No, that was a charge, sir."[152] He had just gone through inconceivable terrors during the retreat which would haunt him for the rest of his life.[153] These horrors began as the command broke from the timber not even a half hour before. Reno left his dead and wounded in the timber, as well as several officers, scouts, and about fifteen troopers. Reno led his battalion to the south and headed for the river about a mile away. The head of the column resembled that of a comet, a compact body of men with a half-mile long tail of stragglers streaming out from behind. Most of the Indians didn't force the issue at either its head or tail, but seemed content to ride along its sides and shoot at the soldiers. Interesting, some of the Sioux thought the soldiers had retreated because they found out they weren't Cheyennes, as they thought the soldiers had been sent to attack this tribe and not them. Therefore, they were satisfied just to see them go.[154] "The soldiers' actions in this regard was constituted by the Indians as meaning the equivalent of: Beg pardon—wrong number—we thought you were Cheyennes!"[155] This was the real reason, the Sioux claimed, why the warriors permitted most of the white men to escape across the river.[156] There was no organized resistance by anyone, nor did Reno make any attempt to provide covering support for the withdrawal. This absence of standard military tactics caused the Court of Inquiry's Recorder to ask when the command left the timber was it "a charge, a retreat, or a stampede?"[157] Had the Indians, at anytime, decided to close on the column, Reno would have had a last stand before Custer.

Private Slaper recalled that not all the Indians fought the troopers from a distance, an Indian had ridden close enough to him that he could have struck him with a saber if he had one.[158] But Reno didn't see anything that was happening behind him. A number of men, riding near him, recalled that the Major was very much excited and had rapidly discharged his revolver at any target which presented itself.[159] The Arikara Red Bear, who cared little for Reno, declared that during the retreat, from the major's "mouth and beard white foam dripped down, and his eyes were wild and rolling."[160] This description of Reno is usually discounted, but Private Burkman told a similar tale in which he said the major's face was smeared with someone else's blood, and that he was bug eyed, and that he shouted orders which no one could understand: "Do this," and then, "Do that." And we didn't know what to do or where to go."[161] Burkman said Private George Penwell, of 'K' Company and assigned as Reno's trumpeter, told him all about the major's demeanor, as he rode near him the whole time. He also claimed Reno was half drunk "leadin' 'em all in retreat."[162] In addition, Private John Fox, 'D' Company, said Reno "appeared to be intoxicated or partially so," when Benteen's battalion arrived.[163] Ben-

[145]Hunt, *I Fought . . .* , 90.

[146]Graham, *Reno Court—Abstract*, 75.

[147]John M. Carroll, *The Custer Scrapbook #4* (Byron, TX: Privately Printed, 1978), 9; Graham, *The Custer Myth*, 291.

[148]Holley, *Once Their Home*, 251.

[149]Graham, *Reno Court—Abstract*, 160.

[150]Graham, *Reno Court*, 510.

[151]Graham, *The Custer Myth*, 291.

[152]Graham, *Reno Court*, 161.　　[153]Hunt, *I Fought . . .* , 175.

[154]Billings *Gazette* (Billings, MT), July 17, 1932.

[155]Thomas B. Marquis, *The Cheyennes of Montana* (Algonac, MI: Reference Publications, 1978), 258.

[156]Ibid.　　　　　　　　　[157]Graham, *Reno Court*, 548.

[158]Brininstool, *Troopers With Custer*, 50.

[159]McClernand, *With Indian and Buffalo in Montana*, 73–74; Graham, *The Custer Myth*, 140.

[160]Libby, *The Arikara Narrative*, 128.

[161]Wagner, *Old Neutriment*, 160–161.

[162]Ibid.　　　　　　　　　[163]Liddic, *Camp on Custer*, 95.

Courtesy of Hastings House Publishers

teen disputed these 'intoxication stories' and always maintained, both privately and publicly, that Reno was not drunk on the bluffs. He stated, "I know there was not enough whiskey in the whole command to make him drunk." However, this could have been a back handed affirmation in that "whiskey was extremely scarce there" or else Benteen "meant that it required plenty of whiskey—and more—to make Reno drunk."[164]

There was a story for each man in the retreat; many went unrecorded, others did not. For example, Private Davern recalled his horse fell before he reached the river, during the time he was passing two dismounted 'G' troopers. There were Indians all around, just waiting to pick off such easy prey. Davern was thrown head first over his stumbling horse. When he got up, he saw that two of the Indians had run their horses into each other in an attempt to be the first to count coup on these men and were now dismounted themselves. Davern's horse regained his feet

---

and Reno's orderly ran over to his animal, mounted and galloped away. He looked behind him and saw the two soldiers "mixed up with the Indians."[165] He supposed they were killed. Private John Meier, Company M, had a bullet wound in his back, and close to the river his horse was also shot, and he was pitched from the animal. The private quickly got to his feet, ran to the river's bank, and jumped into the water. Swimming near him was a riderless mount, and Meier swam to the horse and climbed aboard. The horse and the wounded soldier scrambled up the eastern bank, and with bullets kicking up the dust all around them, they galloped toward the safety of the bluffs. Meier lived another forty-one years.[166] Varnum said during the retreat his orderly, Private Elijah Strode and his horse had been shot, and it fell with him. The Lieutenant halted, got off his mount, caught a loose horse and remounted his orderly and helped him reach the safety of the bluffs.[167] Varnum was assisted by Culbertson; indeed, this was a brave and unselfish act. In the dust smoke and confusion of battle, two of the scouts were wounded by friendly fire. Goose, an Arikara, was shot in the hand, and the Crow, White Swan, was wounded in the leg.[168] It is a wonder they weren't killed because the soldiers, in their panic, fired at anything remotely resembling an Indian. White Swan and Goose, joined by Forked Horn, made it up the bluffs with the soldiers.

It would appear from the direction the column was being led, the object was to recross Ford 'A'. But, with the Indians on the flanks of the long column, it forced them more and more towards the river and a small buffalo trail about a mile from this ford. Recent research has discovered that the troops split into two groups, with the majority going to the quickest crossing point they could find, ford or no ford. Another group of about twenty men took an alternate route and rode southeast, directly to the Little Big Horn instead of skirting one of the river's loops. Although it appeared to be a short cut, the river had to be crossed three times by this group, and they reached the eastern bank at about the same crossing point used by their comrades. At the place the majority crossed, the river was about forty feet in width, with the water up to the saddles. The bank in front of the troopers was about five feet higher than the water, and the only real way to get down to the water was to jump. The soldiers who arrived first and didn't jump in right away were pushed into the river by the momentum of those behind them.

---

[164]Marquis, *Keep the Last Bullet for Yourself*, 128.

[165]Graham, *Reno Court*, 302.
[166]Carroll, *The Sunshine Magazine Articles*, 9.
[167]Graham, *Reno Court*, 124.
[168]Dustin, *The Custer Tragedy*, 131.

The bank on the eastern side was higher than on the western side, so the troopers after crossing over had to scramble up a steep slope.[169] Varnum recalled that the incline was so abrupt his horse nearly threw him "as he jumped up on the other side."[170] Besides the terrain at the crossing point, the Indians were all about and were shooting into the soldiers. Some of the braver warriors even followed the troopers into the river, striking at them with their tomahawks.[171] What little military organization had existed up to this point, now completely dissolved. It had taken the command no more than ten minutes from the time they left the timber to when they arrived at the river and crossed.

With the majority of the soldiers across the river or in the act of crossing, Sergeant Culbertson saw Captain French and Sergeant Frank Lloyd of his company. Lloyd told his fellow sergeant that the men had better stop to provide covering firing for the others and the wounded. Culbertson agreed and told Lloyd to tell French. Lloyd did so, and Culbertson heard French say "'I'll try, I'll try,' and with that he rode up the hill."[172] The only problem with this story is that Lloyd wasn't in the battle, as he was on detached service back at Ft. Lincoln. In the heat of battle, Culbertson could have been confused about the individual with whom he had spoken. If Moylan would have acted on his sergeant's suggestion and laid down a covering fire, it might have saved the lives of a number of soldiers, among them Lt. Hodgson. While attempting to cross the river, a bullet killed his horse and wounded him near his belt line. The Lieutenant slipped off his mount and was thrashing about in the water trying to reach the opposite bank. A number of troopers claimed to have helped Hodgson reach the eastern bank. Hodgson, aware of the number of forsaken men, was said to have cried out to no one in particular, "For God's sake, don't abandon me."[173] Ryan said he saw Trumpeter Charles Fisher, 'M' Company, slow down to assist the young officer. Fisher offered him his stirrup and "the horse drew the lieutenant, in addition to the rider, across the river."[174] For Hodgson, safety was fleeting, as he hadn't gone more than fifty yards when he was shot by Indians from the bluffs above and killed.[175] Culbertson thought the lieutenant had made his way "a little up the hill," before he was killed.

Courtesy of Hastings House Publishers

Godfrey was amazed at the funnel-shaped ravine that led to the bluffs along with the steep inclines men and horses had to clamber to reach the top.[176] The angle of the slopes from the river to the top of the bluffs varies from about 30 to 60 degrees, depending on whether the climb is made via one of the gullies or by way of one of the gradually sloping ridges.[177] It has been recorded, that a person on foot in good physical shape, can make it to the top of the bluffs from the eastern bank of the river in less than ten minutes.[178] Of course, if someone is shooting at you, I am sure that a few minutes could be shaved off this time. With the irregular inclined slopes leading to the bluffs, it was impossible to climb up in any organized manner. The ravines going to the top had narrow deep draws interspersed with a dense tangle of shrubs and small trees. Once again, it was every man for himself. In scaling the bluffs, Dr. James DeWolf and his orderly Private Elihu Clear, 'K' Company, were killed by these same Indians shooting from

[169]Graham, *Reno Court*, 167.   [170]Ibid, 130.

[171]Brininstool, *Troopers With Custer*, 33.

[172]Graham, *Reno Court*, 323.

[173]Graham, *The Custer Myth*, 140.

[174]Barnard, *Ten Years With Custer*, 296.

[175]Brady, *Indian Fights and Fighters*, 273.

[176]Graham, *The Custer Myth*, 140.

[177]Marquis, *Keep the Last Bullet for Yourself*, 122.

[178]Ibid, 122.

above.[179] Private Morris had made it through the wild ride and crossed over the river with Privates William Meyer and David Gordon. Morris said the bluffs were too steep to ascend them mounted, so they were leading their horses and had stopped to rest. The bodies of their comrades were plainly visible down below. The three continued their climb and Morris turned to Gordon and said, "It was pretty hot down there." The older more experienced trooper told Morris he'd get used to it. He had no sooner spoken these words then a hail of bullets descended upon them, and Gordon fell dead, along with Meyer who was hit in the throat. Morris was the only survivor, although he was wounded in the left breast.[180]

Upon reaching the top of the bluffs, Captain Moylan, began to rally what troopers he could muster from the three companies. He began to set up a skirmish line along the bluff's slope. Reno corrected the captain's alignment and moved the men to the crest of the bluff, a little north of where the current Reno Battlefield marker now stands.[181] Luckily for Reno's wounded, Dr. Henry Porter had managed to reach the command, and he set up a field hospital a short distance behind the troops.[182] However, Benteen disputed that there were any battle lines established, and said the men were all scattered about; they were a sorry looking lot. He noted the men must have thought "there was a happier place to be than that."[183] When Moylan was asked at the Court of Inquiry about the dejected appearance of the command, he smartly replied he would "rather be dejected on top of the hill than dead anywhere."[184] The Indians had followed the troops as close as they dared without endangering themselves, and were trying to infiltrate these bluffs to the north, all the while keeping up a constant harassing gunfire. Some of the troopers noted below in the valley that the Indians were no longer crossing the river, but had turned to the north and were riding rapidly in that direction. Heavy clouds of dust were seen hanging over the village, and there was a great deal of back and forth motion by the hostile Indians.[185] Likewise, the warriors who had been seen advancing up the slopes to cut off any further movement by the white men, now broke off their pursuit, as their attention also appeared to be diverted to the north. Furthermore, the troopers began to hear gunfire coming from that direction as well. But not all the war-

riors had moved northward. A number of them were spotted still riding around the crossing point, and others were observed on the bluffs further to the east where they could look down on the troops' position. It was after 4:15 PM.

With the Indians moving away from Reno, few really cared where they were going or why; the fact the warriors were leaving was good enough. However, one officer did think it was strange behavior on the part of the Indians, and he wrote in his diary, "Singular to us it appeared that they made no demonstration against us."[186] The three companies which had moved out so confidentially an hour ago had suffered heavy losses. Thirty-six soldiers were laying dead in the valley, the majority of whom lined the retreat route to the bluffs. Of the wounded, only nine men had managed to reach the bluffs. When these casualty figures are added to those abandoned in the timber, Reno lost 40% of his command. In spite of these terrific losses, Reno could count himself fortunate that the butcher's bill was only this amount. Captain Walter Clifford, of the 7th Infantry and part of Gibbon's column, recorded in his diary: "Had the pursuers been white men, hardly one of the fleeing party could have reached the summit unhurt."[187]

Bringing up the rear of Benteen's battalion was Company K. When they arrived on the bluff, Godfrey was met by his second lieutenant, whom he hadn't seen since Custer detached him before the night march. Hare grabbed Godfrey's hand and exclaimed: "We've had a big fight in the bottom, got licked, and I'm damned glad to see you." In his later years, Godfrey reflected on these events and tried to sort out in his own mind why they "got licked." He reached a conclusion, which even today is difficult to improve upon: "As it turned out I think Custer did make a mistake in going in with a divided force, not that the division of itself would have been fatal, but because Reno failed to hold a leg even if he couldn't skin."[188]

While Reno was giving the order to abandon the timber and retreat to the bluffs, Custer, after speaking with his scouts, caught up with the head of his command which was riding towards Medicine Tail Coulee. After reaching Medicine Trail, the troops rode across the mouth of Cedar Coulee. From the point where Cedar Coulee joins Medicine Tail Coulee, it descends about a mile and a half before it meets a gap a half mile wide in the steep bluffs along the river's eastern banks. This break in the bluffs gave easy access to the Cheyenne camp circle at the upper end of the village and is called Ford 'B'. Custer was heading for

[179]Barnard, *Ten Years With Custer*, 296.

[180]Brady, *Indian Fights and Fighters*, 403; John M. Carroll, *They Rode With Custer* (Mattituck, NY: J. M. Carroll & Company, 1993), 102, 176, 180.   [181]Graham, *Reno Court*, 207.

[182]Ibid, 187.   [183]Ibid, 358.

[184]Ibid, 207.   [185]Hammer, *Custer in '76*, 55.

[186]Stewart, *The Field Diary . . .* , 12.

[187]Koury, *Diaries of the Little Big Horn*, 47.

[188]Brady, *Indian Fights and Fighters*, 374.

this crossing point to cut off any fleeing Indians and to stop any movement to the north caused by Reno's attack. Custer had a good idea of the village's layout and its size from his previous observations. In response to the couriers he had dispatched, the regiment would be concentrated shortly and Reno would have his 'support'. Shortly after crossing the mouth of Cedar Coulee, Custer halted the troops and his men rearranged themselves and tightened their saddles for the action ahead.[189] During this brief halt, Custer ordered Keogh's battalion of two companies forward to take the lead. It was from here, it was reported, that Custer dispatched another messenger. This messenger was said to be mounted on a sorrel-roan horse (Company 'C') and headed north out of the coulee.[190] There are some battle students who question if this incident took place. If Custer did dispatch a messenger to the north, it must have been to Terry, who was thought to be around the Tullock's Forks area, as they were the only other troops in that direction. This could have been Custer's attempt to comply with the General's instructions now that Custer could report accurate intelligence on the hostiles.[191] As Keogh's battalion prepared to move to the front, the lieutenant colonel saw dust rising from a lone rider approaching his command. Boston Custer had taken a steady trot since leaving Benteen a little over an hour ago. He was able to follow the wide distinct trail left by the five company front as it forked off to the right along Reno Creek. His assumption about which trail his brother made was confirmed when he met Martin a few minutes ago. Now he had the main column in sight and he was sure the commanding officer would be surprised and happy to see him. George Custer was indeed surprised to see his youngest brother, as his official duties were with the pack train, and he was happy with the intelligence derived from Boston's arrival.

---

[189]Graham, *The Custer Myth*, 18.

[190]Ibid. Curley reported seeing this messenger dispatched.

[191]Robert E. Doran, "The Man Who Got To The Rosebud," *Research Review—Journal of the Little Big Horn Associates*, Vol. 16, #1, Winter 2002, 11–31.

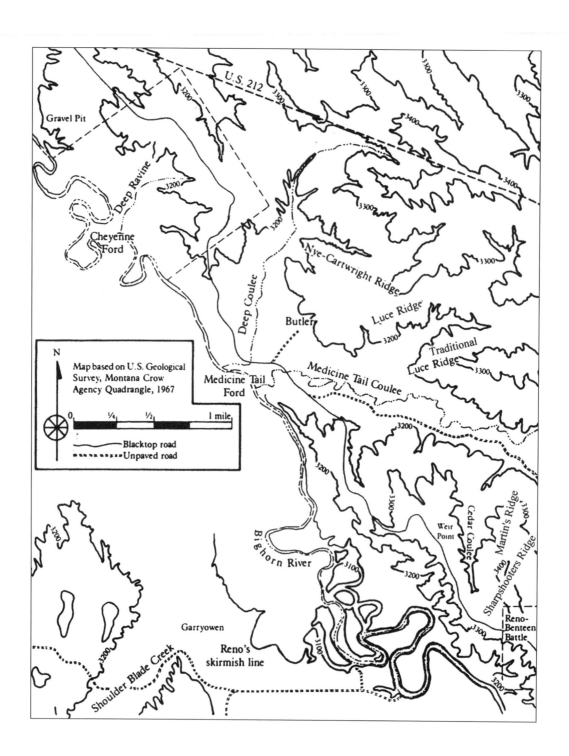

N

Map based on U.S. Geological
Survey, Montana Crow
Agency Quadrangle, 1967

0   ¼   ½   1 mile

——————— Blacktop road
▪▪▪▪▪▪▪▪▪▪▪ Unpaved road

U.S. 212

3200

3300

3300

3400

3400

Gravel Pit

Deep Ravine

3200

Cheyenne
Ford

3300

Nye-Cartwright Ridge

3300

3200

Deep Coulee

Luce Ridge

3200

Butler

Traditional
Luce Ridge

3300

Medicine Tail Coulee

Medicine Tail
Ford

3200

3200

3300

Cedar Coulee

Martin's Ridge

3100

Weir
Point

3400

Sharpshooters Ridge

Reno-
Benteen
Battle

Bighorn River

3200

3100

3300

3200

Garryowen

Reno's
skirmish line

3100

3200

3200

Shoulder Blade Creek

8
Ford 'B' to Calhoun Hill

When Custer identified the lone rider as his youngest brother, he realized the intelligence bonanza just his very presence represented. The five company battalion had just crossed the mouth of Cedar Coulee and was descending Medicine Tail Coulee. They were about a mile and a quarter from a good crossing on the Little Big Horn River now known as Ford 'B;' it had been less than fifteen minutes since Martin had been dispatched. At this point in Medicine Tail, the forward field of vision was limited as if one wore blinders due to the bluffs that rise up on either side. The effect is such that although the Little Big Horn River can be seen in the distance, it appears as if you are seeing it through a card board tube; your distant peripheral vision is very limited. When Boston pulled up beside him, Custer was in the process of riding to the high ground on the northern bluffs, which is today known as Luce Ridge (now referred to as 'traditional' or East Ridge) to better enhance his view of the terrain ahead.

Keogh's two company command was taking the lead with the objective of advancing toward and securing Ford 'B.' That it was Keogh's battalion that was sent forward was verified by both DeRudio and McClernand after the battle. In fact, McClernand had observed a double set of fours, indicating that two companies had approached the ford area.[1] Battle scholars all agree that Custer had the right wing split into two battalions with Keogh in charge of one, and Yates the other. However, there exist much disagreement as to which companies were assigned to what battalion. Lieutenant Mathey mentioned to Walter Camp that Captain Moylan informed him Keogh was given command of three companies and Yates two.[2] However, Martin recalled that as he turned to the rear, with the order to Benteen, 'F' Company was at the head of the command, and "the gray horse company was in the center of the column."[3] Private Coleman recorded in his diary that 'B' Company was originally assigned to the right wing and was part of Keogh's Battalion. In addition, Sergeant James Hill's diary indicated 'C' was assigned to Keogh, and this was confirmed by Knipe who also stated 'C' "was in Keogh's squadron." Thus, declarations of Coleman, Hill, and Knipe led me to propose the division of the regiment as diagrammed in chapter four.[4] Keogh simply went into the

fight with one of his companies detached. Nor was there any overriding reason for Custer to change the wing or battalion assignments, which were made upon leaving Fort Lincoln. At the divide, he and Cooke had to decide how to split up the regiment to conform to the tactics to be employed. Thus, when these two officers went off by themselves for a few minutes to make the hurried division, they simply reverted back to the previous assignments. The left wing, as previously indicated, was to be utilized as two separate battalions. The right wing and its two battalions were going to march as before, except for one company. It was not a rare occurrence to have a company detached from a unit. It would have been highly unusual to remove a company from one battalion just to bring another up to its full compliment. It didn't happen in past campaigns or battles, and it did not happen at the Little Big Horn.[5]

There are a number of students who will take exception to this alignment. The division most frequently assumed to have been made is that Yates was assigned the two-company-battalion of 'F' and 'E,' while Keogh, as senior captain, took 'C', 'I', and 'L.' Charles DuBois took a middle ground and assigned two companies to both Keogh and Yates and split 'C' into platoons, thereby making each battalion of similar strength.[6] He does not explain why Custer would have wanted the two battalions to be equal. As a buttress to their alignment, these students most often cite the Cavalry Tactical Manual of 1874 which states companies are apportioned according to the company commander's seniority. This was true; but what they fail to take into account is all the seniority of army protocol had already been worked out at the beginning of the campaign, temporarily suspended on June 22, and restored a little after noon on June 25th. Cooke, as

---

[1] *Camp, DPL,* #97; *Camp, BYU,* roll 2, #546.

[2] *Camp, IU,* box 2, folder 11, 106.

[3] Graham, *Reno Court—Abstract,* 129.

[4] Liddic, *I Buried Custer,* 13; Richard Hardorff, "The Reno Scout," *Research Review,* Vol. 11, #12, December 1977, 3–12; Greene, *Evidence and the Custer Enigma,* 18; *Camp, IU,* box 2, *(continued)*

folder 8, 35; Camp, BYU, roll 5, box 6, folder 5. However, Captain Moylan stated that Keogh had three companies, including 'C,' and Yates two, see Graham, *Reno Court,* 183.

[5] For example, on the morning of first day's action at the Battle of Gettysburg, Davis' Brigade, Army of Northern Virginia, was ordered along with Archer's Brigade, to move against suspected Union positions to the west of the village. Brigadier General Joseph Davis' Mississippians advanced toward the Union troops with only three of the four regiments in his brigade. The 11th Mississippi had been detached as a guard for the division's wagon train. The division commander, Henry Heath, didn't take another regiment from his other brigades just to bring Davis up to full strength, even with action imminent. David G. Martin, *Gettysburg July 1st* (Conshohocken, PA: Combined Books, 1995), 60–61.

[6] Charles duBois, *The Custer Mystery* (El Segundo, CA: Upton & Sons, 1986), 103.

the regimental adjutant, would be responsible for keeping track of who was senior to whom and make the dispositions hence, and he did. Lastly, as senior battalion, Captain Keogh led his two-company battalion to the ford, as this was where Custer expected the first action would take place. It has been a maxim since the days of Napoleon, perhaps earlier, to grant this privilege to the most senior officer present.[7]

There are a number of battle students who have questioned how Boston, hired as a "guide," although he had limited experience in the west, was able to travel from the pack train, past Benteen's battalion, choose the trail his brother took, meet Martin and successfully join the main command in a journey of seven miles in about an hour and a half. The same journey would have taken Benteen, who had fifteen years of field experience, better than two hours to ride with two miles less in distance. Benteen became confused about which trail to follow, and without Half Yellow Face directing the troops towards the eastern bluffs, he might have crossed the river at Ford 'A'. Other students have also wondered how Mathey, McDougall, Edgerly, and then Benteen could have failed to use Boston as a messenger to appraise his brother about the situation on the back trail.[8] These officers should have surmised where he was headed; McDougall admitted as much to Camp.[9] Boston had followed the trail down Reno Creek until he came to the place where one set of tracks led towards the river, while the other, a heavier more distinct trail, diverted off to the north. It has been suggested Boston either was very lucky in his choice of trails, or he correctly guessed his brother would be with the larger command as indicated by the multiple tracks. His guess was validated about ten minutes later by meeting Martin on Sharpshooters' Ridge. Another possibility is he was pointed in that direction by the Indian scouts returning from the valley. However, there is no indication that these scouts had even seen Boston, let alone communicated with him. That the youngest Custer was able to join the main column, as rapidly as he did, probably indicates he had observed the dust from his brother's troops drifting over the heights. It also demonstrates just what could be accomplished, by experienced officers, who wanted to "come on" and "be quick."

With his brother beside him, Custer would have surely asked three important questions: 1) Did he see Benteen and/or the pack train? 2) Did he see any Indians on the back trail? 3) Did he see anything of the two messengers who had been dispatched? The answers Boston gave would have greatly reassured Custer and confirmed his next move. Boston told his older brother he had passed Benteen and his battalion about an hour and a half ago as he was leaving a watering place back on the main trail. Despite a lack of communication from Benteen, Custer was now assured the village he observed from Sharpshooters' Ridge was the main encampment, and there were no significant villages to the south. He could base his tactical dispositions of his own battalion on this current intelligence rather than on presumptions. This information would allow him the opportunity to formulate a more audacious plan. Custer did not have to relegate any of his wing for a reserve. In addition, by some extrapolations, Custer could determine about where Benteen and the pack train were on his back trail based on the time it took his inexperienced brother to reach the command. Custer also learned the pack train was undisturbed and as compact as could be expected and was within supporting distance of Benteen's battalion. Boston, by conveying this knowledge, had ratified that the dust Custer had seen from Sharpshooters' Ridge was from these units.

With Benteen coming on, the pack train together, and the fact his brother didn't see any hostile Indians, spoke volumes about the location of all the Indians . . . down in the valley, across on the west side of the Little Big Horn River, and apparently unaware of his presence only a mile and a quarter from the north end of the village. For once, the Indian teepees were fairly together and not strung out, to any great extent, along a river's banks. His idea of the village's location proved to be correct, and Custer led the regiment almost to the exact spot he would have preferred. It was 'Custer's Luck' indeed, to happen upon a standing village![10] Boston would also have informed his brother that he had spoken to Martin and that he had probably seen another lone soldier, off to the right, heading in the direction of the pack train. With no Indians on the back trail, Custer could now reasonably conclude that both his messengers had gotten through, and that his orders would be executed. Benteen's three companies would be coming over the bluffs or down the coulee in about thirty minutes. Benteen's anticipated arrival would of course depend on if he was coming with, or without the pack train. Custer could never really be sure what Benteen would do;

---

[7]Letter, Robert Doran to Bruce R. Liddic, January 12, 2002.
[8]Sklenar, *To Hell with Honor*, 226.
[9]Hammer, *Custer in '76*, 69.

[10]It has been speculated that had Custer known the village was intact and standing rather than fleeing, he might not have committed Reno when he did, and Custer might have crossed the river behind Reno instead of turning to the right. By following after Reno, a combined headlong charge could have been made with possibly different results.

if he was with the pack train, it would probably add an hour to the estimate.

One must wonder at this point if Custer had given much thought, when he directed Martin to Benteen, as to how far the pack train would have to travel and how long it would take to "come on" and "be quick," even when Benteen's command was figured into the equation.[11] Consequently, Benteen's statement upon receipt of the message that it was impossible for Custer to expect him to hurry if he had to wait for the pack train and move forward as a combined unit, had merit. Unless Custer was using reverse psychology, about the only way Benteen could possibly "be quick" would be to disobey his commander's preemptory order and ride forward without the pack train. We have no idea if Custer would have computed two different arrival times for Benteen or had even considered the mutually exclusive wording of his order. In all likelihood, Custer expected to chase after the non combatants, wanted the regiment concentrated as soon as possible, and Benteen's troops, with or without the pack train, could be employed as a reserve force to occupy and/or destroy the village. This would free Custer to commit his entire five companies to the enterprise. There are some students who believe Custer delayed his engagement and waited for Benteen to "come on." They cite evidence that Custer waited in Medicine Tail for 45 minutes for the other units to join him.[12] Therefore, they reasoned it was only after Benteen failed to arrive that Custer gave up any thought of attacking the village, at least for the present, and decided on a holding action, leading part of his command up the slopes of traditional Luce Ridge.[13]

Varnum and Edgerly were asked by Colonel Graham about Custer lingering in the coulee for Benteen, and the former said it was improbable, while the latter said Custer couldn't sit still for five minutes under the circumstances, let alone three quarters of an hour.[14] As to Custer going to Luce Ridge, I do not contradict these students that he went there, but it had nothing to do with waiting for reinforcements. Reinforcements, for what purpose? His command had yet to fire a shot, and from the army's past experience, a big village would run as quickly as a small village. Custer now knew the positions of his other units were confirmed, and he started for the low ridges to the northeast that rise above the coulee. These ridges offer a good overall view of the area about Ford 'B.' But, higher above these ridges is a rather steep promontory, traditionally know as Luce Ridge. Custer could have gotten a good view of the ford from the lower ridges but if he wanted to see further up the valley beyond the ford he would have had to climb to the top of Luce Ridge. Custer would climb to the top of this ridge for just this purpose. However, from these lower ridges, Custer saw "a beehive of activity" about a mile ahead on the eastern side of the river in the area of Ford 'B'.[15]

In reaction to Reno's attack, the old men, women, and children from the other camp circles fled in the direction of the Cheyenne camp circle, as it was the nearest and fastest escape route. Soldier Wolf, a Cheyenne warrior, said as the firing from Reno's action became heavier and heavier most of the women and children from the lower camps were moving towards their circle. It was from here that a number of them decided to cross the river to the eastside "and so to get farther away from the fight."[16] Black Elk, later an Ogallala Holy Man, told, "By now women and children were running in a crowd downstream. I looked back and saw them all running and scattering up a hillside down yonder."[17] Gall distinctly recalled the Uncpapa women and children were told to move "down stream where the Cheyennes were camped." He further stated others were " sent scurrying off across the bottom toward the Big Horn" river to the north.[18] Iron Hawk, an Uncpapa, remembered seeing all the women and children running down the valley.[19] Crow King said the only reason why the warriors met Reno was to "give the women and children time to go to a place of safety." Furthermore, they were in the process of retreating when Reno moved into the timber.[20] This is another indication that Custer's presence in Medicine Tail was a surprise to most of the Indians, although some saw the troops on the bluffs. The Indians would never have sent their loved ones into the path of a column of soldiers. Nor would these non-combatants have voluntarily crossed the Little Big Horn had they known of this fact or been warned not to go in that direction. Thomas Disputed, an Ogallala, remembered he

[11]William Hedley, "ps Bring Pacs:" The Order That Trapped the Custer Battalion," *4th Annual Symposium Custer Battlefield Historical & Museum Assn,* June 1990, 48–68.

[12]Graham, *The Custer Myth,* 322.

[13]Hedley, "ps Bring Pacs:" The Order That Trapped the Custer Battalion," 52–55.　　[14]Graham, *The Custer Myth,* 323.

[15]Bob Reece, "1997 CBH&MA Symposium Panel Discussion: The Valley Fight," *11th Annual Symposium Custer Battlefield Historical & Museum Association,* June 1997, 61.

[16]Hardorff, *Cheyenne Memories,* 43.

[17]John G. Neihardt, *Black Elk Speaks* (Lincoln, NE: University of Nebraska Press, 1961) 110.

[18]Graham, *The Custer Myth,* 88; DeLand, "The Sioux Wars," 716.

[19]Neihardt, *Black Elk Speaks,* 122.

[20]Judson Walker, *Campaigns of General Custer in the North-West and the Final Surrender of Sitting Bull* (NY, NY: Arno Press, 1966), 102.

had crossed at Ford 'B' to get behind Reno's soldiers and saw the white men coming down Medicine Tail. He quickly "rode back the way I came" and warned the Indians "that more soldiers were coming."[21] In addition, there were a few horse herds in the area, and some of the warriors and young boys were trying to round them up. There were also a number of mounted warriors who were moving across the ford to try and get around behind Reno. But the non-combatants were of greater interest to Custer. It must be remembered that the mission of the 1876 campaign was to force the hostile Indians back onto the reservations. The army knew and so planned that the most effective way to accomplish this mission was not by fighting the Indians in a pitched battle but by capturing the non-combatants and holding them hostage, followed by and combined with destroying their teepees and property. If he could throw the Indians into a panic and capture the majority of them, he could occupy and destroy the village at his leisure, and the warriors would have no choice but to report to the reservations.

The view presented from the ridges below Luce Ridge confirmed to Custer that the village ended a short distance north of Ford 'B,' and from the activity observed down Medicine Tail Coulee, along with the dust to the north, it appeared that the village was indeed beginning to disperse. So far, Custer's tactics were all he could have hoped. By his movement to the lower end of the village, Reno had drawn the warriors' attention, giving their families time to flee. Custer now had the upper end of the village in sight, undetected by most of the Indians, and he was seeing confusion all around Ford 'B.' It had all the earmarks of a classic double envelopment, and Keogh was already heading to Ford 'B' to begin the action. All Custer had to do now was to gather the threads into his hand and victory would be his reward.

There are a number of battle scholars who believe the village didn't end at Medicine Tail Coulee, but stretched for a number of miles along the Little Big Horn. Although the village consisted of several Sioux tribes arranged in camp circles plus a Northern Cheyenne circle, most everyone agrees the village was defined at the southern end by the Uncpapa circle. This circle began on the north side of what is called the Garryowen Loop of the Little Big Horn River (near Shoulder Blade Creek) which Reno struck. Interestingly, Second Lieutenant Oscar Long, 5th Infantry, in a 1878 interview with a number of former hostile Indians, was told, there was a " small band of disaffected Indians from the Spotted Tail agency" who were

camped on the east bank of the Little Big Horn River a little to the south of the Uncpapa circle.[22] This small group had about twenty warriors and had pitched their teepees north of the Weir Point area. The Cheyenne circle was located at the northern end of the village. There are, however, some accounts that state a few Cheyennes were camped across from Deep Coulee. What has been and is vigorously debated is the length and breath that separated these two distinct circles. This debate tends to follow along the lines of how one evaluates the village's population. Most accounts by the white men portray a village the size of a small city. For example, Dr. Holmes Paulding, a doctor with Gibbon's column, declared the village was eight miles in length by two to three miles in width. In these dimensions, he was somewhat supported by Private Jacob Adams, 'H' Company, who said it was five miles long.[23] Trumpeter Ami Mulford declared it was about four miles long and three quarters of a mile wide. 2nd Lieutenant Hugh Scott, who joined the regiment after the battle, spoke about a village that was four to five miles in length.[24] Reno, who wrote to the New York *Herald*, less than two months after the battle, said the village was three and a half miles long. Benteen told the Reno Court of Inquiry that the Indian camp was between three and four miles in length. This distance was supported by 1st Lt. William English, a member of Gibbon's column, who recorded in his diary that the village was three miles long by three quarters of a mile wide.[25] Likewise, 2nd Lt. Alfred Johnson, of the 7th Infantry, said that the village was four miles long by three quarters of a mile wide.[26] 2nd Lieutenant Charles Roe, 2nd Cavalry, wrote in 1910: "By actual measurement from the circle on one side to the far side of the rectangle on the other side was three miles."[27]

There are a few Indian accounts that agree with the white man's extended village size. Mrs. Spotted Horn told a reporter of the St. Paul *Pioneer Press* that it was a veritable town of teepees which stretched for nearly five miles along the river.[28] Likewise, Fool's Crow said the village was

[21]Liddic, *Camp on Custer*, 122.

[22]James Brust, "Lt. Oscar Long's Early Map Details Terrain, Battle Positions," *Greasy Grass*, Vol. 11, May 1995, 6.

[23]Thomas R. Buecker, "A Surgeon at the Little Big Horn: The Letters of Dr. Holmes O. Paulding," *Montana Magazine of Western History*, Vol. 32, #4, Autumn 1982, 34–49; Horace Ellis, "A Survivor's Story of the Custer Massacre," *Big Horn Yellowstone Journal*, Vol. 2, #2, Spring 1993, 5–11.

[24]Graham, *The Custer Myth*, 379; Tim McCoy, *Tim McCoy Remembers the West* (NY, NY: Doubleday & Company, 1977), 145.

[25]Graham, *The Custer Myth*, 226; *Camp, DPL*, #2.

[26]*Pioneer Press* and *Tribune* (St. Paul, MN), July 22, 1876.

[27]John M. Carroll, *The Two Battles of the Little Big Horn* (NY, NY: Liveright, 1974), 205.   [28]Graham, *The Custer Myth*, 83.

over three miles long.[29] This extended distance was corroborated by both Crow King and Iron Thunder.[30] Hair, an Ogallala warrior, said the village occupied four miles along both sides of the Little Big Horn.[31] However, most Indian accounts do not support these inflated distances between the Uncpapa and the Cheyenne circles. In fact, Major James Walsh of Canada's Northwest Mounted Police remarked from his years of experience that one "cannot certainly depend on any Indian's statement in regard to time or numbers."[32] Respects Nothing, an Ogallala warrior, said the entire camp was situated on a piece of ground a mile square in size.[33] Flying Hawk, another Ogallala, confirmed Respects Nothing's village size and stated that at the furthest points it was equivalent to about one and a half miles. When Flying Hawk told his story to Eli Ricker in 1907, Ricker wanted to check to see if this Indian knew what a mile represented. After several demonstrations, Ricker recorded in his notes "he understands it well."[34] He then sagaciously remarked, however, that had the camp circles been arranged in a strict fashion one after the other, then the village would have stretched for about three and a half miles, but they were not.[35] 2nd Lt. Long was told, two years later, by a number of Indian participants that the village was only 1.32 miles in length, which is very close to Respect Nothing's estimate.[36] Hump recalled the village was not strung out, but was compact, saying the lodges were close together from one camp circle to the next.[37]

Since it is the extent of the Cheyenne circle that is in question, one would expect that the members of this tribe knew where they had camped. As usual, the Cheyenne camp circle was pitched in the form of a crescent moon, opening toward the east.[38] Big Beaver, a Cheyenne warrior, was asked by Dr. Thomas Marquis to show him where his people's circle was on June 25th, and he was led to the mouth of Medicine Tail Coulee. This was confirmed by another warrior, Brave Bear, who anticipated that the soldiers who came down Medicine Tail would cross into the middle of the Cheyenne camp.[39] Two Moons, a

Cheyenne chief, said the teepees followed along the banks of the Little Big Horn, with their camp across from Medicine Tail Coulee.[40] Flying By, a Minneconjou, said his camp was next to the mouth of Medicine Tail.[41] It should be noted Ford 'B' is also known as the Minneconjou Ford. But, with the mouth of this coulee nearly a half mile wide, there would have been more than enough room to accommodate this tribe's circle and still leave room for the Cheyenne lodges. Joseph White Crow Bull might have cleared up the confusing statements by Flying By when White Crow Bull recalled that the Minneconjou and the Sans Arc camp, which are usually placed between the Cheyennes and the Minnieconjous, weren't exactly at the ford, but rather back from it, farther to the west.[42] If this is accurate, then it would explain why all three tribes claimed this area as their own.[43]

There are a number of white accounts that agree with those accounts of Indians who claimed the village extended northward, only to the mouth of Medicine Tail Coulee. Based on his interviews conducted with Cheyenne veterans of the fight, Dr. Marquis, using the Garryowen railroad station as a base line for the southern limit of the village, placed the northern limit or the Cheyenne Circle commencing about the mouth of Medicine Tail Coulee.[44] Being an experienced frontiersman, Fred Girard told the Reno Court of Inquiry that the village was no more than two miles in length from where Major Reno first struck it. Likewise, McDougall told the Court that the village was 2 miles long and very broad.[45] Charles Erlanson, a local rancher since 1911, reported that a number of old Indians showed him both the upper and lower limits of the village, and said that it ended at "a point opposite the mouth of Medicine Tail Creek, less than two miles" in length.[46] Philetus Norris, an early visitor to the battlefield, placed the Cheyennes at Ford 'B.'[47] Private

---

[29]Mails, *Fools Crow*, 161.   [30]Graham, *The Custer Myth*, 77, 79.

[31]Jeff Broome, "Story of the Treacherous Attack," *Little Big Horn Associates Newsletter*, Vol.27, #4, May 1998, 5.

[32]Graham, *The Custer Myth*, 72.

[33]John M. Carroll, *Who Was This Man Ricker And What Are His Tablets That Everyone Is Talking About?* (Bryan, TX: Privately Printed, 1979), 62. Hereinafter cited: *Who Was This . . .*

[34]Ibid, 35.   [35]Ibid.

[36]Brust, "Lt. Oscar Longs' Early Map Details Terrain, Battle Positions," 7.   [37]Upton, *The Custer Adventure*, 83.

[38]Powell, *Sweet Medicine*, 110.

[39]Charles Rankin, *Legacy, New Perspectives on the Battle of the Little Bighorn* (Helena, MT: Montana Historical Press, 1996) 148. Herein after cited: *Legacy*.

[40]Hardorff, *Lakota Recollections*, 134.

[41]*Camp, IU*, box 5, folder 1.

[42]David Miller, "Echoes Of The Little Bighorn," *American Hertiage*, Vol. 22, #4, June 1971, 32–34. There are a number of Little Big Horn students who are suspicious of Miller's writings as historical evidence. However, I don't believe one should overlook references to this battle based upon the fact that some in the scholarly community question their work. I will let the readers decide whether they attach any creditability or not to Miller's research.

[43]Another reported arrangement of the camp circles has the Brules and Ogallalas camped southwest of the Minneconjous at Ford 'B' and north of the Ogallalas were the Cheyennes.

[44]Billing *Gazette* (Billings, MT), July 17, 1932; August 13, 1933.

[45]Graham, *Reno Court*, 379.

[46]Charles B. Erlanson, "Facts About The Custer Battle," *Little Big Horn Associates Newsletter*, Vol. 2, #2, February 1968, 3.

[47]P. W. Norris, *The Calumet Of The Coteau And Other Poetical Legends Of The Border* (Philadelphia, PA: NP, 1884), 37.

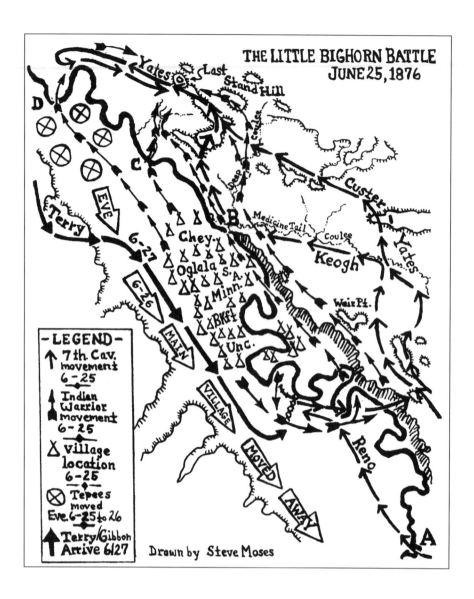

THE LITTLE BIGHORN BATTLE
JUNE 25, 1876

- LEGEND -
↑ 7th. Cav. movement 6-25
▲ Indian Warrior movement 6-25
△ Village location 6-25
⊗ Tepees moved Eve. 6-25 to 26
▲ Terry/Gibbon Arrive 6/27

Drawn by Steve Moses

Thompson, during his adventures on the battlefield, said he had been hiding with Watson in the Medicine Tail ford area, which was opposite the end of the village.[48]

The village was fluid, and this is perhaps a reason why we can have honest men, both red and white, who saw the same Indian camp yet differ on its dimensions. It was evolving even during the time when the battle was being fought. On the afternoon of the 24th, the women were preparing to move the camp the next day to the north and across the Big Horn River.[49] This movement was partially undertaken in the early evening of the 25th, and according to Kill Assiniboine's wife, Hattie Lawrence, many went north, to a point across from Custer Hill, and remained on the west side of the Little Big Horn.[50] After

the Custer phase of the battle, this move was needed, as Doctors Fox and Marquis wrote, to move away from the death lodges, the smell from the white corpses, and to better improve grazing for the animals.[51] Thus, there were really two village sites on June 25th; the complete one which Custer saw from Sharpshooters' Ridge and later from Luce Ridge, and the camps which were moved north about two miles following his defeat. This move would have placed the northern limit of the encampment about opposite last stand hill on the battlefield. For, if we follow the logic by some students of a continuous gargantuan village, ranging anywhere from four to eight miles, as has been indicated by some of the participants, the vil-

[48]Ramkin, *Legacy*, 149.   [49]Dixon, *The Vanishing Race*, 170.
[50]*Camp, IU*, box 5, folder 1, #347.

[51]Richard A. Fox, *Archaeology, History, and Custer's Last Battle* (Norman, OK: University of OK Press, 1993), 372; Marquis, *Keep The Last Bullet For Yourself*, 82.

lage by the shortest measurement would have extended beyond the current highway 212 and by the longest distance reached through the town of Crow Agency. The latter being the case, General Terry's command would have spent the early evening of June 26th socializing with the Sioux and Cheyenne instead of searching for them.

If one reads Lieutenant Edgerly's testimony at the Reno Court very carefully, he stated this very fact. When asked where the bulk of the village was located in relation to Reno's position on the hill, the lieutenant said that it was "Close to the bank of the steam beyond the timber, near where we first saw Major Reno." He was then asked where the bulk of the village was in "reference to ford B?" Edgerly replied: "At first it was higher up the steam, after that it was moved out to the left and down stream."[52] Captain Henry Freeman, of Gibbon's column, arrived on the scene on the 27th and contemporarily recorded in his journal, "On the evening of the 25, the Indians moved the upper part of the village down about two miles and settled down again."[53] Consequently, when the village area was inspected on the 27th by Terry, Gibbon, and Reno, it was perceived to be one camp, protracting from the Garryowen Loop to opposite the current visitor's center, which it was not.

Thus, from the lower slopes of Luce Ridge, Custer saw the northern end of the village, the Cheyenne camp, which was about a mile and a half from the Uncpapa circle, which he had observed near Reno Hill. There is no need to multiply the miles the village occupied along the Little Big Horn any more than one needs to inflate the village's population as a reason for Custer's defeat. The Indians didn't gain this victory with astronomical numbers, swarming from a village rivaling the size of Brooklyn. Because of this, some students believed Custer "attacked a village he could have defeated."[54] Other students are of the opinion Custer's troops had no more hope of successfully attacking this village than did Reno. There were simply too many Indians for the four separate units to overcome. Custer had misread the signs; true, the non-combatants were running, as he perceived and as planned in the campaign, but the warriors were to fight aggressively to save their families. Furthermore, they believed their medicine was strong and were prepared to deliver a crushing blow to these white men. For in less than two hours, the main assault column would be disastrously defeated, and its commander would be dead.

From the lower slopes of Luce Ridge, Custer saw Keogh's battalion advance to the ford and also saw another lone rider coming into Medicine Tail Coulee from the direction of a high peak to the southwest. The rider was Mitch Bouyer, and the intelligence he would bring would not be welcome news for Custer. From Weir Point, Bouyer and the Crow scouts had seen Reno's command abruptly leave the timber in full retreat, and knowing that Custer might be under the impression that Reno was still engaged and would have planned accordingly, they cut diagonally down from the peaks to intercept Custer.[55] The information that Reno had retreated and was heading due south, in the direction of the same ford he had crossed earlier, might change Custer's tactics. Curley told Walter Camp in 1910 that Bouyer informed Custer that Reno had been defeated, and they had a long conversation.[56] Camp learned from Curley that Custer told Bouyer about "seeking a high point to await the arrival of the other troops."[57] But Bouyer reportedly told Curley he didn't think the other troops would join Custer, as they would be frightened, just like Reno had been. Dr. Kuhlman interpreted Curley's story (Curley did not speak English) to mean that Custer was waiting in Medicine Tail for Benteen. He also relied upon this statement to a large extent in his reconstruction of the Custer fight.

Upon learning of Reno's unplanned retreat, I believe it would have been a more logical move for Custer to ride all the way to the top of Luce Ridge, to again reassess the situation. From the apex of this ridge line, Custer had an excellence vantage point of not only the entire ford area, but also of most of the geography to the north. In addition, he could also have scanned the area to the southeast to detect any signs of Benteen or the pack train. From Sharpshooters' Ridge, Custer might have noticed dust clouds to the northwest, but nothing could be clearly distinguished. He would have wanted to know, was it, in fact, the other non-combatants who had chosen this direction rather than crossing at Ford 'B?' Or, was it the population returning to the village in the wake of Reno's retreat? So, he climbed up the steep slopes of Luce Ridge, and upon reaching the ridge, he saw Keogh near the ford. By his very presence, Keogh was clearing out the non-combatants and was forcing them back across the river and was beginning to deploy his battalion about the Ford 'B' area. Two Moons recalled there were more than a few warriors who had crossed at Ford 'B' to attack Reno from

[52]Graham, *Reno Court*, 402.

[53]George A. Schneider, *The Freeman Journal* (San Rafael, CA: Presidio Press, 1977), 64.

[54]Gregory F. Michno, *Lakota Noon* (Missoula, MT: Mountain Press Publishing Company, 1997), 20.

[55]Graham, *The Custer Myth*, 14.

[56]Hammer, *Custer in '76*, 166.

[57]Kuhlman, *Legend into History*, 160.

the rear, but when Custer arrived in Medicine Tail these Indians quickly rode off to the north to hide in the ravines. These soldiers had caught them by surprise.[58] Reno's scattered gunfire to the south was still audible to Custer. However, to the north, in response to Reno's earlier action combined with the pressure Keogh's battalion was exerting, the true source of the dust clouds was revealed. It was a mass of old men, women, and children fleeing the village. Some were moving to the north and the Big Horn River, others were escaping to the west, and a number of them were apparently collecting in a series of bluffs and a stream we now call Squaw Creek.[59] This movement to the north and west, with its tell tale dust, was again confirmed by a number of Indians, among them Respect Nothing who said that "The Indians left their lodges standing. The women fled down the river. . . . The women did not run back to the hills."[60] Four Women said there were about three hundred Indians in her group who were trying to reach safety.[61] But not all the Indians were abandoning their teepees; some were trying to save their possessions. From the top of the high bluffs below where Reno would retreat, the Arikara, Soldier, "saw many Dakota tents go down."[62] This action by the Sioux to break up their camp was also confirmed by Two Strikes who sent Red Bear back to the other scouts with a message to hurry along as he "could see the Dakota tents going down" and feared the Sioux might try and chase after their stolen horses.[63] First Lieutenant Godfrey also wrote about the teepees being dismantled and stated that "the chiefs gave orders for the village to move to break up; at the time of Reno's retreat, this order was being carried out."[64]

There is little doubt that Custer, observing the confusion that by now had permeated the camp circles, was positive the village was breaking up. It was noted its inhabitants were moving away from his command, some of the teepees being struck, travois being hastily loaded, and the fleeing women and children escaping to the north. The Sioux, themselves, were convinced that after "Seeing the Indian women and children fleeing toward the lower end of the village, Custer and his men clearly believed that the hostiles were all on the run."[65] The Lt. Colonel needed to do something and do it now if he was going to inter-

cept this movement. With the information his brother brought him, Custer could now afford to play a bolder hand than before was possible. With definite knowledge of the conditions on his back trail, he could commit the entire battalion to the pursuit of the non-combatants, as Benteen's support would be coming within an hour. After Benteen's arrival, Custer could then order him take control of the village or take charge of the prisoners or confront any lingering warriors so the main column could round up any remaining escapees. The abandoned village could be dealt with at their leisure. It was evident that Keogh's advance had effectively pushed the non-combatants as well as a few warriors out and away from the ford area.[66] In addition, the position taken by this battalion had also blocked any further escape route from Ford 'B.' This was obvious from the magnified movement across the river to the north and west. With his belief that the rest of the command was coming on, Custer decided to commit Yates' Battalion to the pursuit, to be joined by Keogh's Battalion. He no longer considered the village a target; his strategy had changed because of the information Boston Custer conveyed, and by his observations from Sharpshooters' Hill, confirmed from Luce Ridge. He signaled Yates' Battalion to the right, up the slopes of Luce Ridge, and to the north. Custer also needed to provide for an orderly withdrawal of Keogh from the ford, even though there only appeared to be light resistance. He also directed Yates to send a company to the first ridge line overlooking the ford to insure their quick and safe extraction and to provide supporting fire while doing so. Yates, following seniority so dear to the army, ordered First Lt. Algernon Smith, the acting regimental quartermaster and normally assigned to 'A' but now commanding Company 'E,' forward. It is apparent that 'E' rode toward the river from the Indian's attestations. They seemed to remember this company as distinct from the others because they were the only soldiers who rode all gray horses, thereby making their movements on the battlefield easy to recall. White Shield, a Cheyenne, said he could see one company a long way off because their "horses were pretty white. . . . When the Gray Horse Company got pretty close to the river, they dismounted."[67] Frank Bethune, a brother-in-law of the scout Goes Ahead, said he was told much the same thing from the Indians, the Gray Horse Troop was close to the mouth of Medicine Tail Coulee.[68] Other Cheyennes

[58]*Camp, BYU*, box 6, folder 9.

[59]Peter Panzeri, *Little Big Horn 1876* (London, England: Osprey Military, 1995), 71. [60]Hardorff, *Lakota Recollections*, 26.

[61]*Camp, BYU*, box 3, folder 3.

[62]Libby, *The Arikara Narrative*, 117. [63]Ibid, 132.

[64]Graham, *The Custer Myth*, 141.

[65]Richard Hardorff, *Lakota Recollections of the Custer Fight* (Spokane, WA: Arthur H. Clark Company, 1991), 269

[66]Liddic, *Camp on Custer*, 122.

[67]Hardorff, *Cheyenne Memories*, 51–52.

[68]DeLand, *The Sioux Wars*, 447.

spoke about how the gray horse soldiers came near the ford and all dismounted to fire.[69] As 'E' neared the ridge line to the north above where the present day battlefield road crosses Medicine Tail, they saw about twenty 'C' troopers engaged in light skirmish fire which prevented the Indians from crossing to the east side.[70] With 'E's arrival, Company 'C's second platoon mounted and rejoined their fellow soldiers who were now moving back from the ford. Evidence of a cover fire by one company, to mask the withdrawal of another at Ford 'B,' was related to 2nd Lieutenant Long when his Indian interviewees related how "One company started to run when Custer was near the river and the rest fired on them and made them come back."[71] The Indians could not relate to this tactic and misunderstood the maneuver, thinking that Custer shot at his own men.

That Custer probably no longer viewed the village and its warriors as his strategic objective, but instead shifted to the non-combatants is confirmed from a number of Indian accounts. Iron Thunder said that while they were driving Reno away from the village, a report reached them that " they (Custer's soldiers) were coming to head off the women and children from the way they were going, so we turned around and went towards them."[72] Flying Hawk said much the same thing, the warriors being told that Custer was moving to head off the women and children. Red Horse, a Minneconjou, recalled when Reno attacked, the women and children were told to mount their horses and ride to safety. He said they then "fled immediately down the Greasy Grass Creek (Little Big Horn) a little way and crossed over."[73] Soon after Reno retreated, Red Horse and his companions on the bluffs "saw the women and children were in danger of being taken prisoners by another party of troops (Custer) and the warriors quickly turned away from Reno to try and save them.[74] The great Ogallala Crazy Horse summed up what he thought Custer was attempting to accomplish:

When Custer made his charge the women, papooses, children, and in fact all that were not fighters made a stampede in a northerly direction. Custer, seeing so numerous a body, mistook them for the main body of Indians retreating and abandoning their village, and immediately gave pursuit.[75]

Doan Robinson, the long time Secretary of the South Dakota Historical Society and a scholar of the Custer Battle, spoke with a number of Indians who were present. He also came to the conclusion that Custer directed his troops to the north because he mistook the warriors for the non-combatants who were also going in that direction.[76] One might question if Custer didn't know the difference between the warriors and the women and children. However, it would be natural the fighting men would soon follow to join and defend their families. But I believe it was another Ogallala, Charlie Corn, who concisely explained in a letter and with great sagacity what the warriors had experienced that afternoon. He wrote: "You tried to get our children and wives so I was willing to die fighting for them that day."[77] Iron Hawk had similar thoughts as he rode forward to confront the soldiers. He saw an old man and called out to him, "Boys, take courage! Would you see these little children taken away from me like dogs?"[78]

Earlier, Keogh had received his orders to take the lead and proceed to the river and secure the crossing in preparation for an attack by the rest of the wing. Keogh could see the Indians milling about on the east side of the river, and when the Indians detected their presence, the resulting confusion. It was like a covey of quails had been flushed; the Indians began scattering in all directions except toward his companies. The geography around Ford 'B' has changed little since the battle was fought. About a quarter of a mile from the water's edge, the coulee slopes gradually downward, and it narrows considerably. As one nears the ford one finds to the right a high cutbank that stretches northward along the river; to the left a very steep ridge line commences to rise, cresting about two miles to the south at Weir Point. Behind, as one faces the ford, are two major coulees. One is Medicine Tail, already mentioned, to the left, and the other is Deep Coulee situated to the right. These two major drainage areas form a 'V,' with its apex resting on Blummer-(Nye) Cartwright ridge line.

It was after four o'clock when Keogh's battalion began moving down Medicine Tail Coulee, and it's alleged that here occurred a fantastic incident involving a trooper from his company. Like the other soldiers we have mentioned (Knipe, Goldin, Martin, and Thompson), there was supposedly another who rode north with Custer and lived to tell the tale. Private Gustave Korn, a blacksmith, would have the distinction of being the last white man to see Custer and escape death. According to Korn, he

[69]Grinnell, *The Fighting Cheyennes*, 338.
[70]Refer to Greene, *Evidence and the Custer Enigma*, 21, for a listing of the artifacts found in the area.
[71]Brust, "Lt. Oscar Long's Early Map Details Terrain, Battle Positions," 8. [72]Upton, *The Custer Adventure*, 83.
[73]Graham, *The Custer Myth*, 59–60. [74]Ibid, 60–61.
[75]Ibid, 63.

[76]Rankin, *Legacy*, 156.
[77]*Camp, CBNM*, A 312, folder 8, # 11404.
[78]Niehardt, *Black Elk Speaks*, 122.

was one of the advance guard from his company as they rode down the Coulee.[79] He was having problems with his equipment as he couldn't keep his saddle from slipping forward. Korn asked Captain Keogh's permission to halt and adjust his saddle.[80]

After the girth was tightened, the horse became unmanageable, and the animal started on a full run past the battalion and continued on right to the river. The horse didn't stop there, but continued on "going like a train of cars on a down grade." Korn went through the Indians who were shooting at him from all sides and ran into Major Reno's troops on the hilltop. "The horse stopped about three rods from where Major Reno was with 5 bullets in him. Korn escaped without a scratch."[81] He was questioned on Reno Hill about how he had come to leave his company, and Korn said his horse ran away with him. It was reported that his case was investigated, and the private was exonerated afterwards.[82] Korn was considered to be one of the bravest men in the regiment, and his fellow troopers said he was no coward; most of them believed his account of what happened to him in Medicine Tail Coulee.[83] However, many battle students question if Korn's exploits, as he described them, could have occurred. There is no doubt that he was with 'I' Company when it descended into Medicine Tail and through a set of circumstances, believable or not, arrived on Reno Hill to become the last soldier who rode into Medicine Tail Coulee and survived.

As noted, when Keogh approached about three hundred yards from Ford 'B,' he detached a platoon to the heights on his right over-looking the river's crossing, a little below where the Butler marker now stands. This platoon was probably from 'C' and was under the leadership of 1st Sergeant Edwin Bobo. Tom Custer was with his bother, so the actual command of his company would have fallen on 2nd Lt. Henry Harrington, with Bobo as his right hand. Standing Bear, a Minneconjou, said that "The first fighting of all the fighting was down on the river's bottom" and the soldiers were on "the ridge across from the creek—second ridge from the river."[84] These soldiers began to exchange shots with the Indians to clear the area around the mouth of the coulee. That all the warriors didn't flee is evident from the Indians who said some of the men who were still in the camp saw the soldiers and crossed over the ford to meet them and returned their fire. White Shield, an older Cheyenne, reportedly told these young warriors that "No one must charge on the soldiers now; they are too many." So the Indians gradually circled away from the ford.[85] These warriors wanted to prevent any soldiers from crossing to the west bank so as to protect the women and children who were fleeing from the ford and for the others who were hiding in Squaw Creek.[86] With a covering fire established, Keogh motioned for his forward vedettes to continue, and they went right to the river's edge and started across to the western bank in preparation for the arrival of Yates' battalion. 2nd Lt. Roe later wrote that a non-commissioned officer rode into the river even before the Indians had opened fire to check on how suitable the ford was.[87] It was from here, that the opening phase occurred, of what is popularly known as "Custer's Last Stand."

More gunfire was exchanged at Ford 'B' from Keogh's forward vedettes as they pushed against the warriors who had previously crossed the river and from those who had retreated back across in response to the battalion's movement. These troopers rode into the water and reached the other side to secure the western bank in anticipation of the battalion's crossing. The supporting fire from the platoon to their east prevented any of the warriors who had fled to the right and left from flanking the vedettes. There are reports of several troopers killed while trying to cross the river.[88] The Ogallala, White Cow Bull, was more specfic. This warrior said Bobtail Horse killed one soldier who fell into the water, and then he (White Cow Bull) aimed his rifle at another and "fired. I saw him fall out of my saddle and hit the water."[89] Sergeant Ryan told the Hardin *Tribune* that several bodies were found at the ford on the 27th.[90] The body of Sergeant James Bustard of 'I' and his horse were identified across the river. Sergeant Knipe told Camp that he was found "lying across the ford in the Indian village."[91] However, others claim Bustard's body was found with the rest of his company below Calhoun Hill.[92] Trumpeter William Hardy, Company 'A,' recalled Bustard's horse "was found dead on the village side of the river down near the ford."[93] He didn't say if his body was found there as well. In addition, Curley said he saw a trooper from Company 'E' whose horse had

[79]*Camp, IU*, box 2, folder 11.   [80]*Camp, DPL*, #26.

[81]National Tribune (Washington, DC) January 15, 1891; *Camp, BYU*, box 6, folder 10.   [82]*Camp, BYU*, box 1, folder 17.

[83]National Tribune (Washington, DC), January 15, 1891; *Camp, BYU*, box 1, folder 17.   [84]Carroll, *Who Was This . . .* , 38.

[85]Grinnell, *The Fighting Cheyennes*, 350.

[86]Carroll, *Who Was This . . .* , 35–39.

[87]Charles F. Roe, *Custer's Last Battle* (Old Islip, NY: National Highway Association, 1927), 10.

[88]Linderman, *Pretty Shield*, 236; Grinnell, *The Fighting Cheyennes*, 350.

[89]Miller, "Echoes of the Little Big Horn," 33.

[90]Hardin *Tribune* (Hardin, MT), June 22, 1923.

[91]*Camp, BYU*, box 1, folder 3.   [92]Hammer, *Custer in '76*, 58.

[93]*Camp, IU*, box 2, folder 11.

[94]*Army & Navy Journal* (Washington, DC), March 25,1882.

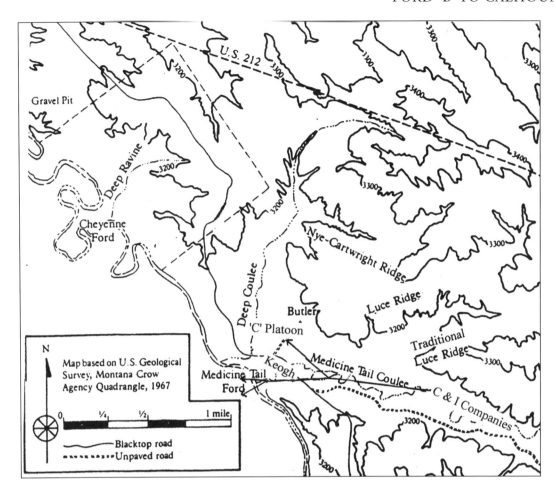

bolted across the river.[94] White Shield also said the soldiers who rode gray horses (Company 'E') were there, but they had halted well before the river.[95] Dr. Paulding and John Finerty, a newspaper reporter with the Crook column, tell a similar story of fighting at the ford, some of his men crossing over but being quickly forced to pull back while losing several men in the river.[96] Girard testified at the Reno Court that when he went over the Custer field on the 28th, he discovered near Ford 'B' signs that Custer tried to cross. He also said he saw the bodies of two white men as well as several dead cavalry horses in the village.[97] He Dog, an Ogalalla, remembered there was no general fighting down near the river. There were "fifteen or twenty Sioux on the east side of the river and some soldiers replied but not much shooting there."[98] Good Voice Elk, an Uncpapa, said Custer got close to the river and fired shots into the teepees, but they were driven off.[99]

Dr. Eastman was also told by the warriors that Custer's soldiers were upon the river's bank, but they discovered it wasn't possible to cross, and they began shooting into the camp. In addition, some of the men had dismounted and were examining the banks very carefully.[100] But suddenly the soldiers were pulling back from the ford, back towards where the others were on the ridge overlooking the ford.

That any company was ever at the ford or exchanged gunfire with the Indians, or crossed to the western side is another contentious point in trying to dertermine the sequence of the Custer fight. Perhaps if it could be proven without a doubt one way or the other, a number of other questions about what transpired later would come into focus. There are a number of Indian accounts which positively state the soldiers, i.e. Custer, never reached the river at all. Gall went so far as to claim the soldiers never got to within a half mile of the ford.[101] However, Gall admitted he reached the scene of the action late, and he could have missed this part of the fight. This was countered by

[95]Grinnell, *The Fighting Cheyennes*, 350.

[96]John F. Finerty, *War-Path and Bivouac* (Lincoln, NE: University of Nebraska, ND), 209.

[97]Graham, *Reno Court—Abstract*, 43.

[98]Hammer, *Custer in '76*, 207.   [99]*Camp, DPL*, #6.

[100]Graham, *The Custer Myth*, 96.   [101]Burdick, *Indian Notes*, 27.

Courtesy of Prentice Hall (Duell, Sloan and Pearce)

George Hyde's Sioux informants, who stated Custer did come right down to the ford, and the Indians opened fire on them, "finally, forcing them to leave the river bank."[102] In fact, some Cheyennes believed that "If the soldiers had not stopped (at the river), they would have killed lots of Indians." He (Custer) could have gone right through the village "and a great victory might have followed."[103] Two Eagles, a Brule, claimed Custer never got down to the river, but then remarked, "it was a short fight only."[104] Two Moons remembered the troops never got to the river, but cut to the north out of Medicine Tail, "came along the ridge and across the mountains from the right of the monument."[105] Godfrey agreed with this, as he, too, saw Custer's trail "on the high ridge back of the field."[106] Kill Eagle, a Blackfoot Sioux, said Custer never got to within 600 yards of the river as the Indians drove the soldiers back and to the north.[107] Respects Nothing, an Ogallala, also stated Custer "did not come to the river or directly attempt to do so." He went from the high ridges to Calhoun Hill.[108] Likewise, Kate Bighead said the troopers were on a high ridge east of the river, and the only shooting done by either side was from long distance.[109] But Sitting Bull, in 1877, told of fighting which took place across the river between the soldiers and the warriors, followed by the white men retreating.[110] This was essentially how the Arapahoe, Waterman, saw the early stages of the Custer fight: "These troops were trying to cross the river and attack the camp but the Indians drove them back."[111]

There are some students who believe it was Custer, himself, who led the troops to the ford and was shot in the river while trying to cross.[112] An account by Pretty Shield described the moment:

He (Custer) went ahead, rode into the water of the Little Big Horn, with Two-bodies (Mitch Bouyer) on one side of him, and his flag on the other—and he died in the waters of the Little Bighorn with Two-bodies and the blue soldier carrying his flag.[113]

She further identified the Sioux, Big-nose, as the warrior who fired the shot that killed the yellow haired

[102]Hyde, *Red Cloud's Folk*, 269.

[103]Grinnell, *The Fighting Cheyennes*, 344–345.

[104]Hardorff, *Lakota Recollections of the Custer Fight*, 145.

[105]Dixon, *The Vanishing Race*, 181.

[106]Graham, *The Custer Myth*, 96.   [107]Ibid, 53.

[108]Hardorff, *Lakota Recollections of the Custer Fight*, 31.

[109]Marquis, *Custer on the Little Big Horn*, 85–86.

[110]Graham, *The Custer Myth*, 72.   [111]Ibid, 109, 111.

[112]There are some accounts which state the officer killed was Lieutenant Algernon Smith of Company E. See Schoenberger, *End of Custer*, 142–143.

[113]Linderman, *Pretty Shield*, 236–237.

chief.[114] David H.Miller in his book *Custer's Fall* related the story of White Cow Bull who we mentioned was one of the Sioux shooting at the soldiers trying to cross the river, and he saw a white man (Custer) on a sorrel horse hit and others held him up to keep him from falling into the water.[115] Jack Pennington, in his study of the battle, presents similar arguments that Custer was shot at the ford, the consequence of which threw the troopers into panic and led to a disorganized retreat northward.[116] Perhaps, one of the strangest accounts of Custer's supposed death in the river, was recorded by Lame Deer, a Sioux Holy Man. He insisted that Custer, because he was dressed in buckskins, was mistaken for a warrior, and his soldiers thought he was an Indian chief coming in for an attack! The troopers were so scared, they knocked him into the water where Custer floated down the river and drowned.[117] The reader can decide for himself what value should be attached to Lame Deer's tale. If Custer had been shot at the ford and unable to command, Keogh would have assumed that role for the right wing. Cooke, as regimental adjutant, would have then accompanied him throughout the fight. This did not happen, as Cooke's body was found with Custer on last stand knoll. In addition, Keogh as the commander of the wing would have probably opted for a defensive position while trying to determine what Custer's overall plan was or would have pulled back in the direction where Reno's command was last seen. It is also highly doubtful, in this situation, if he would have ordered an advance to the north away from his support where the main column was later found.

The white accounts as to what action, if any, took place at the ford are just as confusing. Benteen, as usual, told two different tales. One of which was that most of Custer's command had crossed the Little Big Horn and had gotten into the village "but were driven out immediately—flying in great disorder."[118] Benteen's other story recorded how Custer never even reached the ford, but he did concede Custer rode down Medicine Tail to within "three furlongs" of the river, before turning to the north. In this second story, Benteen agreed with what Gall remembered.[119] Reno, in his official report, wrote "that companies 'C' and 'I' and perhaps part of 'E' crossed into the village, or attempted it at the charge and they were met with a staggering fire, and they fell back."[120] How-

ever, just twenty five days later he wrote a letter to the New York *Herald,* which was published on August 8th, that when Custer arrived at the ford, he had expected to go into the village "with ease," but the Indians were in ambush, and he was forced to the ridges above the river.[121] General Terry, in his report to the Secretary of War, appears to straddle both sides. He said Custer's trail "comes right down to the bank of the river, but at once diverges from it as if he unsuccessfully attempted to cross."[122] In other words, in the expedition commander's opinion, Custer rode to the river and might have or might not have charged crossed the Little Big Horn.

What does all this prove regarding any action or lack of it at the ford and across the river? There are three major points of view. 1) The soldiers didn't go near the river, but turned north out of Medicine Tail about a half mile from the ford. 2) The soldiers went right up to the river's eastern bank, but somehow were forced to retreat to the ridges where they were to die. 3) The soldiers rode to the river, and a number of them crossed over, engaged in a brief but light firefight with the Indians and pulled back the way they came. In short, a student can find in any of the above explanations, plus any number of minor ones, a broad spectrum of viewpoints with a range that permits and induces controversy and is suited to almost any interpretation. I believe the majority of accounts both red and white, combined with physical evidence found in the area, support number three.[123] But it wasn't the overwhelming number of Indians, along with their determination and fire power which caused the soldiers at the river's banks to move back: it was Custer, himself, who ordered their withdrawal. One author succinctly, wrote: "it is extremely doubtful if Custer, who invariably thought offensive tactics, would have turned his battalion away in the face of such weak opposition without another offensive battle plan in mind."[124]

There are many battle accounts that cite Indian stories that claim it was their power and numbers which drove Keogh's troops away from Ford 'B.' Typical among these accounts is one by Tall Bull, a Cheyenne, who remembered that Custer "was driven farther and farther back from the river. Soldiers fell back from the river. Some mounted and some on foot and not in very good order."[125] This is essentially what the Indians had told Nicholas Ruleau, an interpreter at Pine Ridge Reservation in 1879, that the Indians

[114]Ibid, 247.   [115]Miller, *Custer's Fall*, 129.
[116]Pennington, *Battle of the Little Bighorn*, 356.
[117]Jack Walsh, The Globe, ?, 1972, Moses Collection.
[118]Hunt, *I Fought . . .* ,189.
[119]Brininstool, *Troopers With Custer*, 23.
[120]Carroll, *The Federal View*, 105.

[121]Graham, *The Custer Myth*, 227.
[122]Carroll, *The Federal View*, 89.
[123]Greene, *Evidence and the Custer Enigma*, 21–24; Gray, *Custer's Last Campaign*, 363.   [124]Schoenberger, *End of Custer*, 146.
[125]Hammer, *Custer in '76*, 213.

came at the white men like a "flood which could not be checked" and "the soldiers were swept off their feet."[126] A number of authors of the Custer fight have written that what happened next was like a scene from a Greek Tragedy, where Custer in face of staggering odds, attacked down the coulee, only to be repulsed and placed on the defensive. One such author wrote about the hot fire which greeted the soldiers from the other side of the river, after which Chief Gall then led the "forces across the river." The "two companies retreated from the river, returning a ragged defensive fire as they rode, dismounting skirmishers to hold back the Indian advance."[127] There was little the white man could do to offset the hordes of warriors who pushed them away from the ford. The warriors continued to drive the soldiers to their final last stand positions. Upon arrival they selected the best ground they could find to await their fate, as thousands of warriors massed below setting the stage for the world famous conclusion.

But this is not the case. Many other Indian accounts paint a very different picture of the action at the ford. Lights, a Minneconjou, recalled that the action was "not very vigorous but that shooting was indulged by both soldiers and warriors."[128] John Stands in Timber was told the shooting at the ford didn't last very long, and after some gunfire, the Indians pulled back while the soldiers moved out of the area, heading north.[129] Wooden Leg said they only exchanged shots with the troopers "at a long distance, without anybody being hurt."[130] An Ogallala leader, Low Dog, knew it was not any action taken by the Indians at the ford which caused the white man to back away. The soldiers started to cross the river and were going to ride into the village but "Custer changed his mind and moved off."[131] The Indian accounts further state there were few warriors at the ford when the troops arrived. It was only after the soldiers had left that the warriors were joined by many others who rode away from the Reno fight to meet the new threat posed by this second group of white men.

But perception is reality to those who view or experience an event. The Indians believed it was their strong medicine and actions that had forced the white man away from the river. Just as they thought, they had caused Reno to stop his charge in the valley. Likewise, when Reno retreated from the timber, the Indians thought he was going to attack them again, and they pulled back. It was only afterwards that the warriors realized he was retreating, and they closed in for battle; they had 'driven' the soldiers away from the village. Many of Reno's men didn't believe the Indians had ejected them from the timber position, and Keogh's men, probably, didn't believe that they had been forced back by the warriors. Under orders, Keogh had been redirected to the north, picked up his detached platoon and joined Yates' Battalion to pursue the non-combatants to the north. As an analogy, on July 1, 1863 in Gettysburg on McPherson's Ridge, Archer's Confederate Brigade attacked what they assumed to be Pennsylvania Militia, only to discover they had struck the Union Army's veteran Iron Brigade. However, the Iron Brigade believed they were the ones doing the attacking which Archer's men then received. Who was on the defensive, and who was on the offensive? Who retreated to regroup and wait for reinforcements, and who pulled back to realign their ranks and await developments? To the participants, it was all in perception, and historians still debate and study the issue. Thus it's not uncommon when two groups of fighting men meet in battle for each one to think they are the aggressor.[132] So it was at the Little Big Horn.

Custer must have believed Benteen was for once carrying out his orders to bring the pack train with him, or he should have been seen by now to the south. What plans he might have had for these companies couldn't be executed, and the commander would have to use what force he had at hand to chase after the fleeing village. Yates' battalion was now on traditional Luce Ridge with Custer. Custer ordered Yates to dismount a company and prepare to volley fire in response to the Indians who were seen advancing from the hills to the southwest in the direction of where Reno had retreated. Other warriors who had been forced to the right at Ford 'B' by Keogh's battalion were seen moving toward Medicine Tail from the north. This firing would clear the area to the north and keep away the warriors in the lower coulees under cover as the troops reassembled. From this ridge, Yates' battalion fired several volleys. Custer then directed Yates' buglers to sound "recall" in preparation for the move against the non-combatants. Curley told Camp they blew for some time, but he didn't understand their purpose.[133] Mrs. Spotted Horn Bull also heard "the music of the bugles" from her camp.[134]

[126]Hardorff, *Lakota Recollections of the Custer Fight*, 43–44.

[127]Robert Utley, "Last Stand," *The Quarterly Journal Of Military History*, Vol. 1, #1, August, 1988, 121.

[128]Hardorff, *Lakota Recollections of the Custer Fight*, 166

[129]Liberty, *Cheyenne Memories* (New Haven, CT: Yale University Press, 1967), 198.

[130]Marquis, A *Warrior Who Fought Custer*, 229.

[131]*Camp, CBNM*, 11937–11938, #312.

[132]Fox, *Custer's Last Battle*, 279. [133]Hammer, *Custer in '76*, 172.

[134]Graham, *The Custer Myth*, 86.

This firing position, was discovered by Custer Battlefield Superintendent Edward Luce. In 1943, he wrote a letter to Robert Ellison, who had purchased Walter Camp's Notes a decade earlier, that he found these cartridge cases on the "two hills on the north bank of Medicine Tail Coulee." This ridge he went to was higher than Blummer (Nye) Cartwright Ridge and closer to Reno Hill.[135] In total, he uncovered about 150 shell cases in groups about nine to ten feet apart, indicating a dismounted firing line. A month later, he wrote to Colonel Elwood Nye, an early battle student, saying, " 'My Ridge' is ideal for dismounted action with a slight depression behind the skirmishes on the military crest that would be fine for the lead horses." He further said he placed numbered stakes where these cartridges where found.[136] Some students, while not denying that some shooting had taken place along this ridge line, or that Custer troops had either occupied or traveled over its ground, refer to it not as Luce Ridge, but as East Ridge. They claim that what has been traditionally referred to as the place where the former superintendent made his discoveries, was really about a half mile to the north by west from the East Ridge, not far from the southeastern end of Blummer (Nye) Cartwright Ridge. However, whichever ridge one wants to believe upon, Luce found the expended shells, there is little question firing occurred along both ridges.

But other than forcing the Indians he had seen to keep their distance by their gunfire, what other reason(s) did Custer have to go upon the traditional Luce Ridge? Some students think Custer went to this high ground to attempt to draw the warriors away from Reno's beleaguered command.[137] As we mentioned before, others believe Custer was in a holding action waiting for Benteen to "come on," and the crest of Luce Ridge offered a commanding position of the upper reaches of Medicine Tail Coulee. They hold the volley firing from this position was a signal to let Benteen know where the main column was located. These students suggested that Benteen certainly would not expect Custer to be on the high ridges a mile or two back from the river.[138] Still, others believe, following a similar line of thought, that he went to this high ground to see if he could see any sign of Benteen's column before he, in effect, "gave up" expecting him. One of the dedicated students in the current study of the Little Big Horn is Greg Michno. He believes, from his extensive field research, Custer could have seen the troopers and the warriors on Reno Hill from this ridge. If one was to climb up the traditional Luce Ridge and look south from its eastern projection, the other coulee to the east of Sharpshooters' Ridge provides a line of sight right to the Reno Hill area.[139] To test this observation, all one needs to do is ascend the ridge, and even without binoculars, one can see the park service's wayside exhibits while going into the Reno-Benteen battlefield as well as the northeast area of the field.[140]

Without a doubt, Keogh's advance to the ford, besides clearing the area of non-combatants and securing the crossing, would also draw the Indians away from Reno's beaten command. This would give Reno's battalion a chance to reform, and with Benteen joining them, it would enable his second in command to resume the offensive. Therefore, Custer could continue northward after the fleeing village with the assurance, or so he thought, that Reno and Benteen would follow after the Indians who would be drawn to his command to try and prevent the capture of their families. Other students are of the opinion that by Custer moving downstream, for whatever his reason(s), he was not only forcing the warriors to follow after him, but also trapping them between his own column and the expected reinforcements.[141] These Indians were seen moving off the hills to the south to intercept these 'new' soldiers.[142] For if Custer could see the troops on Reno Hill, then it's a sure thing the Indians, who had pursued Reno, could see the soldiers on Luce Ridge.[143] In fact, Michno makes a very good point that Custer continued north along these high ridges, rather than any other route, so as to keep in sight both the ford and the area where he had seen the troops from where the combined battalions would be moving. I believe by doing so, Custer could still pursue his plan to capture their families and at the same time decoy the warriors between the two commands so as to attack them from both directions.[144]

There is little doubt Mr. Michno is correct about the Indians seeing Custer while he was on these ridges from their vantage points a mile or two to the south. The warriors quickly turned their attention away from Reno and responded to the new threat. Their recollections make this very clear. Runs the Enemy, a Two Kettle, had crossed the Little Big Horn and heard other Indians call out that:

[135]W. Donald Horn, "What About Luce Ridge," *Little Big Horn Associates Newsletter*, Vol. 24, #1, February 1995, 6.

[136]Edward Luce, "Custer Battlefield And Some New Discoveries," *Chicago Westerners*, Vol. 4, #1–2, March–April 1947, 8–9. I personally have seen these stakes upon this ridge in the 1970s.

[137]Sklenar, *To Hell With Honor*, 268–269.

[138]Horn, "What About Luce Ridge," 6.

[139]Michno, *Lakota Noon*, 108.   [140]I have done this in May 2002.

[141]Stewart, *Custer's Luck*, 447.

[142]Michno, *Lakota Noon*, 107–108.   [143]Ibid, 107.

[144]Stewart, *Custer's Luck*, 447.

the genuine stuff was coming, and they were going to get our women and children. I went over with the others and peeped over the hills and saw the soldiers advancing. As I looked along the ridge, they seemed to fill the whole hill. It looked as if there were thousands of them, and we would be surely beaten. As I returned, I saw hundreds of Sioux. I looked into their eyes, and they looked different—they were filled with fear.[145]

Short Bull also thought the soldiers were too many. Crazy Horse had pointed out the white men to his fellow tribesman, and when Short Bull looked, he saw Custer's men overrunning a hill to the east. "I thought there were a million of them."[146] Flying Hawk remembered the warriors were beginning to exchange fire with the soldiers on the hill, but soon they left to chase after the soldiers who were "to the east and north on top of a high hill."[147] Wooden Leg had just joined the Indians who were trying to circle around Reno Hill and had only been with them a short time when his attention was called to another body of soldiers. "I saw them on the distant hills down river and on our side of it. Indians began to ride in that direction."[148] The Indians didn't waste any time in rallying their men to prevent Custer from getting to the women and children. Feather Earring said it was only afterwards as Custer moved away from the river that the Indians crossed in great numbers and tried to get around behind him.[149] There was no doubt in White Bull's mind where these new soldiers were headed. "Where we were standing on the side of the hill, (Reno's) we saw another troop moving from the east to the north where the camp was moving."[150]

Company E's covering fire had allowed Keogh's battalion to pull back from the river in an orderly manner. After crossing over the mouth of Deep Ravine, Keogh now ordered Bobo's men to move to the north for the high ground to a position about where the southwestern fence line marks the current boundary of the Custer Battlefield. These troopers would cover the movement of the rest of the battalion as they rode up the slopes to the northeast. It was during this pull back from the ford that Corporal John Foley, Company 'C,' was killed. Sergeant Stanislaus

Roy remembered when he accompanied Major Reno on June 28th, the troops rode down Medicine Tail following the path Keogh took to the ford. On the first small ridge north of the coulee was the body of Foley. Based on what Roy had told him, Camp concluded the corporal was found about eleven hundred feet from the river on the ridge line about a hundred yards to the north of where the path leads to the current marker for Sergeant James Butler.[151] Foley was probably with the platoon providing covering fire until relieved by 'E' and was shot while rejoining the battalion. He Dog, however, said the location where the corporal was found marked the spot where a soldier shot himself.[152] His recollection was supported by Turtle Rib.[153] Keogh had succeeded in reaching the high ground on the other side where the road crosses the present boundary fence. Keogh could see by holding this ground he could control the vicinity around Ford 'B' and Deep Coulee which runs past Calhoun Hill. While waiting for Yates, Company 'C' was deployed facing to the southeast so as to discourage the Indians who were still milling about the ford area from making any advances towards their position. Keogh was right in deploying a company to discourage any movement by the Indians. He Dog said they followed after the soldiers and tried to go over to the other side of the ridge (Deep Ravine?).[154] Flying Hawk told Ricker that "there were also lots of Indians who had followed the river down from Reno without going to their camps," and there were also others who were crossing the river. Foolish Elk said, "The Indians were now getting their horses in from the hills and soon came up in large numbers." Some were crossing the stream farther down, while others were crossing at the ford.[155]

It has been recently suggested this battalion didn't pull back from the ford and ride to the north near Deep Coulee, but instead went back by about the same route as they had approached the ford, that is to the east. Keogh retired from the ford to Blummer-(Nye) Cartwright Ridge and joined the rest of the command there. From this ridge, the united wing rode to Calhoun Hill, arriving there as a single body of troops.[156] This different interpretation is supported by the tactical manuals of the period, which taught combat units were to retreat on their own back trail when an unknown number of entrenched enemy is encountered

[145]Dixon, *The Vanishing Race*, 174.

[146]John M. Carroll, *The Eleanor H. Hinman Interviews On The Life And Death Of Crazy Horse* (NP: The Garry Owen Press, 1976) 40.

[147]M. I. McCreight, *Firewater and Forked Tongues* (Pasadena, CA: Trail's End Publishing Company, 1947), 112.

[148]Marquis, *A Warrior Who Fought Custer*, 226.

[149]Graham, *The Custer Myth*, 97.

[150]Walter S. Campbell Collection, University of OK, box 105, notebook 24.

[151]*Camp, IU*, box 6, folder 19.

[152]Hammer, *Custer in '76*, 20.   [153]Ibid, 207, 254.

[154]Ibid, 207. There has been a long standing Indian tradition that some of the troopers went up and over Greasy Grass Ridge on their way to the battlefield. Letter, Robert Doran to Bruce R. Liddic, February 8, 2003, author's collection.

[155]Ibid, 198.   [156]Michno, *Lakota Noon*, 154.

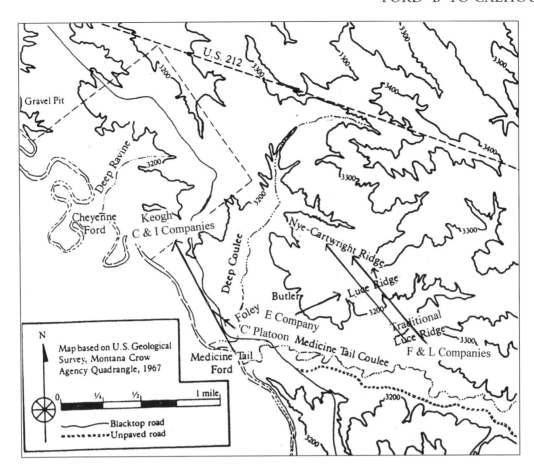

at an obstacle, such as a water crossing.[157] One could also read in what Good Voice Elk said to support the troopers moving in a single body to the north. "Custer and his men at all times were together in one body, and at no time were they formed into a line or at intervals, neither did any part of them become detached for the purpose of holding any particular point."[158] However, other Indian accounts suggest there were two distinct bodies of men, one moving to the north along the high ridges and another moving from Ford 'B' to Calhoun Hill.[159] Brave Wolf, a Cheyenne, said that just as he arrived at the ford, the soldiers began their retreat up the narrow gulch (Deep Coulee) and contradicting Good Voice Elk, remembered the soldiers were drawn up in line of battle.[160] The chief Two Moons also said Custer's men moved forward in two lines.[161] I have based my construction of Keogh's movement to Calhoun Hill on the traditional accounts.

Both Girard and Herendeen, who were left behind in the timber, heard the gunfire from Luce Ridge. The two scouts told Camp it was about a half an hour after Reno's retreat that they began to hear firing down the river.[162] But before this, they said there had been some general shooting, probably coming from the ford area. Now, the men who were in the timber heard "terrific firing."[163] Upon Keogh's move back from the ford and his establishment of a field of fire from the higher ridge line, 'E' Company mounted and rode to the east and took up position upon what is now designated as (new) Luce Ridge. As they were going to be part of the general advance to the north, the company remained mounted and prepared to cover the movement of the rest of the battalion to them. The position assumed by this company would allow Custer to move Yates' two companies safely down from traditional Luce Ridge and up the other side to the high-ridge line that leads to Calhoun Hill. The Cheyennes told of some Indians who the night before the battle were away from the camp and were on the high hills to the northwest. When the soldiers were spotted "the rest went on around a point to cut them off. They caught up there with

---

[157]Letter, Robert Doran to Bruce R. Liddic, November 10, 2001.
[158]*Camp, DPL*, #6.
[159]Hardorff, *Lakota Recollections of the Custer Fight*, 142–143.
[160]Grinnell, *The Fighting Cheyennes*, 340.
[161]*Camp, IU*, box 2, folder 9.

[162]Hammer, *Custer in '76*, 224, 234.
[163]Brininstool, *Troopers With Custer*, 136.

some who were still going down the soldiers starting shooting."[164] The result was the hundred and fifty some cartridges discovered by Luce and others. 'E' Company took thirty-seven enlisted men into the afternoon's action; only about four shots per man would account for these cartridge cases. Tall Bull said, as the soldiers were falling back from the river, he "Heard the volleys."[165]

Custer had moved off traditional Luce Ridge and was riding to the north to link up with Keogh's battalion, already occupying a high point to the north, to begin the pursuit of the non-combatants. Some of these non-combatants were fleeing west towards the Big Horn Mountains, and others were moving to the north. As he moved behind 'E's mounted skirmish line, he was riding parallel to the river about a mile to the west. Custer led the troops to what we now call Blummer-(Nye) Cartwrightt Ridge. This ridge lies to the south and east of Calhoun Hill. It runs essentially east and west and is separated from Calhoun Hill by the upper limits of Deep Coulee and is a little under two miles from last stand hill. Kate Bighead remembered "the soldiers had lined themselves out on a long ridge nearer to the river and a little lower than the ridge far out where we first saw them."[166] This may sound confusing, but if one is looking from the ford area towards this ridge, it appears as she described it. There are a number of battle students who believe Custer moved to Blummer-(Nye) Cartwright Ridge so he could occupy a more commanding position to again wait for Reno and Benteen.[167] However, I believe to facilitate 'E's withdrawal and encourage the warriors to keep their distance, now the Gray Horse company was vacating this vantage point, the two companies of troopers were placed in mounted skirmish order of about nine yards apart on the east side of the ridge's crest.[168] Shell cases have been found for nearly a quarter mile along the crest. Hank Wiebert reported he found a number of shell cases along the crest of Blummer (Nye)-Cartwright Ridge.[169] However, Joseph Blummer wrote to Robert Cartwright in a 1928 letter that he found a number of shells along the northern slope of this ridge about ten feet from the crest.[170] But when

Cartwright wrote to William Boyes, who has devoted a lifetime to the study of this battle, in reply to his questions about these shell cases, Cartwright merely said that "In all over 250 expended cases have been found."[171] He didn't give any details as to exactly where on the ridge line, forward or reverse, these discoveries were made. If military tactics were followed, the cases could have been found along the military crest which is about 30 feet below the true crest; skirmishers were always placed down the slope from a ridge's crest to prevent making a silhouette along its ridge line. Although there had been troopers' gunfire before, and some of it by volley, it was from this position that the distinct, heavy, and very audible gunfire was heard by both the men in the timber and those on Reno Hill. It was after 4:30.

Girard said he began to hear continuous firing about twenty minutes after Reno left the timber, as if some kind of a general engagement was taking place, (Luce Ridge firing ?) then he heard firing to "the left of the village; 3 or 4 volleys as if there were 50 to 100 guns at a volley."[172] Herendeen was even more specific as he stated the firing was very heavy. "There were about nine volleys at intervals and the intermediate firing was quite rapid."[173] This scout might be right in the number of volleys he heard, as over five hundred shell cases have been found along this ridge line since it was discovered by Blummer and Cartwright as noted above. But, was all this firing simply done to prevent infiltration by the Indians and to keep them at a distance? A number of battle authors stated this was not the case. The firing by volleys of three was done as a distress signal to alert the rest of the regiment to Custer's peril.[174] Godfrey wrote, "I have but little doubt now that these volleys were fired by Custer's orders as a signal of distress."[175] Reno in his official report wrote, "We had heard firing in that direction and knew it could only be Custer." Others have thought Custer was laying down a covering fire to help extract his other battalion from the ford area. But all one has to do is travel along this position on Blummer (Nye) Cartwright Ridge, and it is quickly apparent Custer couldn't see the ford area because of hills in front of him. Despite what some believed, Custer wasn't volley firing as a signal for help or to inform the others of his location, he was firing at a small

---

[164]Liberty, *Cheyennes Memories*, 198.

[165]Richard Hardorff, *Cheyenne Memories of the Custer Battle* (Spokane, WA: Arthur H. Clark Co, 1995), 76.

[166]Marquis, *Custer on the Little Bighorn*, 86.

[167]Hedley, "ps Bring Pacs: The Order That Trapped the Custer Battalion," 54.

[168]Richard Hardorff, *Markers, Artifacts and Indian Testimony* (Short Hills, NJ: Don Horn Publications, 1985) 36.

[169]Don Weibert, *Custer, Cases & Cartridges* (NP: NP, 1989), 47–48.

[170]Letter, Joseph Blummer to Robert Cartwright, September 13, 1928, Reference File, Custer Battlefield National Monument.

[171]Letter, Robert Cartwright to William Boyes, Jr. January 1, 1961, Boyes Collection.

[172]Graham, *Reno Court—Abstract*, 173.

[173]Graham, *The Custer Myth*, 264.

[174]The cartridges were reported to have been found by Cartwright in groups of three. See Greene, *Evidence and the Custer Enigma*, 28.

[175]Graham, *The Custer Myth*, 142.

number of Indians who had taken up a position about 400 yards away, who were behind those hills.[176]

These were no doubt the same Indians John Stands in Timber spoke about who were part of Wolf Tooth's band. These fifty or so young Indians were eager for a fight and had the night before slipped out of the camp. These warriors believed the incantations of the blind holy man, Box Elder, who that night said the soldiers were near.[177] They wanted to be the first to confront the white men and win their own battle honors. So they had ridden first to the north, then turned south, finding themselves in the extreme upper reaches of Medicine Tail Coulee. They were then informed by a young Sioux boy who had ridden out to them and shouted, "The soldiers are already at the village."[178] They split into two groups, some going to the north, others to the south, in an attempt to get on both flanks of the white men. Here they were joined by some others who had followed in the wake of 'E' Company when they left the ridgeline overlooking Ford 'B." Hank Weibert discovered these Indian positions from where they had been shooting at the soldiers and where Custer had stopped to reply. A couple of volleys were directed at these Indians, but it was too far away to be effective, and Custer didn't want to advance farther north with an unknown number of Indians sniping at his exposed battalion the whole distance.[179] The companies were ordered about two hundred yards further north by west, and from here they delivered the three volleys heard on Reno Hill and in the valley. The troopers return fire had little effect on the incoming fire as the warriors would shoot, then duck down behind the ridge or move slightly to a new position before shooting again. Custer was in a hurry to capture the non-combatants, and this was delaying him, so to root out the warriors, he sent a company forward to close upon them. It was probably 'E,' as the Indians remembered the gray horses very well along this ridge line.

Custer fired several more volleys as a covering fire while the men advanced towards the Indians. But before the troopers could close upon the warriors, they would retreat. John Stands in Timber said the shooting didn't last long, and the warriors didn't want to get too close to the soldiers. So, "After some shooting, both bunches of Indians retreated back to the hills. The soldiers then crossed over to the south end of the ridge (Calhoun Hill) where the

monument now stands."[180] Stands in Timber remembered for a long time that the white man wouldn't believe him when he said there was fighting at this place.[181] Now the action on this ridge is incorporated into all the battle accounts. One must also note, the Indian accounts don't say they drove Custer off this ridge, they record just the opposite. Custer, after dispersing these Indian snipers to his west, rode on to link up with Keogh on what was to be called Calhoun Hill. In the timing sequence of the Custer fight, it should be noted the Lieutenant Colonel did not leave Blummer-(Nye) Cartwright Ridge until he could see Koegh had safely disengaged from the ford and had arrived on the ridges on the southwestern part of the current National Park Service site. Flying Hawk told Dr. Ricker that the soldiers were on Calhoun Hill before "Custer left the second ridge . . . then Custer came down off the second ridge and went up onto Calhoun Hill."[182] It was now about five o'clock in the afternoon.

After the Indians had been pushed back by the volley fire and the actions of 'E,' Custer decided to try once more to send a messenger through to Benteen or Reno. In all probability, he was telling them of his plan to go to the north and directing them to follow after him and keep the warriors between them and off balance, giving him a free pass to the non-combatants. A set of fours, including Custer's orderly, Trumpeter Henry Dose of Company G, was ordered over the back trail to deliver the message as Yates' Battalion moved towards Calhoun Hill. It would have been too hazardous to dispatch a lone rider with the warriors in the vicinity, even if their numbers were few. The other soldiers were to be the escort for the dispatch rider. Rain in the Face told Dr. Eastman these soldiers had "fled" along this ridge "towards Reno's position."[183] Wooden Leg also spoke about four soldiers who were killed while riding over their back trail. However, in his sequence, it would appear these troopers were killed towards the end of the battle, not in the beginning.[184] Frank Bethune found the bodies not far from the southwestern end of Blummer-(Nye) Cartwright Ridge. Private Henry Petring, Company 'G,' told Camp his friend Dose was found half way between Custer and Reno "with arrows in his back and sides."[185]

And, what of Reno and his command about 2¼ miles

---

[176]Weibert, *Sixty-Six Years in Custer's Shadow*, 53. However, there are others who believe Custer was firing to clear the Indians out of Deep Coulee before he crossed over. See Hardorff, *Markers, Artifacts and Indian Testimony*, 38–39.

[177]Powell, *Sweet Medicine*, 111.   [178]Ibid, 115.

[179]Weibert, *Sixty-Six Years in Custer's Shadow*, 51.

[180]Liberty, *Cheyenne Memories*, 198.   [181]Ibid.

[182]Carroll, *Who Was This . . .* , 36.

[183]Herbert A. Coffeen, *The Custer Battle Book* (NY, NY: Carlton Press, Inc, 1964), 64.

[184]Marquis, *A Warrior Who Fought Custer*, 232.

[185]Hammer, *Custer in '76*, 134. For a different interpetation of where Dose was killed, see Hardorff, *Custer Battle Casualties*, 111–112.

away? Did they have any idea where Custer was and what was happening over the ridges to the north? From post battle recollections of the men, they had a very good idea what was going on and what they should be doing. When the volley firing was happening, Godfrey recalled that some of the officers were asking, "What's the matter with Custer, that he don't send word what we shall do?" and, "Wonder what we are staying here for?"[186] It was also expressed by those on Reno Hill that "our command ought to be doing something or Custer would be after Reno with sharp stick."[187] Varnum also heard the volleys and turned to his friend Wallace and said, "Jesus Christ! Wallace hear that! and that."[188]

---

[186]Graham, *The Custer Myth*, 141. [187]Ibid, 142.
[188]Graham, *Reno Court*, 136.

2
The Trip to Weir Point

Many years later, Trumpeter Martin recalled when he arrived on Reno Hill, Captain Benteen showed Major Reno the order he had carried.[1] The senior captain remembered much the same thing and recorded that "I joined Reno on the hill, my arrival there being only a few moments after Reno."[2] Benteen told the Court of Inquiry that Reno read the order brought by Martin but made no comment on it except to say he had no idea where Custer was, nor did the Major offer any explanation of why he had retreated to the hill or to any of the events which had befallen him in the valley.[3] Custer's message to 'come on, be quick' made little impression upon Reno. In fact, at the time it was thought "Custer will have to look out for himself."[4] There are a number of battle students who believe Benteen was still under Custer's direct order to report to him, and this direct order was not subject to override by Reno or anyone else.[5] General Nelson Miles said much the same thing when asked for his opinion: "It was Benteen's duty to strike out straight for Custer. They saw clouds of dust . . . where Custer was fighting, they knew his location, but no move was made in his direction."[6] However, this belief is counterpointed by more than a few military officers whose judgment holds that after Benteen had shown Reno Custer's order, he was under no further obligation to fulfill its direction. This is because when two separate commands unite, the senior officer present is in de facto and de juro command of the two units. Interestingly, it has been suggested that Custer's own organization of the regiment had dictated that in any combination of the two forces, Benteen would become second in command of the left wing headed by Reno.[7] This would effectively transfer any responsibility to 'come on, be quick' to Major Reno.

It would appear this later military opinion absolves Benteen of any further duty to carry out the order delivered by Martin. Others believed that is was highly unlikely Reno would have stopped Benteen from moving forward, nor would have Benteen listened. One possible scenario is the senior captain might have thought he complied with

orders received, and he had ample justification for letting Custer wait. Any trouble the lieutenant colonel found himself in, was not his concern.[8] Benteen, although a meager company commander, was nevertheless a first class fighter, but his weakness was his vindictiveness, which was pronounced.[9] I submit at the time that Benteen showed Reno the message, the senior captain had made no move nor did he exercise even minimal effort to carry out the order, in part because of this character trait. Until Benteen accomplished this charge or had found it impossible to carry out, he was under no obligation to Reno. In fact, Benteen thought much the same way when his battalion reached the bluffs, because he wrote, "not that I didn't feel free to act in opposition to Reno's wishes, and did so act."[10] Throughout the rest of his life, Benteen never attempted to justify his failure to 'come on, be quick,' and he was to later claim he never asked Reno "for authority to proceed," as "I supposed General Custer was able to take care of himself."[11] However, Benteen candidly admitted to the Reno Court of Inquiry that he could have made an immediate movement, as directed by Custer, but with excellent hindsight added if he had "we would all have been there yet."[12] Contrast this to Edgerly's statement that "I firmly and positively believe we should have gone to 'the sound of the firing' . . . even if at that time we would have shared his fate."[13]

Captain McDougall believed the main reason why Benteen didn't assert the authority given him by the order, when it appeared to most everyone they should have gone to Custer, was because of Reno. The captain said Benteen hesitated because Reno might have set up a technical ground that he was the commanding officer. Reno was habitually jealous of his authority and was rather touchy on that point, and the officers in the regiment were aware of it.[14] McDougall said Benteen didn't want to push the fact because he and Reno weren't on friendly terms. In addition, Benteen might have considered what would have been the ramifications from his disobedience of Reno's orders. If Reno pushed his rank, what would have been the effect on the command in a combat situation with the two senior officers engaged in a confrontation? The

---

[1] Letter, John Martin to David Barry, April 7, 1907, copy in Moses Collection.

[2] Thomas Holmes, "The Little Big Horn—Benteen an Unpblished Letter," *Research Review—Journal of the Little Big Horn Associates*, Vol. 7, #1, January 1993, 4.

[3] Graham, *Reno Court*, 359.   [4] Ibid, 367.

[5] Gray, *Custer's Last Campaign*, 308.

[6] Merrington, *The Custer Story*, 325.

[7] Sklenar, *To Hell With Honor*, 297.

[8] J. L. Beardsley, "Could Custer Have Won," *Outdoor Life*, Vol. 71, #3, March 1933, 56–57; Luther, "Benteen, Reno and Custer," 14.

[9] *Camp, IU*, box 2, folder 1.

[10] Carroll, *The Benteen—Goldin Letters On Custer And His Last Battle*, 246.   [11] Graham, *Reno Court*, 360.

[12] Ibid, 361.

[13] Carroll, *The Gibson and Edgerly Narratives*, 14.

[14] *Camp, BYU*, roll 5, box 5, folder 5.

morale of Reno's battalion was fragile at best and such a spectacle as this, could have put the troops over the edge.[15] Later, McDougall claimed when it became apparent to the senior captain that Reno was "thoroughly incompetent to handle the situation" he (Benteen) resolved to take matters into his own hands. This was also Dr. Porter's view of the status on the bluffs, that "Major Reno was the ranking officer, but I thought that Col. Benteen was the actual commanding officer."[16] After Reno's plea for Benteen to stop and help him reorganize his battalion, he halted his command and ordered them to dismount and deploy as skirmishers on the edge of the bluffs overlooking the valley.[17] Sergeant Windolph said that "It's no use pretending that the men here on the hill, from Reno down, were not disorganized and downright frightened . . . it had only been the grace of God . . . that had let them escape across the river with their lives." In Windolph's opinion, "Benteen more or less assumed command."[18] Dr. Porter said both the officers and men of Reno's Battalion "seemed to think they had been whipped."[19] But, Second Lieutenant Hare saw the situation on the bluffs differently, and stated he was among the last of the men to reach the hill, and when he arrived, Captain Moylan had completed his skirmish line, and in his opinion, the command wasn't "demoralized" at all, and the officers brought the men smartly into line.[20] He maintained Reno was very calm, and although he gave no orders "he was standing there where he could supervise the formation."[21] Hare, who surpressed much of the truth by seeing everything through rose colored glasses, further recalled that when Benteen came up "Major Reno turned around and said in a very inspiring way to his men: 'We have assistance now and we will go and avenge the loss of our comrades.'"[22] However, Private William Taylor, Company 'A,' said all Reno did was walk "around in an excited manner."[23] This testimony of Hare, as to events on Reno Hill, is disputed by Edgerly, who remembered when 'D' arrived on the bluffs, he saw Varnum, whom he described as hatless with a white handkerchief tied about his head. The chief of scouts was very excited, in fact he was crying, and while telling Edgerly about what had happened in the valley, stopped his story, began to swear, all the while yelling for someone to give him a gun so he could shoot Indians.[24]

Edgerly also noted Captain Moylan was among his company begging pitilessly for water, as he was dying of thirst. Benteen was less charitable toward Moylan, as when he first saw Company A's commander, he was "blubbering like a whipped urchin." Benteen thought to himself, it appeared the Captain's bottom had tumbled out, and all the nerve with it.[25] I believe Edgerly's and Benteen's recollections of the conditions on Reno Hill more accurately reflected the true state of Reno's battalion at the time of their arrival.

Reno, after reading Custer's order, thought it was directed more at bringing the pack train up so it could be more accessible and then put it into a safe defensible position rather than commit the pack train to the battle itself.[26] As discussed in a previous chapter, Reno missed the point of Custer's order. True, he wanted the pack train safe, but he also wanted the men who were assigned to the packs. These men would be of no use to Custer holed up far to the rear behind a circle of mules. First, Lieutenant Jesse Lee, the Recorder at the Reno Court of Inquiry, was able to understand the point of Custer's orders, in spite of the fact he wasn't at the battle. In his summation to the Court, he said the order "reveals with equal clearness General Custer's desire to secure the cooperation of all the forces of his command. The place for concentration was on the field of battle against the enemy, and nowhere else."[27] Reno admitted he read Martin's message but it "did not make any impression on me at the time because I was absorbed in getting those packs together, and did not intend to move until I had done so."[28] It would appear in light of the major's mental state, when he reached the top of the bluffs, he was only capable of performing one task at a time and wasn't about to begin another until he completed the one he had currently undertaken. It was clear, the events had spiraled out of of Reno's control, and he was bewildered. The major reason Reno gave for his procrastination and indecision was that his battalion was out of ammunition as a result of the valley fight, and he felt compelled to bring up the ammunition mules before doing anything.[29] Lieutenant Wallace said the men had pretty well used up their ammunition in the valley.[30] Windolph remembered Benteen's battalion was "told to divide ours with them."[31] First Sergeant Ryan, who would be expected to know his company's condition, indicated it was fortunate the ammu-

[15]Hammer, *Custer in '76*, 71. [16]Graham, *Reno Court*, 163.

[17]Graham, *The Custer Myth*, 141.

[18]Hunt, *I Fought With . . .* , 96–97.

[19]Graham, *Reno Court*, 162. [20]Ibid, 240–241.

[21]Ibid, 240. [22]Ibid, 256.

[23]William O. Taylor, *With Custer on the Little Big Horn* (NY, NY: Viking, 1996), 47. [24]Graham, *Reno Court*, 391.

[25]Carroll, *The Benteen—Goldin Letters On Custer And His Last Battle*, 243. [26]Nichols, *In Custer's Shadow*, 190.

[27]Graham, *Reno Court*, 550. [28]Ibid, 517.

[29]Nichols, *In Custer's Shadow*, 190. [30]Graham, *Reno Court*, 45.

[31]Hunt, *I Fought With . . .* , 97.

nition packs had arrived on Reno Hill when they did as "our ammunition was nearly exhausted and we could not get any fresh supplies from any other source."[32] Contradicting Ryan, Sergeant Culbertson said he had only fired twenty-one rounds in the valley.[33] Private Davern said he only fired twenty rounds, and he was shooting every time he had "a good chance."[34] Lieutenant Hare didn't think the battalion was out of ammunition, and when questioned about why he thought so, replied there was plenty of cartridges in the men's saddle pockets.[35] In this statement, the lieutenant was supported by George Herendeen who when specifically asked if the troopers had more than 50 rounds each at the time in their saddle bags replied, "They had all of that. They had more than we wanted."[36] Godfrey wrote in his diary that "We were watching anxiously for our pack train with the reserve ammunition, for the three Cos had expended nearly all they had."[37] Later, after much reflection, the Lieutenant reversed himself and couldn't understand how Reno's troopers could have expended nearly all the one-hundred rounds in their personal possession. He commented that "It has often been a matter of doubt whether this was a fact or the effect of imagination. It seems most improbable."[38] When Benteen was questioned about what he knew about Reno's depleted ammunition supply and the wait for replenishment, he said he never heard anything about it.[39]

All of Benteen's battalion had now arrived on the bluffs, and in view of the condition of Reno's men, Captain Weir dismounted 'D,' and formed them as skirmishers to force any remaining warriors in the vicinity to pull back. Godfrey was then ordered by Benteen to reinforce Weir, and 'K' joined Weir's troopers in a skirmish line along the edge of the bluffs.[40] When the skirmish line was first formed, there was heavy firing, but the Indians had moved so far away, the officers ordered the shooting to stop, as it was a waste of ammunition.[41] It was about 4:30 PM. Godfrey recalled Reno had not given any instructions, leaving Benteen to manage the skirmish line. Godfrey also remembered that Reno's attention was focused elsewhere and was directed towards making arrangements to recover his adjutant's body, Benny Hodgson, from the eastern bank of the Little Big Horn River.[42] Reno had been informed that Hodgson had been shot, and since he was "a great favorite and friend of mine (Reno)" wanted "to do some-

thing for him." With the pack train yet to arrive, the Major left Benteen in command on the bluffs, and with about a dozen troopers, including Sergeant Culbertson, descended the bluffs to look for his adjutant. About this time, Private Edward Davern heard volley firing and turned to Captain Weir and said, "That must be General Custer fighting down in the bottom." Weir then asked the private where, and Davern pointed to the north, and Weir said he believed it was so.[43] But Weir did nothing, nor did any other officer, in part because Major Reno neglected to tell his company commanders, as well as his orderly, that he was leaving the command in an attempt to find his adjutant.[44] Varnum said he never saw Reno until he came up from the river after his search for Hodgson.[45] However, Second Lieutenant Wallace did note Reno's departure down the bluffs, but there is no record that he told anybody about it.[46] Godfrey said he "understood" that Reno was going to check on Hodgson after overhearing him talking to Benteen. Wallace did think it was strange for the Major to check on Hodgson, as he should have sent someone else.[47] For leaving his command in a combat situation, Reno was fortunate not to have faced "charges of misbehavior in the face of the enemy."[48] Davern estimated it was about half an hour after Reno had reached the high ground that he started back down to the river.[49]

This bizarre journey was undertaken in spite of the fact no measures were arranged to speed up the pack train, whose ammunition was supposed to be critical, nor were any steps taken to learn the cause of the heavy gunfire, including volleys, being heard to the north. But what would have precluded this officer with nearly twenty years of service from sending out an officer or a sergeant with a detail of men to ride to the high ground in front of the command to check on the situation? If nothing was observed from Sharpshooters' Ridge, the detail could have proceeded to the twin peaks (Weir Point) further on for a better view of the country. This would have been a relatively safe undertaking, as the detail would have been in visual sight of Reno and Benteen most of the way. One could very well question where were this experienced officer's priorities, as his actions could lead one to conclude he had lost touch with the reality of the situation.[50] In fact, some psychiatrists have explained these strange obsessions, such as Reno's elevating the rescue of Hodg-

[32]Barnard, *Ten Years With Custer*, 296.
[33]Graham, *Reno Court*, 326.   [34]Ibid, 307.
[35]Ibid, 241.   [36]Graham, *Reno Court*, 230.
[37]Stewart, *The Field Diary . . .*, 12.
[38]Graham, *Reno Court*, 141.   [39]Ibid, 365.
[40]Ibid, 428.   [41]Ibid, 429.
[42]Ibid.
[43]Ibid, 305.   [44]Ibid.
[45]Ibid, 124.   [46]Ibid, 33.
[47]Ibid, 50.
[48]Frances B. Taunton, "No Pride In The Little Big Horn," *The English Westerners Society*, 1987, 33.
[49]Graham, *Reno Court*, 305.
[50]Luther, "Benteen, Reno and Custer," 13.

son's body above all his other responsibilities, as evidence of severe mental shock. It is believed, by maintaining this 'idee fixe' permits those who have been traumatized, to retain what sanity they still have available by holding tight to one piece of reality, in relation to the total situation confronting the individual.[51]

That the sounds of gunfire to the north were very audible to the men on Reno Hill, is undeniable. They were plainly heard by the officers, the enlisted men, the scouts, and anybody else who wasn't in denial or trying to obscure the facts. Who said they didn't hear the gunfire? Not surprisingly, it was Major Reno. At his Court of Inquiry, Reno testified he heard only a few scattered shots, but thought they were coming from the direction of the village, but in no manner did the shooting suggest a general battle was taking place. He further stated that the firing was so light it didn't give the impression of a general engagement.[52] Reno's official report suggested otherwise: "We could hear firing in that direction and knew it could only be Custer."[53] In addition, the *Bozeman Avant Courier's* dispatch of July 7, 1876 reported "in the judgment of Major Reno, who heard the first and last volleys of the firing." Lieutenant Wallace testified he didn't hear any gunfire but quickly added, "though others will say they did." He did admit to hearing some scattered shots, backing up Reno's statements, but "no heavy firing."[54] I have already questioned this engineering officer's math skills, and while he was standing right next to his friend, Varnum, his attention was directed to the heavy firing. Now, one can call into question his hearing ability, for it's little wonder he qualified his sworn denial of audible gunfire by remarking others will say the opposite. Captain Benteen supported Reno, and said he heard very little firing at all. "I don't suppose I heard more than 15 or 20 shots."[55] Benteen later did admit to the Court of Inquiry, under further questioning, that he heard the officers talking amongst themselves about the heavy volley firing. But he quickly added, "I heard no volleys."[56] Some officers took a sort of middle ground on whether they could hear the gunfire or not. For example, Moylan said the firing was very faint, but he could still distinguish it as volleys, and it continued for about an hour after he had reached the top of the bluffs.[57] He did admit, however, it was coming from the direction of Custer's field and not the Indian village.

Sergeant Culbertson recalled when he reached the top of the bluffs, his captain asked him about the number of casualties 'A' had taken in the fight. Edgerly and Varnum had joined the two, and while discussing the condition of the company, Culbertson heard heavy volley firing to the north. He remembered Varnum remarked "that General Custer was hotly engaged or was giving it to the Indians hot or words to that effect."[58] Varnum then asked the sergeant for a drink of water and inquired if he had seen anything of Hodgson during the retreat? Culbertson related what he knew about the lieutenant's condition, and they were soon joined by Reno. The major asked if he could find where he had seen him last, and Culbertson replied in the affirmative. Reno was no doubt hoping against hope his adjutant was only wounded and might still be alive. Reno then said he was going to look for his friend and get water and ordered about a dozen men in the vicinity along with the sergeant to accompany him to the river bank below.[59] The little party made its way down the bluffs, and after filling their canteens, came upon the body of Hodgson on a little bench sloping away from the river. Reno examined his adjutant's body and saw he had been shot in the groin and in the temple.[60] The lieutenant's watch and chain had already been taken from his body, but Reno removed a small gold bar which had held the timepiece, as well as a plain gold ring, which was said to be his West Point class ring.[61] Culbertson noted there weren't any Indians to their front, but they did see a few on the hills to their right. Reno and his men then began the climb back up the bluffs to the command.

It was during this return trip on a slope, among the ravine's undergrowth, that Culbertson found a 'G' trooper hiding. The man was apparently scared witless. There are some students of the battle who believe this man was Private Goldin, who claimed he was dispatched by Custer with a message to Reno, and this eighteen year old recruit was physically and mentally unable to carry out his orders. As noted previously, Goldin spent the rest of his life spinning different tales about his role in the Battle of the Little Big Horn. Colonel Graham once remarked each one of the stories was materially different from the other, and the historian could take his choice among them, as they "all are priced the same."[62]

---

[51]Ibid.
[52]Graham, *Reno Court*, 510.
[53]Carroll, *The Federal View*, 103.
[54]Graham, *Reno Court*, 31.
[55]Ibid, 357.
[56]Ibid, 360.
[57]Ibid, 200.

[58]Graham, *Reno Court*, 326.　　[59]Ibid, 325.
[60]Richard G. Hardorff, *On The Little Bighorn With Walter Camp* (El Segundo, CA: Upton & Sons, 2002), 131.
[61]Graham, *Reno Court*, 325.
[62]Graham, *The Custer Myth*, 276. In contrast to this unnamed trooper, who couldn't face the Indians, Pvt. John Wallace, from the same company, pursued a warrior across the river, caught and killed him. This trooper arrived on top of the bluff nonchalantly waving the freshly severed scalp at his fellow soldiers. See, Graham, *The Story of the Little Big Horn*, 59.

After picking up this 'G' Company soldier, who in Culbertson's opinion had hid until an opportunity presented itself to get out, the party returned to the command.[63] In the meantime, Dr. Porter left the hospital area to look for his fellow physician, Dr. DeWolf. He found his body on top of a small ravine below the bluffs and retrieved his pocketbook and a few personal items. Porter was gone only a few minutes and arrived back on the hill about the same time as Reno's party.[64] It was a little before five o'clock in the afternoon when Reno returned to the bluffs. The pack train still had not arrived, so Reno finally decided to try and hurry it along. He appointed Hare his acting adjutant and ordered him to bring the ammunition mules forward. There has been some question as to exactly when Reno gave the order to hurry up these mules. Reno's biographer, Ron Nichols, has Reno appointing Hare shortly after Benteen arrived on the bluffs and immediately ordered him to the pack train.[65] However, this is simply not true. For many different reasons, a number of officers tried to disguise what had happened with misinformation and distortions of the event's sequences. Varnum made it very clear that Reno had returned from his search for Hodgson before dispatching Hare. He remembered this very distinctly because soon after Hare departed, Reno ordered him to take "a detachment and go down and bury Lieut. Hodgson's body." Varnum told Reno it was impossible, as he hadn't any shovels to accomplish the task. He would have to wait until the pack train arrived.[66] Reno told the chief of scouts he could wait. As for Hare, he confused the chronology of the events on Reno Hill by ignoring Reno's half hour absence, as he told Walter Camp, about ten minutes after Benteen came up, Reno sent him to the packs.[67] His confusion (deliberate distortion?) becomes readily apparent when one reads what Reno, himself, told the Court of Inquiry. When asked what orders were sent to the pack train, Reno replied after he returned from examining Hodgson's body, the pack train still wasn't up, "I could not make myself omnipresent. I sent him (Hare) to the pack train to hurry it up all he could. At the time, it was not in sight."[68]

Hare's horse was badly wounded through the jaw, and the poor animal's tongue was hanging outside of its mouth. Godfrey had one of the freshest horses, so Hare borrowed the mount and started for the pack train.[69] The pack train was only about a mile from Reno Hill, but out of sight because of the bluffs, and Hare reached it in about ten minutes. Windolph, however, said the pack train could be plainly seen "coming over the back trail" and Hare rode right to it.[70] But, Godfrey thought Hare was off on a one way mission, alone in Indian infested territory, and he wished him good luck, for Godfrey never expected to see his friend again.[71] Captain Thomas McDougall had the pack train as well closed up as could be expected and was following the trail Custer had taken until he had received Knipe's message, then, as noted, he directed the train to the right. A number of the Arikara scouts had passed him, herding about a dozen Sioux ponies. One of the scouts told McDougall that "The whole Sioux nation is over there in the valley and I am going back to Powder River cantonment."[72] The captain of Company 'B' said he met Hare about a half a mile east of Reno Hill. Lieutenant Mathey directed Benjamin Churchill and Frank Mann, along with two other packers, to cut out two ammunition mules.[73] Each mule was loaded with 2000 rounds, packed into two boxes of one thousand rounds each, one on each side of the mule. With Mann leading the first mule, and Churchill slapping it from behind, the second mule followed, being treated in a like fashion. The little party made their way to Reno's command as fast as they could.[74]

In less than ten minutes, the ammunition resupply had arrived on the bluffs. The packers started to unpack the ammunition boxes, as it was "supposed they wanted it immediately and we unpacked it for their use."[75] But, no sooner had they accomplished this task, then they were ordered to repack the boxes back onto the mules. The packers did not believe the boxes had even been opened and couldn't understand why they had been rushed forward. Mathey agreed with his two packers and didn't remember any ammunition was distributed from the boxes.[76] Private John McGuire, 'C' Company and assigned to the pack train, also recalled no boxes were opened.[77] However, according to Lieutenant Wallace, one box was opened, but not all its contents were taken by the troopers.[78] Wallace later described how when they tried to unpack one of the boxes, the lid was fastened on by screws. "Someone called for an ax and the box was split open about in half, and the men came up and helped themselves to what they wanted till it was all gone."[79] One

[63]Graham, *Reno Court*, 325.   [64]Ibid, 177.
[65]Nichols, *In Custer's Shadow*, 190.
[66]Graham, *Reno Court*, 124.
[67]Hammer, *Custer in '76*, 66. Also see Graham, *Reno Court*, 247.
[68]Graham, *Reno Court*, 505.
[69]Hammer, *Custer in '76*, 66.

[70]Carroll, *The Sunshine Magazine Articles*, 21.
[71]Meketa, *Luther Rector Hare*, 42.
[72]Hammer, *Custer in '76*, 69.   [73]Graham, *Reno Court*, 458.
[74]Ibid, 412.   [75]Ibid, 415.
[76]Ibid, 458.   [77]Hammer, *Custer in '76*, 124.
[78]Graham, *Reno Court*, 52, 550.   [79]Ibid, 484.

might well question how critical was the shortage of ammunition among Reno's command? If Wallace was correct, Reno's troopers took only an average of ten rounds per man. This leads to much speculation regarding the real reason for Reno not responding to the 'come on, be quick' message or to the sound of the guns. In light of what the packers saw and what Wallace recalled, it's doubtful that ammunition had anything to do with Reno's inaction. This wait for ammunition is even more suspect because even with the availability of 4000 additional rounds, Reno still didn't order an advance, as now he decided to wait for the rest of the pack train. Culbertson said it was because of the wounded that Reno waited for the entire pack train to arrive. The troops simply had no way to move the wounded who were not able to ride without blankets to carry them upon.[80] Errors of judgment, panic, and possible mental breakdown may be used to explain Reno's decisions on this afternoon, but they do not excuse them.[81] Wallace did say that there was no uneasiness concerning Custer's command, even though most had heard heavy firing to the north. He did admit, he heard unnamed officers doing "a great deal of swearing about Custer running off and leaving us."[82] Custer might have used the very same oaths regarding the response to his 'come on, be quick' order.

As Hare approached Reno's Hill with the two mules, he noticed Company 'D' advancing toward where the gunfire had been heard. They were some distance out, but still in sight. This would mean they were not over 700 yards away, for Edgerly led them down the ravine, running to the right of and parallel with Sharpshooters' Ridge, which was about the same distance from where the other troops were.[83] If they had passed the head of this ridge, the company would have been out of sight.[84] Shortly after Hare was dispatched to the pack train, when it became apparent no one was doing anything about the gunfire or complying with Custer's orders, Weir lost what little patience he had remaining with both Reno and Benteen. Exactly how Weir came to ride towards the gunfire has been a matter of dispute. Martin said the men all wanted to hurry up and join Custer, but the officers wouldn't let them. Custer's last messenger remembered he saw Captain Weir talking to Reno, and the Captain was excited and appeared angry. Weir kept pointing down the river; soon after this he rode off to the north.[85] Windolph also

stated, "It is known that he had a heated argument with Reno."[86] In addition, Private John Fox, Company 'D,' said he overheard Weir talking with Reno and asking to go to Custer. Fox said Reno told him he could not go, "For if you try to do it, you will get killed and your Company with you." Fox also added he thought Reno was drunk or partially so.[87] Fred Dustin, with a flair for the dramatic, claimed he was told by a soldier of Reno's battalion that Weir went to Reno and was refused permission to advance his troop. At this point, it was reported a hot exchange of uncomplimentary language took place between the two officers to the extent of threats being made by both parties.[88] In spite of all these distinct recollections of a request, a rejection, and an argument, they make for a good story, but that is probably all it is.

If anyone would know the true story of how the company came to move out, it should be Edgerly. In 1886, Godfrey was trying to supplement his reminiscences of the battle, and wrote to Edgerly for the details of how Weir, he, and 'D' Company were the first "to ride to the sound of the guns." Winfield Edgerly told his friend that after arriving on the bluffs, the men had become impatient because no attempt was made to respond to the gunfire so plainly heard. The company's first sergeant, Michael Martin, went to Edgerly with his concerns, and together they approached Weir. With Reno no where in sight, Weir asked them if they were willing to advance with only their company? Edgerly replied he was. It was a little after 5:00 PM, and Reno had returned from his search for Hogdson, and Weir saw Reno speaking to Benteen. Weir started to walk towards the two senior officers, but stopped, returned to his company, and with only his orderly, Private Charles Sanders, mounted his horse and rode to the north. Edgerly, thinking Weir had received the necessary permission, immediately ordered 'D' to mount and followed in his wake.[89] Edgerly learned of his misinterpretation upon reaching Weir Point, when his captain told him "that he was delighted to see me coming and tho't it a sign of personal devotion to him."[90] It wasn't until 1881, that Edgerly finally confirmed what he had personally learned from Weir at the time of the movement. His Captain, it seems, never spoke to either Reno or Benteen, but decided to first ride out to the high point to see if anything could be seen of Custer's command before asking permission

[80]Ibid, 325. [81]Luther, "Benteen, Reno and Custer," 12.
[82]Graham, *Reno Court*, 33.
[83]Hammer, *Custer in '76*, 66.
[84]Kuhlman, *Legend Into History*, 99–100.
[85]Graham, *The Custer Myth*, 291.

[86]Carroll, *The Sunshine Magazine Articles*, 21.
[87]Liddic, *Camp on Custer*, 94–95.
[88]9Dustin, *The Custer Tragedy*, 141–142.
[89]Letter, Winfield Edgerly to Edward Godfrey, January 17, 1886, New York Public Library, Hagner Collection.
[90]Graham, *The Custer Myth*, 217.

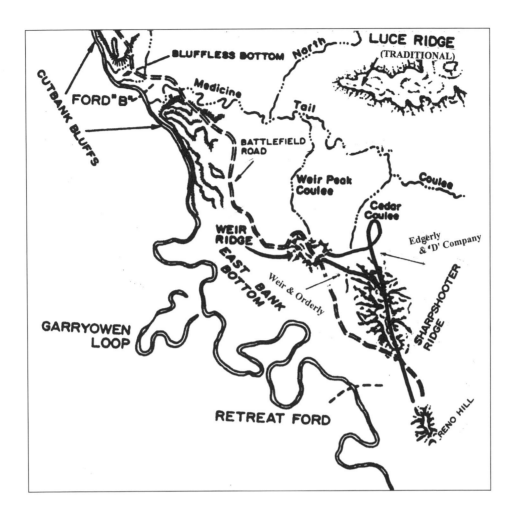

to advance his company. Weir further informed Edgerly that not only did he never speak to Reno about it, but he never even mentioned he was going to leave the command, let alone ask for Reno's permission.[91] In his story, Edgerly is supported by Benteen, who knew of no such request by Weir. In fact, Benteen in his narrative of the battle claimed he never even knew where 'D' Company was and had to inquire of Reno for their whereabouts.[92] He later changed his story, stating, "About this time, I saw one of the troops of my battalion proceeding to the front, mounted. It was Capt. Weir who had sallied out in that direction in a fit of bravado, I think, without orders."[93] One guess is as good as another as to what Benteen really saw, heard or did during the campaign. Neither was Reno aware that one of the companies was riding to the north, and he surely didn't authorize the movement.

Weir moved out about five minutes before he was fol-

lowed by his company, thus it was about quarter after five when 'D' started to the north. That the troopers were still visible from Reno Hill, would mean they had not passed the head of this high hill, for Edgerly led them down the ravine, running to the right of and parallel with Sharpshooters' Ridge.[94] After Weir left Reno Hill, he moved to the first high ground in sight, which is Sharpshooters' Ridge, to try and see what was the situation to the north. After he saw what he could, which wasn't much, Weir noticed the tracks from Custer's battalion and followed them. About a quarter mile past this ridge, he saw the tracks changed from a company front and turned to the east. Weir and his orderly then rode for the high twin peaks which today bear his name. In a highly acclaimed book, published in 2000, Larry Sklenar presented a case for Weir never going to his own peak, as he stopped well before Edgerly on the 'sugarloaf.'[95] He claimed that the 'sugerloaf' ridge described by Sergeant Thomas Harrison,

[91]Ibid, 220.   [92]Ibid, 181.

[93]Brininstool, *Troopers With Custer*, 81; Kuhlman, *Legend Into History*, 99.

[94]Hammer, *Custer in '76*, 66.

[95]Sklemar, *To Hell With Honor*, 305.

Company 'D,' was Sharpshooters' ridge. Sklenar then described Edgerly moving all the way down to the northern slope of Sharpshooters' Ridge and dismounting 'D.' The other companies filled in behind 'D,' except for Benteen, who advanced further than anyone else, all the way to what we know as Weir Point and tried to attract Custer's attention with a guidon.[96]

The evidence in regards to this reconstruction is not favorable to Mr. Sklenar's interpretation. If one reads the testimony of Hare, he said that Weir's troops were on "the highest point around," which describes Weir Point, not Sharpshooters' Ridge.[97] In addition to this verbal testimony, Hare identified (pointed to) high points, on the map used at the Court, as the spot where Weir had advanced. This identification was well north of Sharpshooters' Ridge. Godfrey also agreed with this recognition on the map, as did Edgerly.[98] DeRudio left no doubt as to Weir Point as "it was the highest point down the stream." In addition, "I went to the top of it afterwards on the 27th with Capt. Benteen."[99] What Harrison said was, Edgerly was on the "northeast end of the sugarloaf east of the two peaks."[100] This is not Sharpshooters' Ridge, as there are no "two peaks" east of it. But, it does accurately describe the two peaks of Weir Point west of the present road, and the 'sugarloaf' conforms to the point (ridge) east of these two peaks. In 1986, Jerome Greene identified a number of cartridge finds on Weir Point and concluded that the "soldier activity was concentrated around Weir Point."[101] Futhermore, in 1994 another more detailed archeological survey concluded the number of artifacts discovered on Weir Point were "patterned" and judged as "consistent with Company D's movement . . . and the subsequent retrograde movement back to Reno-Benteen."[102] Lastly, is the location of the Vincent Charley incident, which will be addressed later in this chapter. His body was found about 650 feet south of the eastern 'sugarloaf,' a good quarter mile northwest of Sharpshooters' Ridge, from where Mr. Sklenar believes 'D' was positioned.

If one looks at Camp's Little Big Horn map, drawn on by Edgerly, the lieutenant marked 'D's position, to begin

their movement, some distance north of the rest of the command.[103] This might be true as troops were sent to the area of Sharpshooters' Ridge after Benteen's battalion arrived on the bluffs to dislodge some Indian snipers, which included Wooden Leg. Thus, when Hare said the troops were still in sight, he might have been referring to the rear of 'D' before they disappeared over the ridge line. Edgerly led 'D' company along the same route Weir had taken, but Edgerly, instead of going on to Weir Point, continued on Custer's trail until they were almost at the point where it continued down into Medicine Tail Coulee; very near the spot from where Martin was dispatched. Weir, who had a better view of the whole surrounding country, saw some Indians start to move on the company and signaled his lieutenant to swing to the right.[104] This had the effect of circling 'D' around and doubling over their own trail before turning westward towards Weir on his peaks. This different conjecture of Weir's and Company D's route is confirmed by Edgerly's testimony at the Reno Court. He said Weir kept to the ridge while he led the company down a sort of a valley. After swinging all the way around he came up on the point, reuniting with Weir.[105] Edgerly ratified this route in a letter to Godfrey: Weir "kept to the left along the ridge and I swung off to the right and followed a ravine which led to the Custer field. I think we had gone about a mile" to the north.[106] The above reconstruction of the movement to Weir Point is counter to the traditional view of many battle students, also advocated by the National Park Service (Custer Battlefield), which has Weir riding directly near the edge of the bluffs, along the present battlefield road, straight for Weir Point, followed by Edgerly.[107]

Private George Wylie, Company 'D,' remembered that his company had no sooner started north then they saw the half breed scout Billy Cross coming from the direction of Weir Point.[108] The troopers saw Cross coming in the opposite direction towards them; he had a hand-

---

[96]Ibid., 308.

[97]Graham, *Reno Court*, 247. In 1921, Walter Camp wrote to Godfrey and used the term 'high point,' as did the officers at the Reno Court of Inquiry, which Camp was told designated Weir Point. See Hardorff, *On The Little Bighorn With Walter Camp*, 162–163.

[98]Graham, *Reno Court*, 249, 394, 431.

[99]Ibid, 291.   [100]Liddic, *Camp on Custer*, 97.

[101]Douglas D. Scott and Peter Bleed, *A Good Walk Around The Boundary* (NP : NP, 1997), 29–30.

[102]Ibid, 33–34.

[103]Michael Donahue, "On The Battlefield," *Greasy Grass*, Vol. 14, May 1998, 10–11. It has been questioned whether Edgerly actually drew on this map or that Camp recorded what he was told, over the years, and made the notations himself.

[104]Graham, *Reno Court*, 393. We don't really know what Weir saw from the high point but Edgerly testified, "Pretty soon he (Weir) saw Indians start for me and he signalled me to swing to the right."

[105]Ibid., 393.

[106]Letter, Winfield Edgerly To Edward Godfrey, January 17, 1886, New York Public Library, Hagner Collection.

[107]Stewart, *Custer's Luck*, 397; Gray, *Custer's Last Campaign*, 319–320. Also see Sklenar, *To Hell With Honor*, 307.

[108]For a different account of Cross, see Richard G. Hardorff, *Walter M. Camp's Little Bighorn Rosters* (Spokane, WA: The Arthur H. Clark Company, 2002), 57.

kercheif tied around his head.[109] However, Sergeant Private Stanislas Roy, Company 'A,' said Cross never forded with Reno's battalion when they went into the valley, and he doesn't remember seeing him on the west side of the river at all.[110] If this is true, then Cross and a few Arikaras kept to the east side and climbed the bluffs; while Cross's route, as Wylie seems to indicate, was that of a circle from west side of the river to east. Nevertheless, Herendeen's account agrees with what Wylie recalled about seeing the half-breed scout. It seems Cross had several Arikaras with him, and as Varnum's burial detail reached the top of the bluffs, Herendeen met Cross. Herendeen told Cross, if he wanted a cheap scalp he would "find a dead Sioux a little further down."[111] But, it appeared all Cross and the Arikaras wanted to do was get out of the country; they had their fill of Sioux in the valley and were not seen again until they reached the Powder River.[112]

With the dust from the two ammunition mules rapidly disappearing in the distance, McDougall and Mathey moved the rest of the pack train forward in their wake. It was about 30 minutes (Varnum said 45 minutes) later, or about five thirty, when the head of the pack train arrived among Reno's command, which had done almost nothing since their arrival over an hour ago.[113] McDougall had heard heavy gunfire to the north about five o' clock, and as soon as he arrived on the bluffs, he reported to Reno, informing the major he had not lost a single animal, and that he had heard firing to the north. Reno gave no explanation of the situation and made no reply except to say, "I lost your lieutenant (Hodgson) and he is lying down there," pointing towards the river.[114] It was at this time, right after McDougall arrived on the hill, that Knipe (he rode in with McDougall) saw Private Peter Thompson come walking back. Thompson explained his absence from Company 'C' as "his horse had given out somewhere down in the low country and he had to fall out. He had left the horse standing, wandered around and got lost and finally found his way to Reno on the heights."[115] Knipe, seeing Thompson at this moment, cast a different light on his self described "adventures" beyond Medicine Tail Coulee. It would appear that with the Indian threat subsiding, the skirmish lines had been pulled back, and the

troopers were more or less just standing around on the bluffs. Actually, the first sergeants had their various sergeants going around checking on the men, inquiring who were present and fit for duty, the names of those who were killed, wounded, or missing, and taking an account of government property lost.[116] The officers, meanwhile, were discussing the events and had assembled on the edge of the bluffs overlooking the river. They were talking about the circumstances they found themselves in. Godfrey remembered Moylan, who must have regained his composure, spoke up and said, "Gentlemen, in my opinion General Custer has made the biggest mistake of his life by not taking the whole regiment in at once in the first attack."[117]

McDougall couldn't understand why any firm lines hadn't been formed yet and looked to the north and thought if any Indians were to suddenly come over that ridge line they would have caught the troops entirely unprepared.[118] The warriors could have overrun the whole command. He immediately ordered both platoons of 'B' away from the pack train and established a skirmish line to guard against this possibility.[119] Mathey was equally concerned about the situation, and when questioned at the Reno Court of Inquiry about what everyone was waiting for, after a long pause, replied, "I don't know exactly."[120] McDougall was of the opinion that Reno "did not appear to regard the seriousness of the situation."[121] Twenty years earlier, while a cadet at West Point, Reno received a number of demerits for "destroying a shade tree" that was aside his guard post. In an explanation to the Commandant of Cadets, he wrote: "Thoughtlessness in regard to the safety of anything entrusted to my care is a defect in my character, which I cannot correct."[122] Perhaps this self-assessment is a fitting benediction for Reno's actions on that afternoon. Upon his arrival on the hill, Mathey heard Major Reno giving orders to Captain French to go and bury Hodgson. Captain French wasn't very thrilled with the idea of going back down to the river and requested more men. Mathey noticed Reno becoming impatient with French and " told him to go and he went."[123] But in true army fashion, French turned to Varnum and ordered him to

[109]Hammer, *Custer in '76*, 129.   [110]Ibid, 111.

[111]Ibid, 225.

[112]There are other accounts which claim Cross fought in the valley along with the other scouts. They then went to the river to get water and were unable to rejoin the soldiers, so the next best thing they could do was to return to the Power River Depot.

[113]Graham, *Reno Court*, 124.   [114]Ibid, 470.

[115]*Camp, BYU*, roll 5, box 6, folder 7.

[116]Taylor, *With Custer on the Little Bighorn*, 48.

[117]Fred Dustin, *The Custer Fight* (NP: Privately Printed, 1936), 36.

[118]*Camp, BYU*, roll 5, box 5, folder 5.

[119]Hammer, *Custer in '76*, 70.   [120]Graham, *Reno Court*, 515.

[121]Hammer, *Custer in '76*, 70.

[122]William A. Graham, *The Reno Court of Inquiry Abstract of the Official Record of Proceedings* (Mechanicsburg, PA: Stackpole Books, 1994), xxv.   [123]Graham, *Reno Court*, 459.

go to the pack train to get a couple of spades, take six men, go down to the river and bury Hodgson along with any other bodies which happened to be in the vicinity.[124] It was after 5:30 when Varnum started down the bluffs with his burial detail. Varnum was probably not in the best of humor, as he started back down the bluffs with a detachment of six men and two shovels. The detail had traveled almost two-thirds of the way to the river, when Varnum spotted a number of men emerging from the eastern river's bank. He quickly ordered his troopers to bring their weapons to bear until he could determine what was happening.[125] When it was discovered they were soldiers, Varnum quickly spread the men out to cover their approach from the river.[126]

Herendeen and the troopers who had remained with him had worked their way toward the river, with the intention of crossing it and making for the high ground where they had earlier seen company guidons, and now they could make out the forms of men thought to be soldiers. There were six soldiers from 'G,' three from 'M,' and two from 'A' in the group.[127] The scout and the soldiers had been hearing gunfire for nearly an hour from downstream. Herendeen thought the firing was coming from Custer's command.[128] The party all had turned their horses loose before moving to the river. The men left the little park like place of concealment in the timber, went out to a bend in the river, and crossed over. Herendeen recalled on the eastern side there was a steep cut bank, and the water was up to the men's shoulders. That all the warriors' attention was focused elsewhere, is confirmed by the lack of any serious opposition encountered by the troopers. Herendeen remembered that they only saw five Indians, and just one shot was fired at them. The soldiers responded in kind, and the Indians disappeared. The mere fact that a body of men was able to leave their place of concealment, travel to the river, then cross, and climb the bluffs without being bothered by the Indians is ample proof there was no serious opposition confronting Reno, since the command gained the bluffs an hour before.[129]

After reaching the other side and just starting up a ravine, the men spotted "an officer and some men."[130] It seems both groups saw each other about the same time. Varnum, happy with the reinforcements, now commenced to bury the bodies. He had no sooner started the task, when Wallace appeared on a bank over a ravine and presented Reno's compliments, ordered the entire group back to the bluffs.[131] Varnum had no idea why he was being directed to return, but he immediately started the men back up the hill. He remembered it was a slow hard climb. It was towards six o'clock when they arrived back on the bluffs only to find most of the command was moving down the river along the ridge line.[132]

Upon Hare's return from pushing the ammunition mules forward, Reno called to him and gave him another set of orders. He was told that Weir had advanced while he was gone, and he was to ride after him and inform Weir that he was to open up communication with Custer. The rest of the command would follow as soon as the pack train arrived.[133] It was about 5:30 PM when Hare turned his horse's head to the north and rode out. There is a question as to what Reno was attempting to accomplish when he sent Hare to tell Weir to 'communicate' with Custer? Many years later, Hare told Camp that Reno's order was to 'connect' and not 'communicate' with Custer.[134] Was Weir to seek assistance from Custer, or was he to offer assistance to Custer? Was 'D' supposed to join Custer in any attack? Or was Reno's orginal order to Hare to 'communicate' with Custer correct, so the left wing would know what to do; as it was apparent the second in command didn't? Unfortunately, we'll never know for sure what Reno had in mind when he finally made a small effort to determine what was happening with the main column. The closest indication we have regarding Reno's plan was for Weir to 'communicate' with Custer "if he could, and tell him where we were."[135] Custer, no doubt, would have been pleased to receive this communication!

When Varnum reached the top of the hill, to his surprise, he saw only two companies as the rest of the left wing had departed. Varnum didn't indicate if the major was leading his command forward, but it was assumed he was. In fact, Wallace testified that Reno was out in front leading the command downstream; Moylan agreed.[136] But was he? Again the officers, for various personal reason(s), both confused or screened the sequence of events. Perhaps, as it is strongly believed to protect their own reputations directly and Reno's only indirectly. When Benteen was questioned about where Reno was during the movement, he answered he didn't know if he had still gone to look for Hodgson's body or not. Then realizing what he had said, replied to a follow up question that the Major

[124]Ibid, 124.   [125]Ibid.
[126]Carroll, *I, Varnum*, 68.
[127]Taylor, *With Custer on the Little Bighorn*, 49.
[128]Graham, *Reno Court*, 218.
[129]McClernand, *With the Indian and the Buffalo in Montana*, 80–81.
[130]Graham, *Reno Court*, 220.

[131]Ibid, 124.   [132]Ibid.
[133]Ibid, 247.   [134]Hammer, *Custer in '76*, 66.
[135]Graham, *Reno Court*, 505.   [136]Ibid, 53, 187.

"got to that point about as early as I did, or very nearly."[137] This was a complete lie by the senior captain; Reno never did go to Weir Point. Herendeen, who had nothing to protect or any ulterior motives, said Reno wasn't anywhere near the head of the left wing as it moved down the bluffs. In fact, when he reached the top, with Varnum's burial detail, he was "directly" called to the major's side as Reno wanted him to act as an interpreter to Half-Yellow-Face from whom Reno was trying unsuccessfully to obtain information. Reno had previously motioned the Crow scout over to him and had been attempting to question him regarding the activity in the Indian camp. Reno wanted the scout's opinion about what the Indians were going to do as they were taking down their teepees and were moving away. The Crow said he thought they were going away. Soon after this exchange, Reno summoned Half-Yellow-Face back to him, and asked if they were fleeing, "How is this, the lodges are all up again?" The scout could only stare incredulously into the valley, and said through Herendeen, he didn't know.[138]

Benteen always maintained that he had followed with the rest of his battalion immediately after Weir. However, he could not have left as early as he claimed, which was about 5:15 PM, because Benteen had been waiting for French to resupply his company with ammunition. This was made plain by the testimony of Godfrey and others at the Court of Inquiry. Exactly why French would have to wait for the rest of the pack train to come up with the other ten ammunition mules, when there was already no less then 3,000 rounds available, which hadn't been distributed, is unknown. Even more unexplainable is why Benteen, if he had decided to follow Weir directly, permitted French to delay the whole column. Perhaps what Benteen's lieutenant, Gibson, wrote to his wife nine days after the battle helps explain this officer's thinking. He recorded the command couldn't move to assist Custer any earlier than they did, as "It was impossible as we could neither abandon our wounded men, nor the packs of the whole command."[139] But Hare, in a moment of candor, implied that the command could have moved forward earlier than they did, as it wasn't necessary to wait for the whole pack train. The wounded didn't have to be moved, as they could have been left with the pack train where they were on the hill, there was no need to carry them along. Captain McDougall's company combined with the

pack train guards would have been more than an adequate force to protect these unfortunate individuals.[140]

It was before six o'clock, nearly two hours since Reno's command had scrambled up the bluffs, over 45 minutes since the two ammunition mules had arrived, and 30 minutes since the pack train arrived, yet only one company had moved out to check on the whereabouts of the rest of the regiment. And even this movement was not authorized. But, as Weir rode to the north, with Edgerly following, it had the effect of at last prodding Benteen into action. Now that the packs had arrived, a movement of some sort could be safely undertaken. It has also been suggested, Benteen might have reasoned it would show poorly to have a junior officer with just one company reach Custer before he did.[141] This could very well be close to the truth, or why else would Benteen feel obliged to follow one of his battalion's captains who "had sallied on, having no orders to proceed?"[142] Another explanation, I believe, is Benteen simply did not connect the dots, the 'come on, be quick' order, the absence of Indians around Reno Hill and in the village, and the gunfire —volleys— heard downstream. He, by not doing so, failed to realize the enormity of what was taking place to the north. Consequently, when Benteen did finally move out, the action was without a plan and lacked decisiveness. There are a few students of the battle who believe Benteen was "a wholesale murderer." It was a well-known fact that he despised Custer. They believe Custer and his "gang" were uppermost in Benteen's mind, and he used the warriors at the Little Big Horn as "hit men" to rid himself of Custer. One went so far as to write, Benteen was provoked to such an extent that "sacrificing the lives of 225 other men was wholly immaterial."[143] I do not subscribe to this assessment of Benteen's motives, as it is neither sound nor rational. At best, it's difficult enough to try to ascertain what motivates a person you know, let alone one who has been long dead that you never even knew.

After French was resupplied, Benteen motioned for Company 'M' to follow him and started downstream, with Companies 'K' and 'H' falling in behind.[144] Benteen said he went after Weir "to see for myself what was

---

[137]Ibid, 361.

[138]Ibid, 221. As noted previously, the dismantling of the lodges was also seen by the Arikara Scouts.

[139]Fougera, *With Custer's Cavalry*, 269.

[140]Stewart, *Custer's Luck*, 403.

[141]Eric Bacopulos, "Captain Frederick W. Benteen's Response to Custer's Last Message," *7th Annual Symposium Custer Battlefield Historical & Museum Assn.*, 1993, 39.

[142]Carroll, *The Benteen—Goldin Letters On Custer And His Last Battle*, 215.

[143]Georg Wenzel Schneider-Wettengel, "Murder Most Foul," *Research Review* (Little Big Horn Associates, Inc.), Vol. 15, # 6, June, 1981, 3.   [144]Hammer, *Custer in '76*, 56.

Courtesy of Hastings House Publishers

going on around the whole country that could be seen."[145] Reno was dismayed when he saw these troops moving off. Two of his senior company commanders were no longer acting under his authority. Now, an additional three companies had left him without orders, and he had his trumpeter sound recall "continuously and assiduously."[146] Benteen paid no attention to the call and just continued with the troops, heading north directly for Weir Point, "to get in sight then of what I had left my valley-hunting mission for."[147] It is unfortunate Benteen didn't decide time was of the essence earlier. Twenty years later, Benteen came to this same conclusion and wrote that "Too much time had been lost."[148] But, he never acknowledged by whom was it lost. The lack of information or misunderstanding, indecision, disregard of orders, personal feelings, and general inefficiency brought about by the lack of leadership had all conspired to delay this going to the 'sound of the guns' until it was too late to successfully challenge the battle's outcome.[149]

Reno, of course, had a different view of the troops moving downstream. Even though Weir had "on his own hook moved out his," Reno now regarded Weir's company as the advance guard. This would give the other companies, he ordered out for their support, time to get into position. To accomplish this support, Reno said that "After the pack train came up I formed the column with three companies on the left, the pack train in the middle and two companies on the right and started down the river."[150] The only detail the major omitted was where he would have positioned the regimental band! Reno also said he was at the head of the combined battalions and was leading them in the direction Custer had taken. This account by Reno is pure and simple moonshine. However, he now admitted to the Court of Inquiry that he did know where Custer had gone as his trail had been "found."[151]

In spite of Reno's described detailed formation, the reality is that the three separate troop movements to Weir Point were done independently of each other. The advance was disjointed, and there wasn't any coordination from one move to the next. The foregoing fairly represents how the command moved north. Company 'D' moved out first, and about a half an hour later, Benteen followed, with Company 'M' at the head of the movement and succeeded, as noted, by Companies 'K' and 'H.' Reno was still on the hill about six o'clock with Herendeen and Half-Yellow-Face. Company 'B' delayed their advance, to help 'A' make ready to carry the seven wounded men who were

[145]Graham, *Reno Court*, 361.
[146]Brininstool, *Troopers With Custer*, 81.   [147]Ibid.
[148]Holmes, "The Little Big Horn—Benteen: An Unpublished Letter," 4.   [149]*Camp, BYU*, box 5, folder 5.
[150]Graham, *Reno Court*, 505–506.   [151]Ibid, 505.

unable to mount.[152] Most of the wounded who reached the bluffs were from 'A,' and these troopers were carried on a blanket by six men, mostly from their own company. The pack train was set to bring up the rear. After going only about a quarter of a mile or a little beyond, where the current boundary fence line crosses the road, Moylan rode out to McDougall and said he couldn't keep up with the movement because of the wounded. He needed help. McDougall then detached his second platoon and personally accompanied it back to Company 'A.' Upon rejoining the first platoon, he noticed that the whole forward movement was stopped, and the troops were being directed to "left about."[153] The pack train never really moved and probably didn't cross the current northern boundary of the Reno-Benteen Battlefield. After Company 'A' moved out, Reno finally mounted up and rode towards Company 'B.' It was before 6:15 PM. Even as the pack train had begun to move, one man, Private Thomas Blake, Company 'A,' was left behind. He was so stricken with fear that he refused to move by claiming he was too injured. His disgusted fellow troopers simply left without him.[154]

Weir Point rises rather steeply about a mile and a quarter from Reno Hill. The point is in effect a group of three promontories that resemble a sort of an 'L' on its side. There are two points along the river's bluffs, west of the present road and parallel with the river. The other peak lies east of the road and presents a round 'sugarloaf' appearance. At the time of the battle, the eastern and western projections were connected by gradual sloping sides that have since been graded down for the present road bed. Before the road was improved in 1954, the graveled roadbed simply went up and over the connecting slanting sides. With the paving of the road, the area between the peaks was cut down, and in 2001 the eastern projection was cut back about six feet further to accommodate traffic access for the Weir Point interpretive marker. It was to these peaks that Weir and his orderly arrived about 5:30. It was a little after 5:45 PM when Edgerly led Company 'D' up the slopes of Weir's Point, arriving up over the projection in front of Weir as he was on the "second peak farthest north."[155] Wylie recalled that Edgerly dismounted the men, sent the horses back over the peak to the south, and formed a line running east to west. There are some accounts that have Edgerly meeting Weir about where the present road cuts through the peaks, and he continued to lead them in an easterly direction and turned to the

north. Edgerly rode along this ridge line for about another half mile before stopping.[156] Weir looked downstream, saw what he thought to be guidons, and said he could see Custer over there.[157] As he prepared to advance the troop, Sergeant James Flanagan quickly spoke up: "Here Captain, you had better take a look through the glasses; I think they are Indians."[158] Weir did so and changed his mind about leaving the point.

It was shortly after Edgerly reported to Weir that they noticed a lone rider approaching from Reno position. It was Lieutenant Hare; he arrived to find Edgerly and 'D' out ahead of Weir.[159] Hare delivered Reno's order to Weir to open up 'communication' with Custer. He then turned his horse back to the command and found it coming down stream. Benteen had moved about a mile.[160] Hare stopped to tell Benteen about the situation ahead, but he hadn't finished when he looked up and saw Captain Weir joining them.[161] Weir had seen the dust of the troops and assuming Reno was at the head, rode to meet the column, as he knew reinforcements were necessary if they were to carry out the major's orders. Edgerly confirmed right after Hare spoke to his captain, Weir left the hill by himself going towards Reno Hill.[162]

Benteen's expanded battalion continued on, climbed the peak's slopes, and the troops deployed in the order they had marched along the peaks. Edgerly with 'D' was already in line on the eastern most projection, and French deployed his command to the west and slightly behind 'D.' Later, the remnants of Company 'G' under Wallace filled in next to 'D's left flank.[163] Godfrey halted 'K' before they reached the crest on the south side of the western point. He wanted to see what was ahead and rode to the top by himself. After looking around, Godfrey ordered 'K' onto the point to connect with 'M.' Company 'K' was following the contour of the peak and was positioned a little to the rear of 'M's line.[164] Benteen led 'H' to the two peaks which paralleled the river, taking a forward position on the northern most point.[165] For whatever reason, Benteen apparently was only exercising command over his own company at this point. None of the other three company commanders indicated that Benteen gave them any orders or attempted to direct them once they turned

[152]Ibid, 52.   [153]Ibid, 471–472.
[154]Sklenar, *To Hell With Honor*, 219.   [155]Hammer, *Custer in '76*, 56.

[156]Joe Sills, "Weir Point Perspective," *7th Annual Symposium Custer Battlefield Historical & Museum Assn.*, 1993, 45.
[157]Hammer, *Custer in '76*, 56.   [158]Ibid, 129.
[159]Ibid, 66.   [160]Graham, *Reno Court*, 247.
[161]Ibid, 260.
[162]Ibid, 394; Carroll, *The Gibson and Edgerly Narratives*, 11.
[163]Graham, *Reno Court*, 53–54.   [164]Ibid, 431.
[165]Ibid, 360.

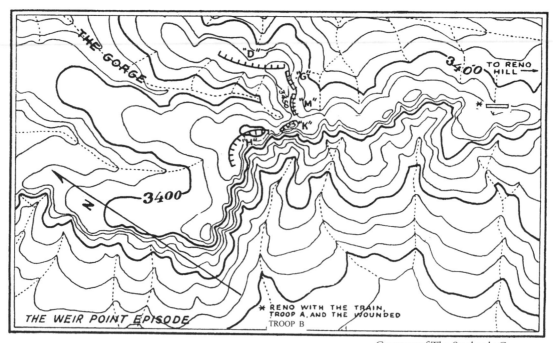

to the north. Benteen said the other troops were at a right angle to his on the other ridge, "with the intention of showing to General Custer . . . our exact location as near as possible."[166] Benteen further elaborated that when he arrived at the elevations, he had his "first glimpse" of the Indian encampment.

> I saw enough to cause me to think that perhaps this time we had bitten off quite as much as we would be able to chew. Then I got the guidon of my own troop and jammed it down in a pile of stones which were on the high point, thinking perhaps the fluttering of same might attract attention from Custer's command if any were in close proximity.[167]

Private George Glenn of 'H' told how he and others had looked down and saw the country thick with Indians, "and some of the men said to Benteen, 'Captain, the Indians are getting around us.'"[168] Benteen had also been observing the country downstream and noticed the number of Indians moving in the direction of the troops. He turned to Gibson and said, "This is a hell of a place to fight Indians. I am going to see Reno and propose that we go back to where we lay before starting out here."[169] With that, he rode down off the peaks to find Reno.

Varnum remembered that when he reached the top of the bluffs, Reno had only Companies 'A' and 'B,' plus the pack train personnel remaining with him. Since Varnum had no command, he remained awhile and tried to help Moylan, but it was very slow work as Moylan didn't have enough men to carry the wounded. Company 'A' was still struggling along the bluffs when Varnum left them and rode ahead to Weir Point "about a mile and a half there I joined Capt. Weir's company."[170] Wallace and what was left of Company 'G,' about seven men, had departed to join the other companies a short time before. When Varnum arrived, 'D' was dismounted out on the far point of the extended eastern ridge, and they were exchanging long range gunfire with the Indians, "who seemed to be coming from out on the prairie."[171] There were a good many shots being fired. Later, the Lieutenant back-tracked on this story he told to the Court of Inquiry and said the country in front of 'D' was badly broken up into gullies, and there was no sound of firing by either the Indians or the troopers.[172] Other officers agreed and said there was very little firing done by the troops while at Weir Point.[173] Varnum also testified from this advance point he couldn't ignore "All the Indians in the country seemed to be coming a little distance off, as fast as they could travel in that direction."[174] But later he informed Camp, the Indi-

[166]Ibid, 260.
[167]Carroll, *The Benteen—Goldin Letters On Custer And His Last Battle*, 215; Graham, *Reno Court*, 374.
[168]Hammer, *Custer in '76*, 136.   [169]Ibid, 81.

[170]Graham, *Reno Court*, 125.   [171]Ibid.
[172]Carroll, *I, Varnum*, 70.   [173]Graham, *The Custer Myth*, 319.
[174]Graham, *Reno Court*, 125.

ans weren't all that numerous while at Weir Point and "they were not hard pressed," while there. It wasn't until after the troops had pulled back and had reestablished themselves on Reno Hill that the area to the north became "black with Indians."[175] That the soldiers suffered only one casualty during the whole Weir Point episode, tends to support what Varnum later remembered and not what he testified to before the Reno Court.

Reno had ridden past 'B,' which had only advanced about a half of a mile and was about an equal distance from Weir Point, when Hare "came back." Reno never maintained he had been on Weir Point. There was really no reason for him to go there, as Reno received all the information he would need from the report of Hare, his acting adjutant. This, when combined with what Weir, then Benteen told him, only added to his knowledge.[176] Hare heard Benteen tell Reno that they needed to fall back as the peaks weren't a good place for defense. Another officer commented that since the command occupied the two almost parallel ridges of the peaks, there was no practical way of defending the space between them.[177] In Benteen's opinion, the Indians could also pass around the troops to the east and also by the river's valley to the west. If the warriors undertook these movements, they would soon be in their rear and then the real trouble would start.[178] But, upon further reflection of what Benteen had told his lieutenant, he (Benteen) changed his mind. Benteen suggested to Reno, the best course for them to take was to pull the troops off the peaks. They could then be deployed in a heavy skirmish line across the bluffs to give him time "to select a better place . . . and not be rushed over by them."[179] Reno listened to what Benteen proposed and agreed the peaks weren't a very good place to make a stand. But, he rejected Benteen's offer to delay the Indians while the senior captain surveyed the country for a more defensible spot.[180] Reno said he "had been impressed with the position 'I' had first reached on the hill." He later recalled his main reason for the return to this position was that it was nearer to the water for resupply than was Weir Point.[181] Interestingly, Benteen later said he agreed with this decision.[182] Reno turned to Hare and gave the order for the command to retreat from the peaks; McDougall arrived to see the beginning of this "left about." Hare saluted and turned once again for the troops on the high ground.

It was about this time there occurred another one of those fantastic episodes which seem to characterize the Battle of the Little Big Horn. After Captain French received Reno's order to retreat, Private Edward Pigford of Company 'M' said he was told by this officer he wanted to know something definite about Custer's whereabouts. French instructed Pigford and two other 'M' troopers to ride north "and find out how Custer was faring."[183] The three left as the companies were departing Weir Point. They concealed themselves in the numerous ravines all the while working their way downstream. They managed to avoid detection by the warriors and arrived in the vicinity of Calhoun Hill; close enough to clearly hear the sounds of their fellow troopers in their death throes. Through the dust and smoke of the battle, Pigford saw "a little group of white men fighting desperately."[184] The three spectators "knew, that there was no escaping death that was circling around and closing upon them."[185] Soon there was a wild rush and "the Sioux war cry of victory split the late afternoon air;" it was all over. Pigford knew they had stayed too long and told his two companions it was time to leave.

Pigford remembered that as they mounted their horses "a big band of two or three hundred Indians" spotted the interlopers and attacked. Pigford recalled it was "the hottest corner" he was ever in, and the other two soldiers, he had forgotten their names by the time he related his story, were shot and fell from their mounts. The private credited his escape to his horse that he described as a "splendid animal." The Indians pursued Pigford all the way from the Custer field almost to Reno Hill. When he arrived amongst his fellow troopers, he dismounted in front of French and made his report: "Captain there ain't a man left; they're all butchered."[186] Pigford told his interviewer, "How I ever got away from that horde of yelling, shooting red devils I can't tell you."[187] And neither, I might add, can this author or anyone else!

Hare always maintained he never ordered the companies off of Weir Point, in spite of the fact Reno said he did. Reno told the Court of Inquiry Hare had acted on his own responsibility and used his name to order the retreat. But, when pressed to affirm this point, Reno admitted the retreat order was given by him.[188] However, Reno's orderly supported Hare's statement about not receiving the retreat order from Reno. Private Davern said

[175]Hammer, *Custer in '76*, 62.

[176]Graham, *Reno Court*, 506; Hammer, *Custer in '76*, 67.

[177]Graham, *Reno Court*, 71.   [178]Hammer, *Custer in '76*, 67.

[179]Graham, *Reno Court*, 361.   [180]Ibid, 361.

[181]Ibid, 506.   [182]Ibid, 361.

[183]Washington *Observer* (Washington, PA), October 7, 1932.
[184]Ibid.   [185]Ibid.
[186]Washington *Observer* (Washington, PA), October 8, 1932.
[187]Washington *Observer* (Washington, PA), October 7, 1932.
[188]Graham, *Reno Court*, 506.

he heard no orders and he saw Reno and Benteen talking together, but heard nothing."[189] It was virtually a repeat of how the order to leave the timber was communicated to the officers in the valley nearly two and half hours ago. Again, no trumpet calls were made, and as in the valley, most of the officers found out only by hearsay or when they saw their troops on the flank departing. Benteen rode back and signaled to his lieutenant to pull back.

It must be remembered that no one who was on Weir Point ever claimed it was the Indians who forced them off of these ridges. It was reported, Benteen's company never even fired a round while they were on the peaks, and the only Indians that could be seen were several miles away.[190] The four companies spread across Weir Point were not really bothered by the warriors until they began the retreat. But, Reno in his official report, wrote the Indians nearly overwhelmed the troops, and only "a heavy fire from the skirmish line" kept them at bay.[191] As 'H' withdrew, they passed Godfrey's company. Godfrey was confused. 'H' was moving south with not so much as a word to him, and he now observed the pack train and two companies who were with Reno "moving to the rear." Godfrey remained in position as he had no orders to leave.[192] It was generally understood that when part of a command moves, the rest were to follow if no orders to the contrary are received. But, Godfrey waited, uncertain as to what was happening. Lieutenant Hare had ridden over to his friend and said the command had been ordered back and "I should mount my company and follow the command."[193] French must have been watching Hare speaking to Godfrey, and when he saw 'K' mounting and preparing to leave, he deduced the discussion was about a withdrawal.[194] Why Hare didn't inform French, Wallace, and Edgerly is unexplained; as the adjutant, it was his duty to carry out Reno's directions.

Like falling dominoes, with 'H' already gone, 'K' mounted and leaving, French ordered 'M' to mount and rode over to Edgerly. He told Edgerly the order had been given to fall back. Edgerly looked around, and there were no longer that many Indians to their front, and he told French, "I think not, . . . I heard no such order."[195] French assured him it was true and spent the next several minutes trying to convince Edgerly to withdraw. With his company mounted and ready, the Captain told the Lieutenant the order had been given, and Edgerly could do whatever he wanted, but "he was going."[196] With that, French returned to his company and moved off at a gallop. Edgerly always maintained that with the manpower they had available on Weir Point, they could have gone much farther, but if they had crossed Medicine Tail, they all probably would still be there.[197] Reluctantly, the Lieutenant gave the order for 'D' to mount and withdraw. That each company commander was at Wier Point on "his own hook" is very plain. No one in authority (Reno) ordered their forward movement. Reno tried to deny he ordered the withdrawal, and no officer was assigned for a rear guard. It was a familiar formula with Reno, but this time he was lucky. Hare tried to cover for Reno on this last point and stated Reno had ordered Weir and French to cover the retreat, and they did so almost right up to Reno Hill.[198] This was a complete falsehood, as we shall read, for Hare was with Godfrey's company the whole time. French was headed to safety at a gallop, and Weir was with Reno moving back to the position on the bluffs. In 1910, Hare confided to Camp that he, in effect, had not told the truth to the Court of Inquiry. He admitted that these two companies "came tearing along (so fast) and passed Co. 'K'" who had left about ten minutes before.[199] So much for a rear guard.

Company 'D' rode down off the point leaving Edgerly and several enlisted men as the last remaining soldiers. Instead of acting as a company commander, which in effect he was, the Lieutenant did a foolish thing that almost cost him his life. As Edgerly prepared to mount, he saw an Indian who was so tantalizingly close that he couldn't resist stopping to take a shot at the warrior. After he fired a round at this Indian, Edgerly tried to mount his horse, but the animal was terrified with the close shooting and with the carbine still in his hand, the horse whirled in a circle, throwing him to the ground. Edgerly then handed the carbine to his orderly and literally jumped into the saddle. The Indians, on another knoll, seeing the confusion on the part of these foolish white men less than twenty paces away, fired their guns rapidly. While this was happening, the lieutenant's orderly sat on his mount with "a broad grin on his face" as placidly as if at dinner "in a perfect shower of

---

[189]Ibid, 308. Benteen, always ready to take credit for anything which turned out positive, claimed he had ordered the withdrawal from Weir Point to avoid the panic which had taken place in the valley fight. See Carroll, *The Benteen—Goldin Letters On Custer And His Last Battle*, 215–216.

[190]Kuhlman, *Legend Into History*, 105–106.

[191]Carroll, *The Federal View*, 103; Graham, *Reno Court*, 539.

[192]Ibid, 431.   [193]Ibid, 432.

[194]Edgerly claimed at one time, 'K' left dismounted from the point. See Carroll, *The Gibson and Edgerly Narratives*, 11.

[195]Hammer, *Custer in '76*, 56; Graham, *Reno Court*, 394.

[196]Graham, *Reno Court*, 394.   [197]Hammer, *Custer in '76*, 57.

[198]Graham, *Reno Court*, 247.   [199]Hammer, *Custer in '76*, 67.

bullets."[200] The Indians got so close . . . Sergeant Thomas Harrison remembered they "threw the bridles over their head" drew their Colt .45's, and prepared to fight their way clear.[201] It was before 6:30 PM when Edgerly rode off the point. Without an officer in charge, 'D' departed Weir Point in a column of twos, and the men began to gallop to join their retreating comrades. As Edgerly reached his company, he "yelled, Bring those horses down to a trot" and conditioned to obey, 'D' dropped down to a fast trot. Later in the battle, Edgerly approached Private Sanders and asked him what was so funny at such a time when the Indians on that ridge were trying their best to kill them. The orderly, after first begging the lieutenant's pardon, replied: "I was laughing to see what poor shots those Indians were; they were shooting too low and their bullets were spattering dust like drops of rain."[202] Even a decade later, when Edgerly penned his narrative, he still had never seen a cooler man under fire than this trooper.

During Company 'D's withdrawal, there occurred an incident which reflected little credit on those involved, and some appeared to spend the rest of their lives trying to cover up what had really happened to the company's farrier, Vincent Charley.[203] Charley had been born in Switzerland in 1849 and was in his second enlistment at the time of the battle. Charley was riding toward the rear of the company as it descended the peaks. Probably the same Indians who had been trading gunfire with Edgerly were also shooting at the retreating soldiers. About an eighth of a mile from Weir Point, above the west slope on Cedar Coulee, Charley took a bullet that came from his right and behind him, piercing the bone above the hip and presumably exiting through the soft tissue of the abdomen.[204] Charley fell from his horse, struck his head on the ground causing a bloody wound.[205] The Private called out to the last soldiers as they rode past "that he was hit and implored them not to go off and leave him."[206] But, they just continued on past the wounded man. Charley tried to keep up with his retreating comrades as best he could, half crawling on his feet and one hand.[207] It was at this point that Edgerly, accompanied by Harrison and Wylie rode up to the dis-

abled man and Charley cried out he was wounded and needed assistance. The Lieutenant stopped, but didn't dismount, and "told him to get into the ravine near him and he would try to come back and save him as soon as they could get reinforcements."[208] The same Indians who had shot Charley continued to fire, and one bullet passed through Wylie's canteen and another cut the staff of the guidon he was carrying, and the flag dropped to the ground. Wylie quickly dismounted and retrieved the guidon, then the party continued on.[209] Harrison remembered, "After going a piece they looked back and saw the Indians finishing up Charley."[210] Standing Bear, a Minneconjou, confirmed what Harrison witnessed. The sixteen year old warrior said they chased the soldiers off the hill and "One got killed, and many of us got off and couped him."[211] After the battle, Charley's remains were found with a stick rammed down his throat.

What makes the story of this unfortunate soldier even more pathetic and depressing, is that Edgerly, throughout his life, always claimed and even so testified under oath at the Reno Court of Inquiry that he had asked Captain Weir for reinforcements to rescue a man who had been wounded and whom he promised to save. Weir replied, according to Edgerly, "he was sorry but he couldn't stop our movement." Harrison's statements to Camp claim both he and Edgerly knew Charley was dead shortly after they left him. Edgerly would have no reason to ask Weir to "save a man" who was already dead. To avoid taking the blame for abandoning a wounded man to the Indians, Edgerly shifted the responsibility for the decision on to Weir. This was convenient, as Weir died in December 1876, and Harrison was discharged in August of the same year. Just nine days after the battle, Edgerly wrote to his wife and said the thing he "regretted more than any other thing that happened to me, for I had promised that wounded man I would get him out and wasn't able to raise a finger for him."[212] Without a doubt, his close call on

---

[200]Carroll, *The Gibson and Edgerly Narratives*, 11.

[201]Liddic, *Camp on Custer*, 97–98. It's possible he meant they took the reins in their teeth.

[202]Carroll, *The Gibson and Edgerly Narratives*, 11.

[203]Vincent Charley's name has also been spelled Charlie. On the Custer Battle Monument he is listed as Chas. Vincent.

[204]Douglas Scott, etal, *They Died With Custer* (Norman, OK: University of OK Press, 1998), 306.

[205]Scott & Blood, *A Good Walk Around the Boundary*, 34; Hammer, *Custer in '76*, 57.   [206]Liddic, *Camp on Custer*, 96.

[207]Hardorff, *Custer Battle Causalities*, 160.

[208]Liddic, *Camp on Custer*, 98.   [209]Hammer, *Custer in '76*, 130.

[210]Liddic, *Camp on Custer*, 98.

[211]Neihardt, *Black Elk Speaks*, 119.

[212]George M. Clark, *Scalp Dance : The Edgerly Papers on the Battle of the Little Big Horn* (Oswego, NY: Privately Printed, 1985), 25. It has been suggested why would Edgerly, in a private letter to his wife, lie about his trying to rescue this trooper? I would counter, why would Harrison lie? He claimed they all knew Charley was dead soon after they left him. Harrison had no motive to prevaricate. He wasn't in command, the army could do nothing to him as he received his discharge that year (1876), and he probably never knew there was any attempt to claim Charley was not dead after they left him. Edgerly had a motive to shade the truth; the others did not.

Weir Point affected Edgerly's judgment, and this thirty year old lieutenant was scared and probably oblivious to everything except self preservation. But, even given these conditions, he was troubled by this incident for the rest of his life.[213] This was evident in his interview thirty years later when he spoke to Camp about the episode.[214]

It has been suggested that it wouldn't have made any difference if Edgerly rescued Charley or not, because with the wound through the hips, peritonitis would have set in and sealed his fate. He would have died either way.[215] I believe this is both a shallow and callous interpretation of the circumstances. No one could know what the future would have held for Charley, but his fate was sealed when no one attempted to lend him a hand. Furthermore, if there was enough time for Edgerly and his small party to stop and talk to the private, there was probably enough time to try and get him on a horse.[216] In light of the above, one might question Colonel Graham's characterization of Edgerly as "a man of immaculate character and a knightly gentleman of the old school."[217] There were many officers of the 7th Cavalry who wished the entire Weir Point episode would be gone and forgotten; in light of the above, this was especially true for Lieutenant Edgerly.

The name of this wounded man wasn't revealed for many years, and although Camp recorded the name in his notes, as late as 1967 there was still speculation over the abandoned man's identity.[218] In 1903, Henry Mecklin, a Medal of Honor winner at the battle, returned to the area and accompanied by Custer Battlefield Superintendent A. N. Grover, they uncovered several graves on the battlefield and the remains were transferred to the National Cemetery. The skeletons were interred within a few days of their discovery, and although Mecklin told Grover the names of these individuals, they were recorded as "Unknown;" among these soldiers was Vincent Charley.[219] When Walter Camp learned about this, he wanted the spot where Charley was killed marked, but nothing was done about it. To assist in locating the place, Camp recorded the distance from Weir Point to where the private was found to be 650 feet.[220] It was nearly 90

years before a government tombstone was erected. However, this current battlefield marker for Charley is next to the east side of the Reno-Benteen Road about two thousand feet south of Weir Point. The National Park Service placed this marker here for the benefit of the visitors driving along the road; although there is some evidence which points to this marker as being near his original burial site which was possibly under the road.[221] However, the place where he was killed is located to the north by east about a quarter mile. In 1992, the Custer National Cemetery's "unknown" grave 455 was exhumed, as well as four others, as part of "a full physical anthropological examination of the remains with the express goal of individually identifying the remains."[222] After a careful examination of the bones, it was concluded they were indeed Charley's, and marker 454 was changed from "unknown" to "Vincent Charley."[223] It is a fitting tribute for a faithful soldier who gave his life for his adopted country.

What exactly did Weir see during the nearly fifteen minutes he was almost alone on the point? This is one of the great mysteries of the battle. There are as many theories as there are students. On one extreme, some believe Weir saw most of the Custer fight, but did nothing; those who subscribe to the opposite viewpoint believe he only saw a rear guard action, as Custer had moved away to the north. Of the former, these students believe Weir witnessed the fighting about Calhoun Hill; others, who subscribe to Custer's delay of 45 minutes in Medicine Tail Coulee, say he saw the troops on Blummer-(Nye) Cartwright Ridge. One student took this supposed sighting a step farther and suggested Custer communicated with Weir through semaphore, telling him to 'come on.'[224] This was the reason given, answering the question as to why it is believed he left the point so abruptly after Hare delivered Reno's order. Others have countered there is no way Weir saw anything other than what he thought was . . . a rear guard action. There was never even so much as a hint from Weir nor anyone else, who reached this high ground, that they

---

[213]Hardorff, *Camp, Custer and the Little Bighorn*, 63.

[214]Hammer, *Custer in '76*, 56–57.

[215]Douglas Scott and P. Willey, "Custer's Men Took Names To Their Graves," *Greasy Grass*, Vol. 12, May 1996, 22

[216]Sills, "Weir Point Perspective," 49.

[217]Graham, *The Custer Myth*, 217.

[218]Gordon Bateman, "Who Was Left To Die On Weir Point?" *Little Big Horn Associates Newsletter*, Vol. 1, #7, July 1967. Walter Camp's papers weren't readily available to the general public until the early 1970s.   [219]Scott, *They Died With Custer*, 124.

[220]*Camp, IU*, box 6, folder 17.

[221]Scott & Willey, "Custer's Men Took Names to Their Graves," 22. There is a question as to who actually placed Charley's marker on this spot. A former historian at the Custer Battlefield, said that the Custer Battlefield Historical & Museum Association was responsible for its placement. However, one of the past presidents of this association said that they were not involved in this marker project. Letter, Richard G. Hardorff to Bruce R. Liddic, January 13, 2003, author's collection.

[222]Scott & Willey, *They Died With Custer*, 113.

[223]Ibid, 201–202. Since there is no known photograph of Charley, the approximate reconstruction of his face, done at the time, is of interest. See Ibid, 202.

[224]Letter, Jay Smith to Bruce R. Liddic, August 26, 1982, author's collection.

believed they witnessed the destruction of any part of Custer's command. If they had, at some future point it would have come out, as did the other 'secrets' the participants tried to hide.[225] Some did observe action to the north, but that's all they assumed it was, a running fight moving away from them. In addition, no one, neither officer nor enlisted man, ever said publicly or privately they saw any soldiers trying to reach their position. To believe this was an all encompassing conspiracy, as to what some subscribe the soldiers should have seen/known, is stretching credibility beyond what is reasonable. Some students, following Kuhlman's thesis, believe Custer seeing the troops on Weir Point made a "premature move that turned a safe holding action into a series of ambuscades" which destroyed his command.[226] For if Weir could see troops on the Custer field, Custer could surely see troops on Weir Point. To paraphrase Benjamin Franklin, "Two can keep a secret if one is dead." This said, if Wylie was correct and Weir did see guidons, (he didn't say where to the north or how close) and the captain subsequently verified the Indians had them, he had to assume a disaster of some sort had befallen Custer's command. The army of the past placed the utmost importance on the colors they took into battle; they were usually only relinquished upon death. Could it have, after the battle, become too easy for the surviving officers to convince themselves they had no idea of Custer's fate despite the presence of Indians carrying his guidons?[227] Could this have been his justification for leaving the point so quickly and riding back to Reno to report what he had seen? Weir died six months after the Little Big Horn battle. Weir never left behind any account of the Little Big Horn, but it's very possible what he discussed with Godfrey that night is about as close to the truth as we'll arrive at. Godfrey recalled Weir told him Custer had been repulsed, and that is why he was unable to make a juncture with their wing.[228] Three months later, this Lieutenant wrote in *The Army and Navy Journal*, Weir " to a high point from which he had a good view of the country. From it, could be seen Custer's battlefield, but there was nothing to indicate the result."[229] Over the years, Godfrey never changed his opinion that the story Weir told him was the truth. In 1892, he wrote, "The conclusion was arrived at that Custer had been replused, and the firing was the parting shots of the rear guard."[230] Godfrey said while he was on the point he could see stationary

groups of horsemen, and individual horsemen moving about and knew they were Indians. He also said although he had seen this large group of Indians mulling around about two miles away, (Calhoun Hill) he saw no evidence of fighting.[231] Edgerly said when they got up on the point all they saw "was a good many Indians riding up and down firing at objects on the ground 'around.'"[232] Edgerly's observation was verified during the 1984 archaeological dig when a number of bullets uncovered around the soldiers' positions were "found vertically impacted, or nearly so, in the ground." It was concluded this would most likely have occurred as the Indians fired downward into the bodies.[233] Windolph was also of the opinion that Custer had attacked and had been repulsed. Then, Custer had ridden on downstream towards where Terry and Gibbon would soon arrive.[234] First Sergeant Ryan recalled when he arrived at Weir Point, they "could see Indians riding back and forth firing scattered shots. We thought they were disposing of Custer's wounded men, which afterwards proved true."[235] This seems to be the prevailing sentiment among the witnesses. Lieutenant Hare being the exception, as he said, "the Indians were especially thick over on Custer Ridge and Custer . . . was fighting them." In contradiction to Godfrey's statements, Hare said he pointed this fact out to Weir when he arrived on the point from Reno.[236] Hare's quick observations for the limited time he was on Weir Point might be more accurate than what has generally been believed. In an 1877 letter, Lieutenant John Garland wrote that: "Capt. Nowlan told me last winter that he heard Mr. Edgerly tell Gen. Sturgis at the camp fire last fall at Standing Rock that he saw and heard the General's devoted band from where he and Weir stood."

The Indians' stories tend to back up what the soldiers thought they saw from Weir Point. Gall told the participants who had attended the Tenth Anniversary of the battle: "When the skirmishers reached the high point overlooking Custer's field, the Indians were galloping around and over the wounded, dying and dead, popping bullets and arrows into them."[237] Black Elk, a youth at the time of the battle, said when he was on the Custer field to loot the bodies, the rest of the warriors left to chase the soldiers back to the hill.[238] John Stands in Timber was told the Indians didn't start for the troops on Weir Point until most of Custer's men had been killed. He said his

[225]Sills, "Weir Point Perspective," 46.
[226]Kuhlman, *Legend Into History*, 117.
[227]Discussion, Bruce R. Liddic with David Evans, June 22, 2001.
[228]Graham, *Reno Court*, 435.
[229]*Army and Navy Journal* (Washington, DC), September 29, 1876.
[230]Graham, *The Custer Myth*, 142.

[231]Ibid, 446. [232]Ibid, 393.
[233]Douglas Scott, Richard Fox, Jr., etal., *Archaeological Insights into The Custer Battle* (Norman, OK: University of OK Press, 1987), 123. [234]Hunt, *I Fought With . . .* , 102.
[235]Barnard, *Ten Years With Custer*, 297.
[236]Hammer, *Custer in '76*, 67; Kuhlman, *Legend Into History*, 226.
[237]Graham, *Reno Court*, 89.

informants thought the troops didn't come off these ridges as they sensed "an ambush, as the Indians were just waiting for them to advance a little farther before falling on them from the flank."[239] Standing Bear said after the Custer fight the warriors about Calhoun Hill were standing around and they "saw soldiers coming on a hill toward the south and east. Everybody began yelling: 'Hurry!' and we started for the soldiers." This warrior was sure the advance towards the other soldiers occurred only "after we wiped out Custer."[240] However, Two Moons remembered the Custer fight was still being contested when a number of Indians charged after Reno's men.[241]

There were other officers on Weir Point who saw very little, or at least claimed they did, and appearently understood even less. For example, Benteen recalled while some officers said they could see the Custer Battlefield from that vantage point, he for one "knew positively that it (the battlefield) was not, having gone over it two or three times since."[242] Today, the reader can judge for himself the utter fallaciousness of this pronunciation by standing on Weir Point and looking at the Custer Battlefield. Benteen wrote to his wife nine days after the battle and said they could see nothing of Custer from the peaks and hear very little firing, but they did see numbers of Indians in that direction.[243] If true, then most of the action on the Custer field was over about six o'clock, and many students so believe. Without a doubt, many of the men on Weir Point had witnessed the last stage of the Custer fight. Weir, himself, might have seen the earlier action by 'C' Company on Finley Ridge and later Calhoun Hill as he arrived on this point before 5:30 PM. From the above recollections and testimony of both the officers and enlisted men, it becomes clear that action was still going on at Custer's battlefield while they were on Weir Point. But, to what extent has been the question? Of the officers, Hare, for one and probably Weir and maybe Edgerly, saw the fight but couldn't or wouldn't psychologically connect what they were seeing to the disaster which was befalling their commanding officer. What the soldiers saw from Weir Point and the interpretation given the evidence, perhaps doesn't reflect well on their analytical ability, but this has nothing to do with their credibility as to what they thought (or wanted to think) they had observed.[244]

An experienced combat officer, Godfrey knew panic when he saw it, and it was right in front of his company, as the rest of the troops came galloping down from the high point. Godfrey had gone some distance in his withdrawal when he looked back and saw French's Company come "tearing over the bluffs, and soon after Weir's followed in hot haste."[245] He saw Edgerly having trouble extracting himself, and the Indians were beginning to pour over Weir Point with the intention of following after the troops. He also noted a heavy fire was commenced by the Indians on the troops in the rear.[246] Godfrey knew from past battles he needed to do something and quick. There was a real danger the panic and confusion would spread "and perhaps prove disastrous.[247] Godfrey recognized with no rear guard established it would be the valley fight all over again, only this time above on the bluffs. Godfrey halted 'K' Company's movement and ordered the troopers to dismount, prepare to fight on foot and sent the 'fours' with the led horses back to the main column. Hare, who had ridden down from Weir Point with Godfrey, also noted what was happening and told his friend that he was going to stay with Godfrey, "Adjutant or no adjutant."[248] Hare said this occurred when the company was about 500 yards from Reno Hill.[249] The two officers had about twenty-five men on the line when the 'fours' departed.[250] Godfrey wrote in his often quoted *Century Magazine* article, his objective was to "compel the Indians to halt and take cover," so as to permit an orderly retreat to Reno Hill.

However, in 1918, Godfrey told Walter Camp the real reason he halted and formed a skirmish line. He had, upon looking back, seen a man (Vincent Charley) had been hit and fallen from his horse. 'D' Company was coming on, and he supposed they would want to send a detachment back to rescue him. Godfrey thought he ought to make a stand to enable Company 'D' to do so.[251] In addition, Godfrey privately told Captain Robert Carter, 5th Cavalry, he expected not only 'D' but also 'M' to rally behind his company, but "Did they rally? Not much! But left me to hold the sack!"[252] Charley's abandonment was a very sensitive subject then and later. All the officers knew of the charges (and later court-martial) brought against Colonel John J. Reynolds, 3rd Cavalry, for abandoning

[238]Neihardt, *Black Elk Speaks*, 128–129.

[239]Hardorff, *Cheyenne Memories*, 172.

[240]Neihardt, *Black Elk Speaks*, 119.

[241]Wayne Wells, "Little Big Horn Notes," *Greasy Grass*, Vol. 5, May 1989, 11.   [242]Graham, *Reno Court*, 374.

[243]Graham, *The Custer Myth*, 300.

[244]Sills, "Weir Point Perspective," 50.

[245]Graham, *The Custer Myth*, 143.

[246]Edward S. Godfrey, "Cavalry Fire Discipline," *Military Service Institution*, Vol. 19, September 1896, 257–258.

[247]Graham, *The Custer Myth*, 143.   [248]Ibid.

[249]Hammer, *Custer in '76*, 67.

[250]Graham, *The Custer Myth*, 319.

[251]*Camp, IU*, box 5, folder 17.

[252]Graham, *The Custer Myth*, 319.

Courtesy of Hastings House Publishers

his wounded three months prior at the Powder River fight. And didn't General Terry tell Custer, "And whatever you do, Custer, hold on to your wounded?"[253] Neither Charley's name nor the circumstances of his death was brought out to the Reno Court of Inquiry, other than the barest particulars.[254] Nor did anyone on the Court probe the witnesses to reveal additional details on this touchy matter. Even forty-two years later, Godfrey didn't tell Camp the name of this trooper; it was Camp who put Charlie's name in brackets in his recorded notes of their conversation.[255]

When Godfrey saw no rescue was to be undertaken, and with some warriors less than a half mile away, he began to move the men of 'K' back toward Reno Hill, alternately, by odd and even numbers. But, with the continued gunfire, his troopers started to panic, and they tended to bunch up into one long line. The men would quickly fire their carbines and move hastily to the rear. Godfrey attributed this to their inexperience and "many had not

been under fire before."[256] With Hare's assistance, he got them reformed again into proper intervals. The Indians took advantage of the lull in the troopers' return fire to close upon the soldiers.[257] With a revamped skirmish line, the soldiers opened fire and once more drove the warriors back. Godfrey directed Hare to take some men and climb "a high point on the right (Sharpshooters' Ridge)," to protect the company's flank as the ridge line dominated the surrounding area. Hare had just begun the move when Trumpeter George Penwell reined his mount beside the lieutenant and presented Major Reno's compliments, and he was to immediately fall back to the command . . . now! Godfrey motioned for Hare to rejoin him.[258] Godfrey later wrote, "I had not only the attack to meet but was harassed by Reno's repeated orders 'to retire at once'. But he made no attempt to give me reinforcement." Godfrey concluded Reno was "insensate."[259] But, the battle proven lieutenant's troubles were far from over. Godfrey finally gave the order to fall back "Double time March." But, like Cross and the Arikaras, the men of 'K' had their fill of Sioux and took off like sprinters. His line broken, the men running, and the warriors dreaming of many coups, Godfrey reached the last of his self-control. He got in front of the men and pointed his Colt revolver directly at his

[253]Manion, *Last Statement To Custer*, 26.
[254]Graham, *Reno Court*, 394.
[255]There is always the possiblity that Godfrey did not know the name of this trooper.

[256]Stewart, *The Field Diary . . .* , 13.
[257]Godfrey, "Cavalry Fire Discipline," 258.
[258]Graham, *Reno Court*, 432.
[259]Graham, *The Custer Myth*, 319.

soldiers and made "the air blue."[260] Through the lieutenant's "tall swearing" the men understood they might as well stop right now and take their chances of being killed by the Indians, for if the troopers persisted they would most certainly be shot by him. The men looked at their commander "aghast" but stopped in their tracks about where the National Park's northwest boundary fence crosses the road. The company retired the rest of the way with their carbines and faces to the Indians.[261] 'K' Company didn't suffer a single casualty nor did anyone else in the command.[262] Godfrey's actions in retiring from Weir Point are in stark contrast to Reno's actions in the valley. It only serves to illustrate what a determined and competent officer could accomplish to minimize casualties during a retreat.

Godfrey reaped well-deserved praise from his fellow officers for his accomplishment. Edgerly wrote his wife a few days after the battle that "Godfrey and Hare had their skirmish line, and they did splendidly driving the Indians back enough to cover us until we got in position."[263] Three years later, at the Court of Inquiry, Edgerly publicly declared that "Capt. Godfrey had turned back and covered our retreat in the most brave and fearless manner."[264] Hare thought Godfrey was very "clever" in his directing the skirmish

line.[265] Captain Weir on the evening of the 25th walked over to Godfrey's position and shook the Lieutenant's hand saying, "I want to thank you, Godfrey, for saving my troop," during the retreat.[266] However, Wallace said the few men of 'G' Company returned to Reno Hill at a walk.[267] One must wonder if this twenty-seven-year-old second lieutenant was in the same battle as everyone else. Benteen, as Godfrey's battalion commander, tried to take the credit and said it was he who told Godfrey "to check the Indians" and "he (Godfrey) was all right and he (Benteen) would look out for him."[268] As would be expected, Reno didn't mention Godfrey's initiative in his official report nor in his testimony at his Court of Inquiry.[269]

The pack train was the first to arrive back at the place they had left just a short time before. It was before 6:45 PM. Reno and Weir came in next with Companies 'A' and 'B' followed by Benteen and 'H.' The officers began to work on a defensive perimeter. They were soon joined by the few troopers of 'G' then 'M', 'D', and finally Godfrey and 'K' arrived with their guns still pointing at the warriors. For the officers and enlisted men who were being positioned along the perimeter's line, their long difficult afternoon was about to become an even more arduous evening.

---

[260]Godfrey, "Cavalry Fire Discipline," 258.

[261]Ibid. [262]With the exception of Vincent Charley.

[263]Clark, *Scalp Dance*, 25. [264]Graham, *Reno Court*, 394.

[265]Hammer, *Custer in '76*, 67.

[266]Graham, *The Custer Myth*, 334. [267]Graham, *Reno Court*, 54.

[268]Ibid, 362. [269]Ibid, 506.

10
Last Stand Knoll

In the past nine chapters I have made note of the many controversies which permeate the Battle of the Little Big Horn. These points, whether significant, insignificant or very insignificant, are argued long and hard by the legion of students. But this three-ring-circus of imbroglio really amounts to very little when compared to the debate about the various sundry points of the famous "Last Stand." To paraphrase the late Don Russell, one of the founders of the Chicago Westerners, one can add to this circus the hippodrome track, the menagerie, and any number of sideshows. There are two major (and many minor) schools of thought when the 'Last Stand' stage is reached in the battle's discussion. One of which addresses how Custer arrived at the last stand field; the other involves the condition of Custer's command. Each one of these theories consists of two parts. Regarding the perception of how or why Custer reached his final position, one, the fatalistic theme, contends that Custer's companies were forced back to the last stand hill by hordes of warriors. Because of this overwhelming pressure, Custer was given little choice in the direction or manner in which the troops arrived. It was only just a matter of time before his force was deluged by the following red wave. The other perception is that Custer arrived at the last stand area because he chose to go in that direction for a purpose. His movement was not forced, it was voluntary. The second school of conflicting thoughts involves the condition of the main column. One perception is that a disintegration of the regiment's command structure had set in, which spiraled out of the officers' control in the combat that followed.[1] The other perception contends that the five companies remained cohesive and well handled until the very end atop last stand knoll.[2] I believe the facts demonstrate that a more accurate assumption would be a combination of the two thoughts, a part from one school and a part from the other. Custer's command arrived at the last stand area under their own volition for a specific purpose; the main column was intact, had suffered very few casualties, and the companies were under the control of their officers and noncommissioned officers.

The above brief outline portrays some of the current thinking; however, there are as many other theories, re-

constructions, and purported answers to what happened over the next sixty minutes as there are students and books on this battle. Any author would have to be very pretentious, indeed, to claim he or she knows what really transpired to create one of American history's greatest mysteries. Those who attempt to understand these events, can only present the circumstances as he or she comprehends them. In the end, however, one person's conjecture is as good (perhaps better) as another's; that said . . .

It was before five o'clock when Custer arrived in the vicinity of Calhoun Hill. It had been about 45 minutes since he had dispatched Keogh's Battalion to Ford B. Custer had seen nothing during that charge, the subsequent recall, or his own action on Nye (Blummer)-Cartwright Ridge that indicated that the warriors had changed or even threatened to change, to an aggressive posture. It still appeared the warriors were only interested in delaying his movements so the noncombatants could escape. The campaign's objective was to compel the Indians to return to the reservation. Whether they arrived at the reservations with or without their teepees and possessions was immaterial so long as they arrived. His objective, similar to Grant at Richmond eleven years earlier, wasn't a fixed Indian village (city), but its inhabitants (Lee's Army).[3] Walter Camp compared Custer at this point of the battle to being like a man "tracking a bear through the brush — the main thing is to catch up, the fight could come afterward."[4] As Company 'C' had pulled back from the ford, Keogh ordered the company to assume firing positions on the northern higher ground to discourage any attempt by warriors to charge the command as it attempted to reconcentrate. This position was to the west of the present road after it crossed the present National Park fence line. According to recent archeological discoveries, the artifact pattern and distribution suggests that these troops moved up along the south side of Deep Coulee. This pattern is found "adjacent and parallel to the park's boundary fence from Greasy Grass Ridge to Calhoun Hill."[5] White Bull said the Indians were content to let the soldiers move to the north from Ford B while attempting to keep them on the east side of the river, away from their women and children.[6] Also, as an incentive,

[1]Jacob Adams, "A Survivor's Story of the Custer Massacre on the American Frontier," *Journal of American History*, Vol. 3, April 1909, 230.

[2]See Fox, *Archaeology, and Custer's Last Battle* and Gray, *Centennial Campaign*, 223–226.

[3]Dennis Clark, "Surprise at the Little Big Horn," *10th Annual Symposium Custer Battlefield Historical & Museum Association*, June 1996, 44.

[4]Hardorff, *On The Little Big Horn With Walter Camp*, 214.

[5]Scott and Bleed, *A Good Walk Around the Boundary*, 39.

[6]Wells, "Little Big Horn Notes," 15.

the further north the soldiers went, the further they were separated from Reno's soldiers on the bluffs to the south.

There are some Indian accounts which, by their perception, suggest they were the militants, causing the soldiers to retreat and become disorganized. Tall Bull, a Cheyenne warrior, said there had been hard fighting at Ford B, and the troops had stood their ground until they backed off. The soldiers fought all the way while retreating up the hill. Soldier Wolf agreed with his fellow tribesman and recalled that the heavy fighting at the ford had kept Custer out of the village, and as a result, the ground was covered with the bodies of their ponies and the soldiers' horses. "But the Indians overpowered the soldiers and they began to give way, retreating up the hill towards where the monument now is."[7] But, other Indian accounts speak of "several charges [that] had been made but no fighting had been done," at the ford, and the soldiers just moved away to the north.[8] One reason why the Indians didn't press their confrontation with the soldiers until later was their lack of mobility. Most of the Indians at this point in the fight were on foot and the soldiers, in their retreat from the ford, simply out-distanced them on horseback. In addition, the troopers' longer range Springfield carbines kept the warriors from any serious pursuit over the open flats near the river. Because of a lack of forage, very few horses were kept in the village itself; most of the animals were out grazing to the north and west. Black Elk recalled that everybody was trying to catch a horse. He was lucky to find his pony fairly quick, as "most of the people's horses were out grazing yet and they were running after them."[9] Tall Bull said, the warriors who had first gotten to their horses all went off to fight Reno, leaving only those who were delayed or were unable to find their horses to confront Custer's surprise foray at Ford B.[10] Foolish Elk, an Ogalalla, recalled that most of the Indians were still catching their horses when Custer moved back from the ford. It was only after they had obtained their ponies that they "followed on after Custer in overwhelming numbers."[11] Standing Bear wasn't successful in securing a pony and returned to the village to wait for the horses to be brought in.[12] Young Two Moon, a Cheyenne and nephew of Chief Two Moon, told how the Indians came rushing like "ants out of a hill," but "were struggling (my italicizing) up the gulches northeast of the soldiers."[13]

The archeological evidence found toward Calhoun Hill evidence gives the appearance of light or at least limited firing.[14] This was confirmed by Kate Bighead who said that after the attack at the ford there was a long period of "slow fighting with not much harm to either side."[15] This was about to change in a very short time as the Indians, in ever increasing numbers both on foot and horseback, were coming after the soldiers. They were infiltrating Medicine Tail Coulee and working their way up to get behind Keogh's lines on Calhoun Hill to a position now called Henryville Ridge.[16] The Indians were also traveling along the east side of the river and approaching Greasy Grass Ridge from the west. The pattern and distribution of their artifacts makes it clear that the warriors were seeking any available cover to fire into the front, rear, right and left flanks of the soldiers.[17] Their numbers were swelling by the minute as Reno was no longer perceived as a threat, and these warriors now turned about and were riding as quickly as they could to the north. Gall was even more specific about the reason for the sudden increase in the number of warriors confronting the troops on Calhoun Hill. He said, as soon as the Indians had forced Reno's men up the bluffs, the warriors turned to the north to repeat the same process to this second group of white men.[18] Fred Girard also agreed with Gall, stating that "It is certain that if Reno had held out against these Indians, hundreds of them would have remained to hold him in the timber, and Custer would have had a better show."[19]

Without a doubt, these warriors, many on foot and few on horseback, drew the attention of Company 'C.' The troopers could see the Indians beginning to move on either side of them, taking advantage of the natural contours of the land to avoid the soldiers' gunfire. To keep the warriors from coming any closer, Keogh ordered the platoons of Company 'C' to deploy into two parallel skirmish lines, one looking to the southeast, the other to the southwest. The 'number fours' with the led horses were positioned

[7]Jerome A. Greene, *Lakota and Cheyenne* (Norman, OK: University of OK Press, 1994), 52–53.

[8]Hardorff, *Lakota Recollections*, 59, 68, 75. Standing Bear recalled it wasn't until the soldiers arrived at what would be Keogh's position that the soldiers stopped to fight. See Hammer, *Custer in '76*, 215. However, these warriors might have arrived late and didn't witness any of the earlier fighting.

[9]DeMallie, *The Sixth Grandfather*, 181.

[10]Hammer, *Custer in '76*, 213.   [11]Ibid, 198.

[12]DeMallie, *The Sixth Grandfather*, 185.

[13]Greene, *Lakota and Cheyenne*, 68.

[14]Scott and Bleed, *A Good Walk Around the Boundary*, 39.

[15]Marquis, *Custer On The Little Bighorn*, 87.

[16]This ridge was so named because of the many .44 caliber Henry/Winchester shell cases which were found, on the first ridge from the southeast corner of the NPS fence line, during the 1984 archaeology survey.

[17]Scott and Bleed, *A Good Walk Around the Boundary*, 41.

[18]Barry, *Indian Notes . . .* , 13; *Army & Navy Journal* (Washington, DC), July 3, 1886.   [19]Hammer, *Custer in '76*, 233.

Yate's Battalion Movement Along Battle Ridge

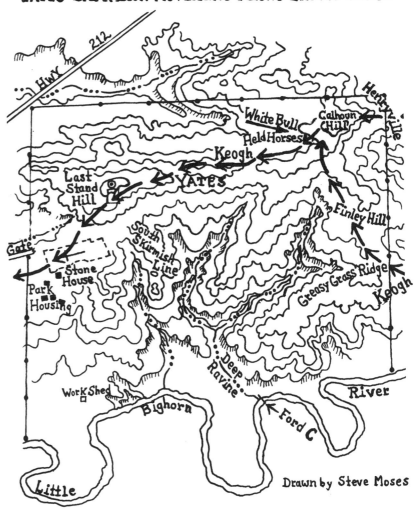

Drawn by Steve Moses

between the platoons' lines. This tactic was employed before by the Seventh Cavalry in June 1867, when their supply train was attacked by Indians on the Kansas prairie.[20] Just like nine years earlier, this mobile skirmish line kept the Indians at a distance while they moved towards even higher ground, Finley Hill. White Bull declared the soldiers' fire was so effective that the Indians had no choice but to fall back toward the south.[21] Keogh and Company 'I' had proceeded to join Custer on Calhoun Hill. Once on Finley Hill, if one can believe Private Thompson's narrative, the position that was then undertaken by 'C' was even more unusual for a company of cavalry. They had evolved into an infantry formation when they fired. Thompson said there were two ranks, in a sort of a semi-circle.[22] They had gray hats on their heads, which many in 'C' Company wore.[23] This formation was confirmed by Two Moon who further elaborated that some of the soldiers were down on their knees firing, while some were standing.[24]

It was after five o'clock when the officers assembled near the backside of Calhoun Hill for an "officer's call." Custer had made some crucial decisions and he was about to make his final one, which would prove to be the most important. He had decided to continue after the village's inhabitants, and he needed to communicate his determination. Many students of the battle have visited the last stand area, some, dozens of times, and have walked over its terrain and studied it until they knew the ground as their own backyard. As a result, these students have an advantage over Custer in knowing almost every feature of its terrain. He only saw the topography once and had to make troop depositions in an instant. Custer saw an area that would become his battlefield, which was roughly a mile square, with the Little Big Horn River flowing to the northwest. Near the southeast corner of this field rose the little knoll (Calhoun Hill) where the officers had assembled. Looking to the north, he saw a hog-back ridge, which ran about a half a mile, to another slight elevation, which would become Last Stand Hill. The land generally slopes down toward the river from right to left, and there are numerous crests (or ridges) separated by arroyos. The

major crests are delineated by bottom drainage channels, which have been named so students can have common reference points. The most prominent and most referenced of the draining courses is Deep Ravine, which from head to mouth is about one thousand yards. This ravine is a superficial depression and stretches from near the markers for the Keogh's company (about four hundred yards from Last Stand Hill) and becomes progressively deeper and deeper as it travels westward. There are two branches; the one to the south is called Calhoun Ravine. Its head rests at Calhoun Hill, and curves to the northwest to join Deep Ravine. The other branch runs northeast out of Deep Ravine and reaches almost to Last Stand Hill. There is another small anonymous depression that runs slightly to the north of what has been termed the 'South Skirmish Line.' This concavity drains more or less directly into the Little Big Horn River.[25]

[20]Stan Hoig, *The Battle of the Washita* (Garden City, NJ : Doubleday & Company, 1976), 10. In this engagement, the horses were also protected by the wagons. [21]Vestal, *Warpath*, 195.
[22]Magnussen, *Peter Thompson's Narrative*, 160.
[23]Liddic, *Camp on Custer*, 86.
[24]Graham, *The Custer Myth*, 102–103.

[25]Gray, *Custer's Last Campaign*, 389

Custer could see that some Indians had gotten between him and the river, but this would have been only natural to place themselves between the soldiers and their families. What Custer probably didn't understand was the nuances of the terrain to the north and west, which, indeed, made it very formidable. The land was severely cut up by ravines and was formed into narrow ridges with small knolls. Too, small, in fact, for any type of positioning for five companies of cavalry. When traveling over this domain, the view offered is deceiving. A point of reference which one can see very clearly one minute can in just another minute disappear entirely from visual sight. This territory is not well suited for any type of cavalry charge, nor is it particularly adaptable to establishing a defensive posture. The landscape simply afforded too many opportunities for the warriors to slink, slide, and hide all over the ground while remaining largely unseen by the troopers until it was too late to prevent their ambush tactics. Mitch Bouyer was no doubt familiar with the land, but it is unknown what information he was able to impart to Custer and whether this information fit into the tactical plan Custer had composed.[26]

That tactical plan which Custer put together was one that was both offensive and defensive. I believe Custer intended to hold the high ground around Calhoun Hill as his base. For by occupying this site, he had just the position he needed to hold a corridor open for Benteen. Because of his tardiness, Custer could reasonably assume Benteen had first linked up with Reno before proceeding, and they would arrive together. I'm sure he never once thought his order to 'come on' would be ignored.[27] Custer could see Indians around Ford B and their movements towards the troops. By establishing a position on the crest of Calhoun Hill, support could be given to Benteen, especially if the warriors tried to interdict him and the pack train as they crossed over the ground. From Calhoun Hill, Custer could also deny the use of Deep Coulee to the warriors, thus facilitating Reno's and Benteen's arrival.[28] In addition, occupation of this hill would serve two additional purposes. One would be to act as a blocking force to cut off any Indian pursuit of his troops. The second purpose would be to act as an anvil to Benteen's hammer and catch those warriors who had been bold enough to follow between two fires. There are some reconstructions of the battle which hold that there was no offensive part to Custer's tactics, and a panic route was about to begin.[29] But, logical thinking dictates that if Custer believed he was about to be overwhelmed by Indian hordes, he would not divide the right wing again and lead two (or three depending on your view point) companies north to Last Stand Hill.[30] Not only would this put about a half a mile between him and any support, but it would also increase the distance from the expected arrival of Benteen and the packs. Furthermore, if the Indians were to position themselves between Benteen and Keogh and Yates, the regiment would surely be defeated in detail. It has been asked what use would this defensive position serve to those who couldn't get there?[31] Finally, if Custer was thinking defensively, wouldn't Blummer (Nye)-Cartwright Ridge be a better choice as Custer would be closer to his expected support where he had a commanding ridge with excellent visibility all around? I will say again, neither the size of the village nor the number of Indians figured greatly into Custer's thinking. His overriding concern was the escape of the Indians, especially the non-combatants. And to this end, Custer remained committed to offensive operations until he realized how wrong his judgment was in both the temperament, determination, and numbers of his foe.

The offensive part of his plan involved his moving to the north with Yates' Battalion in pursuit of the non-combatants. The vedettes had reported that there were numerous women and children hiding in a ravine on the east side of the river about a mile to north and west of Calhoun Hill.[32] In addition, heavy moving dust clouds were still noted to the north on the west side of the Little Big Horn River. From past experience, Custer knew that the warriors would retreat when pushed, they always had, and as soon as their families were clear, they would melt into the prairie. But this day it was to be different, and when pushed, the warriors would push back . . . only harder. This time, the Indians would not simply go away. Lieutenant General Philip Sheridan, upon reading the after battle reports and interviewing the survivors, correctly surmised what had happened:

The Indians were actually surprised and in the confu-

---

[26]Ibid, 383.

[27]It is true the order did not say to 'come on' to Custer and a possible argument could be made that Reno's position was the 'front' where Benteen was needed. But Benteen, I believe, knew very well what the intent of the order to 'come on' meant.

[28]Wayne Wells, "The Fight on Calhoun Hill," *2nd Annual Symposium Custer Battlefiled Historical & Museum, Assn*, 1988, 27.

[29]Scott, Fox, etal., *Archaeological Insights . . .*, 114.

[30]There are some students, in their reconstruction, who think Custer, instead of going after the women and children, left the Calhoun Hill area to seek a better defensive position to the north.

[31]Wells, "The Fight on Calhoun Hill," 19.

[32]John P. Hart, Ed., *Custer and his Times, Book Four* (NP: Little Big Horn Associates, Inc, 2002), 215.

sion arising from the surprise and the attempt of the women and children to get out of the way, Col. Custer was led to believe that the Indians were retreating and would escape him.... I do not attribute Colonel Custer's action to either recklessness or want of judgment but to a misapprehension of the situation.[33]

Another re-construction of Custer's decision to go to the north, holds that he observed the movement of the warriors to the north and sensed they were attempting to flank and destroy his command. In order to forestall this tactic, Custer gave up the thought of chasing the non-combatants and turned Yates' Battalion at about a 45 degree angle to the right and moved downstream to counteract their design.[34]

Custer decided to take only two of Yates' companies, 'E' and 'F.' northward. He would detach a company to increase both the manpower and the firepower of the blocking force and to give him the insurance of a free rein without having to worry about warriors coming in behind him. It would have been natural to select 'L' from Yates' Battalion to help support Keogh, as this company was commanded by Custer's brother in law, in whom he had great confidence.[35] Many might think Custer was foolhardy in chasing after all these Indians with only about ninety men. But, the frontier army had a propensity for going after any number of Indians with a small body of troops with little forethought to the consequences. Some of the encounters ended in disaster for the white men, such as the Grattan and Fetterman fights. However, there were also successes as well. In 1874, Colonel Ranald Mackenzie, 4th Cavalry, at the Battle of Palo Duro was only able to put two companies on the canyon's floor "against an unknown but very large number of Indians," with no advance planning.[36] The two companies charged through the entire village which contained about 800 Indians, keeping them at bay until the other companies were able to reach the bottom.

Before he left, Custer probably ordered Keogh to posi-

tion his battalion, along with 'L,' along Calhoun Ridge, in order to assure a domination of the area around Deep Coulee, the western end of Calhoun Ridge. This deployment would also give them command of the ford area as well. Second Lieutenant Harrington detached the second platoon of Company 'C' under the command of First Sergeant Edwin Bobo to establish a position around Finley Hill facing to the southwest. In addition, a detail was sent to the western edge of this hill, about two hundred yards away, as it neared Greasy Grass Ridge.[37] This detail would cover the portion of Deep Coulee which leads to Ford B and attempt to prevent its use by the warriors.[38] Wooden Leg related that these white men (Company 'C') had come from the other group of soldiers on Calhoun Hill.[39] Keogh began to deploy 'L' around Calhoun Hill and kept 'I' as the reserve. The horses were probably placed in a small ravine between 'L' and 'I' Companies. Custer no doubt expected this augmented battalion to do little more than engage in long distance skirmishing. This type of action usually results in few casualties to either side. But any potential skirmishing would come to a quick end as soon as Benteen's Battalion showed up and moved to join the main column.

It was about 5:15 PM, and Custer, with headquarters staff, and 'E' and 'F' were moving away from Calhoun Hill, traveling along the back side of the ridge line (Custer Ridge) towards where the non-combatants were reported. It must be noted that Custer Ridge doesn't end at Last Stand Hill, but drops away to the northwest. The reduced battalion followed this ridge until they were past what was to be Last Stand Knoll. The troopers continued moving slightly to the northwest, crossing right through the present parking area and through the cemetery and continued on towards where the present stone house is located when one enters the battlefield. That Custer didn't deploy any troops along his ridgeline, as some students believe, but moved straight toward his objective, is confirmed by Little Wolf, a Cheyenne. He recalled there was only one group of soldiers who was deployed, and that was on Calhoun Hill. There were no soldiers from Calhoun Hill to Last Stand Hill; "the soldiers moved right along."[40] Gall had spoken to both Crow King and Crazy Horse about the battle, and he related what they had told him, they:

---

[33]Graham, *The Custer Myth*, 116–117.

[34]Stewart, *Custer's Luck*, 447.

[35]Sklenar, *To Hell With Honor*, 84. As for Custer's move to the north, Dr. Gray concluded: "But why had Custer attempted so much with so little? The ultimate reason was simply inadequate enemy intelligence.... Up to the very last minute, the evidence Custer was so assiduously gathering seemed to conceal the true strength of the hostiles, and to indicate that they were in flight.... Custer attacked separately from Reno because he thought the village was in flight, and then the terrain features delayed and displaced his attack." See, *Centennial Campaign*, 183.

[36]Michael D. Pierce, *The Most Promising Young Officer* (Norman, OK: University of OK Press, 1993), 150–151.

[37]Gray, *Custer's Last Campaign*, 367–369; *Camp, BYU*, roll 2 box 2 folder 4 & 5.

[38]It might have been asking these men to do too much, as Ford B was about 1300 yards away. It would have been difficult at this distance.

[39]Marquis, *A Warrior Who Fought Custer*, 231.

[40]*Camp IU*, box 7, folder 7.

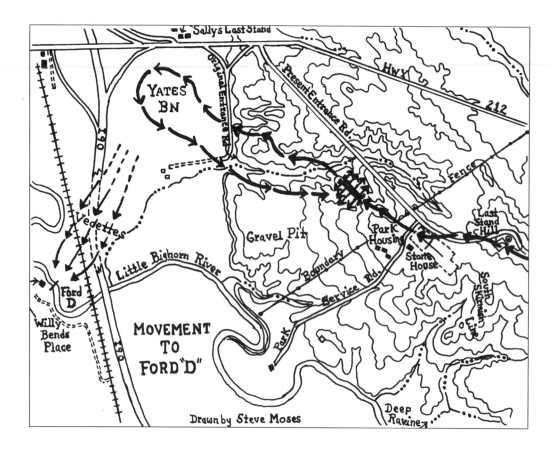

Drawn by Steve Moses

were afraid the soldiers, that we had seen march in the direction . . . north might kill our women and children. They (Crow King and Crazy Horse) went back the way they came (from the Reno fight). Their ponies were racing.[41]

As noted, Custer could see the movement of the Indians on the west side of the river. He led the two companies down onto the first long, hogback ridge to the west of the battlefield's entrance road, then down onto the flats near Route 212. Julia Face, the wife of Thunder Hawk, a Brule, said, "None of the warriors reached the high ridge ahead of Custer."[42] But she must not have known about the Cheyennes with Wolf Tooth, who were already to the east of the troops and were riding north, parallel to their route. This band of Indians almost caught up with Yates' Battalion. As Custer moved down off his ridge, the command came under fire from Wolf Tooth's warriors who had circled around from their previous action at Blummer-(Nye) Cartwright Ridge and were now on Last Stand Hill. But, the only thing their bullets hit was the earth, as the rear of the column had passed out of sight.[43] Bouyer

probably told Custer about the ford near the present iron railroad bridge, across from the former Willy Bends' place (Ford D). This was the ford Custer was trying to reach; the non-combatants were within his reach. White Bull said the women and children were only about a half mile away.[44] That Custer was headed for this ford, is verified by the account of John Stands in Timber.[45] He even indicated the Bends' place, by name, as Custer's objective.[46] In addition, Lieutenant Philo Clark was told in 1877, by the former warriors who had surrendered, Custer was trying to reach Ford D to cross over the river. One Indian even drew a map on the floor of the Lieutenant's room to illustrate his account.[47] White Bull also drew a map which showed this body of soldiers headed straight to the north beyond the battle ridge. Furthermore, in his summation, at the Reno Court of Inquiry, Jesse Lee concluded that Custer had attempted to cross the river further down and had led his troops in that direction for this purpose.[48] This determination is similar to what Reno told Lieu-

[41]Barry, *Indian Notes . . .* , 25–27.
[42]Hardorff, *Lakota Recollections*, 128.
[43]Liberty, *Cheyenne Memories*, 199.

[44]Wells, "Little Big Horn Notes," 15.
[45]Liberty, *Cheyenne Memories*, 199.
[46]Don Rickey, John Stands in Timber Interview, Custer Battlefield Collection, August 8, 1956, folder 15878.
[47]Wells, "Little Big Horn Notes," 17–18.
[48]Graham, *Reno Court—Abstract*, 259.

tenant Frank D. Baldwin, 5th Infantry, in the summer of 1876. Baldwin noted in his diary that "from the signs along his (Custer's) trail Reno thinks that Custer made several efforts to get down to the village."[49]

I don't believe Custer's two companies tried to force a crossing at Ford D. As was customary, his vedettes had advanced ahead of the companies, who were about 300 yards behind on the south side of Route 212 in the flats across from the present-day gas station complex. These advanced troopers now met up with a heavy resistance from the Indians who had raced ahead and also from the camp police and old men who had escorted the non-combatants northward. "The Custer men tried to cross the river at a ford west of the railroad tracks . . . Cheyenne hidden in the brush on the south side of the ford drove the soldiers back and killed a couple of them in the bush by the river."[50]

Kills Eagle, a Blackfoot, said the soldiers didn't come within sixty yards of the ford before they drove them off and up the hill.[51] Other Indian accounts record they had massed in the timber and had opened such a terrific fire from all sides that the troops gave way.[52]

There are some students who believe Custer had a double envelopment planned, which is why he attempted to keep going north. These students believe, there were two distinct Indian camps, separated by about two miles. An upper camp, which Reno struck, and a lower camp, located on the south side of Onion Creek on the west side of the river, across from the mouth of Deep Coulee. Custer, according to their reconstruction, had already dispatched his 1st battalion under Keogh across the river at Ford B to attack this separate village from the south. The 1st battalion was repulsed and sought the high ground. Custer with the 2nd battalion (Companies 'F' and 'L;' 'E' was detached) was likewise repulsed from Ford D and was now isolated from the rest of the column. The Custer battle then became one of two distinct actions about a half mile apart.[53] There are other students who believe a variation of the above is more accurate. They claim Custer was planning to march to Ford D all along, cross over and make an attack on the village from the north. This attack was to be a signal to Reno to leave his position in the valley and "press forward" as soon as he heard the gunfire. Custer expected that "the combined pressure would stampede the Indians out of their village."[54] This viewpoint finds some support in the diary of Private Thomas Coleman who wrote that he (Custer) ordered "Reno to charge the village at the upper end and he would go down and ford it at the lower end in order to cut them."[55] Custer, according to these students' re-constructions, did successfully cross at Ford D with his whole command. Custer's troops then drove through the pony herd and killed a number of them before being forced back across the river at Ford C (Cheyenne Ford at the mouth of Deep Ravine) and from there ascended to Custer Ridge where they were then deployed.[56]

Yates' vedettes were forced back via the flats from their attempted crossing, towards the rest of the battalion that moved to their support, and covered their retreat with well-placed fire support. One student believed this action was, instead, toward a position the troops had taken on Cemetery Ridge rather than on the flats below.[57] He believes the two companies retreated from the ford area to the southeast, and crossed the present boundary fence south of the present gravel pit below the park housing for the rangers. The two companies then proceeded to Last Stand Knoll from the west.[58] However, the maps from both the red and white men record this action down on the flats between Route 212 and the cemetery on the bluffs.[59] No doubt, the squad graphically described to the officers what lay ahead at the ford. I believe at this point, Custer finally realized he had misread the situation. It wasn't just the non-combatants who were this far north of the village, but also hundreds of warriors who had rushed downstream to oppose his movement. When Custer pulled back from Ford B and kept moving to the north, the Indians correctly surmised the soldiers were heading to cross at Ford D and to cut off the non-combatants.

[49]James Brust, "Baldwin Talks with Reno, writes about Custer's Final Battle," *Greasy Grass*, Vol. 9, May 1993, 22.

[50]Rickey, John Stands in Timber Interview.

[51]Edward Milligan, *High Noon on the Greasy Grass* (NP: NP, 1972), 8.

[52]Thomas R. Buecker, "Sioiux War Report," *Greasy Grass*, Vol. 7, May 1991, 18.

[53]Bob Doran, "Battalion Formation on the Custer Trail," *3rd Annual Symposium Custer Battlefield Historical & Museum Assn.*, 1989, 9–23.

[54]Letter, Henry Lemly to Robert Carter, July 15, 1921, Ghent Collection, Library of Congress.

[55]Liddic, *I Buried Custer*, 17. However, Coleman could have only known this from second hand information, as he was with Company B.

[56]It is beyond the scope of this book to go into the sources or further details of these various battle re-constructions. Suffice to say, the students have extracted from the accounts 'facts' which they believe support their views.

[57]Fox, *Archaeology, History, and Custer's Last Battle*, 188.

[58]Ibid, 185.

[59]George A. Schneider, *The Freeman Journal* (San Rafel, CA: Presidio Press, 1977), 65; Wells, "Little Big Horn Notes," 14.

Not only weren't they going to permit him anywhere near their women and children, but they were suddenly displaying an aggressive posture which had up to this point been lacking. The warriors were not falling back, as a shield for the non-combatants, but instead they just kept pressing towards the battalion's flanks. They didn't act as Custer had expected, and instead of rushing to remove their families and horses from harm's way, then try to flee, the warriors were counterattacking. Custer had surprised the village all too well. They did not have the time, even if they wanted, to send away their women and children. Therefore, they had to fight to protect them; the warriors had no other choice.[60] Custer could see more and more warriors crossing Ford D all the time.[61] Custer knew he couldn't force this changed situation with only ninety men, and his gunfire didn't appear to be as effective as before. He ordered a retreat back to the high ground, the hogback ridge (Custer Ridge Extension) overlooking the flats. Custer could have reasoned that heavy volley fire should discourage the ever growing number of warriors from pressing too close, all the while he hoped to see the reunited regiment appear to the south.

A great number of shell cases have been found all along this ridge line, as well as along the original, now abandoned, battlefield entrance road which Custer crossed on his way to the higher hogback. It has been reported that there were hundreds of cases found along this ridge about four to five hundred yards north of the cemetery.[62] Most of these cases were removed in the mid 1960s and were not recorded by the park personnel.[63] It must be remembered that the Custer Battlefield was a very different place in the 1950s and '60's. One could saunter about on any part of the field (outside the fence) and do about whatever one wished. It was a simple matter to find these shells and put them in your pocket; the battlefield 's environs were virtually unprotected during this period.[64] Most of these shell cases that were uncovered and picked up

found their way for sale to private collectors.[65] However, there were still a number of these cartridge cases that were discovered and documented by Park Rangers, indicating a volume of fire rivaling that on the better known Blummer-(Nye) Cartwright Ridge.[66]

John Stands in Timber said that after Custer retreated to below the stone house, he waited there for awhile. The Indians continued to press the soldiers and answered the soldiers' volleys with gunfire of their own from the ridges north of the battle monument.[67] White Bull also said the soldiers were on these northern ridges. He told Stanley Vestal, a later interviewer of Indians, that the Gray Horse Soldiers (Company 'E') were deployed well north of the monument. He even drew Vestal a map so his story would not be misunderstood.[68] Dr. Don Rickey, who had interviewed John Stands in Timber on the battlefield, noted that the real action started, at least from the Cheyenne viewpoint, below and west of the cemetery. After this, the action moved to Custer Hill.[69] The warriors told Stands in Timber they often wondered "why the soldiers did not move south to rejoin the others, and if the Custer men had not delayed so long they could have gotten back to the other soldiers."[70] To the south, heavy firing was heard coming from the Calhoun Hill area, and this could have been the cause of the lieutenant colonels' delay. Custer had been expecting Benteen for nearly an hour, and he probably thought they would be making an appearance at any minute, sweeping the Indians before them. Custer, probably never entertained the thought this gunfire from Keogh's position was an indication of a serious problem involving Benteen's/Reno's anticipated arrival. But, as he was beginning to take casualties and there was no sign of support, Custer decided to pull back. The decision to abandon this forward position might have been hastened by Wolf Tooth, Big Foot, and their followers. These Indians had moved in, from the Last Stand Hill area, behind a ridge line above the white men to the east and were firing down into Custer's men.[71] He ordered a movement back towards Keogh's position on Calhoun Hill area to reunite the two battalions for the second time and to undertake a defensive stance until the situation could be stabilized.[72]

[60]DeCost Smith, *Indian Experiences* (Caldwell, ID: Caxton Printers, 1942), 232.

[61]Liberty, *Cheyenne Memories*, 199.

[62]Letter, J. W. Vaughn to Superintendent, Custer Battlefield National Monument, July 2, 1963, Custer Battlefield Collection.

[63]Letter, Robert Doran to Bruce R. Liddic, August 30, 2001, author's collection. Mr. Doran said there were nearly a thousand cases discovered. Others have countered these shell cases could have come from the firing during the various anniversary celebrations, as well as the ones former Superintendent Edward Luce 'salted' for the benefit of the visitors.

[64]Michael Koury & Dr Richard Fox, "Debate—Nature of Fighting at the Little Big Horn," *12th Annual Symposium Custer Battlefield Historical & Museum Assn.*, 1998, 79.

[65]Ibid.

[66]Scott and Bleed, *A Good Walk Around the Boundary*, 27–28.

[67]Rickey, John Stands in Timber Interview.

[68]Wells, "Little Big Horn Notes," 14–15.

[69]Rickey, John Stand in Timber Interview.   [70]Ibid.

[71]Powell, *Sweet Medicine*, 116.

[72]There are a number of students who do not believe Custer would have left these men on Calhoun Hill and moved north with only two companies. He probably would not have, if he (*continued*)

As some students have correctly summarized, there were two separate "last stands" taking place. One 'stand' at Calhoun Hill, as the Indians moved to surround Keogh's battalion, and another 'stand,' that for the present, involved a moving fight wherever Yates' battalion went. These two units were never able to rejoin each other, and the closest they came was about a half a mile. If one believes what Crazy Horse said, the Indians on purpose tried to keep the units isolated after they had split apart.[73] He said when they rushed northward after the Reno fight, the warriors divided into two groups in their pursuit of the northward bound troops. One would try to intercept Custer before he could get to Ford D and the women and children. The other crossed over the river (Ford C?) to get in Custer's rear.[74] It is not necessary to inflate the numbers of Indians (or the village's population) who overwhelmed the soldiers. Individually, the two battalions would be outnumbered 12 to 1, if only twelve hundred warriors confronted them. The soldiers were divided by faulty command decisions which committed one to a holding action and the other to an offensive operation without either having sufficient manpower to accomplish their objective. This was compounded by Custer's failure to grasp the Indians' frame of mind. Thus, his two battalions became separated by a couple of thousand yards that consigned the two groups of white men to fight and die alone.

Custer ordered 'E' Company to pull out and take up positions in the present cemetery to the south and west of the visitors center, to protect the retreat of 'F.'[75] Company 'F' reached the crest of last stand hill and positioned itself along this ground and extended into the slight depression just to the west of the battlefield road. This move would cover both the area to the northeast as well as the column's flank to the southwest. It was about 5:30 that afternoon when Custer, with the two companies, retreated through the cemetery. Many battle re-constructions have the troopers going back to the Last Stand Hill area following the general direction they had trav-

eled a short time before. Gall told the participants at the tenth anniversary ceremony this very fact. He said that Custer stopped at the down slope location from Last Stand Hill (near the visitors center) before he came back to his final place.[76] But, Cheyenne accounts are more detailed and have the soldiers retreating through the cemetery to the southwest, "riding to a dry gulch and following it up to the center of the basin (near the head of Deep Coulee), below where the monument now stands."[77] The Indians took advantage of this elongated movement to cover the ridges behind Last Stand Hill so the soldiers couldn't continue in that direction. The two companies moved toward the upper banks of the basin below the present Stone House. The Indian pressure continued to increase, and Custer ordered Company 'E' to dismount with 'number fours' to the center and cover the rear of 'F' as it advanced up the slope of Last Stand Hill. The Indians remembered: "Some of the soldiers lay down on the ground, firing from that position. Others advanced for a distance, running, covered by the rifles of the men already hugging the earth."[78]

Moving Robe, an Uncpapa woman, saw that the white men were trapped. "There were Indians everywhere." She noted the Cheyennes were beginning their attack from the north, and the Sioux were starting from the south. The soldiers were just about surrounded.[79]

The continued gunfire Custer heard coming from the south wasn't very reassuring when he reached the top of his hill. There was no sign of Benteen, the pack train or Reno, and there was nothing but gun smoke and dust a half mile away, with shadowy figures emerging, moving towards this rise of ground which would become Last Stand Hill. Almost as soon as Yates' battalion had departed, Keogh found himself between a rock and a hard place. The Indians hadn't really receded back to their camps. They were being continuously strengthened and were constantly moving in his direction, taking advantage of the geography, so neither Keogh nor Calhoun could ever be really sure where the warriors were concentrating. So, instead of seeing Reno and Benteen riding to Keogh's position, there appeared nothing but angry and aggressive warriors. If Keogh abandoned the Calhoun Hill area to move toward Custer, Benteen and Reno could very well find themselves ambushed in Medicine Tail or when they crossed Deep Coulee. However, if Keogh mounted his expanded battalion and fought his way through to the

---

thought these troops were going to encounter the resistance they did, nor did he expect these two companies to be in a fight. In my reconstruction Custer thought he was going north to chase after and capture the noncombatants.

[73]There are other accounts which state Crazy Horse went up Deep Ravine and killed some of the horse holders behind Calhoun Hill. He then crossed the battle ridge to join the Minneconjous on the east side. A little later, Crazy Horse followed White Bull and charged through Keogh's Company at the gap on the battle ridge.

[74]Charles Diehl, "Crazy Horse's Story of Custer Battle," *South Dakota Historical Collections*, Vol. 6, 1912, 227.

[75]Rickey, John Stands in Timber Interview.

[76]Scott and Bleed, *A Good Walk Around the Boundary*, 44.

[77]Powell, *Sweet Medicine*, 116; Fox, *Archaeology, History, and Custer's Last Battle*, 186.   [78]Powell, *Sweet Medicine*, 116.

[79]Wells, "Little Big Horn Notes," 12.

south, where Reno was supposed to be, Custer might find himself cut off by Indians moving in behind his departing companies. But, if he stayed where he was, in light of the increased Indian activity, his companies might be encircled and decimated before he could receive any support. It was a difficult decision for Captain Myles W. Keogh. With the very real possibility that the twilight of eternity would close down around his command, he chose to remain where Custer had ordered him. Keogh (and Calhoun) could have reasoned, at least from the way they had positioned their troops, that they could provide some measure of support to Yates' battalion, while at the same time keeping the way clear for the expected and now prayed for reinforcements from Reno and Benteen.[80]

Standing Bear, a Minneconjou, reported that most of the Indians, he saw, went to the northeast up Deep Coulee and then spread out to the east (Greasy Grass Ridge) and to the rear of the white men, "completely encircling his (Custer's) troops on both hills."[81] By both hills, Standing Bear was referring to Last Stand Hill and Calhoun Hill. These Indians were working their way all long the ridges and ravines on the east side of the river, while others moved to the east, then north to complete the circle. In 1908, Foolish Elk repeated much the same story, but in more detail:

> The Indians were now getting their horses in from the hills and soon came up in large numbers. Some crossed the stream farther down (Ford C or D?) and others crossed the ford (B) and followed . . . in overwhelming numbers. The Indians were between Custer and the river and all the time coming up and getting around to the east of him, passing around both his front and rear.[82]

It was these Indians that drew the attention of Calhoun as well as the soldiers on Finley Ridge.

The squad of troopers a few hundred yards west of Finley Hill were the first to feel the full effects of the warriors' fighting qualities this day.[83] This detail had tried to prevent the Indians from using the ford area and Greasy Grass Ridge, but the Indians charged and overran this position. He Dog said the real "fighting began in the Finley area and kept up all along."[84] The small squad couldn't fire their carbines fast enough to keep the warriors at bay, and as the Indians closed on the troops, revolvers were employed and the few who were left struggled to reach

Finley Hill.[85] The Company 'C' troopers on Finley Hill were under the command of First Sergeant Bobo and Sergeants Jeremiah Finley and August Finckle. As the warriors overran this squad and were pressing the soldiers from the west, Crow King and his followers, who had left the Reno fight, rode through the village then turned to the east at Deep Ravine. They followed a branch of Deep Ravine, to the southeast, which brought them very close to 'C' platoon's right flank.[86] The fire from the Indian positions on Greasy Grass Ridge, as well as this assault on their flank broke apart the troop's formation, and the result was the sixteen marble markers which are placed around this hill. It should be noted, the thickest concentration of dead horses on the southern part of the battlefield was on Calhoun Hill, extending down to Finley Hill.[87] Sergeant Finley's badly mutilated body, with twelve arrows in it, was found next to the head of Carlo, his horse.[88] Bobo was able to ride back, at least part of the way, to Keogh's position on the east side of Custer Ridge. His horse was found about two thirds of the way there, as it had been killed and "had slidden down the bank into a gully." The first sergeant's body was found in a "pile of men around Keogh."[89] A possible explanation for Bobo's presence with Keogh could be that he was seeking reinforcements, but no sooner had he left, than his platoon was broken, and he was only able to arrive on foot to report to Keogh.[90]

It was noted that his body wasn't mutilated.[91] Daniel Knipe believed Finley was only wounded during the action and wasn't able to reach safety. He said you could tell from the mutilations, which men were wounded and which were just killed. The squaws and children would first strip and shoot the wounded full of arrows, then chop their faces with hatchets.[92] Sergeant Finckle almost made it to Calhoun Hill, as his body was found between Finley and Calhoun. He was severely mutilated as well. The archeological evidence supports the possibility of Greasy Grass Ridge being a strong Indian position. A large number of shell cases, mostly fired from Henry/Winchester Rifles and Spencer carbines, were found on the western slope of this ridge. After disposing of 'C' Company's second platoon, these Indians then used this position to fire at the eastern side of Calhoun Hill, while others moved back towards

[80]Joe Sills, "Were There Two Last Stands," *2nd Annual Symposium Custer Battlefield Historical & Museum Assn.*, 1988, 17.

[81]Hardorff, *Lakota Recollections*, 59.

[82]Hammer, *Custer in '76*, 198.

[83]Marquis, *A Warrior Who Fought Custer*, 231; Evans, *Custer's Last Fight*, 270–271.   [84]Michno, *Lakota Noon*, 208.

[85]Greene, *Evidence and the Custer Enigma*, 66–67.

[86]Barry, *Indian Notes . . .*, 25–27.

[87]*Camp, BYU*, box 2, folder 9.

[88]Hardorff, *Custer Battle Casualties*, 113.

[89]*Camp, IU*, box 2, folder 8.

[90]Another possibility is that Bobo was seeking safety and wound up with Keogh's Company.

[91]*Camp, BYU*, roll 1, box 1, folder 2.   [92]Ibid.

the river through the ravines and underbrush to assault the other group of soldiers around Last Stand Hill.[93] It was originally thought that a good part of the warriors who fought Custer were only armed with bows and arrows, war clubs and lances plus an odd assortment of older firearms, mostly muzzel-loaders. It was believed the best weapons the Indians had were the ones captured from the soldiers. This was the standard interpretation of the arsenal of Indian arms and equipment. The interpretation was changed in 1984 due to the archaeological investigations conducted at the battlefield. This survey revealed a number of very interesting facts. Of the 209 Indian weapons identified, 119 or 56% were 'modern' repeating weapons. Sixty-six of these were either Henry or Winchester rifles, which could discharge up to sixteen rounds without reloading. By extrapolation, the archaeologists determined there were nearly 400 firearms employed against Custer, of which about 192 were repeating rifles or about one of these fast firing weapons for every trooper in Custer's command.[94] This impressive warrior firepower was arrayed against the soldiers' single shot Springfield carbine. After a careful study, both Drs. Douglas Scott and Richard Fox concluded when all the data is taken into account, "it becomes readily apparent that Custer and his men were outgunned, if not in range or stopping power, then certainly in firepower."[95] The two archaeologists also believed that these Indian weapons would be more effective than the more powerful and longer range Springfield carbines as the warriors drew progressively closer and closer to the troopers' positions.[96] It would be only natural that those warriors who were the best armed (with repeating rifles) would be in the forefront of any fire fight.[97] From the shell case evidence found during the 1984 archaeological survey, it appears this was the case.

This survey also found that at least seven of the Indian weapons which were used to break the soldier's line on Finley Hill were also fired against Calhoun's position from Henryville Ridge, southeast of this hill.[98] One possible explanation for the Indians shifting their firing positions from Greasy Grass Ridge to Calhoun Hill would be that the bullets from their shorter range Henrys and Winchesters were not very effective against Company L's location, about seven hundred yards away. However,

when their firepower was directed at Finley Hill, it proved very effective as it was only about three hundred and fifty yards away. Also, the warriors could have simply lacked any other good closer targets, so they moved to the east using the land's natural cover to move in close.[99] Another point to consider is that the disintegration of Company C's platoon on Finley Hill didn't trigger the subsequent breakdown on Calhoun Hill. If it had, the Indians who opposed 'C' would not have had enough time to move to 'L,' take up positions, and begin their firing again.[100] Thus Company L's status, no matter how precarious at the time, was not the primary result of Finley Hill being overrun. But, when Calhoun tried to counter the Indian threat coming from Greasy Grass Ridge/Finley Hill area by repositioning his line, he exposed the company to the increased firepower originating from Henryville Ridge without a corresponding counter response. More and more warriors then moved to take advantage of the too few soldiers who tried to adequately cover both the south and west sectors. Calhoun's line was stretched to the breaking point.

For a number of years, it has been accepted as battle dogma that Crazy Horse swept down from "the north in a great arc" and got around and behind Last Stand Knoll. With Crazy Horse's charge, any chance Custer might have had, vanished.[101] In 1985, Richard Hardorff took exception to this standard interpretation, and in a groundbreaking correction to these long held beliefs, explained how Crazy Horse used a route up Deep Ravine.[102] It wasn't possible for Crazy Horse to have ridden the distance, nearly seven miles, from the Reno fight to make the northern sweep across Ford D in time to confront Custer on last stand hill. As Michno concisely pointed out, "Pegasus was not his (Crazy Horse's) to command that day."[103] After participating in the Reno fight, Crazy Horse and his followers moved up Deep Coulee to help block any soldiers from retreating back south and east to Reno.[104] With this additional movement by the Ogallalas, the Indians had now succeeded in isolating the three units of the regiment from each other with hundreds of warriors in

---

[93]Greene, *Evidence and the Custer Enigma*, 66–67.

[94]Scott, Fox, etal., *Archaeological Insights into the Custer Battle*, 112.

[95]Ibid.   [96]Ibid, 113.

[97]Another explanation could be the Indians always claimed their young men were wild with excitement and had rushed to the forefront of the fight. They could not be restrained.

[98]Ibid, 62–63, 113.

[99]Wells, "The Fight on Calhoun Hill," 27–28.

[100]Ibid, 28.

[101]Robert Utley, *Custer Battlefield* (Washington, DC: National Park Service, 1969), 33.

[102]Hardorff, *Markers, Artifacts & Indian Testimony*, 43–45. Eight years later, Greg Michno further elabrated on Crazy Horse's traditional route and demonstated it just could not have happened in this manner. See, Greg Michno, "Crazy Horse, Custer, and the Sweep to the North," *Montana The Magazine of Western History*, Vol. 43, #3, Summer 1993, 42–53.   [103]Ibid, 52.

[104]Graham, *The Custer Myth*, 97–98.

Courtesy of Warren Van Ess

red men right through the soldiers' line. White Bull said that the last time he took a 'run' at the soldiers he did not turn back but rode right into them.[108] The rest of the warriors followed, and this bunch of soldiers started to run back to the other bunch of soldiers (Keogh).[109] The 'run' had turned into a major and unexpected penetration of the soldier's line.[110] There was no longer any time to reload the single shot carbines, and the soldiers drew their Colt .45s as the skirmish line fell apart. By reading White Bull's account, one could interpret his charge occurred between Keogh's position and Calhoun's. There is a ravine in this area which might present an obstacle to anyone riding from the east to west across the soldiers' front. White Bull could have ridden up this ravine to its head and near to a place between the soldiers and the 'set of fours.'[111] With Indians to the south, east, and west, this sudden breakthrough was possibly more than the invested troopers could entertain. There is no way to determine if the soldiers were ordered to fall back or were overrun and forced back. But, even if they were ordered to withdraw, it requires little imagination to envision the cavalrymen breaking ranks and running for any perceived place of safety they could find. The Indians directed particular attention to the horse holders in the depression between Calhoun Hill and Company 'I.' According to Moving Robe, it was easy to stampede these horses as their holders were trying to control as many as ten animals apiece. "An Indian waived his blanket and scared all the horses," and they ran right towards the Indians. If Moving Robe was correct that each horse holder was responsible for up to ten mounts, then the need for more firepower on Calhoun's line must have been acute as the action reached its climax. Calhoun needed men to cover the two fronts, and he was forced to borrow from the 'set of fours' for his only reinforcements.

between them. Crazy Horse and White Bull both joined in the fighting against the troops on Calhoun Hill from near Henryville Ridge. It was here White Bull made another 'run' against the soldiers to show his bravery. He leaned on the top of his horse while riding near the troopers, holding onto his horse's mane with both hands, and afterwards returned to the warriors.[105] But, there was more to the fight on Calhoun Hill than just feats of bravado by the Indians against the cavalrymen. The Indians had 'L' company outnumbered by better than 20 to 1, and there was no escape for the beleaguered soldiers. It was just the type of a fight in which the Indians excelled.

Gall claimed he led the attack on Calhoun's left flank from the area of the southeast corner post of the current park's fence line. Red Feather, an Ogallala, recalled that arrows were freely used, as well as the repeating rifles.[106] The soldiers were on one side of the hill and the Indians were on the other, with a slight rise between them.[107] After Crazy Horse made his 'run' against the white men, the warriors charged, and their force of numbers carried the

There is little doubt the troopers on Calhoun Hill gave a good account of themselves. Their position was only overrun after a heavy, intense fight. Almost to the last moment, the soldiers stood their ground as indicated by the numerous piles of Springfield cartridges cases that were found beside the bodies. Just how good of an account 'L' gave is evident from the statements the Indians made after the battle. Many of the warrior casualties occurred around

---

[105]Hardorff, *Lakota Recollections*, 115. Mr. Hardorff concluded this 'run' took place north of Custer Ridge, between Custer and Calhoun Hill. Upon looking at a topography map, one can see the two hillocks between where this gap is located.

[106]Ibid, 87.   [107]Ibid.

[108]Some students have placed this action north of Calhoun Hill, near where Keogh was killed.

[109]Wells, "Little Big Horn Notes," 15.

[110]Michno, *Lakota Noon*, 213.

[111]Wells,"The Fight on Calhoun Hill," 30.

the Calhoun Hill area.[112] Runs the Enemy, a Two Kettle, said the Sioux tried to charge this position more than once, but "The return fire was so strong that the Sioux had to retreat back over the hill again."[113] Red Feather said it was a hard battle for this hill "because both sides were brave warriors."[114] Red Horse, a Minneconjou who fought at Calhoun Hill, had seen too much death on both sides that afternoon, and the memory remained with him for the rest of his life. He said later, "I don't like to talk about that fight. If I hear any of my people talking about it, I always move away."[115] Sitting Bull took a more pragmatic approach to the numbers of dead and was said to have remarked nobly: "My heart is full of sorrow that so many were killed on each side, but when they compel us to fight, we must fight."[116]

After the battle when Captain Moylan examined Calhoun Hill, he commented that the dead were found lying in the "regular position as skirmishers." Near one of the bodies, the captain counted twenty-eight expended shells, with numerous other cartridges cases found between the other bodies.[117] In spite of all the firing these troopers did, the soldiers still had more than enough ammunition. Red Feather caught several of the soldiers' spooked horses and found many cartridges in the saddlebags, along with coffee.[118] This was one of the few places on the battlefield where the white men were found in a formal battle line. Edgerly thought that from the location of the bodies, Calhoun's troopers had been positioned "for a cooly planned resistance."[119] Calhoun's body was found exactly where it should have been, in the rear of the first platoon.[120] Second Lieutenant John Crittenden, the company's second in command, was found about thirty feet from his company commander. Varnum told Camp that the only way Calhoun's mutilated body could be identified was by the fillings in his teeth.[121] However, Edgerly recalled Calhoun was not mutilated at all.[122] Crittenden was similarly reported butchered, and his body was only recognized by the "fragments of his glass eye, into which an arrow had been shot."[123] Edgerly didn't comment on Crittenden's condition, except to say there were numerous arrows sticking in his body.[124]

This close up fighting no doubt wiped Company 'L' and whatever other troopers who previously had managed to reach Calhoun Hill. The few who escaped this onslaught fell back, keeping below the ridge line, going toward the support of 'I' Company. This movement is confirmed by archaeological evidence, which has uncovered several .45/55 Springfield cases fired by carbines used on Calhoun Hill and which were also fired from Keogh's position.[125] It is possible that at least one trooper fled to the east, toward Reno. In 1904, a boot bearing the initials of *J. D.*, with human bones still encased, was uncovered in Deep Coulee. Twenty-four years later a skeleton was found near where the boot was discovered, with an arrowhead in its vertebrae. A number of shell cases were found near the bones. This could have been the remains of Private John Duggan of Company 'L.'[126] Private Charles Graham succeeded in fleeing Calhoun Hill, but he never made it to Keogh and temporary safety. His body was found half way between the two positions.[127]

Some students have theorized that First Sergeant James Butler of Company 'L,' when there was no further hope, in self-preservation, took off on his horse and rode through the lines to the south.[128] After riding into Deep Coulee, he galloped up the other side, putting a good distance between him and the warriors. Several Indians gave chase, but couldn't catch up due to the head start Butler had. Low Dog, an Ogallala, took a shot at the fleeing soldier and managed to hit his horse as it crossed a small knoll about six hundred yards to the northeast of Ford B and nearly a mile and a half from Weir Point. Butler scrambled to his feet and continued to move toward the high ground, but he didn't get far. When his body was found, there were many spent Springfield cases laying beside it. Godfrey said it was apparent that "he had sold his life dearly."[129] Gall related what might have been the end of this brave soldier:

> There was a soldier on the hill southeast of us still fighting when the battle ended and we had a hard time to kill him. He killed several of our braves. Finally some of the braves crawled up the hill on all sides. Those behind him finally killed him.[130]

If the soldier Gall spoke about was Butler, it shows that

[112]Hardorff, *Markers, Artifacts and Indian Testimony*, 46.
[113]Dixon, *The Vanishing Race*, 175.
[114]Hardorff, *Lakota Recollections*, 88.
[115]Graham, *The Custer Myth*, 60.   [116]Vestal, *Sitting Bull*, 174.
[117]Graham, *Reno Court*, 201.
[118]Hardorff, *Lakota Recollections*, 88
[119]Hammer, *Custer in '76*, 58.   [120]Stewart, *Custer's Luck*, 451.
[121]Hammer, *Custer in '76*, 63.   [122]Ibid, 58.
[123]Hardorff, *Custer Battle Casualties*, II, 17.
[124]Hammer, *Custer in '76*, 58.

[125]Scott, Fox, etal., *Archaeological Insights into The Custer Battle*, 117.
[126]Hardorff, *Custer Battle Casualties*, II, 56–58.
[127]*Camp, IU*, box 2, folder 11.
[128]Butler was not riding a thoroughbred horse, as some have thought but the horse of former Sergeant Milton Delacy who had deserted. See, Schoenberger, *End of Custer*, 196.
[129]Liberty, *Cheyenne Memories*, 207–208; Marquis, *A Warrior Who Fought Custer*, 236; Hardorff, *Custer Battle Casualties*, 110–111.
[130]Barry, *Indian Notes . . .* , 27–28.

the first sergeant wasn't killed early in the fight, but rather towards the end.[131] Other theories regarding Butler, whose body was found the farthest from the Custer field and the closest to Reno, speculate he was sent from Calhoun as a messenger to Benteen.[132] Private Martin said that he didn't think Butler, as a First Sergeant, would have been sent as a messenger.[133] However, in desperation to get a courier through to Benteen, any mounted man could have been selected. Or is it just possible before 5:30 PM, as Calhoun was desperately engaged, that troop movements were seen on Weir Point? Consequentially, could Butler have been dispatched in response to this sighting to hasten the long expected reinforcements? [134] If so, then from Weir Point, Captain Weir and 'D' Company could have seen exactly what they thought they saw. Which in truth was the end of a fight, with Indians milling about Calhoun Hill, finishing off any wounded soldiers, looting the dead, while heavy dust clouds moved to the north, away from the scene.

And what of Company 'C'? No one has been able for certain to explain where this company met its end. Knipe was at a loss to understand why his company's men were found on all parts of the Custer field.[135] Benteen was equally perplexed when he examined the battlefield on the 27th. He wrote his wife: "What became of 'C' Company no one knows—they must have charged below the village . . . or have been killed on the bluffs—as very few of 'C' Co. horses are found."[136] The survivors tried to understand the movement and positions of the right wing by the location of their dead horses. It's clear that the mounts of this company were found everywhere; from Finley Hill on the south to last stand hill on the north, where six dead 'sorrels' were found.[137] As Benteen asked, what of Company 'C'? No one has been able for certain to explain where this company met its fate. Another possible reason why 'C' seemed to disintegrate on the Custer field, was the lack of officers and noncommissioned officers to direct them. Tom Custer was on his brother's staff. Harrington was inexperienced, and Bobo and most of his sergeants became casualties early in the fight. This would certainly lead to a loss of the company's effectiveness and cohesion. However, there are literally as many theories as there were men in Company 'C' to interpret this dispersion. Charles Du Bois

put forth an interesting hypothesis that 'C' fought the battle in two separate platoons which were at a distance from each other. The first platoon was employed to cover the gap between 'I' and 'L' on Calhoun Hill. The other companies fought as a single unit. This, he concluded, would explain why their bodies were found all along battle ridge.[138] I have remarked on how 'C's second platoon had been sent to Finley Hill, so DuBois' theory might be more accurate than previously thought.

Keogh's company had deployed below the east side of Custer Ridge about a quarter mile north of Calhoun Hill. It's possible they were being held as a reserve, or they were in the process of moving to assist Calhoun or tried to cover his front as the few survivors fled over the ridgeline. But, it's clear from the evidence, 'I' had not been positioned or had moved along the ridge top.[139] If at one time they had occupied this high ground, Keogh probably would have ordered the troops to the east side to escape the fire from both Greasy Grass Ridge and Henryville Ridge. There was little agreement of his intent from the officers and men who inspected Keogh's position after the battle. Private Goldin thought 'I', whose bodies lay in a slight depression, had been formed into a hollow square, with Keogh in the center to resist the Indians.[140] Edgerly disputed this assessment and believed the captain was falling back towards Custer in a fighting retreat.[141] Lieutenant McClernard, who was with Gibbon's column, thought the gap he observed in the bodies between Keogh and Calhoun was the result of Custer ordering Keogh to fall back to his position. He believed the captain was in the process of so doing when he was attacked.[142]

Wallace was of the opinion Keogh's troopers had been killed while running in file. But he wasn't sure if Keogh had ever formed them into a true skirmish line. Wallace did admit "They were killed at intervals, but from their position, I don't think they could have been in a skirmish line."[143] Edgerly, in his scrutiny of this part of the field agreed with Wallace but only to a point. He stated, "There were no regular lines, but still evidence that there had been a line."[144] Lieutenant Roe said, "We found Captain Keogh and thirty nine of his Troop in another comparatively small space. The dead men were stretched out all along and back of this ridge."[145] Homer Wheeler, who

---

[131]For another explaination, see Stewart, *Custer's Luck*, 448–449.

[132]Edward Godfrey, "Custer's Last Battle," *Contributions to the Historical Society of Montana*, Vol. 9, 199.

[133]Hammer, *Custer in '76*, 102.   [134]Taunton, *Custer Field*, 38.

[135]Hammer, *Custer in '76*, 164.

[136]Graham, *The Custer Myth*, 298.

[137]Hammer, *Custer in '76*, 87. Company C rode sorrel colored horses.

[138]Graham, *The Custer Myth*, 102–103.

[139]Scott, Fox, etal., *Archaeological Insights into The Custer Battle*, 115.

[140]Carroll, *The Benteen-Goldin Letters*, 32.

[141]Graham, *The Custer Myth*, 219.

[142]McClernand, *With Indian and Buffalo in Montana*, 93.

[143]Graham, *Reno Court*, 61.   [144]Ibid, 401.

[145]Roe, *Custer's Last Battle*, 10.

was with the reburial detail in 1877, thought that this was the only position which was found where it appeared a defense had been made.[146]

Archaeological data has reportedly demonstrated that whatever Keogh's plan for his troop's disposition was, it was probably Keogh's own decision for his company to be where they were later found. He was not forced into this position. The Indians didn't push his company to the eastside of the ridgeline. This data has recorded very few artifacts found on either side of the ridge top above his position which would indicate a fight.[147] Nevertheless, no matter how 'I' came to be deployed on the reverse side of Custer's Ridge, it was now this company's turn to confront the victory flushed warriors. One minute, the troops on Calhoun Hill were holding out, and the next, their line was broken, and there was bedlam. This disintegration happened in a sufficiently short enough time span that Company I, as the reserve, could not be mobilized with any effect.[148] Their first bodies were found about 30 yards from where Calhoun's remains lay. McClernand was of the opinion there was a slight pause between the Indians overrunning Calhoun and their advance against Keogh. His belief was based on the distance between the dead led horses of the two companies, which would have been closer if they had acted in concert.[149]

Archaeological evidence tends to support the beliefs of Edgerly and McClernard that the company was in retreat. There have been very few Springfield cases found in this area, nor have there been many Indian artifacts uncovered.[150] This tends to support the conclusion the troops didn't have time to fire more than a round or two before they were cut off and destroyed. The carbines were not very effective as close range weapons, as they couldn't be fired fast enough. Red Feather said the Indians charged when they thought the soldiers' guns were empty. It's more probable, the troopers didn't have time to reload and resorted to their revolvers. Gall said the soldiers discarded their guns, then "fought with their little guns.[151] Grinnell's informants told him, as the soldiers made their way towards the other soldiers, about a half a mile behind them, "They fought with six-shooters, close fighting—almost hand to hand" as they tried to fall back.[152] White Bull described one such incident of man-to-man confrontation he had with an 'I' trooper. The soldier fired his Springfield at him and missed. The soldier didn't have enough time to reload, and White Bull was so close, he threw his carbine at the Minneconjou's head. White Bull knocked him down with the butt of his rifle. The warrior complemented this unknown soldier, and said he was a brave man who put up a good fight.[153] When the army fought as a unit(s), they always had the advantage over the warriors because of their organization and discipline. However, when it became a man-to-man fight, the warriors were superior. As individuals, they were simply better fighters than the soldiers. The Indians knew that they could kill more soldiers in hand-to-hand fighting than they could shoot down from a distance. In the Reno fight, for the most part, they stayed back shooting at the troopers and didn't charge in among them.[154] This time, it would be different; they would close in on these white men who had come to capture their women and children.

This close up fighting, according to He Dog, was initiated by Crazy Horse. He charged and broke through "and split the soldiers into two bunches." This part of the line that was cut off, fought their way to the others (Custer) at the end of the ridge. The soldiers from the second part who couldn't fight their way through, tried to get away toward the river, but "were all killed."[155] It has been suggested that perhaps He Dog wasn't referring to a formal skirmish line, as such, but rather a line of men in retreat.[156] Standing Bear said Keogh wasn't in retreat when he was confronted. The men on Calhoun Hill gave way and moved back to Keogh's position, and he made a desperate stand. Then Keogh and all his men were killed.[157] Upon a visit to the battlefield, Lieutenant John Bourke agreed with Standing Bear. He said it appeared to him Keogh attempted to make a stand as he and his company died in one compact mass, whereas, the other graves are "scattered in irregular clumps admid intervals."[158] This was contradicted by Foolish Elk who said the men from 'I' and what few of 'L' and 'C' who were still mounted, tried to retreat:

The men on the horses did not stop to fight, but went on ahead (towards Custer) as fast as they could go. The

---

[146]Homer W. Wheeler, *Buffalo Days* (NY, NY: A. L. Burt, 1925), 185.

[147]Scott, Fox, etal., *Archaeological Insights into The Custer Battle*, 115. However, other students have countered the ridge top was disturbed by the road. In addition, these shell cases could have been picked up by early visitors who generally followed the contour of the present road to Calhoun Hill. See, Richard Hardorff, "Burials, Exhumations and Reinterments," *Custer and his Times, Book Two* (NP : NP, 1984), 54.

[148]John P. Langellier, *Myles Keogh* (El Segundo, CA: Upton & Sons, 1991), 144.   [149]Roe, *Custer's Last Battle*, 38.

[150]Langellier, *Myles Keogh*, 150.

[151]Graham, *The Custer Myth*, 91.

[152]Grinnell, *The Fighting Cheyennes*, 315.

[153]Miller, "Echoes of the Little Big Horn," 36.

[154]Powell, *Sweet Medicine*, 119.

[155]Hardorff, *Lakota Recollections*, 75.

[156]Langellier, *Myles Keogh*, 146.   [157]Ibid, 59.

[158]Ibid, 134.

men on foot, however were shooting as they passed along ...The Indians were so numerous that the soldiers could not go any further, and they knew that they had to die.[159]

After this action very little is known about Crazy Horse's role, if any, at Last Stand Knoll. It has been speculated that because of a lack of Indian statements regarding his presence following the assault on Keogh, Crazy Horse left the battlefield to secure a fresh horse.[160] But, at this point in the fight, little leadership was required; the warriors were in overwhelming numbers, and all were eager to finish the battle.

Keogh's body was found in a slight depression along with a number of troopers. It would appear the soldiers there were all killed in a bunch. Some have concluded the closeness of the markers placed here foretold of men shot down in a volley of fire delivered from close range.[161] It's possible this was the group of soldiers Gall said were shot down in one bunch.[162] Perhaps First Sergeant Bobo, First Sergeant Frank Varden, Corporal John Wild, Trumpeter John Patton, and possibly Sergeant James Bustard had rallied around Keogh in an effort to hold the warriors back.[163] Keogh's left knee and leg was shattered, probably while mounted, as this wound corresponded to one found on his horse Comanche. Three other bullet wounds were discovered on his body that was found stripped, except for one sock, but otherwise not mutilated. It has been generally conceded that the body of Keogh's second in command, First Lieutenant James Porter, was never found, or at least positively identified. After a trip to the battlefield two days later, Benteen said he saw Porter's body, but gave no indication where.[164] Godfrey disputed Benteen's claim that he saw his body and said Porter was not found.[165] But, that he was dead was a certainty, as his buckskin jacket, complete with a bloody bullet hole near the side of his heart, was found in the Indian village.[166] Private Goldin was of the opinion Porter's body was burned in the village that evening.[167] Even Benteen admitted he could not find the body of 'C's Second Lieutenant Henry Harrington. Benteen's observation was confirmed by both Moylan and Gibson, who also failed to discover Harrington's remains.

The bodies of Bobo and Bustard were reported as untouched, and no comment was made on the condition of Varden's.[168] Wild was one of the tallest men in the company, and Patton the shortest, and they were identified because of this disparity. However, Private Frank Kennedy, Company 'I' and assigned to the pack train, looked for his fellow troopers and made no further comment on their bodies' condition.[169] Marker number 174 stands apart from the rest of 'I' Company near the eastern boundary fence. Three Springfield cases, all fired from the same carbine, were uncovered around this trooper's gravestone. According to the archaeologists, the data is consistent with the trooper trying to escape the Keogh fight. He "dashed across the ravines and up the final side slope" drawing the fire of the Indians, as he tried to get away. After discharging the rounds from his carbine, he resorted to his Colt .45. The archaeologists tell us he fired his Colt just as he was hit by an Indian bullet. "His colt round struck the ground where he fell.[170] It has been speculated this 'I' trooper was Private Henry Bailey.[171]

Recent re-constructions of the action in this sector have the noted Cheyenne Chief Lame White Man joining in from the west, while Crazy Horse and White Bull were splitting the area held by 'I' and possibly the first platoon of 'C'. Dr. Fox presents what appears to be very compelling evidence to support his explanation. In view of this revision, the National Park Service in the late 1980s changed the way they now interpret the events in this area to correspond with Dr. Fox's, among others,' views. But, I don't think this 'new' explanation is correct. I believe, the park service was too quick in a rush to judgment on this point. They could very well have been influenced by trying to show the public a return on their investment for all their time and effort from the massive archeological projects in the mid 1980s. The park service's opinion was probably along the lines of, if nothing new is uncovered and nothing is changed, what is the purpose of these projects?[172] Traditionally, Lame White Man's attack took place against 'E' Company on the south skirmish line down from Last Stand Knoll. I believe the testimony of the Indians are best interpreted when compared with the military accounts, combined with the terrain, and the resulting casualties from

[159]Hammer, Custer in '76, 199.
[160]Jim Holly, "Crazy Horse on the Greasy Grass," 8th Annual Symposium Custer Battlefield Historical & Museum Assn., 1994, 112. Also see, Mike Sajna, Crazy Horse (NY,NY: John Wiley & Sons, 2000), 288–289.   [161]Stewart, Custer's Luck, 452.
[162]Army and Navy Journal (Washington, DC), July 3, 1886.
[163]As noted, some accounts have Bustard's body found across from Ford B.   [164]Camp, IU, box 2, folder 16.
[165]Camp, BYU, roll 1, box, folder 7.
[166]Hardorff, Custer Battle Casualties, 16.
[167]Ibid, 105; Hardorff, Custer Battle Casualties, II, 32, 46–47.

[168]Hardorff, Custer Battle Casualties, 108–109, 116.
[169]Hardorff, Custer Battle Casualties, II, 68–69. Wild was 5'10" and Patton was 5'3".
[170]Scott, Fox, et al., Archaeological Insights into The Custer Battle, 124.
[171]Schoenberger, End of Custer, 199.
[172]Michno, Lakota Noon, 212, fn. 390.

such an assault.[173] As such, it is my belief Lame White Man's charge occurred just as it had been related in the past by the Indian narratives, and this action will be covered in its proper context on the South Skirmish Line.[174] Today, 'I' company markers appears to be little more than "knots of soldiers," who were surrounded by Indians.[175] This knot was composed of mostly Company 'I' troopers, but with a few survivors from 'L' and 'C.' The various Indian accounts state there were no formal lines, as Edgerly, Wallace and Wheeler believed. The warriors, Turtle Rib, Two Eagles, and Foolish Elk, among others, said this was a running fight, and the soldiers didn't make a stand.[176] This is consistent with the archaeological evidence. This compact mass of soldiers could reflect the beginning of a breakdown in the command and control of 'I.' If one views the marker arrangements on the Keogh's sector of Custer's Field, their distribution doesn't reflect any sense of a tactical distribution. This is logical, with Keogh having little warning of the impending collapse of Calhoun Hill, which as noted, was suddenly subjected to a heavier volume of fire from Henryville Ridge and an aggressive attack. This was coupled with increased pressure from the Greasy Grass Ridge quarter, and the combination was too great for the manpower available in 'L.' Nor, at this time, was Keogh aware of any immediate threats to his company. This sudden stress eroded Calhoun's direction of his company, and he no longer had resources to respond to the threat. Their panicky flight was about to begin, which would soon deluge 'I' and in turn sealed the fate of Yates' battalion. George Custer's last stand started with the confluence of these two events.

The officers and men crowded on Last Stand Hill saw figures emerging amid swirling alkaline dust and thick sulfur-smelling gunsmoke, which hugged the ground in huge billows before it rose skyward. The atmosphere had darkened and took on the appearance of a premature sunset, but it was the sunset of cavalry's defeat and the sunrise of victory for the warriors. The dust-covered men who were now becoming more distinguishable were clearly white men. Upon seeing these fugitives, Custer probably knew there would be no support from Keogh's battalion or little relief for the few men who had managed to reach his position at the top of a small knoll. This flight numbered perhaps only twenty men, who less than a quarter of an hour

before had been three companies of his cavalry. White Bull said some of the soldiers did not flee towards Last Stand Knoll, but instead ran towards the river. This is consistent with the stories the Indians told to Hugh Scott. Some of the bodies later found in Deep Ravine may have come from 'L' and 'I.'[177] It was before six o'clock. The forty some men on Last Stand Hill would be dead in fifteen minutes; it had only been less than two hours since Keogh had advanced so confidently towards Ford 'B.'

One of the benefits derived from the archaeological investigations from the 1980s, resulted in the establishment of the Indians' movements about Custer Battlefield. It has been concluded these movements were along two general courses. One from the south to the north, or from Finley Hill to Calhoun, then to Keogh and Last Stand Hill. The other course took the Indians from positions near Calhoun Hill to the South Skirmish Line linking up with the Indians who chased the troopers from the flats near Route 212 and were now attacking from the north and west. These two general avenues of Indian movement were converging on Last Stand Knoll, and present, the best evidence that this area was the final position occupied by the cavalrymen.[178] With the Cheyennes to the north and east and the Sioux to the south and west, and less than two companies remaining, it wouldn't take long until the white men were overwhelmed. As Yates' Battalion climbed up the slopes of Last Stand Ridge, Moving Robe was right, these soldiers were just about surrounded. Company 'E' was dismounted in the battalion's ascent to provide cover for 'F.' 'E' Company took up position about 200 yards south of the current visitor center in a line now referred to as the South Skirmish Line. These troops were probably deployed to try and halt the Indian pursuit not only from the present cemetery area, but also to try and stop the flow of warriors up Deep Ravine. Custer knew his only short term safety lay in keeping the warriors at carbine distance. Archaeological evidence indicates as soon as Calhoun's position was overrun, the Indians began to move northwest to the Deep Ravine area and from 500 yards away began to fire into these soldiers on the South Skirmish Line. The warriors were joining a battle that had already begun.[179] Custer had reached his last stand toward six o'clock. Company 'F' could not continue further south because of the collapse of Keogh's position, and, any movement east was effectively blocked by the Indians behind

[173]Ibid, 212.

[174]For a detailed discussion of these various re-constructions refer to Michno, *Lakota Noon*, 209–212.

[175]Miller, *Custer's Fall*, 140; Langellier, *Myles Keogh*, 148.

[176]Hammer, *Custer in '76*, 199, 201. Hardorff, *Lakota Recollections*, 148–149.

[177]Wells, "Little Big Horn Notes," 15–16.

[178]Scott, Fox, etal., *Archaeological Insights into The Custer Battle*, 120.

[179]Ibid, 118–119. White Bull, however, who was near Deep Ravine never mentioned any south skirmish line. He did note the soldiers who ran towards this ravine at the end of the battle.

Last Stand Knoll. Consequently, with the collapse of his base at Calhoun Hill, any slim hope that Custer could have held out in a defensive position on last stand hill was doomed. Custer deployed 'F,' as noted, along the hog back ridge. As the retreat had been effectively stopped, 'E' Company was ordered to extend further down the slope, even though there was little cover, to near the head of Deep Ravine. Two Moon remembered "those who were on the hill . . . had gray horses and they were all in the open."[180] Each company would try to support the other in this sort of an upside 'L' formation, but there simply weren't enough men to cover the length and width of the 'L.' The warriors had forced Custer to reluctantly halt on this barren ridge. Without any cover, the lieutenant colonel could only pray for support from Benteen/Reno and hope his longer-range carbines kept the warriors from closing too quickly.

It is possible that for a little while, 'E' kept the Indian attackers, to the north and west, at bay. Very few Indian cartridge cases were uncovered in this area.[181] The increased pressure from the warriors released from the Calhoun fight to the south is demonstrated by seven separate, identifiable Indian firing positions against 'E's skirmish line. Dr. Kuhlman first brought to the battle students' attention the South Skirmish Line. He concluded after careful study that these troopers fought along this area at fairly regular intervals.[182] However, over the years this South Skirmish Line has been called into question. Second Lieutenant Richard Thompson, 6th Infantry, said there were only 9 or 10 men down the slope from Custer towards the gully. This number of men couldn't have been much of a skirmish line.[183] However, other students thought there wasn't any skirmish line in this area because of a lack of bodies and the accounts of the various participants, and also because the markers which were erected there didn't accurately reflect the condition of the field. They concluded Company 'E' "as a whole was never involved in the alleged maneuver at this location."[184] However, the archaeological evidence tends to support Kuhlman's theory of this skirmish line, and clearly it was

"a zone of combat."[185] But, the pattern of artifacts isn't able to finally settle the debate about a line in regular skirmish order, and the archeologists suggested a better term might be "South Defensive Area."[186] It has been said of Dr. Kuhlman "that he is right one hundred times for every time he is wrong."[187]

That a heavy fight took place is documented from the discovery of expended Springfield cases all along the area. In addition, bullets fired from the troopers' carbines were found embedded in the ground in front of corresponding Indian positions near where a number of Indian shell cases were uncovered.[188] Most of these Indian cases were found on the south and east side of 'E's line. There were fewer found to the north and west which suggests that the Indians attacking from this quarter were not as well armed" as the ones on the other side."[189] However, Powell's Indian informants recalled, "The Indian fire was heavy from both sides."[190] Wooden Leg remembered a band of soldiers rode down and dismounted near the head of Deep Ravine. The Indians reacted as expected and pulled back.[191] Both sides then exchanged long range fire; it was inevitable something had to give, and under the leadership, of Lame White Man and the determination of the "Suicide Boys," it was the destruction of Company 'E.'

John Stands in Timber told the story of the "suicide boys" who the evening before pledged "to throw away their lives to never return from the next battle."[192] The five Cheyennes who made this covenant were all under twenty years of age, and some of them had lost relatives a week before at the Rosebud Battle. Lame White Man knew every one of these young warriors. This Cheyenne leader, at the time of the Custer fight, was thirty-seven years old and exercised a great deal of influence with his people. He was also the head soldier of his tribe's Elk Society, and was known among the Sioux by the name of Bearded Man, from the presence of facial hair.[193] His maternal grandson was John Stands in Timber. The soldiers' appearance the afternoon of June 25th was a surprise to the vil-

---

[180]Dixon, *The Vanishing Race*, 181.

[181]A number of students claim the reason why so few shell cases were found here was because of the disturbance, over the years, around the cemetery and visitors center.

[182]Kuhlman, *Legend Into History*, 186–188. A few students believe Dr. Kuhlman, in some instances, used faulty methodology to manipulate his conclusions. They cite his theory of the 'south skirmish line' as an example.

[183]Hammer, *Custer in '76*, 248. At the time, Thompson was on the Far West so his knowledge was only second hand.

[184]Hardorff, *Markers, Artifacts and Indian Testimony*, 58.

[185]There are other re-constructions, support by some Indian testimony, which claim this 'zone of combat' was the result of the twenty-eight runaways at the end of the battle who were trying to seek safety.

[186]Scott, Fox, etal, *Archaeological Perspectives on the Battle of the Little Bighorn*, 123–124.

[187]Letter, Dr. Edgar Stewart to Frank Mercatante, January 29, 1962. Steve Moses Collection.

[188]Scott and Fox, *Archaeological Insights into The Custer Battle*, 124.

[189]Ibid.   [190]Powell, *Sweet Medicine*, 116.

[191]Marquis, *A Warrior Who Fought Custer*, 230–232.

[192]Powell, *Sweet Medicine*, 112.

[193]Hardorff, *Lakota Recollections*, 139–140.

lagers as well as Lame White Man. He had just entered a sweat lodge when he heard the cry the soldiers were attacking the camp. Lame White Man went back to his lodge but he didn't have time to put on his war clothing. But instead, he wrapped a blanket about his body, grabbed his weapons and jumped on to his pony and raced north to join the other Cheyenne fighters who trailed along after the white men. He told his wife, Twin Woman, "I must go across. I must follow my boys."[194] It was the last words she would ever hear her husband speak.

The Indians shooting at these soldiers were told by the 'criers' to watch out for the "suicide boys." When they began to attack the white men and the soldiers started to fight the boys, everyone was to jump up and go in close. The warriors were told not to give the troopers time to reload, but fight them hand to hand.[195] The "suicide boys" were among the last warriors to enter the fight, and they attacked up the level area from the national cemetery and charged right into the Gray Horse Company. The Indians were beginning to swarm all around the soldiers. Lame White Man called out: "Come. We can kill all of them."[196] Standing Bear remembered, "There were about four or five Indians to every white man here."[197] Some of the Indians turned their attention to the horse holders and stampeded the animals. By this time, most of the horses that hadn't been shot, broke loose from the 'set of fours' and were captured. In the confusion, a few troopers tried to mount and ride towards last stand hill. But the warriors cut them off about a quarter of a mile from the hill and killed them all.[198] One trooper might have managed to escape this assult. He Dog and Flying Hwak remembered one soldier, after he had made it back up to Custer hill, kept on riding. He got away "around the big body of Indians toward the north. . . . He was beating his horse with the revolver and was yelling away. He fired backward now and then." The soldier was getting away, then he was seen to fall. He Dog thought "the revolver went off accidentally in the beating of the horse."[199] There is speculation this individual was Second Lieutenant Jack Sturgis, second in command of 'E.' In addition, as an argument that all of 'E' weren't killed on the South Skirmish Line, Black Elk, following the battle, said he saw dead gray horses on the top of Custer hill.[200] There was hand to hand fighting everywhere. The cavalrymen took heavy casualties, but

so did the Indians; every one of the "suicide boys" was dead or dying. They had begun the hand-to-hand combat, and true to their vows, had paid the price. In the end, "it was a mess. They could not tell which was this man or that man, they were so mixed up."[201]

The warriors had their tomahawks and war clubs, but the soldiers only had their single shot Springfields. Once they had fired their carbines, there was no time to reload, and the soldiers drew their Colts. Stinking Bear saw one of his fellow Sioux charge a soldier who resorted to defend himself by taking his carbine by the barrel, turning it into a club. This unknown trooper swung the carbine so hard that he knocked over not only his assailant but himself as well in the process.[202] There was dust and gun smoke everywhere. It was so thick and pervasive that Yellow Nose, a Cheyenne, said he couldn't see what was happening. In fact, the Indians told John Stands in Timber that it was because no one could see what was happening, they modified their coup counting order. No warrior could claim 'first coup,' in this fight, only 'second' and 'third' coup was allowed.[203] It's no wonder the Indians suspended their normal coup counting, as everyone was going 'crazy' at this time.[204] Standing Bear said it was so insane that Indians were being killed by their own people, so "I began to retreat."[205] Horned Horse, an Ogallala, was more specific about the friendly fire and intertwined his fingers and said, "Just like this, Indians and white men."[206] He said, because of the smoke and dust, no one could tell friend from foe. "It is an absolute fact that the young bucks in their excitement and fury, killed each other, several dead Indians being found killed by arrows." Incredibly, Runs The Enemy, a Two Kettle, said he saw one Indian who had been killed "with a war axe."[207] It was told after the "suicide boys" struck 'E,' the rest of the fight didn't take long. In less than thirty minutes, the Custer fight was all over. Wolf Tooth said if it hadn't been for these brave young men, the Custer fight might have ended like Renos,' with the soldiers holding the higher ground, keeping the Indians at bay, and each side seemly content with long distance sniping. "The Custer fight was different because those boys went in that way, and it was their rule to be killed."[208] Respects Noth-

[194]Ibid, 115–116.　　　[195]Liberty, *Cheyenne Memories*, 201.
[196]Marquis, *A Warrior Who Fought Custer*, 231.
[197]DeMallie, *The Sixth Grandfather*, 188.
[198]Powell, *Sweet Medicine*, 117.
[199]Hardorff, *Lakota Recollections*, 52, 75–76.
[200]Neihardt, *Black Elk Speaks*, 126.

[201]Liberty, *Cheyenne Memories*, 201.　　[202]Ibid, 202.
[203]Ibid.　　　　　　　　[204]DeMallie, *The Sixth Grandfather*, 186.
[205]Ibid, 188.　　　　　　[206]Graham, *The Custer Myth*, 63.
[207]Dixon, *The Vanishing Race*, 177.
[208]John Stands in Timber, "Last Ghastly Moments At The Little Bighorn," *American Heritage*, Vol. 17, #3, April 1966, 72. Some students think too much emphasis has been placed on the story of the action at Ford D and the 'suicide boys' as it comes *(continued)*

ing said one Indian continued on from the attack on the gray horses and dashed through the soldiers at Custer Hill on horseback. He said he thought this Indian was killed, but he wasn't sure.[209] This Indian was probably Lame White Man, as he was killed just south of Last Stand Knoll. Little Wolf, a Cheyenne, said Lame White Man charged the soldiers and chased them back up the ridge "where he was killed."[210] When the bullet struck him, he fell headlong from his horse.[211] It has been assumed by many students that nearby lay the body of a mortally wounded Cheyenne, Noisy Walking.[212] His body was said to be found due west of Lame White Mans' about half way between Last Stand Knoll and Deep Ravine. However, Howling Woman, Noisy Walking's aunt, said his body was found at the bottom of Deep Ravine, near the river. His aunt was the one who placed Noisy Walking's body on a pony travois and brought him back to the village where he died that night.[213]

After the fighting was over, Tall Bull, Lame White Man's brother in law, approached Twin Woman, who had been sheltering her children, and informed her that her husband was dead. The leader of the Elk Society had followed his young warriors to the death. Together they made a travois and crossed the river to place his corpse upon it. When his naked body was found, partially hidden by some brush, it was covered with dust, and he had been shot through the right breast with the bullet coming out the back.[214] Little Crow, an Uncpapa, had mistaken him for one of Custer's scouts and removed his scalp.[215] In addition, there were also numerous stab wounds on Lame White Man' body.[216] His remains were brought back into the camp and dressed in his finest buckskins and taken north "to the sand rocks."[217] About 1916, the site of his death was marked by a small pile of stones as was the Cheyenne tradition. In 1956, John Stands in Timber had the National Park Service place a small wooden interpretative sign at this pile of stones.[218] This simple trib-

ute has since been replaced by a formal red stone marker, just off the west side of the battlefield road, a short distance south from the monument.

Kate Bighead implied, there was a different sequence to the fighting on Custer Battlefield. She maintained there was still fighting going on in other parts of the field, besides Last Stand Hill, after the South Skirmish Line had been overrun. She claimed that she traveled toward Calhoun Hill in time to see the fighting there; this was after 'E' had collapsed. Kate Bighead remembered the action then shifted to Keogh's quarter.[219] After Keogh was destroyed, the only group of white men which remained was on Last Stand Knoll. This contradicts the battle sequence I have presented. Without a doubt, the Indian accounts present the researcher with a broad spectrum of viewpoints, which permits and encourages different interpretations by students, while still generating controversy. I have tried to determine the truth of these Indian accounts by checking them against the physical evidence available. In doing so, this evidence can be checked by both the military and other Indian accounts. It has been said that the labyrinth of contradiction and incertitude presented in these Indian accounts reduces their value. I believe, however, it also strengthens them. These different accounts, which seem to contravene each other, are a better indication of the underlying truth of the interviewees, than if all their accounts were in total agreement. "No two people see the same incident in the same way and it would be only natural to see this magnified where thousands of participants are involved in a battle comprising several rather than just one field of action."[220]

There are a number of re-constructions of the battle which state the soldiers were not able to maintain a sufficient volume of fire to keep the warriors at a distance. This was due in part because of all the shooting done by the troopers. Their carbines began to overheat, and the shell extractors began to cut through the rims of the soft copper cases. This would make it impossible to reload the weapon until the shell could be removed by the use of a knife to pry out the case or a ram rod inserted down the barrel to push out the case. Either method would not be conducive to keeping ones' scalp when a reliance was placed on the carbine as the principal weapon. Another reason, besides overheating, was also presented as a cause of the

from basically one source, that of John Stands in Timber. I would reply, it should also be remembered this same source is the only Indian account that told about the firing on Blummer-(Nye) Cartwright Ridge.

[209]Hardorff, *Lakota Recollections*, 33.

[210]*Camp, IU*, box 7, folder 5.

[211]Billings *Gazette* (Billings, MT), May 26, 1927.

[212]Liberty, *Cheyenne Memories*, 203. Today, this spot is marked with a red stone marker.

[213]Hardorff, *Hokahey!*, 77–78.   [214]Ibid, 68.

[215]Hardorff, *Lakota Recollections*, 140; Liberty, *Cheyenne Memories*, 203.

[216]Marquis, *A Warrior Who Fought Custer*, 261.

[217]Powell, *Sweet Medicine*, 119.

[218]Hardorff, *Cheyenne Memories*, 167.

[219]Marquis, *Custer On The Little Big Horn*, 39–40. Also see Bruce A. Trinque, "The Cartridge Case Evidence on the Custer Field: An Analysis and Re-interpretation," *5th Annual Symposium Custer Battlefield Historical & Museum Assn.*, 1991, 69–83.

[220]Clifford L. Nelson, *The Custer Battalion At The Little Big Horn*, History Honors Thesis, Concordia College, 1969, 44.

Courtesy of Hastings House Publishers

extractor failure. The copper cases were generally carried in a leather belt. As such, there can occur a chemical reaction between the leather and copper, called verdigris, which would prevent a flawless ejection.[221] Both Gall and Rain in the Face related how the soldiers got shells stuck in their guns and then just discarded them.[222] This might account for some Indian stories which mentioned the soldiers appeared "panic stricken."[223] That carbines were found after the battle with crammed shell cases, was verified by the soldiers in Gibbon's command. Although the Indians did a very systematic job of cleaning up the battlefield of anything useful, "a number of carbines were found. Many had defective shell extractors, and some were loaded but not fired." Captain C. E. Dutton, in his report to the Chief of Ordnance, questioned the officers of the whole 1876 campaign, and he wrote all of them had observed at least one example of extractor failure; some officers reported six or seven failures.[224] Godfrey later wrote when he was asked what caused Custer's defeat, he listed as his third reason: "The defective extraction of the empty cartridge shells from the carbines."[225] But, regardless of the extraction failures and the effect, if any, they had on the battle, there was more than enough ammunition to keep the carbines that could, firing. There were a number of full cartridge belts captured by the warriors, and the Indians didn't find any belts that were completely empty.[226] But, like all other aspects of the Custer Battle, this also is in dispute.

Lone Bear, an Ogallala, reported, "The ammunition found on the men at 'Last Stand Hill' was not plenty."[227]

There is no doubt that some of the carbines failed to function properly; this is confirmed by the historical evidence from both sides. But, what exactly was the extent of the problem, and was it really one of the major reasons for Custer's defeat as Godfrey and others believed? Recent archaeological evidence also confirmed the failure to eject the shell cases, but in agreement with a 1973 study, Drs. Scott and Fox concluded there was only "an average of 5% as an overall failure rate." This was determined by examining the recovered cases from both the Reno engagement and the Custer Battlefield.[228] This 5% figure was projected

[221]Mills, *My Story,* 334.

[222]Brady, *Indian Fights and Fighters*, 285; Army and Navy Journal (Washington, DC), July 3, 1876; Marquis, *A Warrior Who Fought Custer,* 266.

[223]Thomas B. Marquis, *She Watched Custer's Last Battle* (Hardin, MT: NP, 1933), 5.

[224]Scott, Fox, etal., *Archaeological Perspectives On The Battle Of The Little Bighorn,* 113.   [225]Graham, *The Custer Myth,* 146.

[226]Marquis, *A Warrior Who Fought Custer,* 264, Army and Navy Journal (Washington, DC), July 3, 1886.

[227]Hardorff, *Lakota Recollections,* 162.

[228]Paul Hedren, "Carbine Extractor Failure at the Little Big Horn: A New Examination, *Military Collector and Historian*, Vol. 25, #2, 1973, 66–68. Scott, Fox, etal, *Archaeological Perspectives On The Battle of The Little Bighorn,* 114.

to involve ten carbines with the right wing and twenty with the left wing. The archeologists, after their analysis, decided after allowing for some biases, "the number of guns involved is not statistically significant," and "it was not significant to the outcome of the battle."[229] Interestingly, one of the reasons why in 1872 the Springfield system was selected as the primary weapon for the Army, was the low failure rate for cartridge case extraction.[230] Based on this study, there is little doubt the ejection failure as one of the overall outcome determents of the Battle of the Little Big Horn ranks as a non event. But, to those ten soldiers who faced overwhelming odds, whose carbines failed, it was an event of monumental proportions and may very well have contributed to their deaths.

At the same time 'E' was being assaulted, White Bull and possibly Crazy Horse continued north along the ridge and confronted the last of Custer's men who were making the final stand on Last Stand Knoll.[231] These soldiers on last stand hill were the remnants of four companies who didn't total thirty soldiers; added to this was the largely intact Company 'F.' Godfrey, however, said he counted forty-two bodies and thirty-nine horses on Last Stand Hill.[232] Moving Robe was never more prophetic: "Long Hair's Troopers were trapped in an enclosure. There were Indians everywhere. It was not a massacre, but a hotly contested battle between two armed forces."[233] It was a little after six o'clock, and there is little question at this stage of the battle that disorganization was a major problem. The troopers could sense the Indians were moving in closer and closer. The dust and smoke made it appear as late in the evening.[234] The Indians were shooting their arrows in a long arc from about 200 yards away, causing them to fall indiscriminately among the near-panicked soldiers. The soldiers probably killed the remaining horses that were still standing, to form a makeshift breastworks, but it would only give them a few more minutes of life. DeRudio remembered that many of these horses were 'sorrels' from 'C.'[235] If so, and DeRudio was quite positive about this, they could have been from a couple of 'sets of fours' who had retreated to this position.

There is a theory the last stand area at the top of the hill was in reality a hospital area for the wounded, and the barricade of horses found in a semi circle, was an attempt to protect these wounded. It has been suggested this is the best reason to explain why most of the officers from the right wing were found there, surrounded by less than a company of enlisted men. One author explained it would have been only natural for the wounded officers and men to be taken to headquarters on Custer Hill for treatment by Dr. Lord.[236] In support of this theory, it was pointed out that the body of Dr. George Lord, assistant surgeon, was found about twenty feet southeast of Custer's remains.[237] However, one student discounted that this was any type of hospital area. He suggested, instead, that Custer had positioned seven of his best marksmen at the top of the knoll and concluded they "must have taken their toll on any warrior who exposed himself too much."[238] Another suggested this circle of horses was intended not only for the wounded, but for the other non-combatants as well, "to afford them maximum protection."[239] Command and control had vanished, and company integrity no longer existed. The troopers on the hill, who were still able to move, abandoned their wounded and dying comrades and fled towards the river. Hare later confided to Camp, he thought Custer's men had been struck in a panic, and they didn't fight very well.[240] There were perhaps twenty-eight of these men. They were trying to reach any place where they perceived safety lay. They headed towards Deep Ravine. Two Moon said maybe forty men broke away and started for the river.[241] "They did not get far, because many Indians were all around them." White Bull and a group of Cheyennes saw the men running towards them. These Indians shot a number of them, and the rest were forced into this ravine where the soldiers were all killed.[242] Big Beaver, a Cheyenne, agreed with White Bull. He said these soldiers, about 15 or 20, started for the river and down the ravine, and mounted Indians killed them. Black Elk was even more graphic. He said they saw soldiers starting to run down hill towards us. All or most of them were on foot, and he thought they were so scared that they didn't know what they were doing. This Ogallala said the warriors yelled, "Hoka hey," and charged towards the white men. Black Elk personally met a soldier on horse back and sent an arrow through him:

> He screamed and took hold of his saddle horn . . . with his head hanging down, I took my heavy bow and struck

[229]Ibid, 114–115. [230]Ibid, 115.

[231]Thomas B. Marquis, *The Cheyennes Of Montana* (Algonac, MI: Reference Publications, 1978), 51–52.

[232]Graham, *The Custer Myth*, 377.

[233]Hardorff, *Lakota Recollections*, 95.

[234]Graham, *The Custer Myth*, 93.

[235]Hammer, *Custer in '76*, 87.

[236]Gray, *Custer's Last Campaign*, 292.

[237]Gray, *Centennial Campaign*, 392–393. Hardorff, *Custer Battle Casualties*, 105. [238]Schoenberger, *End of Custer*, 205.

[239]Sklenar, *To Hell With Honor*, 324.

[240]*Camp, IU*, box 2, folder 11.

[241]Graham, *The Custer Myth*, 103.

[242]Marquis, *A Warrior Who Fought Custer*, 237–238.

him across the back of the neck. He fell from his saddle, I got off and beat him to death with my bow. I kept on beating him after he was dead. I was mad, because I was thinking of the women and children running down there, all scared and out of breath.[243]

Upon his inspection of the battlefield, Lt. Bourke said he thought a frightened party of about 30 men ran and tried to gain the bank of the river. They were killed like wolves.[244] Red Horse, a Minneconjou, remembered, "We finished up this party right there in the ravine."[245] Sergeant Knipe said most of these troopers must have reached the ravine as he counted 28 bodies lying in it about 2000 yards from the monument.[246] But, Private Coleman said he helped bury thirty men of 'E' Company, and they weren't in a ravine but "in a line not ten feet apart."[247] It was believed Mitch Bouyer had led these soldiers in their attempted breakout, as his body was found among the cavalrymen.[248] That it was Bouyer, was positively confirmed during the archaeological survey when grave markers 33 and 34 were excavated. This brave, faithful, and talented scout survived longer than most of the other men of Custer's command whom he guided into battle.

Two Moons said the Indians were shooting quick, and they were circling all around, the warriors would shoot and shoot again, the "soldiers drop."[249] The warriors knew the end was near for these white men; Gall said, "finally . . . we charged through them with our ponies. When we had done this, right here on this ground and just a few rods south of us, the fight was over."[250] Tall Bull related much the same story of how he raced the other warriors to the top of the hill: "They (the soldiers) were quickly killed."[251] Wooden Leg said the Indians didn't charge the hill until the soldiers had stopped shooting; too many warriors had already been killed. It was only then that the Indians jumped up and rushed forward. This is consistent with the stories told by most of the Cheyenne and Sioux warriors. They always insisted, the soldiers were not killed by riding over them, as depicted in most movies. The warriors killed the whites by shooting at them from behind every hill or bush that offered cover.[252] It was only when the return fire slackened from the few stragglers

remaining, did the Indians charge and clear the knoll. The scene upon Last Stand Knoll "looked like thousands of dogs might look if all of them were mixed together in a fight."[253] Even at this last stage, there were a few soldiers who were still capable of mounting a defense. Tall Bull said he raced his horse up the knoll's slope to beat the others to the top. His horse was hit by seven bullets and fell dead. He reported as the Indians gained the top, a sergeant and six others jumped up and ran back along both sides of the ridge. Tall Bull remembered these last white men didn't last long.[254]

Many of the warriors claimed these soldiers were braver than the ones they had fought in the valley. Sitting Bull stated, "I tell no lies about dead men. Those men who came with the 'long hair' were as good men who ever fought."[255] Crow King agreed with his fellow Uncpapa and expressed his admiration for Custer's bravery.[256] Brave Wolf said he had been in many hard fights throughout his life, but Custer's soldiers were the bravest he had fought.[257] Red Horse mentioned one man who he had seen several times during the battle and declared him the bravest man the Indians had ever fought.[258] Low Dog also commented on these white men and the brave manner in which they held their ground.[259] "Many Indian eyewitness are in agreement as to the unflinching valor of Custer's men."[260]

Custer's body was found on the top of Last Stand Knoll a little to the southeast of the hill, surrounded by ten men behind a make shift breastworks of six dead 'sorrel' horses, laid nose to tail about 30 feet in diameter.[261] Custer had several wounds. One bullet entered near his left temple, about halfway between the eyes and ears, and traveled through his head; a second bullet struck his left breast. A recently uncovered story, supposedly told by Dr Porter, reported, when he examined Custer, the chest wound wasn't, as has been commonly thought, near the center. It was higher up on the left shoulder and would not be necessarily fatal.[262] His body was stripped except for one sock, and according to most eyewitnesses, Custer wasn't muti-

---

[243]Neihardt, *Black Elk Speaks*, 127.

[244]Gray, *Custer's Last Campaign*, 397.

[245]Graham, *The Custer Myth*, 60.

[246]Hammer, *Custer in '76*, 95.

[247]Liddic, *I Buried Custer*, 21–22.

[248]Hammer, *Custer in '76*, 95.

[249]Graham, *The Custer Myth*, 101.

[250]Barry, *Indian Notes . . .* , 27.

[251]Powell, *People of the Sacred Mountain*, 1028.

[252]Grinnell, *The Fighting Cheyennes*, 339.

[253]Marquis, *A Warrior Who Fought Custer*, 237.

[254]Powell, *People of the Sacred Mountain*, 1028.

[255]Graham, *The Custer Myth*, 71.   [256]Ibid, 78.

[257]Grinnell, *The Fighting Cheyennes*, 340.

[258]There has been much speculation over who was this man, see Stewart, *Custer's Luck*, 460–461 for a discussion over his identity.

[259]Graham, *The Custer Myth*, 75.

[260]Veatal, *Warpath*, 247. There is no doubt a number of Indians did comment on the bravery of Custer's soldiers to their white interviewers, for obvious reasons. However, other warriors made it clear Custer's men panicked as much as did Reno's.

[261]Hardorff, *Custer Battle Casualties*. 98, 103.

[262]W. Don Horn, "Fifty Years On Custer's Trail," *Greasy Grass*, Vol. 18, May 2002, 48.

lated. Dr. Porter said Custer was "stark naked and clean as a baby."[263] But, Sergeant Windolph, who was with Captain Benteen when he identified Custer, said he was fully clothed in his buckskin suit, the same one he wore the morning of the battle, and he was not scalped.[264] Private O'Neil gave even more details and said when he saw the body, Custer's head was positioned higher than his feet, and his face was calm without any distortion. The bullet that struck his chest entered a little behind and below the left breast. The bullet traveled between the back and the breastbone and exited on the right side near the lower ribs. O'Neil theorized, this wound was made by an Indian on horseback, while Custer was on foot. Custer's head wound, he thought, was made by an Indian on foot at the same level as the commander.[265] The Arapaho, Waterman, seemed to confirm some of O'Neil's speculations:

> When I reached the top of the hill I saw Custer. He was dressed in buckskin coat and pants, and he was on his hands and knees. He had been shot through the side and there was blood coming from his mouth. . . . Four soldiers were sitting up around him, but they were all badly wounded. . . . Then the Indians closed in around him, and I did not see anymore.[266]

Tom Custer's corpse, according to Fred Girard, was found on the highest point of the knoll about 15 feet from his brother. Dr. Porter said that this officer was very badly mutilated, perhaps the worse example on the field. The doctor recorded he was disemboweled, and his head had been crushed in by a blow from a war club. Godfrey agreed with the doctor that his head had been horribly smashed in, his whole scalp was missing, and his body was shot through with dozens of arrows. Godfrey said identification of the body would have been impossible if they had not discovered the initials 'T.W.C.' tattooed on his arm.[267] Private Slaper said Tom Custer's body was the most dismembered of any he had seen. This condition of Custer's body has been the standard interpretation of the captain's remains. However, there are others who claim this body was in no worse condition than the other soldiers. O'Neil said he recognized Tom Custer by looking at his face. Captain McDougall said Tom was easily identified; he had no problem when he saw the remains. He noticed a scar on his left cheek due to an old wound, and he had a split forefinger on the left hand.[268] One must wonder if these individuals had viewed the same body.

Among those who were identified, grouped near Custer, around the top of the knoll were: Adjutant Cooke, Private Edward Driscoll, Company 'I,' Private John Parker, Company 'I,' 'E' company's commander, First Lieutenant Smith, Sergeant John Vickory, Company 'F,' Trumpeter Henry Voss, Headquarters Staff, and Private Charles McCarthy, Company 'L.' There were a number of soldiers who had been on this knoll but were able to flee the position before it was completely overrun. Sergeant Robert Hughes, who carried Custer's personal flag, was found in Deep Ravine and identified by Captain McDougall.[269] Private Tim Donnelly, Company 'F,' was also found in Deep Ravine.[270] In addition, two other 'F' troopers were found in this area. One, Private William Brown, might have possibly reached the Little Big Horn River at the mouth of Deep Coulee as his body was found about 250 yards across the river. The other, Corporal John Briody's remains, were found on a rise above Deep Ravine. His right leg had been cut off and placed under his head.[271] Sergeant Major William Sharrow's body was discovered furthest north on the battlefield.[272] He was found opposite the present parking lot on the east side of the service entrance road. The youngest Custer, Boston, was found on the lower west side down the slope from the monument, about 100 yards from George and Tom. He had been shot several times and his body was "mutilated some."[273] Their young nephew, Autie Reed, lay nearby. Dr. Lord's body was identified about twenty feet southeast of Custer's on a side hill.[274] Most accounts claim Lieutenants Porter of 'I,' and Sturgis serving with 'E,' were not found or at least recognized on the battlefield.[275]

How long did the action on Custer field last? This is another point that has been debated almost as soon as the dust and gun smoke had settled. This reconstruction portrays the Custer fight lasting about two hours, from the time Custer descended into Medicine Tail Coulee until the last few troopers were overrun on Last Stand Knoll, after 6:15 PM. The action on Custer field itself, from Finley Hill to Last Stand Knoll, in my opinion, was a little over an hour's duration. The Indians originally said the battle was fairly even until the very end. They estimated it was about two hours before the last soldiers were

---

[263]Hardorff, *Custer Battle Casualties, II*, 27.   [264]Ibid, 24–25.

[265]Ibid, 26.   [266]Ibid, 19.

[267]Hardorff, *Custer Battle Casualties*, 99.

[268]Hardorff, *Custer Battle Casualties, II*, 99; Hardorff, *Custer Battle Casualties*, 31.

[269]Hammer, *Custer in '76*, 72.   [270]Ibid, 139.

[271]*Camp, BYU*, roll 1, box 1, folder 8.

[272]*Camp, IU*, box 2, folder 10.

[273]Lawrence A. Frost, *General Custer's Libbie* (Seattle WA: Superior Publishing Company, 1976), 246.

[274]Hammer, *Custer in '76*, 248. Others accounts say he was not identified, see Hardorff, *Custer Battle Casualties*, 104–105.

[275]Ibid, 105.

killed.[276] Other Indians said the action didn't last anywhere near that long. Gall said the fight was over in about thirty minutes, maybe a little longer.[277] A Cheyenne agreed with Gall and said the fight lasted about as long as it would take the sun to travel the width of a lodge pole or about twenty minutes. Although there are others who claim the shorter time span referred to the struggle just for Custer Hill.[278] However, Flying Hawk's statement indicated the fight lasted well over an hour. This is the time it took him to drive the horses he captured into the village and return to the fighting.[279] But, whatever time frames the Indians used, it was only a rough estimate, "as they neither had clocks nor watches and their only method of measuring time being purely by the position of the sun."[280]

The testimony at the Reno Court of Inquiry indicates the officers tended to use the shorter time estimates. It would be to their advantage to believe and so state that the Custer fight was over quickly to demonstrate there would have been no way they could have responded even if they had known. Hare said the fight was over in forty-five minutes; Wallace said Custer was heavily engaged by the time Reno reached the bluffs or a little after 4 o'clock, in this he was seconded by Varnum. Edgerly, who would have been in one of the best positions to know, said it

was all over in twenty minutes or a half hour at most; Benteen said Custer was probably finished in a half hour, but on a guess, an hour at the very most. However, the scouts said the fight lasted much longer. Girard stated the action lasted until about dark; Herendeen said it was more than an hour. That the shooting continued until about dark, as reported by Girard, could have been the sporadic shooting the Indians conducted while looting the battlefield. Private O'Neil sided with the scouts and recorded the battle lasted better than an hour.

Thus Custer and all the men who followed him across Medicine Tail Coulee passed through that one way portal separating life from death from which no one has returned. But it has been said a person doesn't really die as long as they are remembered by the living. If this is true, then Custer and these troopers are as much alive today, although not in flesh and blood, as they were when they so confidently rode into battle. In my reconstruction of the Custer Fight, I have questioned many of the acts of commission and omission of Custer's subordinate officers, especially Reno and Benteen. This is not meant to gloss over the decisions and actions of Lieutenant Colonel George A. Custer. As commanding officer, he was predominantly responsible for the situation he found himself in late on the afternoon of June 25th. This accountability extends to not only his own violent death, but also to the total destruction of the five companies of his beloved regiment.[281]

[276]Nelson A. Miles, *Personal Recollections and Observations of General Nelson A. Miles* (NY, NY: DaCapo Press, 1969), 286–289.

[277]Barry, *Indian Notes . . .* , 21.

[278]Linderman, *American*, 179; Smith, *Indian Experiences*, 232.

[279]*Camp, IU*, box 2, folder 6.

[280]Smith, *Indian Experiences*, 232.

[281]Luther, *Reno, Benteen and Custer*, 17.

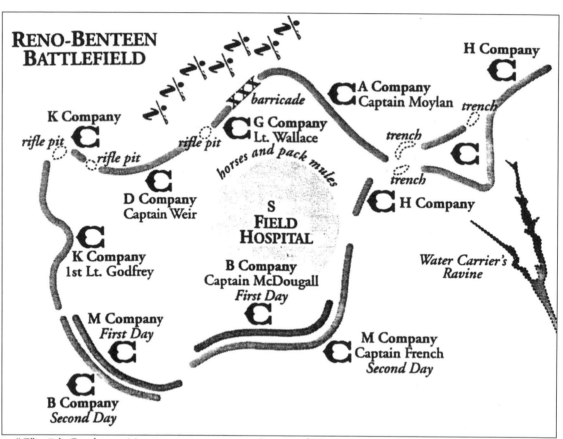

RENO-BENTEEN BATTLEFIELD

H Company

C A Company
Captain Moylan

barricade

K Company

rifle pit

rifle pit

rifle pit

C G Company
Lt. Wallace

trench

trench

trench

D Company
Captain Weir

horses and pack mules

S
FIELD
HOSPITAL

C H Company

K Company
1st Lt. Godfrey

B Company
Captain McDougall
First Day

Water Carrier's Ravine

M Company
First Day

M Company
Captain French
Second Day

B Company
Second Day

"C"—7th Cavalry positions
"i"—Indian positions

Courtesy of John D. Mackintosh from "Custer's Southern Officer"

11
Reno Hill

As men from Godfrey's 'K' rejoined the rest of their comrades on Reno Hill, there was already a rudimentary defensive perimeter being established. But, even more importantly for the survival of the 7th Cavalry was the transformation that Benteen had undergone in just the past few minutes. From a carping, fractious, contemptuous company and battalion commander, he now became the leader these shaken soldiers desperately needed. For the next two days, Benteen was an inspiring officer whose heroic actions inspired many and who more than any other individual held the regiment together in its darkest period. There are many who wonder what led to this change and how was it accomplished? I have already written of possible reasons for Benteen's earlier reluctance to assume any semblance of command authority in the presence of Major Reno. Captain McDougall, an officer with many years of experience, provided some insight into this conversion. He told Camp that he personally went to Benteen as soon as they reached Reno Hill because he (McDougall) was disgusted and afraid that Reno was doing nothing for the command and was "thoroughly incompetent." If the situation persisted it "would be a second Ft. Phil Kearney affair."[1] McDougall told Benteen he had better take charge as the ranking captain "and run the thing." McDougall recalled Benteen just smiled at him and proceeded to do as he suggested. McDougall said for the rest of the battle Benteen kept a watch over Reno, "going frequently over to Reno . . . and when he (Benteen) saw the need for action anywhere about the lines he either suggested it be done or else positively ordered it done."[2] Apparently McDougall wasn't the only captain who was concerned about Major Reno's capabilities. Godfrey reported that evening Captain Weir had approached him with a question. Weir asked if there was a conflict between the judgment of Benteen and Reno, whose orders would he obey? Godfrey didn't hesitate a second and replied, "Benteen's."[3] Thus was the state of command which existed upon Reno Hill the evening of the 25th.

Most students have described Reno's Hill, about one hundred feet above the river, as a saucer with its edges broken off, or a horseshoe with one prong bent inward at right angles to the other prong.[4] This is accurate as far as it goes, but it lacks the in-depth description of its terrain. The area is really two parallel crests running about east and west with a small swale or valley separating the crests. It has also been suggested that a more accurate and complete description would be a sort of a triangle with a tail from its apex.[5] The northern base of this triangle is about 175 yards in width and a length of 350 yards from its base to its apex. A narrow ridge runs in a southeasterly direction, and this ridge is long and narrow upon the crest. The ridge has steep slopes and a fairly flat crest, about thirty feet wide, and projects 500 feet southward from the rest of the position. It is the highest point on the hill and dominated the defensive perimeter.[6]

As Wallace reached the perimeter, Benteen ordered him to place his company in the manner he indicated. Wallace replied he had no company—only three men. Benteen said then place yourself and these three troopers where he had pointed. Major Reno was seen in about the middle of the position.[7] 'H' Company was ordered to the hill's key position, that of the long ridge to the south. Benteen must have realized this was the most exposed position, and that is why he assigned his company to defend it. The troops were arranged about in the order they reached the hill, i.e., the northern point was Company 'K,' to their right was 'D,' to the left 'M,' to 'M's left was 'B' which linked up with 'H.' 'A' was to the east and to their left was 'G,' which in turn linked up with 'K.' All this sounds very neat and orderly, but in the initial stages it was anything but neat and orderly. This was because the Indians were no longer kept at bay by Company 'K' and began to press their advantage. So fast had the Indians closed the gap, that 'K' didn't have time to assume any formal designated place, but just fell in with the other troopers. The officers believed the Indians were about to mount an all-out attack and ordered all available troopers to the perimeter, leaving a few others and the civilian packers and horse holders to watch the pack train. The pack animals and mounts, which remained saddled, were placed in two semi-circles around the wounded in the depression or swale between the two ridges, as it afforded the most cover. Here, Dr. Porter with the help of his attendants and the civilian packers established a field hospital.

The soldiers on Reno Hill were now about to experience the same intensity and enthusiasm for battle that Custer must have discovered among the warriors. The

---

[1]Hammer, *Custer in '76*, 71.   [2]Ibid.
[3]Graham, *The Custer Myth*, 334.
[4]Stewart, *Custer's Luck*, 408.

[5]William G. Rector, "The Reno-Benteen Defense Perimeter," *Montana Magazine of Western History*, Vol. 16, #2, Spring 1966, 70.
[6]Ibid.   [7]Graham, *Reno Court*, 362.

Indians took possession of all the surrounding high points and opened up a heavy volume of fire.[8] It was now about 7 PM. Shortly after the Indians started shooting, Major Reno came over to McDougall and told him, "Captain, be sure to hold that point at all hazards."[9] The situation was critical. There was little cover for the men, as there hadn't been enough time to construct anything sturdy enough to stop a bullet. Private Slaper remembered the officers told the men to get down and lay flat on their stomachs so as not to expose themselves. The troopers obeyed this order to the letter as they found out that "the least sight of any portion of the body was the signal for a volley from the Indians."[10] Slaper managed to use his knife to cut some of the earth loose in front of him to form a little ridge on which to rest his carbine. The Indians had spotted this movement and bullets struck his little mound of dirt in such numbers and force as to blind him "so, he could scarcely see for an hour or more."[11] Godfrey remembered laying on the hill, and after a few minutes wondering if the small sagebrush he was behind "would turn a bullet." Since it was only as thick as his finger, he decided to get up and walk around the line to direct the firing.[12] As he walked the line behind his men, he found himself standing over Sergeant DeWitt Winney, when a bullet went through this non-commissioned officer. The sergeant gave a quick jerk and cried out he was hit. Godfrey's other men implored him to get down or he would be hit as well, and Godfrey reluctantly did so, next to Winney, and discovered he [Winney] was dead. Godfrey recorded it was the first time since 1861 he had seen a man killed in battle.[13]

However, there were several officers who didn't expose themselves at all; they took little part in the battle that evening, and in fact simply disappeared. Moylan spent most of the time among the packs. While Benteen was all around his company's position, his lieutenant, Gibson, spent his time hugging the ground, lying low, and gave little inspiration to the men of his company. Mathey was said to have hid in the hospital area, safely overseeing the animals all that evening, and didn't show up for any of the fight.[14] Other officers, like Godfrey, were right out on the front line with their men sharing their fate. Captain French, likewise, was in the center of his company's line that was taking heavy fire from the warriors on Sharpshooters' Hill. He reportedly gave orders and

directed 'M' as "coolly as though it was a Sunday school picnic.[15] He sat tailor style while bullets sprayed all around him as he extracted jammed shells from any carbine handed to him, then passed them back reloaded.[16]

The Indians on Sharpshooters' Ridge (about 900 yards away from the soldiers' position) directed some of the heaviest fire on the troops. Wooden Leg personally wasn't one of the warriors who went to fight the "first soldiers," even though he had captured a carbine and plenty of ammunition. But, he remembered there were many other young men who joined in the battle.[17] First Sergeant Ryan recalled that by now the firing had become general all along the line. The company on his right had several men killed in just a few minutes of this exchange.[18] Ryan said one of the Indians who occupied this hill was a particularly good shot, as he had killed the fourth man on the sergeant's right. The third man was the next to get hit, then the man next to Ryan took a bullet. Ryan said he figured his turn was next, so along with Captain French, Ryan and six others jumped up and instead of shooting to their front, made a quick turn to the right from where the expert shooting was originating, and together delivered a devastating volley. Ryan believed they put an end to that particular Indian marksman, as no further men were killed from that spot.[19]

The Indians paid special attention to the hundreds of horses and mules that were picketed in and around the hospital swale. Dozens of these animals were shot where they had been positioned. However, Young Two Moon said the Indians did not necessarily target the animals. Moylan, however, thought that the horses were the object of the Indians' fire. If they couldn't shoot the men, they could shoot the animals.[20] Eventually, forty-six horses and mules were killed, but some of these could have been mercy killings by the packers.[21] Mathey began to have the horses unsaddled and the mules unpacked. He then gathered picket ropes in order to create a make shift corral. As soon as a horse or mule was killed, he had the men roll the animal on its back and the picket ropes were attached to their lifeless legs. This freed the horse holders who were then ordered to report to the perimeter.[22] Eventually, a more formal corral was created by threading the combined ropes around the legs of the dead ani-

[8]Graham, *The Custer Myth*, 143.

[9]Graham, *Reno Court*, 472.

[10]Brininstool, *Troopers With Custer*, 55. [11]Ibid.

[12]Graham, *The Custer Myth*, 143.

[13]Stewart, *The Field Diary . . .*, 14.

[14]Carroll, *The Benteen-Goldin Letters*, 206, 210, 243.

[15]Brininstool, *Troopers With Custer*, 55.

[16]Ibid.   [17]Marquis, *A Warrior Who Fought Custer*, 256–257.

[18]Barnard, *Ten Years With Custer*, 298.   [19]Ibid.

[20]Graham, *Reno Court*, 188.

[21]Hardorff, *Cheyenne Memories*, 154.

[22]Hammer, *Custer in '76*, 71.

mals establishing a fence like enclosure. After dark, the surviving animals were repositioned so they would be more protected from the hostile fire from all directions, except from the open area to the east.[23] The packs and boxes taken from the mules were placed around the wounded to provide the best possible protection.

The Indian firepower was increased even further with the addition of over 200 captured carbines along with thousands of rounds of 45/55 ammunition. As more and more warriors joined in the firefight, the bullets descended upon Reno Hill in an ever increasing volume. Further back, the "hills were black with Indians looking on while warriors were as thick as could get within firing range."[24] It would appear there were more Indians than there were places for them to shoot at the white men. Benteen was reported to have seen nothing but "black heads," sticking up all around the perimeter. Ryan said the Indians made several charges upon their line, but each time were thrown back by the gunfire, which all along the line was "very rapid and at close range."[25] Varnum concurred with Ryan and recalled the Indians were anywhere from two to five hundred yards from the soldiers, and they would direct a heavy volume of fire for fifteen to thirty minutes and then charge their line. When the Indians got close, the soldiers "let them have it and drove them back."[26] Windolph said he didn't recall any real charges that were made, but "little groups of Indians would creep up as close as they could get, and behind bushes or little knolls open fire."[27] Godfrey said the firing was "very heavy," and he directed only the best marksmen in 'K' to respond, and the others were to keep these marksmen well supplied with pre-loaded carbines.[28] Wallace said the Indian gunfire was "continuous." Benteen said the troopers had a very warm time of it as long as there was enough light for the Indians to "draw a bead on us."[29] Windolph thought if the Indians "had used their heads," and made a charge against the soldiers all at the same time, they would have swept over the command.[30] Perhaps this could have happened, but the Indians weren't about to waste more lives in an all out assault. With no water on the hill, they could have assumed that sooner or later the white men would have to go to the river, and when they did, they could be killed with little risk.[31]

The ammunition was packed on packsaddles (appareros) and not on the more traditional sawbucks as were the other supplies. During this firefight, one old crusty pack mule by the name of "Barnum" had enough of the noise and broke loose from the corral.[32] He headed straight for the warriors past Captain Moylan's company on the northern end of the line. Sergeant Richard Hanley, Company 'C' and assigned to the pack train, saw this attempted escape and the dangerous potential of delivering an additional 2000 rounds of ammunition into the hands of the Indians. Hanley felt responsible for the mule and thought he'd be blamed if the mule got away, so he took off on horseback after "Barnum." He thought he would be killed as "the shots from the Indians cut the ground all around." Drawing his Colt .45 he intended to shoot the mule down if he couldn't catch him. But, he was able to get the animal turned after he had gotten about half way between the two lines and ran him back to the herd in the swale.[33] Hanley was assisted in this recovery by Private John McGuire of Company 'C,' who was also assigned to the pack train. For this courage in the face of enemy fire, the sergeant was awarded the Medal of Honor. This was not the only mule who had managed to leave the improvised corral area. Benteen reported he personally stopped three ammunition mules who were heading for the Little Big Horn River to get a drink. The senior captain said he personally returned the animals to Mathey and saw he had been paying no attention to the animals. Benteen then tore into this lieutenant and said there was never "an officer of the army who ever got such a 'cussing out' as I gave Mathey . . . before enlisted men, officers, and packs."[34] But some mules, mad with thirst, did escape from Reno Hill and were not recaptured or perhaps even noticed by the soldiers. At least one ammunition mule managed to reach the river, and its cargo was secured by the Indians and later used against the troopers.[35]

Darkness set in around 9 PM, and with it the firing died off, except for an occasional shot or two, and in another hour the fire from the Indian position stopped entirely. Five men had been killed and six wounded, with most of these casualties coming from Reno's already battered battalion.[36] The casualties weren't all one-sided. White Bull

[23]Graham, *The Story of the Little Big Horn*, 67.

[24]Hammer, *Custer in '76*, 71.

[25]Barnard, *Ten Years With Custer*, 298.

[26]Carroll, *I, Varnum*, 71.   [27]Hunt, *I Fought . . .*, 101.

[28]Graham, *The Custer Myth*, 143.

[29]Graham, *Reno Court*, 65, 181.   [30]Hunt, *I Fought . . .*, 101.

[31]Eastman, "The Story Of The Little Big Horn," 358.

[32]Some accounts have this incident occurring when the pack train first arrived on Reno Hill. Hanley, himself, told Camp it was after they returned from their attempt to reach Weir Point. Hammer, *Custer in '76*, 127; *Camp, BYU*, roll 1, box 1, folder 4. Other accounts have this mule stampeding on the 26th. Sklenar, *To Hell With Honor*, 316.   [33]Hammer, *Custer in '76*, 127.

[34]Carroll, *The Benteen-Goldin Letters*, 198–199.

[35]Hardorff, *Cheyenne Memories*, 158; Marquis, *A Warrior Who Fought Custer*, 262–263.   [36]Panzeri, *Custer's Last Stand*, 81.

had been on the northeast side of Reno Hill when his friend Dog's Back Bone was killed.[37] Dog's Back Bone was killed when he yelled a warning to another warrior. He told his tribesman to "Be careful. It's a long way from here, but their bullets are coming fierce." Indeed, the bullets were, as no sooner than the words were spoken than Dog's Back Bone was shot in the head and died instantly.[38] A fifteen year old Sioux warrior named Breech Cloth was killed on the east side of Reno Hill during his attempt to make a "run" against the soldiers' line. His horse threw him, and when he tried to get up, the youth was shot dead.[39] White Bull said they did not try to crush Reno, as they did Custer, on purpose. The Indians thought they could starve him out, and they didn't want to lose any more braves, by "recklessly charging the fortifications."

---

[37]Hardorff, *Lakota Recollections*, 123. Other accounts have this warrior killed on the 26th but the details are the same, Hardorff, *Hokahey!*, 87–88.   [38]Ibid, 91.   [39]Ibid, 86.

In addition, the Cheyenne claimed they were not sure of their odds, as they didn't exactly know how many men were with Reno. Therefore, they were very cautious.[40] When Sitting Bull arrived on the bluffs above the soldiers, he saw the warriors were assembled to the south and northeast. He and the chiefs then ordered the young men to leave a lane open on the east side, in case the soldiers wished to leave the country![41]

The accurate gunfire from the Indian positions was something of a surprise to the soldiers. They didn't think the Indians could shoot that accurately. So the men assumed they must be fighting white renegades, squaw men, and half breeds. Reno surely thought so and said so in his report.[42] Years after the battle, an ex-confederate who lived with the Sioux, Frank Huston, said there were white men in the village. Many thought it was Huston himself who was in the village and took up arms again against the Yankees.[43] Private Martin told Camp he saw the dead body of a white man in the village; Knipe said it was in a teepee.[44] Sergeant M. H. Wilson, 7th Infantry, who was with Gibbon's command, told Camp, he personally found the body of a white man dressed in Indian clothing and buried in a tree. This occurred on June 27th near the present day Crow Agency. This man had a long beard and had been shot in five or six places, and it was evident he had fought with the warriors on Reno hill.

---

[40]Hardorff, *Cheyenne Memories*, 80–81.
[41]Vestal, *Sitting Bull*, 173.   [42]Carroll, *The Federal View*, 103.
[43]Graham, *The Custer Myth*, 79–80.
[44]Hammer, *Custer in '76*, 105.

Courtesy of Hastings House Publishers

Wilson said the cavalrymen told him of seeing a white man fighting against them while they were on the hill.[45] Captain Poland wrote "that Sitting Bull has as aides and special advisors, five renegade white men."[46] The captain stated one was a Spaniard, another a discharged soldier from 22nd Infantry. Private James Pym, Company 'B' and a Medal of Honor recipient, knew there were a number of white men helping the Indians. Pym said he saw these renegade whites bearing Custer's guidons as they circled Reno Hill. These men also swore a blue streak at the troopers, "calling the men vile names (in perfect English) and daring them to leave their works."[47]

He Dog eventually acknowledged there was a white man in the village with the Ogallalas, but that he was only a Canadian half breed. He wasn't aware of any others.[48] In spite of He Dog's recollections, there was at least one other half breed in the Indian village, and he was in the Uncpapa circle. His name was John Brughier, a half breed Santee Sioux. He was a fugitive from Standing Rock Agency as a result of an outstanding arrest warrant for a murder which took place in December 1875, and had fled to his relatives in Sitting Bull's camp.[49] His wife always insisted that although he was in the Uncpapa circle during the battle, he never fought against his father's people.[50] There is little doubt there were others besides full blooded Indians in the village by the Little Big Horn. But, at this late date, it's impossible to determine how many and to what extent, if any, they assisted the warriors in their fight with the soldiers, and if this assistance was in any way material.

After the Indian gunfire had died away, an on-and-off rain shower that evening only added to the soldiers' woes. Some of the troopers went back to the pack train to retrieve their overcoats from "the cantles of our McClellan saddles" for a little protection.[51] But the rain did little to cut through the sultry air of a moonless night. There wasn't to be much rest, only more work to be undertaken. Some men were sent to help assist with the animals and to secure the hospital area. The rest of the command was directed to establish a stronger defensible perimeter. To this end, each company's line was straightened out and

reassigned a specific area to safeguard. Moylan's company was assigned to defend the sector to the west across from the hospital area. They used packsaddles and boxes to provided breastworks of sorts. 'H' didn't move their position and still held the southern end of the hill all by themselves. This company covered as much ground as four of the other companies combined.[52] At the time, the companies were shifting their lines, it was no doubt expected the heaviest attacks would come from the north, as had been previously experienced. This was because the warriors would no doubt want to keep themselves between the soldiers and their families. This assumption would almost prove disastrous the next day when the Indians converged against the perimeter's weak spot.

Reno claimed he ordered the company commanders to provide as much protection for the men as possible. However, there were very few entrenching tools available, and the men had to make do with tin cups, knives, and folded mess plates. Ryan recalled his company formed breastworks out of boxes of hard tack, sacks of bacon, corn or oats, "and, in fact, everything that we could possibly get a hold of."[53] The First Sergeant said rations were distributed, but it was the lack of water that caused the greatest suffering. The western side of the line really needed no additional defenses, as it had a natural protection from the steep sloping sides that ran all the way down to the river. Reno suggested Benteen build some breastworks along his extended line. Benteen was very tired, and he didn't think it was necessary as he thought the Indians would leave by morning. Benteen, however, did request that the few spades available be sent to him, but they never arrived, so the senior captain let his men sleep. Benteen thought his position would have no serious problem the next day, but to his chagrin, the Indians concentrated against his line and "I had a good deal of trouble keeping my men on the line."[54] Slaper said they tried to strengthen their breastworks, but met with varying degrees of success.[55] But, the men and officers were exhausted; the soil was fluffy and porous, and there were only three spades in the whole command![56] Not unexpectedly, Wallace saw the situation differently. He said the men worked willingly through the night, "digging little rifle pits and I heard no grumbling." Godfrey said some did work diligently digging breastworks, and they were still at the task when day broke.[57] Varnum, probably more accurately, said

[45] Camp, IU, box 2, folder 10.
[46] Chicago Tribune (Chicago, Il), July 15, 1876.
[47] Cox, Five Years in the United States Army, 152–153.
[48] Hammer, Custer in '76, 206.
[49] Camp, IU, box 2, folder 11; John S. Gray, "What Made Johnnie Bruguier Run?" Montana Magazine of Western History, Vol. 14, #2, April 1964, 34–49.
[50] Camp, BYU, roll 1, box 1, folder 9.
[51] Hunt, I Fought . . . , 103.

[52] Graham, The Custer Myth, 181.
[53] Barnard, Ten Years With Custer, 299.
[54] Brininstool, Troopers With Custer, 83.   [55] Ibid, 56.
[56] Graham, Reno Court, 56.
[57] Ibid, 35; Graham, The Custer Myth, 144.

most of the command simply fell asleep. Private Slaper recalled the men were so tired that the only way they could be kept awake was when the officers walked among them all night long and tried to keep them alert.[58] How successful the officers were is open to question.

It was toward 10 PM when Moylan was ordered to assign a non-commissioned officer and six men for picket duty to the north of the command. After several of his sergeants asked to be excused from the duty, the captain settled on Sergeant Stanislaus Roy. Roy told his captain he would go out, but only if the men under his command also volunteered. Five troopers did so, and Roy was told to report to Major Reno for his orders. Reno told Roy to have the men sneak out from the line one at a time, to always have two stay awake at a time, and to keep up a constant conversation so as to be sure to keep awake. Roy's detachment would be a trip wire, should the warriors attempt a night attack on the perimeter. Reno then said if the Indians began shooting again the next day, the men were to scatter and run back to the line from different directions and not to bunch up for easy targets. Roy said all the men were badly in need of sleep, but they carried out their orders to the letter. At first light, the warriors opened fire again, and the detail quickly retreated back to their line as directed, and suffered no casualties. Moylan later came over to Roy and complimented him on his adherence to duty and performance.[59] The soldiers weren't the only ones out on picket duty that night. Late in the evening, Wooden Leg was selected along with five others to guard the village from any surprise attack by the white men. They went over to where the soldiers were and climbed upon hills and points higher than the soldiers from where they could look down on them. Wooden Leg said they could have easily "shot among them, but we did not do this." These scouts just watched the whites and made sure "they were yet there."[60]

For any of the weary troopers who remained awake, the night was one of alarms, and some of these men began to hallucinate. There were reports that a column of troops could be seen moving over the hills, coming to their assistance, but in the directly opposite direction from which any such help would come.[61] This apparition was so strong, the buglers of the command were assembled to let this body of troops know their location.[62] When a rumor started that General Crook might be near, a civil-

ian packer jumped bareback on a horse and rode around the area yelling: "Don't be discouraged, boys. Crook is coming."[63] In the phantasms of imagination, men heard the calls of officers, the tramp of horses, and trumpet calls. These spectral trumpet calls were then answered by the trumpeters on the hill.[64] Ryan insisted the trumpet calls weren't all in their imagination. He said about midnight he and others heard a trumpet call, and the men thinking it was Custer, began to cheer. A trumpeter was ordered to sound a call, but there was no response. It was decided, it was just a trick by the warriors to get the men "out of our works."[65] Godfrey offered a possible explanation for what the men thought they had seen or heard. He recalled the long shadows of the hills and the refracted light gave a supernatural aspect to the surrounding country. He speculated this might account for the illusions experienced by some of the men.[66]

But, even more disturbing than their fear, sore muscles, hunger, thirst, and the mind numbing fatigue, was the "high carnival" being held by the Indians in the village below. Only through sheer exhaustion would any of the troopers be able to sleep that night, as from the valley floor below they heard and saw an authentic "monster's ball" taking place. Varnum said it was a scene of "demoniacal celebration and frantic revel." Godfrey wrote, the village was "a veritable pandemonium. All night long they continued . . . beating their tom-toms, dancing, whooping, yelling . . . we knew they were having a scalp dance."[67] Reno said he and some other officers while looking through field glasses saw the Indians engaged in a war dance around three captive soldiers. They had been tied to a stake, and Reno had an impression Lieutenant Harrington was one of the unfortunate souls. Godfrey, however, said they found no evidence of this sort afterwards in the village.[68]

What some soldiers saw take place in the village was confirmed in 1879 by Little Knife, an Uncpapa. He said a soldier was in fact tortured to death in the village during a wild dance.[69] Two Moon said some dead soldiers "were afterwards dragged into the village, dismembered and burned at a big dance that night."[70] Rain in the Face said there was a big feast and scalp dance that night.[71] Black Elk reported everybody was up all night in the village. "All over the camp there were big fires and kill dances

[58]Ibid, 144; Brininstool, *Troopers With Custer*, 56–57.
[59]Hammer, *Custer in '76*, 113.
[60]Marquis, *A Warrior Who Fought Custer*, 257.
[61]John Gibbon, *Gibbon on the Sioux Campaign of 1876* (Bellevue, NE: The Old Army Press, 1969), 32.
[62]Ibid.
[63]Graham, *The Custer Myth*, 144.
[64]Ibid.
[65]Barnard, *Ten Years With Custer*, 299.
[66]Graham, *The Custer Myth*, 144.
[67]Ibid.
[68]Ibid.
[69]Hardorff, *Lakota Recollections*, 96.
[70]*Camp, BYU*, box 6, folder 9.
[71]Brady, *Indian Fights and Fighters*, 290.

all night long."[72] Ryan was of the opinion a few troopers were taken prisoner, as later in the village human bones and parts of blue uniforms were found where men had been tied to stakes and trees. Goldin also thought a few of his fellow soldiers had been burned at the stake. He said they found a large fire at the lower end of the village and several skulls burned beyond recognition. In addition, a piece of a blue flannel shirt was discovered nearby with the initials of Lieutenant Sturgis embroidered on it.[73] Windolph recorded he saw the great bonfires and heard the steady rhythm of the tom-toms beating for their wild victory dances. He also recalled hearing the high pitched wailing of the squaws crying for their dead and wounded.[74] Private Harry Jones, Company 'I' and assigned to the pack train, wrote, "The Indians must have captured some of Custer's men and tortured them to death, although I saw no evidence of this. . . . This is all hearsay."[75]

But, Moving Robe contradicted the torture stories. She emphatically said, "Not a single soldier was burned at the stake. Sioux Indians do not torture their victims." Foolish Elk said, categorically, no soldiers were taken captive. He said the white men who think so should have seen the amount of firing that was done on the battlefield. If they had, they would "never suppose that any of the soldiers could come out alive." Turtle Rib told they took no soldiers off the battlefield. They were all killed where they laid.[76] Wooden Leg disputed the fact there was any celebration in the village that evening. He recalled, "There was no dancing or celebrating of any kind in any of the camps that night. Too many people were in mourning among all the Sioux as well as among the Cheyenne." However, Wooden Leg did admit "There was much noise and confusion, but it was from other causes."[77] He never told what the "other causes," were.

Sitting Bull said there were no celebrations that night, and he was indignant at this suggestion. This was not the time for rejoicing. The Uncpapa medicine man said it never was "the custom to hold a victory dance, under such circumstances, until after four days had elapsed and the mourners had given permission." Sitting Bull "commanded, tonight we shall mourn for our dead, and for

those brave white men lying up yonder on the hillside."[78] In spite of Sitting Bull's and others' protestations, I believe there were victory celebrations going on in the village that night. The older, wiser chiefs and warriors probably followed the dictates of their customs and quietly mourned and reflected; there were no wild celebrations in their presence. But, the young braves and the inexperienced youth had much to commemorate, and they probably kept the night pretty lively in the areas where they assembled. It was this activity that was observed by the men on Reno Hill.

There is no doubt there was much discussion among both officers and enlisted regarding the whereabouts of Lieutenant Colonel George A. Custer. Some were of the opinion their commander had ridden off and left them. A few of the older veterans recalled the rumors that were prevalent after the Battle of the Washita regarding the fate of Major Joel Elliott. Others thought at the very least, Custer should have sent a messenger to them saying where he was and what had happened.[79] Along these lines, Benteen said he and some of the officers thought "Custer had gone to General Terry, and we were abandoned to our fate." Godfrey thought Custer had attacked the Indians and had been repulsed, as was Reno, and he simply was "unable to make a junction with us." The lieutenant also heard similar sentiments among the enlisted men that evening.[80] Sergeant Culbertson said there had been a rumor that Custer had wounded men, including Lieutenant Calhoun, and couldn't make contact with Reno. Moylan heard the rumor, and as Calhoun was his brother-in-law, tried to trace down the information. He was told a scout had brought the news in. Moylan said he didn't think it was true.[81]

McDougall believed Custer had run across the same bunch of Indians, as had Reno, and they were following him, preventing him from coming back to Reno Hill, or he had retreated to Terry's command. There was no hint from anyone that Custer had been destroyed.[82] It's no surprise that Benteen heartily agreed with these feelings, and added, "not a soul in the command imagined that Custer had been destroyed until General Terry came up. That was our first intimation."[83] Culbertson backed up Benteen's recollections, as he said no one entertained the

[72]Neihardt, *Black Elk Speaks*, 131, 133. Black Elk even remembered one of the songs they sung that night and recorded it, see page 134.

[73]*Camp, BYU*, roll 1, box 1, folder 2.

[74]Hunt, *I Fought . . .* , 102.

[75]*Camp, BYU*, roll 1, box 1, folder 18.

[76]Hammer, *Custer in '76*, 199, 202.

[77]Marquis, *A Warrior Who Fought Custer*, 256.

[78]Vestal, *Sitting Bull*, 174.

[79]Marquis, *Keep The Last Bullet For Yourself*, 119.

[80]Graham, *Reno Court—Abstract*, 149; Graham, *Reno Court*, 435, 445.

[81]Ibid, 330.   [82]Ibid, 478.

[83]E. A. Brininstool, *The Custer Fight. Captain Benteen's Story Of The Little Big Horn, June 25–26, 1876* (Hollywood, CA: Privately Printed, 1933), 26.

slightest impression that Custer and his command could have possibly been destroyed. He was asked at the Reno Court of Inquiry to further elaborate upon this impression and replied: "The impression was that General Custer had wounded and was not able to come to us, as we were not able to go to him."[84] But, a few men began to have suspicions of what might have happened to Custer. Windolph said as time passed and still no word from Custer reached Reno Hill, there was a feeling "that some terrible fate might have overtaken him. What it was, we could only guess."[85] Surprisingly, Reno best captured, in his official report, what the vast majority of the cavalrymen felt about Custer's possible fate. "The awful fate that did befall him never occurred to any of us as within the limits of possibility."

The conduct of Major Marcus Reno the afternoon and night of June 25th, has been the subject of much controversy and variance. Some had reported that after the troops had returned to the hill, the Major disappeared, and if a hole had been available, he would have crawled into it and pulled the hole in after him.[86] French said he never really saw the major on the hill that night, and he couldn't find anyone else who did.[87] Godfrey told the Court of Inquiry he received no orders from Reno that night, nor did he recall seeing him.[88] Wallace told the Court much the same thing. The major also had his defenders who said he was walking around the line most of the night. Edgerly, Porter, and Benteen contradicted the other officers, and said Reno was about, if anyone bothered to look for him.[89]

In addition, Reno's drinking was perceived once again. Private Corcoran said that night Reno walked past his position and inquired about how he was getting along. He saw Reno with a quart bottle of whiskey in his hand.[90] Mathey confirmed Reno had a "flask" of whiskey with very little left, but this was on the morning of the 26th. Mathey quickly added he saw no evidence of drunkenness on his part during the battle.[91] McDougall reported he saw nothing to indicate Reno was drunk, nor did he see any whiskey in Reno's possession.[92] Girard countered these statements by McDougall by saying "that McDougall was a good soldier, but he did not dare tell the truth."[93] Godfrey, one of Reno's severest critics, did-

n't believe the stories that Reno was drunk and questioned if there was any whiskey in the command.[94]

Benjamin Churchill and John Frett, two civilian packers, certainly did not vouch for Reno's temperance. Frett, who in 1879 was the manager of the Commercial Hotel in St. Paul, told the Reno Court of Inquiry about 10 PM, on the 25th, he went to the pack train to obtain a blanket as well as some hardtack. While there, he turned and saw the major, and said, "Good Evening," and Reno asked him whether the mules were "tight or not?" Frett either didn't understand what Reno wanted or misunderstood the question; the packer asked Reno what he meant "by tight." According to Frett, Reno said, "Tight, God Dam you," and slapped his face. Reno then grabbed a carbine and threatened to shoot him. Frett noticed a bottle of whiskey in Reno's hand, and some of its contents flew onto the packer when Reno slapped him.[95] He said the major was drunk. This story was confirmed by Churchill, who had accompanied Frett, to the pack train. He said he didn't hear the whole conversation between his friend and Reno, but he did see Reno strike out towards Frett, and some of Reno's whiskey spilled on him as well. He saw a carbine in Reno's hands, and it was at this point he took his fellow packer by the shoulders and pulled him away. Churchill testified before the Court of Inquiry that it was his "impression at the time that he was a little under the influence of whiskey or liquor."

It was sometime in the late hours of the 25th or very early on the 26th, that according to Benteen, Reno brought up the subject of abandoning the wounded to him. In essence, this tale relates how Reno wanted to escape from the Indians, thought the men should be mounted, the property destroyed that couldn't be carried off, and a night march made to their base camp at the Powder River. Those who were wounded and were able to stay on a horse would be taken along; those who couldn't would be left to the tender mercy of Sitting Bull's warriors.[96]

Benteen said he wouldn't agree to any such undertaking. Did Reno think it was the only way to save the command, or was it just an option, one of many, which was discussed by the two officers? Godfrey recalled: "We thought the command ought to move that night and effect a junction with him (Custer)."[97] He believed it was better to move all the men now, as later there would probably be more casualties.[98] Colonel Graham, a lifetime student of the battle, was of the opinion that what Reno

[84]Graham, *Reno Court*, 331.
[85]Hunt, *I Fought . . .* , 107.
[86]Stewart, *The Field Diary . . .* , 15; Brown and Willard, *The Black Hills Trails*, 191–192.
[87]Stewart, *Custer's Luck*, 416.
[88]Graham, *Reno Court*, 436.
[89]Ibid, 163, 365, 395.
[90]Hammer, *Custer in '76*, 150.
[91]Graham, *Reno Court*, 464.
[92]Holley, *Once Their Home*, 246.
[93]Ibid, 266.

[94]Brady, *Indian and Fighters*, 376.
[95]Graham, *Reno Court*, 450.
[96]Stewart, *Custer's Luck*, 420.
[97]Graham, *Reno Court*, 436.
[98]Ibid, 436.

really said (or meant) was "if the command was moved, the helpless wounded must be left behind."[99] To which Benteen probably replied, "You can't do that." Graham thought that way too much was being made by partisans on both sides of this "abandon the wounded," tale. Graham's opinion might have merit. Private Taylor had written to Walter Camp, that on the evening of the 25th he had asked the first sergeant of his company what was going to happen? Were they going to stay or try to move away? Neither noticed Major Reno was standing near by and had overheard their conversation. Reno quickly told both men, "I would like to know how the hell we are going to move away."[100]

Private John McGuire, Company 'C' and assigned to the pack train, did overhear some officers talking about escaping from their predicament. He said an improvised officer's council took place near where he was positioned. At the time that McGuire related his recollections, he could only recall the name of one officer, Major Reno. He said the officers spoke about pulling back from the line and trying to break out under the cover of darkness. McGuire said it was Reno, himself, who replied to this proposal by stating he had a number of wounded men that couldn't be moved, and he would stand by them until the end.[101] However, if Reno (or whomever made this suggestion) wasn't serious about this option, and if in fact he only discussed moving the command with Benteen, there must have been others within hearing distance who thought otherwise and had eavesdropped or learned by gossip about this discussion. Consequently, there was a very strong rumor going around on that long and weary night that "to save the balance of the command, they (the wounded) were to be abandoned."[102] One might well imagine the emotions these men experienced during the rest of the bat-

tle. When Terry's column arrived on the 27th, it was noticed by these soldiers, the wounded "appeared to feel that they were stepping from death back to life again."[103] But, if what McGuire and Taylor heard was an accurate reflection of Reno's rejection of this proposal, why would Benteen fabricate such a fictitious story, keep the fire smoldering, and occasionally fan the flame over the years? Is it possible, Benteen knew he'd find a receptive audience to this tale, because most of the survivors would believe Reno was capable of advocating just such a proposition? An early Reno biographer noted: "Reno had his faults undoubtedly; one of which was his inability to cope with liars."[104]

Today, there are many people who think that the Custer Battlefield is a haunted place.[105] It has been said over the years some National Park Service personnel have even told of seeing apparitions and other strange phenomenon associated with the battle.[106] These employees "reported seeing scenes 'in vivid detail' of soldiers being massacred by hordes of Indians." Visitors also reported hearing gunshots and sights of a battle taking place right before their eyes.[107] In all probability, Reno thought the same way about this blighted landscape. These specters not only frequented the land, but they also inhabited his mind as well. Even a decade later, Major Marcus Reno graphically recalled: "the horror of Custer's battlefield is still vividly before me, and the harrowing sight of those mutilated and decomposing bodies crowning the heights on which poor Custer fell will linger in my memory till death."[108]

The casualties of Custer's Last Stand weren't just the dead bodies that littered the valley floor and the bluffs above the Little Big Horn River. The victims also included many of those who, by the grace of God, had survived.

[99]Graham, *The Custer Myth*, 338.

[100]*Camp, BYU*, roll 1, box 1, folder 11.

[101]*Camp, BYU*, roll 1, box 1, folder 4.

[102]Gibbon, *Gibbon on the Sioux Campaign of 1876*, 37.

[103]Ibid.

[104]E. A. Brininstool, "A Letter from E. A. Brininstool," *Montana Magazine of Western History*, Vol. 4, #4, Fall 1954, 63.

[105]Earl Murray, *Ghosts Of The Old West* (NY, NY: Dorset Press, 1988), 27.   [106]Ibid, 18–27.

[107]Undated, unnamed newspaper clipping, Steve Moses Collection.

[108]Hunt, *I Fought . . .* , 175.

12
Conclusion

After forty-eight hours with no sleep, Second Lieutenant Varnum was so exhausted that he collapsed around midnight, at the spot where he had been standing. He awoke to find himself being carried by Private Anton Seibelder, a Company 'A' trooper, to a more secure area on Reno Hill. It was about 3 AM on June 26th, and the faint streaks of daylight were just beginning to make their appearance to the east. From Sharpshooters' Hill two shots rang out, which appeared to be a signal for the Indians to open fire. At first, there wasn't enough light to clearly distinguish their targets. But as dawn became more and more pronounced, a regular fusillade descended from the hills surrounding the soldiers' positions. There was no doubt the warriors fully intended to overrun the white men and take the hill. As the firing began, Private Seibelder had noticed Varnum was lying in an exposed position and moved him to an area of safety. The lieutenant promptly fell back to sleep in spite of the gunfire and didn't awake until well after sunrise. [1] When he awoke about 5:00 AM, he saw the Indians had moved closer and were now behind the ridges which were only two to five hundred yards from their lines. Some of the bolder warriors positioned themselves less than one hundred yards away, and there was a continuous ring of gunsmoke surrounding the command. The Indians were firing very rapidly, trying to draw the soldier's fire to their positions. [2]

Godfrey, among other officers, realized what the warriors were trying to accomplish by the these tactics. They wanted to exhaust the soldiers' ammunition and were waiting for the replenishment lull when they would rush the line. Godfrey ordered only the best marksmen in the company to return the fire. [3] Seeing the gunfire diminish, the Indians started to rush the troopers' position. Varnum recalled the men held their fire until the warriors began their charge, and then "we would get up and open on them." [4] This back and forth between the Indians and the soldiers continued throughout the early morning. Realizing this tactic wasn't working, the Indians would suddenly jump up from their hiding places, and then drive for cover before the soldiers were able to get a good fix. In addition, the warriors employed the old ruse of placing a hat or a shirt on a stick and holding it up to draw the troopers' gunfire. [5] The Indians also concentrated their fire at those soldiers who hadn't entrenched their positions or had done a poor job of providing cover for themselves.

These Indians made life particularly miserable for the men posted in Benteen's section of the line. After the battle, Benteen tried to determine how many Indians were around Reno Hill. He was never able to arrive at a satisfactory answer about "how many of the miscreants there were;—probably we shall never know,—but there were enough." [6] As the gunfire intensified, these men were taking fire from three different directions on the battlefield. The lack of preparation the night before was now coming back to haunt the regiment's senior captain. On this day, Benteen's casualties would total more than any of the other companies on Reno Hill. [7] It was toward mid-morning when a sergeant reported to Benteen, with Lieutenant Gibson's compliments, and said the company was "having a regular monkey and parrot time of it" on the line. [8] Gibson wrote in a letter to his wife, dated July 4, 1876:

> We occupied the most exposed position and the Indians had a clear fire at us from four sides, my only wonder is not every one of us wasn't killed. The bullets fell like a perfect shower of hail, and every instance I thought I certainly would be the next struck. [9]

Benteen went over to one part of his line near the head of a small ravine that ran all the way to the river. He observed the Indians seemed to be gathering in greater and greater numbers in front of his position, and were using this natural cover to organize for an overwhelming charge. Benteen ran to the pack train and mustered everyone he could reach and had them carry anything that might stop a bullet aimed at his position. Soon, about sixteen men were seen transporting a variety of materials, to Company 'H's position, "sacks of bacon, boxes of hard bread, pack saddles" to erect a makeshift breastworks. The Captain told Gibson to take charge of this "Falstaffian crowd," and hold the position at all hazards. [10] The struggle for Reno Hill was approaching a finality.

Company 'H' was down to a handful of cartridges, and re-supply was sporadic, the warriors were seen massing for a charge, and the casualties were mounting by the minute. Realizing his predicament and the need to hold this sector, Benteen went to look for Reno to request reinforcements. He found the Major in a sort of a foxhole with Captain Weir, but he wasn't very sympa-

---

[1] Carroll, *I Varnum*, 71–72.
[2] Graham, *Reno Court*, 141.
[3] Graham, *The Custer Myth*, 144
[4] Graham, *Reno Court*, 141.
[5] Graham, *The Custer Myth*, 144.
[6] Ibid, 181.
[7] Willert, *Little Big Horn Diary*, 400.
[8] Graham, *The Custer Myth*, 182.
[9] Fougera, *With Custer's Cavalry*, 269.
[10] Graham, *The Custer Myth*, 182.

thetic to his second in command asking for more men. Reno told Benteen the Indians were pressing the whole command, and he had no men to spare. Benteen looked directly at the Major and told him repeatedly in no uncertain terms he needed a company of men and he needed them now or the whole perimeter would be carried by the Indians.[11] Reno reluctantly ordered Captain French's company off their part of the line and to report to Benteen's section. Reno never moved from his foxhole, and as French passed, he just motioned for him to go on.[12] French's men weren't very happy to leave their rifle pits to assist another company who had neglected to entrench their position the night before. Forty years later, Private Morris could still recall the grumbling the men of 'M' did as they made their way to the hottest part of the battlefield.[13] Without a doubt, Benteen heard the dissatisfaction expressed by the ranks. After the battle, when French submitted his first sergeant's name (John Ryan) for the Medal of Honor, Benteen refused to endorse the recommendation, apparently, because Ryan had failed to immediately order his men out of their rifle pits at Benteen's direction.[14]

Benteen quickly returned to his position, with French and 'M' company following in his wake. The additional men arrived just in time, because a few minutes earlier one of the soldiers had been shot and killed. Long Road, a Sans Arc warrior, was able to rush in to count coup on this soldier's body. He was promptly shot and killed, but his body was so close to the cavalrymen, the other Indians couldn't get near enough to carry the warrior off.[15] The Indians were so close to the soldiers' lines that they were able to contemptuously throw stones and clumps of dirt while mockingly flinging arrows by hand at the defenders. Benteen, with the 'M' troopers filling in around 'H,' told the men he was getting tired of this game, and he was going to charge these Indians. When he did, the men were to follow him and yell like fiends and shoot as fast as they could.[16] The Captain gave a cheer and started towards where the Indians were massing for the final charge. Discharging their carbines in a volley, the soldiers drew their Colt 45s and yelled at the top of their voices and started down the slope. The actions of the Indians in receiving this charge was recalled fondly by Benteen: "to say that 'twas a surprise to them, is mild form, for they somersaulted and vaulted as so many trained acro-

bats, having no order in getting down those ravines, but quickly getting; de'il take the hindmost."[17]

Benteen quickly ordered recall sounded, and the soldiers climbed back up the hill and dropped down behind their makeshift barricades. Sergeant Windolph remembered that they had cleared the Indians out for a good hundred yards down the slope, after which the troopers "hustled back to their holes."[18] Gibson and Company 'H,' who had been on the receiving end of the gunfire all morning, were very pleased. Not only had this charge enlivened the men's spirits and restored some measure of morale, but also "the Indians had lost heavily, so they thought it wise to give us a little wider berth."[19] With the threat decreased from this direction, the men of 'H' worked to construct breastworks on the southwestern side of their ridge line. The Indian fire had slackened and the need for water was more acute than ever. Both the men and the wounded were suffering from the lack of water. The sun seemed to cook the blood in the veins of the men manning the line, while the gunsmoke stung their parched throats.[20] It was especially difficult to endure, when the cool waters of the river were visible and seemly within reach of the command. But "It was impossible for a man to go to the river without getting killed or wounded."[21] In spite of this, a number of men volunteered to follow the ravine, now cleared of warriors, to reach the river and secure as much water as they could carry. Godfrey remembered that, it was a little before noon when this was undertaken.[22] Benteen ordered four of his best marksmen to follow these volunteers and provide cover fire. But, even with heavy fire suppression, it was still a dangerous task. During the efforts to obtain water, one man was killed and six wounded. The Cheyennes told about one soldier who was so desperate for water that before approaching the river he stripped down to his underwear and with a cup in one hand and a canteen in the other, jumped into the river. He was filling his containers all the while his head was buried in the Little Big Horn River, drinking. At the same time, the Indians on the opposite bank were shooting at him. The warriors said part of the time the white man couldn't be seen for all the water being splashed up by the bullets. After getting all the water he could carry and his belly could hold, he started up the hill with Indian bullets still impacting all around him. The Cheyennes

[11]Graham, *Reno Court*, 436.　　　　[12]Ibid.

[13]Brady, *Indian Fights and Fighters*, 404.　　　　[14]Ibid.

[15]Other accounts claim this soldier and warrior were killed at the conclusion of the charge and not before it, see Stewart, *Custer's Luck*, 424.　　　[16]Graham, *The Custer Myth*, 182.

[17]Ibid.　　　　　　　　　　　[18]Hunt, *I Fought . . .* , 106.

[19]Fougera, *With Custer's Cavalry*, 270.

[20]Edward Pickard, "I Rode With Custer," *Montana Magazine of Western History*, Vol. 4, #3, Summer 1954, 28.

[21]Liddic, *I Buried Custer*, 18.

[22]Stewart, *The Field Diary . . .* , 16.

believed this white man's medicine was strong, as he reached the top of the hill untouched.[23] Twenty-five 7th Cavalrymen would later be awarded the Medal of Honor for their actions (and others) that were "above and beyond the call of duty."

Company 'H' continued to work on their rifle pits and strengthen their position, but in the early afternoon the soldiers were again suddenly under heavy fire. This time it was from the north and east. In the morning, Benteen had put an end to the gunfire descending upon him from the river flank; but now the bullets were darting into his position from another direction. Once more, Benteen left his men and went to Major Reno and found him still near Captain Weir. Edgerly noted the bullets were flying very fast around 'D' Company's sector, and he was amazed Benteen wasn't "riddled" while he stood on the line talking to Reno.[24] Benteen told the Major about the charge he had led and its effect upon the warriors. Now "They are coming to your left, and you ought to drive them out.[25] Reno, in his foxhole on the left of 'D's line, raised himself up on his elbow and asked Benteen, "Can you see the Indians from there?" Benteen answered, "Yes." Reno gave some thought to the request, but never bothered to leave his foxhole to see for himself, and told Benteen, "If you can see them, give the command to charge."[26]

Benteen led Companies 'B,' 'D,' 'G,' and 'K' forward in another charge. [27] It was about 3 PM. However, Godfrey said that Reno led this charge, and Benteen accompanied the Major.[28] Private Coleman, whose Company 'B' was at the apex of the charge, recorded Major Reno was the leader.[29] In all probability, Reno did lead the men in this charge, as Benteen's 'H' wasn't involved nor was it in his sector. The Indians opened a heavy fire upon the advancing soldiers, and they charged about 70 yards before the order was given to fall back. Not a single man was hit during this charge and retreat, and all the soldiers made it back to their foxholes. McDougall agreed with how Benteen recalled the action. He said that Benteen came over to his company and said, "get your men ready and start out." McDougall further recalled it wasn't the order to fall back that halted his company but "the fire was so heavy on my right and rear that I had to return."[30] The Indians were not going to surrender any of the high ground

to white men. But, it was noted the Indian fire was now decreasing in both intensity and energy. By late afternoon, it almost ceased, except for some scattered pot shots. About this time, Reno had attempted to send a message through to Terry, but the scouts "either failed to get through the hostile lines or else they didn't even try to do so." Actually, the scouts did succeed in leaving the hill, but they soon returned, "saying the country was full of Sioux" and they couldn't get through.[31]

The troopers soon saw the reason for the lack of gunfire. The warriors were breaking camp. The warriors had set fire to the grass to hide their movements. It was about 7 PM when the soldiers noticed the inhabitants of this great camp moving through and out of their smoke screen and across the plateau towards the Big Horn Mountains. Although the troopers were elated to see the Indians departing, they were suspicious and feared it was a trap. There were a number of "explanations" expounded on for the warriors leaving the field of battle to them. Some thought that Custer had linked up with Terry, and that together they were coming to their relief, others believed the Indians were short on ammunition and therefore broke off the engagement. Not a few were of the opinion it was only a trick to get them to leave their position, and then the warriors would make "a final desperate effort to overwhelm us." [32] The soldiers, now, started to stand up and began to move about the hill, but always near their foxholes should the gunfire again commence. About sundown, there were no Indians to be seen, and the men were ordered to take the horses and mules down to the river for a much needed watering. "Their rush for the river when they got near to it was very pathetic."[33] The cooks were directed to start fires and prepare the first real meal the soldiers would have in the past forty-eight hours. Those who weren't involved in these activities relaxed, counting themselves lucky to have come through this Indian fight in one piece.

After the horses had been watered and the evening meal eaten, the command was moved a short distance closer to the river. This move was necessary to get away from the dead animals, the hastily dug graves, and the stench of their prior position. In addition, the new line would better command the approaches to the Little Big Horn. The body of Lieutenant Hodgson was finally recovered and buried by a small party on a little knoll "overlooking the river with a cedar tree at his head."[34] Before midnight,

---

[23]Grinnell, *The Fighting Cheyennes*, 342. The identity of this trooper is Private William D. Nugent of Company A; his story was published in *Winners of the West*, June 24, 1926.

[24]Graham, *Reno Court*, 397.   [25]Ibid.

[26]Ibid, 397–398.   [27]Graham, *The Custer Myth*, 185.

[28]Stewart, *The Field Diary . . .* , 17.

[29]Liddic, *I Buried Custer*, 18.   [30]Holley, *Once Their Homes*, 245.

[31]Stewart, *Custer's Luck*, 427; Nichols, *In Custer's Shadow*, 200.

[32]Liddic, *I Buried Custer*, 19; Graham, *The Custer Myth*, 145.

[33]Hammer, *Custer in '76*, 58.   [34]Liddic, *I Buried Custer*, 20.

Billy Jackson and Fred Girard scrambled up the bluffs and rejoined the 7th Cavalry, happy to be alive. The command bedded down for the evening and except for the extra guards slept soundly until morning.[35] About 3 AM on the 27th, Lieutenant DeRudio and Private O'Neil made their presence known as they approached the command's picket line. They had tried before to reach the hill, but with the Indians guarding all the avenues, found it impossible until now. Both were heartily welcomed, as they had been given up as dead.[36] The men were up and about early, reworking their positions and taking stock of their situation. About mid-morning, a cloud of dust was seen a few miles down the valley, and the men were recalled to their entrenchment and the command put into shape to renew the battle. The dust cloud was moving too slowly to be Indians, and it was correctly concluded that the cause of the cloud was a relief column. It was thought that this was Crook's column because they couldn't see any gray horses, and so they knew it couldn't be Custer.[37] Soon a white scout, Muggins Taylor, arrived with a note to Custer from Terry telling him of their expected arrival. According to Godfrey, the dispatch also noted that several Crow scouts had reported the defeat of the 7th Cavalry.[38] Reno ordered both Hare and Wallace to ride to the approaching column and guide them back to Reno Hill.

Terry had made every effort to reach the designated area by the 26th. The first few days of the march started off well enough, and Terry kept the infantry to their task. On June 24th, they camped on lower Tullock's Creek. The following day was to prove disastrous to the timetable to which Terry was trying to adhere. For reasons never satisfactorily explained, the command left the trail for a short cut and then got hopelessly bogged down in a labyrinth of hills and ravines while marching west towards the Big Horn River. Despite a night march, the command still found itself some distance from where they were supposed to be the following morning. In fact, they were twelve miles from the mouth of the Little Big Horn River. Terry had his scouts out early on the 26th, and Bradley met several of Custer's Crow scouts. Little Face told the lieutenant that these Custer scouts said that the white soldiers had met with death and defeat; Bradley relayed this information to General Terry. Upon hearing this story, most of the officers thought that although a battle had been fought, the army was victorious. Custer, however, had

probably taken casualties and was camped somewhere down stream with his wounded. Terry made every effort to hurry the troops along, but as night fell they made bivouac in the present town of Crow Agency, Montana. Terry was a day late on his perceived schedule.

As Terry pushed up the valley on the west side of the Little Big Horn River, early on the morning of the 27th, Bradley and the scouts swung off to the left among the hills above the eastern bank of the river. There they made a shocking discovery. Little Face had been right; the 7th Cavalry had met with disaster. Bradley rode back to Terry and made an emotional report. He told the General, "I have a sad report to make. I have counted 197 bodies lying in the hills." Terry asked if they were white men. The lieutenant answered with a husky voice, "Yes."[39] It was after 10 AM when Hare and Wallace pulled up in front of General Terry. The first question they asked was the whereabouts of Custer, and if they had seen him? After hearing the reply to their question, the officers were "dumbfounded," it seemed impossible for them to comprehend what they had just been told.[40] By 11 AM, Terry had arrived on Reno Hill, and it was officially confirmed that five companies of the regiment, including its field commander, laid in death a few miles away. The troops on Reno Hill had thought they fought the major part of the battle; now they realized it was only a side show to what had taken place to the north.[41] The meeting between the Montana Column and the remnant of the Dakota Column "triggered an emotional binge for all concerned."[42]

The remaining part of the day was spent in policing the hill to gather up the government property, destroy what was no longer serviceable, and move the wounded down to the Montana Column's camp site in the valley. This campsite was located just to the east of the present day gas station and museum complex at Garryowen, Montana.[43] Detachments from both columns were dispatched to search for any possible survivors from the five companies, while others were given the duty of burying the dead. Captain Benteen was assigned to follow Custer's trail and try to determine what had happened and to gain some insight into how the battle was fought. However, Benteen testified at the Reno Court of Inquiry that it was he

[35]Ibid.

[36]Clyde McLermore (ed), "My Personal Story," by Lt. Charles deRudio, *Frontier and Midland Magazine*, Vol. 14, January 1934, 159.

[37]Stewart, *The Field Diary . . .* , 18.

[38]Graham, *The Custer Myth*, 146.

[39]Gibbon, *Gibbon on the Sioux Campaign*, 29. However, Roe said Bradley sent a note to Terry with this information. Roe, *Custer's Last Battle*, 11.

[40]Stewart, *The Field Diary . . .* , 19.

[41]James P. Murphy, "The Campaign of the Little Big Horn," *Infantry Journal*, Vol. 34, June 1929, 638.

[42]Gray, *Centennial Campaign*, 193.

[43]Marquis, *Custer On The Little Bighorn*, 34.

who went to Terry and requested permission to take the lead in going over the Custer field.[44] Lieutenant Roe told a different story of how Benteen was chosen to explore the Custer field. The lieutenant remembered that Benteen went over to Terry when he saw him approaching the hill and inquired about Custer. Terry told him Custer was dead with his command about four miles away. Benteen said he didn't believe it, and he told Terry, "I think he is somewhere down the Big Horn grazing his horses. At the Washita, he went off and left part of his command, and I think he would do it again."[45] The general was in no mood to debate the facts with the infallible Benteen and replied: "I think you are mistaken, and you will take your company and go down where the dead are lying and investigate for yourself."[46] So much for Benteen's testimony about asking for permission.

After a careful investigation of the field, Benteen said that he reached a conclusion, which he never changed, that the battle "was a route, a panic, till the last man was killed."[47] The senior captain based his opinion that the battle was a debacle because Custer's officers, with the exception of three, were not found with their companies, but with Custer at his last stand position. This indicated to Benteen the five companies did not fight as cohesive units.[48] He also believed that Custer did not approach close to the river, and the Custer part of the fight didn't last anymore than an hour.[49] Benteen had his company bury the soldiers found on Calhoun Hill and then continued along the battle ridge to the last stand area. Upon Benteen's return, it was noted he was pale, subdued, and had a troubled look on his face. Still, not fully comprehending what he had discovered, he said to Lieutenant Roe, "We found them, but I did not expect we would."[50]

During the afternoon, General Terry was busy debriefing the 7th Cavalry officers in an attempt to learn the circumstances of the Custer battle and the fight for Reno Hill. No doubt, Terry had heard the rumblings from the survivors on the hill concerning the fate of Custer and the conduct of Major Reno.[51] By early evening, the first preliminary examination of the Custer field had been concluded; no survivors were found, and the fifty wounded men had been successfully transferred to the valley camp. To the cavalrymen, this move represented a vast improvement over their prior accommodations. But, the men of the 7th infantry were appalled at the conditions surrounding them. First Lieutenant William English, 7th Infantry, recorded in his diary that the "Stench of dead bodies and horses, fearful around us."[52] Captain Clifford graphically described the scene near them:

> Our camp is surrounded with ghastly remains of the recent butchery . . . the air is thick with the stench of festering bodies. . . . The repulsive looking green flies that have been feasting on the swollen bodies of the dead are attracted to our camp fires . . . let us bury our dead and flee from this rotten atmosphere. . . . A little delay on this death stricken ground and we will remain forever.[53]

On the 28th, a concerted effort was undertaken to conduct a systematic and complete search of the Custer field and Reno's valley fight for bodies, to identify and bury them. Three of the officers were never identified, along with, a great many of the enlisted men. Captain Ball was ordered to take his company of the 2nd Cavalry to learn what had become of the Indians. He tracked their trail for about fifteen miles, as it headed north towards the Big Horn Mountains. Here, the trail split into two parts, one going southeast, the other southwest.[54] In the early evening, Terry ordered a move to the junction of the Big Horn River where it was expected the steamboat 'Far West' would be waiting to take the wounded aboard. Terry had dispatched two of his scouts the day before to make the advance arrangements. The combined columns started out, but trying to transport the wounded by hand simply overwhelmed the command. They only managed to travel four miles in nearly five hours. It was apparent that moving the wounded by hand litters wasn't feasible, and it was about midnight when camp was made for the night. The next morning the troops set about to construct both mule litters and Indian style travois. This would prove to be a vast improvement. The command then continued their journey in the early evening to take advantage of the cooler temperatures.

The two scouts returned to the column a few hours later and reported that the 'Far West' was in fact waiting and ready for them at the mouth of the Little Big Horn River. Terry decided to push on and reach the steamboat as soon as possible. They arrived at the boat early on the morning of the 30th. The wounded were loaded on board, and shortly after noon, Terry with his staff, and Major Brisbin of Gibbon's command, began the journey to their base camp on the Yellowstone River. Gibbon was ordered

[44]Graham, *Reno Court*, 368.
[45]Hammer, *Custer in '76*, 249.
[46]Ibid.
[47]Ibid.
[48]Graham, *Reno Court*, 386.
[49]Ibid, 375.
[50]Hammer, *Custer in '76*, 250. Other accounts have this burial taking place on the 28th.
[51]W. J. Ghent, "Varnum, Reno, and the Little Big Horn," *Winners of the West*, April, 1936.
[52]Taunton, *Custer Field*, 22.
[53]Ibid, 22–23.
[54]Stewart, *Custer's Luck*, 475.

to assume command of the remainder of the Dakota column as well as his own Montana column. He was to ford the troops to the north side of the Big Horn and to follow the 'Far West' back to the base camp. Terry reached the camp late in the afternoon, and he began to write his official report. The officers knew that Custer's defeat spelled a dismal failure for the campaign, and that someone was going to be blamed.[55] It was entirely possible President Grant, as well as the American public, would look for a scape-goat. The hunt for cover had begun. General Terry would have to walk a fine line in his construction of the events on the hills above the Little Big Horn, and pray that his explanations would satisfy his superiors and the Grant Administration. That day, Terry sent the scout Muggins Taylor to Fort Ellis to carry other dispatches. Unfortunately for Terry, Taylor reached civilization before his official dispatches, and on July 4th the Helena *Daily Herald* published an 'extra' edition, and the news was quickly telegraphed east. On July 2nd, Gibbon's combined command arrived and bivouacked around the camp at the junction of the Rosebud and Yellowstone Rivers.

The integrated columns were to remain in the field to rest, refit and await reinforcements. All the men knew, it would only be a matter of time before they would be ordered "once more into the breach." Lieutenant Hare wrote his father on July 3rd that he expected the command to remain at this camp for about three weeks, "fitting-up for another trail." He said, the massacre the 7th Cavalry experienced, hadn't any parallel in the country, and he was unsure of the effect it would have on the people. He concluded:

> The 7th Cavalry, the boast and pride of the Army both to its personnel and material, is almost annihilated by a lot of infernal devils, and we cannot convince ourselves of it. We will try them once more and if we don't wipe out old scores we will certainly get wiped out ourselves.[56]

However, it wasn't until August 8th that Terry felt strong (confident?) enough to lead the command out of his base camp and up the Rosebud to again pursue the Indians.

Colonel Gibbon took a different view of the "infernal devils," who had fought and defeated the 7th Cavalry. Soon after the battle, he wrote, it was the fraud and deceit practiced upon the Indians by the government and their agents which left the Red Man to suffer "for the actual necessities of life. When, then, the Indian, driven to desperation by neglect or want and his sense of wrong, goes

to war (and even a Christian will fight before he will starve), the army is called in to whip 'these wards of the nation' into subjection." Once the army completes the task, then another round of fraud and deceit begins until the next war is thrust upon the military, "for the purpose of bringing into subjection a people forced into war by the very agents of the government which make war upon them."[57] These unvarnished and insightful comments by Gibbon represent a higher understanding of the Indian situation then was ever exhibited by the politicos in far distant Washington. In the end, the faults of the Battle of the Little Big Horn were those of our government and war, not the warriors . . . be they white or red.

Terry completed his official report and entrusted it to his adjutant. He instructed him on its delivery and ordered him to board the 'Far West' with the wounded for the trip to Fort Lincoln and Bismarck. About mid-morning, on July 3rd, Grant Marsh, the boat's captain, left the bank for the river's mid-channel and began the seven-hundred-mile run to Fort Lincoln. In a record-breaking trip in just fifty-four hours, the steamboat reached Bismarck and the fort. Although it was 11 PM on July 5th, the crew-members rushed from the boat and awoke the whole town to break the news. Captain Marsh went to the telegraph officer and began to tell the story of the battle as it had been related to him. The story coming out of Bismarck, Dakota Territory would create newspaper headlines for weeks. It wouldn't be until July 5th that Terry's own report would reach Chicago and then be forwarded on to General Sheridan. The Lieutenant General was in Philadelphia at the Continental Hotel while he attended the Centennial Exposition along with other Grant Administration dignitaries. It was said, Sheridan's grief over the death of his close friend, Custer, and the partial destruction of the 7th Cavalry, was only exceeded by his anger over Terry's report. Instead of a report on the battle with a list of casualties, it was a defense of Terry's conduct of the campaign.[58]

The troops who had remained at Fort Lincoln, as well as the families who had been left behind, had heard earlier the rumors of a big fight with the Indians, and the army didn't come out on top. The days from June 25th on were remembered as a time of suspense. "The atmosphere was charged with depression."[59] George Custer's wife was to later write what most of the other dependents, as well, had felt. There was "a premonition of dis-

---

[55]Gray, *Centennial Campaign*, 196.

[56]Meketa, *Luther Rector Hare*, 40.

[57]Gibbon, *Gibbon on the Sioux Campaign*, 62.

[58]Paul A. Hutton, *Phil Sheridan and His Army* (Lincoln, NE: University of Nebraska, 1985), 315.

[59]Frost, *General Custer's Libbie*, 226–227.

aster that I had never known before weighed me down. I could not shake off the baleful influence of depressing thoughts."[60] The inhabitants of the fort had heard the late night whistle of the 'Far West' as it docked at Bismarck and knew their days of waiting for information was about to end. Captain William McCaskey, 20th Infantry and acting commander of the fort, was officially notified before sunrise on July 6. It was up to him and the officers he selected to break the news to the new widows and fatherless children, of both officer and enlisted, as to what happened eleven days prior. Elizabeth Bacon Custer probably best summarized the emotions of the wives, when she was informed of the fate of her husband: "I wanted to die." No doubt the same could be said for what Twin Women probably felt when she was told about her husband, Lame White Man; as well as the rest of the Sioux and Cheyenne who had lost loved ones.

The citizens of Syracuse heard the dark rumors coming out of the West almost as soon as the fireworks celebrating the nation's 100th birthday had faded away. Undoubtedly, some sort of disaster, was suffered by the army, but the details and confirmation were lacking. But, as they opened the Syracuse *Morning Standard* on July 6th, Syracusans began to read that General Custer had a "fight with the redskins and many were killed and wounded." The next day in large type, the headlines declared, "War With Sioux Indians—Death of Custer Confirmed." The rumors were true. In the following days, the public was given a steady diet of "Additional Details of the Slaughter of Custer and his Men," and of "Reinforcements Hastily Going Forward." How the "Tribes Inclined to Join Sitting Bull," and "The Causes of the War." These headline stories continued for nearly a week in an effort to feed the insatiable public demand, not only in Syracuse, but the entire country as well, for more and more information.

This demand for information and answers to 'why' and 'how' resonate down to us today. Except for the result, exactly what happened to Custer and his five companies will never be known with certainty. Out of this unknown, there grew the fantastic tales, speculations, perjuries at the Reno Court of Inquiry, and the imaginary inventions of events by the participants, that all form part of this unsolvable mystery. For many western history students of the battle, it's "More than journey's end, it is the journey itself that enchants us." The Battle of the Little Big Horn was of no great historical consequence in the scope of the American experience. But, it has been the subject of more controversy, dissension, dispute than almost any other event in our history.[61] As one historian noted, while the battle itself is of little importance, 'Custer's Last Stand,' is another matter. It's George Armstrong Custer's figure that sets this event apart and provides the starting point in an endless search. In the American conscience, he stands forever, frozen in time, on that "dusty Montana slope."

Years ago, a story was told of a Custer scholar who went to pay a call on a little old lady who reportedly had information relating to the Battle of the Little Big Horn. This information was supposed to be in the form of some letters by several of the participants. Upon answering the knock on her door, the scholar inquired about General Custer. The lady, hard of hearing, quickly replied, "Custer! He's dead. The Indians killed him," and promptly closed the door. Perhaps she conveyed in two concise sentences the unarguable truth of what happened, that, over the years, a sea of ink upon a library full of books has yet to achieve.

---

[60] Elizabeth B. Custer, *"Boots and Saddles," or, Life in Dakota with General Custer* (NY, NY: Harper and Brothers, 1885), 265.

[61] Graham, *The Custer Myth*, XI.

Men's evil manners live in brass;
their virtues we write in water.
—*William Shakespeare*

Bibliography

Books

Barnard, Sandy. *Ten Years with General Custer*. Terre Haute, IN: AST Press, 2001.

Custer's First Sergeant. Terre Haute, IN: AST Press, 1996.

Barry, David F. *Indian Notes on Custer And His Last Battle*. Baltimore, MD: Wirth Press, 1947.

Bergamini, John D. *The Hundredth Year* NY, NY: G. P. Putnam's Sons, 1976.

Bookwalter, Thomas E. *Honor Tarnished*. N.P. : Little Horn Press, 1979.

———. *The Search For The Lone Tepee*. N.P.: Little Horn Press, 1983.

Boyes, W. *Cheyenne Tribal Historian John Stands In Timber's Account Of The Custer Battle*. N.P.: Little Big Horn Associates, Inc., 1991.

Brady, Charles T. *Indian Fights and Fighters*. NY, NY: Doubleday, 1904.

Brininstool, E. A. *Troopers With Custer*. Harrisburgh, PA: The Stackpole Company, 1952.

———. *The Custer Fight. Captain Benteen's Story of The Little Big Horn, June 25–26, 1876*. Hollywood, CA: Privately Printed, 1933.

Brown, Jesse and A. M. Willard. *The Black Hills Trails*. NY, NY: Arno Press, 1975.

Brown, Mark. *The Plainsmen of The Yellowstone* NY, NY: G. P. Putnam's Sons, 1961.

Byrne, P. E. *Soldiers of The Plains*. NY, NY: Minton, Balch & Co., 1926.

Carroll, John M. *The Gibson and Edgerly Narratives*. Bryan, Texas: Privately Printed, N.D.

———. *The Benteen–Goldin Letters on Custer and His Last Battle*. NY, NY: Liveright, 1974.

———. *General Custer And The Battle Of The Little Big Horn : The Federal View*. New Brunswick, NJ: The Garry Owen Press, 1976.

———. *I Varnum*. Glendale, CA: The Arthur H. Clark Company, 1982.

———. *The Custer Autograph Album*. College, TX: The Early West, 1994.

———. *The Sunshine Magazine Articles*. Bryan, TX: N.P., 1979

———. *The Custer Scrapbook, #4*. Bryan, TX: N.P., 1978.

———. *They Rode With Custer*. Mattituck, NY: J. M. Carroll & Company, 1993.

———. *The Two Battles Of The Little Big Horn*. NY, NY: Liveright, 1974.

———. *Who Was This Man Ricker And What Are His Tablets That Everyone Is Talking About?* Bryan, TX: Privately printed, 1979.

———. *The Eleanor H. Hinman Interviews On the Life And Death Of Crazy Horse*. N. P.: Garry Owen Press, 1976.

———. *Three Hits and a Miss*, Bryan, TX: privately printed, 1981.

Chandler, Lt. Col. Melbourne C. *Of Garryowen in Glory*. Annadale, VA: Turnpike Press, 1960.

Clark, George M. *Scalp Dance: The Edgerly Papers On the Battle of the Little Big Horn*. Oswego, NY: Privately Printed, 1985.

Coffeen, Herbert A. *The Custer Battle Book*. NY, NY: Carlton Press, 1964.

Connell, Evan S. *Son of the Morning Star*. San Francisco, CA: North Point Press, 1984.

Cox, Rev. John E. *Five Years In The United States Army*. NY, NY: Sol Lewis, 1973.

Crawford, Lewis F. *Rekindling Camp Fires*. Bismarck, ND: Capital Book Comapny, 1926.

Custer, Elizabeth C. *Boots and Saddles*. Norman, OK: University of OKPress,1966.

Darling, Roger. *General Custer's Final Hours*. Vienna, VA: Potomac-Western Press, 1992.

———. *Benteen's Scout to the Left*. El Segundo, CA: Upton & Sons, 1987.

———. *Sad and Terrible Blunder*. Vienna, VA: Potomac-Western Press, 1990.

DeLand, Charles. *The Sioux Wars*. Pierre, SD: South Dakota Historical Collections, 1930.

DeMallie, Raymond J. *The Sixth Grandfather*. Lincoln, NE: University of Neb. Press, 1984.

Dixon, Dr. Joseph. *The Vanishing Race*. NY, NY: Bonanza Books, 1975.

———. *The Vanishing Race*. Glorieta, NM: The Rio Grand Press, 1973.

du Bois, Charles. *The Custer Mystery*. El Segundo, CA: Upton & Sons, 1986.

Dustin, Fred. *The Custer Tragedy*. Hollywood: Privately Printed, 1936.

———. *The Custer Tragedy*. N.P.: N.P, 1965. *The Custer Tragedy*. El Segundo, CA, Upton & Sons, 1987.

Evans, David C. *Custer's Last Fight : The Story Of The Battle Of The Little Big Horn*. El Segundo, CA: Upton & Sons, 1999.

Finerty, John F. *War-Path And Bivouac*. Lincoln, NE: University of Nebraska Press, N.D.

Forrest, Earle R. *Witnesses At the Battle Of The Little Big Horn*. Monroe, MI: Monroe County Library System, 1986.

Fougera, Katherine Gibson. *With Custer's Cavalry*. Caldwell, ID: The Caxton Printers, 1942.

Fox, Richard A. *Archaeology, History, And Custer's Last Battle*. Norman, OK: University of OK Press, 1973.

Frost, Lawrence A. *General Custer's Libbie*. Seattle, WA: Superior Publishing Company, 1976.

Gibbon, Col. John. Gibbon *On The Sioux Campaign*. Bellevue, NE: The Old Army Press, 1969.

Graham, Col. William A. *The Custer Myth*. Harrisburgh, PA: Stackpole Company, 1953.

———. *The Story Of The Little Big Horn*. Harrisburg, PA: Stackpole Company, 1959.

———. *The Reno Court Of Inquiry, Abstract Of The Official Proceedings*. Harrisburgh, PA: Stackpole Company, 1954.

———. *The Reno Court Of Inquiry, Abstract of the Official Proceedings*. Harrisburgh, PA: Stackpole Company, 1994.

———. *The Official Record Of A Court Of Inquiry Convened At Chicago, Illinois, January 13, 1879, By The President Of The United States Upon The Request Of Major Marcus A. Reno, 7th U. S. Cavalry, To Investigate His Conduct At The Battle Of The Little Big Horn, June 25–26, 1876*. Pacific Palisades, CA: Privately Printed, 1951.

Gray, Dr. John S. *Custer's Last Campaign*. Lincoln, NE: University of Neb. Press, 1991.

———. *Centennial Campaign*. Fort Collins, CO: Old Army Press, 1976.

Greene, Jerome A. *Evidence and The Custer Enigma*. Kansas City, KS: The Lowell Press, 1973.

———. *Evidence and The Custer Enigma*. Goldin, CO.: Outlooks, Inc., 1986.

———. *Lakota and Cheyenne*. Norman, OK: University of OK Press, 1994.

Grinnell, George B. *The Fighting Cheyennes*. New Haven, CT: Yale University: 1915.

Hammer, Dr. Kenneth M. *Custer In '76*. Provo, UT: Brigham Young University Press, 1976.

———. *Biographies Of the 7th Cavalry*. Fort Collins, CO: Old Army Press, 1972.

———. *Men With Custer*. N.P.: Custer Battlefield Historical & Museum Assn., 1995.

Hanson, Joseph Mills. *The Conquest of the Missouri*. NY, NY: Murray Hill Books. 1946.

Hardorff, Richard G. *Markers, Artifacts, And Indian Testimony*. Short Hills, NJ: Don Horn Publications, 1985.

———. *The Custer Battle Casualties*. El Segundo, CA: Upton & Sons, 1989.

———. *The Custer Battle Casualties, II*. El Segundo, CA: Upton & Sons, 1999.

———. *Camp, Custer, And The Little Big Horn*. El Segundo, CA: Upton & Sons, 1997.

———. *Lakota Recollections of The Custer Fight*. Spokane, WA: The Arthur H. Clark Company, 1991.

———. *Hokahey! A Good Day!* Spokane, WA. The Arthur H. Clark Company, 1993.

———. *Cheyenne Memories of the Custer Fight*. Spokane, WA: The Arthur H. Clark Company, 1995.

———. *On The Little Big Horn With Walter Camp*. El Segundo, CA: Upton & Sons, 2002.

———. *Walter M. Camp's Little Bighorn Rosters*. Spokane, WA: The Arthur H. Clark Company, 2002.

Hart, John P. (Ed) *Custer and His Times, Book Four*. N.P: Little Big Horn Associates, Inc, 2002.

Hein, Lt. Col. O. L. *Memories of Long Ago By An Old Army Officer*. NY, NY: G. P. Putnam's Sons, 1925.

Hilton, Suzanne. *The Way It Was—1876*. Philadelphia, PA: The Westminster Press, 1975.

Hoig, Stan. *The Battle of the Washita*. Garden City, NJ: Doubleday & Company, 1976.

Holley, Frances Chamberlain. *Once Their Home*. Chicago, IL: Donohue & Henneberry, 1892.

Hunt, Robert & Frazier. *I Fought With Custer*. NY, NY: Charles Scribner & Sons, 1947.

Hutchins, James S. *The Papers Of Edward S. Curtis Relating To Custer's Last Battle*. El Segundo, CA: Upton & Sons, 2000.

Hutton, Dr. Paul A. *Phil Sheridan and His Army*. Lincoln, NE: University Of Neb. Press, 1985.

Hyde, George. *Red Cloud's Folk*. Norman, OK: University Of Ok Press, 1967.

Judd, A. N. *Campaigning Against The Sioux*. NY, NY: John M. Carroll & Co. 1973.

King, W. Kent. *Massacre: The Custer Cover-Up*. El Segundo, CA: Upton & Sons, 1989.

Koury, Michael J. *Diaries of the Little Big Horn*. N.P: The Old Army Press, 1968.

Kuhlman, Dr. Charles. *Legend Into History*. Harrisburgh, PA: Stackpole Company, 1952.

———. *Custer And The Gall Saga*. Billlings, MT: N. P., 1940.

———. *Massacre Survivor*. Fort Collins, CO: Old Army Press, 1972.

Langellier, John P. *Myles Keogh*. El Segundo, CA: Upton & Sons, 1991.

Liberty, Margot. *Cheyenne Memories*. New Haven, CT: Yale University Press, 1967.

Libby, Orin. (Ed) *The Arikara Narrative of the Campaign Against the Hostile Dakotas, 1876*. Bismarck, ND: North Dakota Historical Society, Vol. 6, 1920.

Liddic, Bruce R. *I Buried Custer*. College Station, TX: Creative Publishing Co., 1979.

———. *Camp On Custer*. Spokane, WA: Arthur H. Clark Co., 1995.

Linderman, Frank B. *Pretty-Shield*. NY, NY: The John Day Company, 1972.

Mc Clernard, Edward J. *With Indian and The Buffalo in Montana, 1870–1878*. Glendale, Ca: Arthur H. Clark Company, 1969.

Mc Creight, M. I. *Chief Flying Hawk's Tails*. NY, NY: Alliance Press, 1936.

———. *Firewater and Forked Tongues*. Pasadena, Ca: Trail's End Publishing Company, 1947.

Mc Coy, Tim, *Tim McCoy Remembers the West*. NY, NY: Doubleday & Company, 1977.

Mc Laughlin, James. *My Friend the Indian*. Seattle, WA: Superior Publishing Co, 1970.

———. *My Friend the Indian*. Boston, MA: Houghton Mifflin Company, 1920.

Mails, Thomas E. *Fools Crow*. Garden City, NY: Doubleday & Company, 1979.

Magnussen, Daniel O. *Peter Thompson's Narrative of The Little Big Horn Campaign 1876*. Glendale, CA: Arthur H. Clark Company, 1974.

Manion, John S. *General Terry's Last Statement to Custer*. El Segundo, CA: Upton & Sons, 2000.

Marquis, Thomas B. *A Warrior Who Fought Custer*. Minneapolis, MN: The Midwest Company, 1931.

———. *Memories Of A White Crow Indian*. NY, NY: The Century Company, 1928.

———. *Keep the Last Bullet For Yourself*. NY, NY: Two Continents Publishing Co., 1976.

———. *Custer on the Little Bighorn*. Algonac, MI: Reference Publications: 1986.

———. *Cheyennes Of Montana*. Algonac, MI: Reference Publications: 1978.

———. *She Watched Custer's Last Battle*. Hardin, MT: N.P., 1933.

Martin, Albert. *Sitting Bull and His World*. NY, NY: Dutton Books, 2000.

Martin, David G. *Gettysburg July 1st*. Conshohocken, PA: Combined Books, 1995.

Michno, Gregory. *Lakota Noon*. Missoula, MT: Mountain Press, 1997.

Miles, Nelson A. *Personal Recollections*. NY, NY: Dacapo Press, 1969.

———. *Serving the Republic*. NY, NY: Harper & Brothers Publishers, 1911.

Milligan, Edward. *High Noon on the Greasy Grass*. N.P.: N.P., 1972.

Miller, David Humphreys. *Custer's Fall*. NY, NY: Duell, Sloan, And Pearce, 1957.

Mills, Anson. *My Story*. Washington, DC: 1918.

Mills, Charles K. *Harvest of Barren Regrets*. Glendale, CA: Arthur H. Clark Company, 1985.

Murray, Earl. *Ghosts of the Old West*. NY, NY: Dorset Press, 1988.

Nichols, Ron. (Ed) *Men With Custer*. N.P.: Custer Battlefield Historical & Museum Association, 2000.

———. *In Custer's Shadow: Major Marcus Reno*. Fort Collins, CO: Old Army Press, 1999.

Neihardt, John G. *Black Elk Speaks*. NY, NY: William Morrow & Company, 1932.

Norris, P. W. *The Calmut Of The Coteau And Other Poetical Legends Of The Border*. Philadelphia, PA: N.P., 1884.

Nye, Lt. Col. Elwood. *Marching With Custer*. Glendale, CA: Arthur H. Clark Company, 1964.

Overfield, Loyd J. II. *The Little Big Horn 1876, The Official Communications, Documents And Reports*. Glendale, CA: Arthur H. Clark Company, 1971.

Panzeri, Peter. *The Little Big Horn, 1876, Custer's Last Stand*. Ny, Ny: Reed International Books, 1995

Pennington, Jack. *The Battle of the Little Bighorn: A Comprehensive Study*. El Segundo, CA: Upton & Sons, 2001.

Pierce, Michael D. *The Most Promising Young Officer*. Norman, OK: University Of OK Press, 1993.

Powell, Father Peter J. *People Of the Sacred Mountain*. NY, NY: Harper & Row, 1976.

———. *Sweet Medicine: The Continuous Role of The Sacred Arrows, The Sun Dance, And The Sacred Buffalo Hat In Northern Cheyenne*. Norman, OK: University Of OK Press, 1969.

Rankin, Charles. *New Perspectives on The Battle Of The Little Bighorn*. Helena, MT: Montana Historical Press, 1996.

Robinson, Charles III. *General George Crook*. Norman, OK: University Of OK Press, 1998.

Roe, Charles F. *Custer's Last Battle*. Old Slip, NY: National Highway Assoc., 1927.

Sajna, Mike. *Crazy Horse*. NY, NY: John Wiley & Sons, 2000.

Sandoz, Mari. *Crazy Horse, Strange Man of The Ogallalas*. NY, NY: Alfred Knopf, 1942.

Sarf, Wayne. *The Little Big Horn Campaign*. Conshohocken, PA: Combined Books, 1993.

Schoenberger, Dale T. *End Of Custer*. Blaine WA: Hancock House, 1995.

Schneider, George A. *The Freeman Journal*. San Rafael, CA: Presidio Press, 1974.

Schultz, James Willard. *William Jackson, Indian Scout*. Boston, MA: Houghton & Mifflin & Co., 1926.

Scott, Douglas D., Etal. *Archaeological Perspectives on the Battle of The Little Big Horn*. Norman, OK: University Of OK Press, 1982.

———. *A Good Walk Around The Boundary*. N.P.: Nebraska State Historical Society, 1997.

———. *Archaeological Insights into The Custer Battle*. Norman, OK: University Of OK Press, 1987.

———. *They Died With Custer*. Norman, OK: University Of OK Press, 1998.

Scott, Hugh L. *Some Memories of a Soldier*. NY, NY: N.P., 1928.

Sharp, Paul F. *Whoop-Up Country*. Helena, MT: Historical Society Of Montana, 1960.

Sklenar, Larry. *To Hell With Honor*. Norman, OK, University Of OK Press, 2000.

Smith, Decost. *Indian Experiences*. Caldwell, ID: Caxton Printers, 1942.

Stewart, Dr. Edgar I. *Custer's Luck*. Norman, OK: University Of OK Press, 1955.

———. *The Field Diary of Lt. Edward S. Godfrey*. Portland, OR: Champoeg Press, 1957.

Taunton, Francis B. *Custer's Field*. London, England: Johnson-Taunton Military Press, 1984.

Taylor, William O. *With Custer on The Little Big Horn*. NY, NY: Viking Press, 1996.

Upton, Richard. *The Custer Adventure*. Fort Collins, CO: Old Army Press, 1975.

Urwin, Gregory J. W. *Custer And His Times—Book Three*. N.P.: N. P., 1987.

Utley, Robert M. (Ed) *The Reno Court Of Inquiry*. Fort Collins, CO: Old Army Press, 1972.

———. *Custer and The Great Controversy*. Los Angles, CA: Westernlore Press, 1962.

———. *Cavalier In Buckskin*. Norman, OK: University Of OK Press, 1976.

———. *Custer Battlefield*. Washington, DC: National Park Service, 1969.

Van De Water, Frederic F. *Glory Hunter*, Indianapolis, IN: Bobbs-Merrill, 1934.

Vaughn, J. W. *Indian Fights. New Facts on Seven Encounters*. Norman, OK: University Of OK Press, 1966.

Vestal Stanley. *Sitting Bull*. Norman, OK: University Of OK Press, 1965.

———. *Warpath and Council Fire*. NY, NY: Random House, 1948

———. *Warpath*. Boston, Ma; Houghton & Mifflin, 1934.

Wagner, Glendolin, D. *Old Nuetriment*. NY, NY: Sol Lewis, 1973

Walker, Judson. *Campaigns Of General Custer In The North-West And The Final Surrender Of Sitting Bull*. NY, NY: Arno Press, 1966.

Weibert, Don. *Custer, Cases, & Cartridges*. N.P.: N.P, 1989.

Weibert, Hank. *Sixty-Six Years In Custer's Shadow*. Billings, MT: Privately Printed, 1985.

Wheeler, Homer W. *Buffalo Days*. Indianapolis, IN: Bobbs-Merrill, 1923.

Willert, James. *Little Big Horn Diary*. La Mirada, CA: Privately Printed, 1977.

———. *To The Edge of Darkness*. El Segundo, CA: Upton & Sons, 1998.

Articles

Adams, Jacob, "A Survivor's Story of The Custer Massacre On The American Frontier," *Journal Of American History*, Vol. 3 (April 1909).

Beardsley, J. L., "Could Custer Have Won?" *Outdoor Life*, Vol. 71, # 3 (March 1933).

Brininstool, E. A., "A Letter From E. A. Brininstool," *Montana, Magazine Of Western History*, Vol. 4, # 4 (Fall 1954).

Buecker, Thomas R., "A Surgeon At The Little Big Horn," *Montana, Magazine Of Western History*, Vol. 32, # 4 (Autumn 1982). Coughlin, Col. T. M. "The Battle of The Little Big Horn," *Cavalry Journal*, Vol. 43, # 181 (Jan.–Feb. 1934).

Diehl, Charles. "Crazy Horse's Story of the Custer Battle," *South Dakota Historical Collections*, Vol. 6 (1912).

Ellis, Horace. "A Survivor's Story Of The Custer Massacre," *Big Horn Yellowstone Journal*, Vol. 2, # 2 (Spring 1993). Hanson, Maj. Joseph M. "The Civil War Custer," *Cavalry Journal*, Vol. 43, # 183 (May–June 1934).

Hedren, Paul, "Carbine Extractor Failure At The Little Big Horn: A New Examination," *Military Collector And Historian*, Vol. 25, # 2 (1973).

Hughes, Robert P. "The Campaign Against The Sioux," *Journal Of The Military Service Institution*, Vol. 43, # 79 (January, 1896).

Godfrey, Edward S. "Cavalry Fire Discipline," Military Service Institution, Vol. 19, (September 1896). "Custer's Last Battle," *Contributions To The Historical Society Of Montana*, Vol. 9, (1909).

Graham, Col. William A. "Come On! Be Quick! Bring Packs!" *The Cavalry Journal*, Vol. 32, # 132,(July 1932).

Gray, John S. "Arikara Scouts With Custer," *Dakota History*, Vol. 35, # 2,(Spring 1968). "The Pack Train On Geroge A. Custer's Last Campaign," *Nebraska History*, Vol. 57, # 1, (Spring 1976). "What Made Johnnie Bruguier Run?" *Montana, Magazine Of Western History*, Vol. 14, # 2, (April 1964). John Stands In Timber. "Last Ghastly Moments At The Little Big Horn," *American Heritage*, Vol. 17, (April 1966).

Johnson, Barry C. "A Captain Of Chivalric Courage," *English Westerners*, Vol. 25, #'s 1 & 2, (1987/1988).

King, Charles. "Custer's Last Battle," *Harper's*, # 81, (August 1890).

Knipe, Daniel A. "A New Story Of Custer's Last Battle," *Contributions To The Historical Society Of Montana*, Vol. 4, (1903).

Luce, Edward. "Custer Battlefield And Some New Discoveries," *Chicago Westerners*, Vol. 4, # 1–2, (March–April 1947).

Luther, Tal. "Benteen, Reno, And Custer," *The Trail Guide*, Vol. 5, # 1, (March 1960).

Mclemore, Clyde (Ed). "My Personal Story," By Lt. Charles DeRudio, *Frontier and Midland*, Vol. 14, (January 1934).

Michno, Greg. "Crazy Horse, Custer And The Sweep To The North," *Montana, Magazine Of Western History*, Vol. 43, # 3, (Summer 1993).

Miller, David. "Echoes Of The Little Big Horn," *American Heritage*, Vol. 22, # 4, (June 1971).

Morris, Maj. Robert E. "Custer Made A Good Decision: A Leavenworth Appreciation," *Journal Of The West*, Vol. 16, # 4, (Oct. 1977).

Murphy, James P. "The Campaign Of The Little Big Horn," *Infantry Journal*, Vol. 34, (June 1929).

Noyes, Lee. "The Guns Custer Left Behind," *The English Westerners Society*, (Summer 1999).

Pickard, Edward. "I Rode With Custer," *Montana, Magazine Of Western History*, Vol. 4, # 3, (Summer 1954).

Rector, Willam G. "The Reno-Benteen Defense Perimeter," *Montana, Magazine Of Western History*, Vol. 16, # 2, (Spring 1966).

Taunton, Frances B. "No Pride In The Little Big Horn," *The English Westerners Society*, (1987).

Utley, Robert. "Last Stand," *The Quarterly Journal Of Military History*, Vol. 1, # 1, (August 1988).

Newspapers

Army and Navy Journal. Washington, DC.
Billings *Gazette*. Billings, MT.
Bismarck *Daily Tribune*. Bismarck, ND.
Fort Benton *Weekly Record*. Ft. Benton, ND.
Janesville *Gazette*. Janesville, WI.
Leavenworth *Times*. Leavenworth, KS.
Morning Standard. Syracuse, NY.
New York *Herald*. NY, NY.
National Tribune. Washington, DC
The *Globe*.
Washington *Observer*. Washington, PA.

Publications

Custer Battlefield Historical & Museum, Association Symposiums. Hardin, MT.
Greasy Grass Custer Battlefield Historical & Museum Association. Hardin, MT.
Little Big Horn Associates Newsletter. Lombard, IL.
Research Review Journal of the Little Big Horn Associates. El Paso, TX.
The Battlefield Dispatch. A Quarterly Newsletter of the Custer Battlefield Historical & Museum Association. Hardin, MT.
Winners of the West. St. Joseph, MO.

Government Publications.

Report of Chief Engineers, 1877. Washington, D.C.

Manuscript.

Custer Battlefield National Monument Collection (Little Big Horn National Monument). Crow Agency, MT.
Dustin Collection. Custer Battlefield National Monument (Little Big Horn National Monument). Crow Agency, MT.
Hagner Collection. New York Public Library. NY, NY.
Frank L. Mercatante Collection. Grand Rapids, MI.
William Ghent Collection. Library of Congress. Washington, D.C.
J. Blummer Manuscript. Custer Battlefield National Monument (Little Big Horn National Monument). Crow Agency, MT.
Onondaga County Historical Society. Syracuse, NY
Roger Darling Collection (Darling Research). Vienna, VA.
Steve Moses Collection. Otsego, MI.
Walter M. Camp Papers. Indiana University. Bloomington, IN.
Walter M. Camp Papers. Brigham Young University. Provo, UT.
Walter M. Camp Papers. Denver Public Library. Denver CO.
Walter M. Camp Papers. Custer Battlefield National Monument (Little Big Horn National Monument). Crow Agency, MT.
Walter S. Campbell Collection. University Of OK. Norman, OK.
William Boyes, Jr. Collection. Rockville, MD.

Unpublished Sources.

Nelson, Clifford L. *The Custer Battalion At The Little Big Horn. History Honors Thesis*, Concordoia College, 1969.

Index

There are three notable exceptions to the entries in this index. They are the names of Frederick W. Benteen, George A. Custer, and Marcus A. Reno. In the case of these individuals, they are referred to so frequently that any attempt to cite every mention would result in a rather unwieldy index. However, each of the three is listed under key events regarding the often referred to and significant aspects of the battle.

Vanishing Victory: Custer's Final March
by Bruce R. Liddic, volume five of the Battle of the Little Bighorn Series
of Upton and Sons, Publishers, has been published in an edition of
1,050 copies, of which 50 copies have been specially bound,
signed by the author, and numbered.
Publication supervision by The Arthur H. Clark Company,
Spokane, Washington, design by Robert A. Clark.
Printing and binding have been completed by
Thomson-Shore, Inc., of Dexter, Michigan.